THEORIES OF LEARNING
AND INSTRUCTION

Officers of the Society
1963–64

(Term of office expires March 1 of the year indicated.)

WALTER W. COOK
(Deceased)

STEPHEN M. COREY
(1964)
Teachers College, Columbia University, New York, New York

EDGAR DALE
(1964)
Ohio State University, Columbus, Ohio

JOHN I. GOODLAD
(1966)
University of California, Los Angeles, California

HERMAN G. RICHEY
(1965) *(Ex-officio)*
University of Chicago, Chicago, Illinois

RALPH W. TYLER
(1965)
Center for Advanced Study in Behavioral Sciences, Stanford, California

PAUL A. WITTY
(1966)
Northwestern University, Evanston, Illinois

Secretary-Treasurer
HERMAN G. RICHEY
5835 Kimbark Avenue, Chicago, Illinois 60637

THEORIES OF LEARNING
AND INSTRUCTION

*The Sixty-third Yearbook of the
National Society for the Study of Education*

PART I

By
THE YEARBOOK COMMITTEE
and
ASSOCIATED CONTRIBUTORS

Edited by
ERNEST R. HILGARD

Editor for the Society
HERMAN G. RICHEY

19  64

Distributed by THE UNIVERSITY OF CHICAGO PRESS · CHICAGO, ILLINOIS

The responsibilities of the Board of Directors of the National Society for the Study of Education in the case of yearbooks prepared by the Society's committees are (1) to select the subjects to be investigated, (2) to appoint committees calculated in their personnel to insure consideration of all significant points of view, (3) to provide appropriate subsidies for necessary expenses, (4) to publish and distribute the committees' reports, and (5) to arrange for their discussion at the annual meeting.

The responsibility of the Society's editor is to prepare the submitted manuscripts for publication in accordance with the principles and regulations approved by the Board of Directors.

Neither the Board of Directors, nor the Society's editor, nor the Society is responsible for the conclusions reached or the opinions expressed by the Society's yearbook committees.

Published 1964 by

THE NATIONAL SOCIETY FOR THE STUDY OF EDUCATION
5835 Kimbark Avenue, Chicago, Illinois 60637

First printing, 10,000 Copies

Printed in the United States of America

The Society's Committee on Theories of Learning and Instruction

JEROME S. BRUNER

Professor of Psychology
Director, Center for Cognitive Studies
Harvard University
Cambridge, Massachusetts

N. L. GAGE

Professor of Education and Psychology
Stanford University
Stanford, California

ERNEST R. HILGARD
(Chairman)

Professor of Psychology and Education
Stanford University
Stanford, California

A. A. LUMSDAINE

Professor of Educational Psychology
University of California
Los Angeles, California

T. R. McCONNELL

Chairman, Center for the Study of Higher Education
University of California
Berkeley, California

PAUL WOODRING

Distinguished Service Professor of the College
Western Washington State College
Bellingham, Washington

Associated Contributors

JOHN B. CARROLL

Roy E. Larsen Professor of Educational Psychology
Harvard University
Cambridge, Massachusetts

J. W. GETZELS

Professor of Educational Psychology
Departments of Education and Psychology
University of Chicago
Chicago, Illinois

v

ROBERT GLASER

Professor of Education and Psychology
Director of Research, Learning Research and Development Center
University of Pittsburgh
Pittsburgh, Pennsylvania

WINFRED F. HILL

Associate Professor of Psychology
Northwestern University
Evanston, Illinois

FREDERICK J. McDONALD

Associate Professor of Education and Psychology
Stanford University
Stanford, California

SIDNEY L. PRESSEY

Visiting Professor
College of Education, University of Arizona
Tucson, Arizona

KARL H. PRIBRAM

USPHS Research Professor
Departments of Psychiatry and Psychology
Stanford University School of Medicine
Palo Alto, California

FRANK RESTLE

Professor of Psychology
Indiana University
Bloomington, Indiana

PAULINE S. SEARS

Associate Professor of Education
Stanford University
Stanford, California

FRED. T. TYLER

Professor of Education
University of California
Berkeley, California

BENTON J. UNDERWOOD

Professor of Psychology
Northwestern University
Evanston, Illinois

Editor's Preface

At the February, 1960, meeting of the Board of Directors of the National Society for the Study of Education, Professor T. R. McConnell, a member of the Board, noted that nearly twenty years had elapsed since the publication of *The Psychology of Learning* (1942), the last publication of the Society to deal, in any comprehensive way, with theories of learning. At the June meeting of the same year, the Board voted to bring out a new yearbook on the subject, provided Professor Ernest R. Hilgard of Stanford University would accept the chairmanship of a committee to plan and prepare the volume for publication in 1963. Professor Hilgard agreed to serve as chairman on the condition that publication be delayed until 1964 to make it possible for the scholars that he wanted as committee members and contributing authors to arrange their very full schedules to give the time that would be required for the undertaking. The Board promptly accepted Professor Hilgard's condition, and work on the yearbook began. Professor Hilgard, as had Professor McConnell, chairman of the committee on the 1942 yearbook, enlisted the help of a group of America's leading behavioral scientists. Their endeavors are presented in this yearbook, *Theories of Learning and Instruction*.

Professor Hilgard's closing section, "Postscript: Twenty Years of Learning Theory in Relation to Education," should be read as a preface as well as a concluding statement. He explains the plan and purpose of the volume, notes our progress in developing learning theory and our failure to make the most of what we have, and presents the somewhat different views of 1942 and 1964 regarding the approaches from theory to the solution of instructional, organizational, curricular, and other problems of education.

Educators, psychologists, and laymen will find the reading of the yearbook a rewarding experience.

HERMAN G. RICHEY
Editor for the Society

Table of Contents

CHAPTER I

The Influence of Learning Theories on Education (1900–1950)

FREDERICK J. MC DONALD

Introduction

The historical influence of psychological theory on educational theory and practice will be discussed in this chapter. The distinction between psychological theory and learning theory (as an aspect of psychological theory) is not useful in describing the interaction of psychological and educational thinking in the early part of this century. The major ideas dominating that period were social Darwinism, pragmatism, and, finally, metaphysical behaviorism. The yeast of these ideas created an intellectual ferment which yielded a new conception of the learning organism that has greatly influenced thinking in psychology and philosophy and, in turn, in education.

Two distinct developments are significant for the relation of psychological and educational theory through the decades of the twenties and the thirties. The first of these is the predominant position of John Dewey's philosophy in educational thought. The roots of this philosophy in pragmatism, Dewey's early association with functionalism in psychology, and the continued relation of this philosophy to progressive social thought in America were critical factors in shaping a psychology of the educational process. Other psychological systems were weighed in the balance of Dewey's experimentalism.

Contemporaneously, Watson achieved the final separation of psychology from the vestiges of traditional philosophical thought, providing in the process what was judged to be a modern, scientific, philosophic position.[1] From this point on, one had learning theories

1. See Gustav Bergmann, "The Contribution of John B. Watson," *Psychological Review*, LXIII (July, 1956), 265–76, for an analysis of Watson's contribution to psychology in contrast to his own and others' conception of this con-

from which to choose. Watson substituted the laws of frequency and recency for Thorndike's law of effect.[2] Skinner and Hull presented their variations of Thorndike's law of effect.[3] The issues among these various theories were clear and stimulated a vigorous experimental attack that gave modern psychology its principal characteristics.

The introduction of Gestalt psychology and field theory into American psychology was an event as significant for education as for psychology. These theories presented themselves as the antagonists of the associationism that dominated American psychology and its applications in education. Gestalt psychology and field theory were attractive alternatives to American educators. By the later thirties these competing psychologies came to be regarded as competing learning theories. The Forty-first Yearbook of the National Society for the Study of Education describes the choices available to educators, and the yearbook committee presented what it viewed as the "principal protagonists," conditioning theory, connectionism, and field theory.[4] This conflict became critical for a profession that had been taught by James that teaching must everywhere agree with psychology.[5] The stated intent of the committee was "to show that although there are differences among them, these systems possess many fundamental points of agreement . . . and to present in a manner primarily constructive and only incidentally controversial, a discussion of some of the more important phases and conditions of human learning which are particularly significant for education."[6]

---

tribution. Watson's professed contributions were as significant for the social thought of his times as the more permanent effects of his work in psychological science.

2. Ernest R. Hilgard, *Theories of Learning*, p. 49. New York: Appleton-Century-Crofts, 1956 (second edition).

3. *Ibid.*, pp. 82 and 121.

4. *The Psychology of Learning.* Forty-first Yearbook of the National Society for the Study of Education, Part II. Edited by Nelson B. Henry. Chicago: Distributed by the University of Chicago Press, 1942. See particularly, T. R. McConnell, "Introduction," pp. 3–13.

5. James' statement in this respect is not infrequently cited without his qualifications. But he spelled out the essence of the relation of psychology to education—one that Dewey substantially used. See William James, *Talks to Teachers*, pp. 21–27. New York: W. W. Norton & Co., 1958.

6. *The Psychology of Learning, op. cit.*, p. 3.

The committee's statement represents a manifesto for what appears to be the major effort of the forties and early fifties, the attempt to reconcile, to find the common. It was a period of eclecticism, but also a period when the influence of learning theory on education reached its nadir.[7]

The major question which this chapter will attempt to answer is, why did a particular psychological theory come to dominate educational thinking? The history of this development is embedded in the climate of intellectual and social thought of a period. One answer to this question will be that the acceptance of a learning theory depends only in part on its evidences of validity, its prescriptiveness for educational practice, or its "practicality." The acceptance appears to depend in large part on its consistency with the thinking of influential educational and social theorists, and more subtly on the *Zeitgeist*. It is not surprising that educators' preferences for a learning theory are not simply matters of rational choice. An analysis of the determinants of acceptance is instructive, for they have shifted from period to period and suggest a characteristic of the relation of psychology and education that is likely to persist.

The Early Period: Thorndike and Connectionism

William James[8] and G. Stanley Hall[9] must be credited with bringing scientific psychology to the attention of the educational profession generally. While James went on to philosophy, Hall's production of data and psychological theory were prodigious, and his influence spread into American education. Child study, initiated by Hall, has been a characteristic of American education since his time. Hall provided the data and the ideas that were one of the roots of the child-centered school.

While Hall's influence was great, he cannot be said to have pro-

7. David G. Ryans, "Educational Psychology," in *Annual Review of Psychology*, p. 432. Edited by Calvin P. Stone and Quinn McNemar. Stanford, California: Annual Reviews, Inc., 1955.

8. James, *op. cit.*

9. G. Stanley Hall, *Educational Problems* (New York: D. Appleton & Co., 1911) and *Adolescence* (New York: D. Appleton & Co., 1904). Hall's work was voluminous; the above are representative and were influential. Hall's journal articles should not be overlooked, nor should his founding and editing of the *Pedagogical Seminary*.

duced a *systematic* psychological or educational theory. He was an evolutionist, and his psychological and educational theories were essentially an application of evolutionary concepts to mind and to education (social Darwinism, as it has been called). His major theoretical contribution was the general psychonomic law: ontogeny, the development of the individual, recapitulates phylogeny, the evolution of the race. The educational application of this principle was the recapitulation theory. This theory stated that the individual lives through the cycles of racial development and that educational procedures should be geared to this developmental pattern.

Herein lies the link between Hall's general psychology and its application to pedagogy. For he was ready to judge a civilization by the way its children grew, and a school system by the way it adapted itself to the natural growth of individuals. Nature was right, he insisted, particularly in the lives of children. To a nation about to celebrate "the century of the child," his doctrines had enormous appeal.[10]

Hall's significance so far as the discussion of this chapter is concerned is that he put into the mainstream of educational thinking a core of ideas that constituted for many educators a "learning theory." Today we usually designate his kind of theory a developmental theory and contrast such theories with learning theories. The juxtaposition of developmental and learning theories has been as important for educational theory as the debates over learning theories.

More importantly, Hall's evolutionary concepts posed real difficulties for a society that was becoming increasingly committed to the notion that education was the key to social progress. These ideas were the chief obstacle to the democratization of education. Hall's basic conceptions stressed the determining force of heredity, though for Hall heredity was essentially racial heredity. Heredity placed limits on the power of education to change man. Such a limitation was to become unacceptable to the social thought that prevailed in this country through the early decades of this century.

The struggle to clarify the influence of inherited determining tendencies was a principal component of the debate in the early part of this century. This debate had its counterpart in psychology

10. Lawrence A. Cremin, *The Transformation of the School*, p. 102. New York: Alfred A. Knopf, 1961.

and education in the nature-nurture controversy.[11] The side of this issue one chose was an important determinant of the kind of learning theory one was likely to accept.

The early phases of this debate were carried by Thorndike who posed the issues clearly in terms of their relevance to educational theory. Thorndike perhaps more than any other individual made "learning" a central concept in American psychology. His position must be regarded as central in the debates that issued over learning theory.

THORNDIKE AND THE SCIENCE OF EDUCATION MOVEMENT

The origins of the science of education movement are complex[12] and are rooted in the comprehensive changes in American intellectual life at the turn of the century. Thorndike cannot be credited with beginning the movement, but he was the prototype of the successful applier of scientific methods to educational problems. His approach to the problems of education was straightforward.

A true educational science must be inductive, must be made up from the study of the particular facts in answer to thousands of different questions.[13]

And, shortly after writing the foregoing statement, he wrote:

The final test of the scientific quality of the notions we have, the hypotheses we frame, the experiments we devise, the records we take, and the like, is of course their power to progress toward verification and prophecy and control.[14]

Objectivity was the key. Induction from the data was the method.

. . . there is no chance for any simple general theory. . . . The true general theory must be the helpless one that there can be no general theory, or be made up of such extremely vague conclusions as the fea-

11. See Richard Hofstadter, *Social Darwinism in American Thought*, pp. 170–204 (Boston: Beacon Press, 1955 [revised edition]) for a discussion of the eugenics movement and its place in American social thought.

12. See Cremin, *op. cit.*, pp. 90–126 and 179–239.

13. Edward L. Thorndike, *Educational Psychology*, p. 164. New York: Lemcke & Buechner, 1903.

14. Edward L. Thorndike, "What Is 'Scientific' Method in the Study of Education?" *On the Teaching of English in Elementary and High Schools*, p. 82. Fifth Yearbook, National Society for the Scientific Study of Education, Part I. Edited by Manfred J. Holmes. Chicago: Distributed by the University of Chicago Press, 1906.

tures common to all human natures and the changes everywhere desirable allow. Such conclusions are on a level for helpfulness and illumination with the inane tautologies of hygiene books. "Good air, nutritious food and proper exercise are sure to assist health."[15]

An educational science was the product of hard work and careful thought. Thorndike got on with the work of answering the thousand questions. His unquestioned influence on American education must be attributed in part to the scientific respectability he gave to educational practices. He provided answers. He exemplified the pragmatic, utilitarian, American mind in action.

THE SOCIAL SIGNIFICANCE OF THORNDIKE'S WORK

By the turn of the century America had embarked on the great experiment in universal mass education. Progressive social thought had developed into a powerful force in American intellectual life.[16] Exciting educational experiments were being tried; progressivism was on the rise in American education.[17] The school was to be, had to be, adapted to the needs of an urban-industrial and an increasingly democratic society.

The story of how Thorndike slew the dragon of formal discipline is well known.[18] His experimental work provided the scientific basis for the liberalization of the curriculum. That the curriculum would have been liberalized in any case seems apparent. Courtis credits the mental-test movement with focusing the public's attention on the spread of ability in the schools. He also states that methods for individualizing instruction were justified mainly on philosophical

15. Thorndike, *Educational Psychology* (1903), *op. cit.*, pp. 163–64.

16. See Henry Steele Commager, *The American Mind*, particularly Part II. (New Haven, Connecticut: Yale University Press, 1950) and Hofstadter, *op. cit.*, chaps. vi, vii, and viii.

17. Cremin, *op. cit.*, Part II. See also John Dewey and Evelyn Dewey, *Schools of Tomorrow* (New York: E. P. Dutton & Co., 1915; paperback edition, 1962).

18. An example of a presentation of the topic of transfer of learning to prospective teachers may be found in S. L. Pressey, *Psychology and the New Education*, chap. xiv. New York: Harper & Bros., 1933. Pressey presents the issues and relevant data as of the thirties. Thorndike's educational studies figure prominently in Pressey's analysis. The early critical experimental work may be found in Edward L. Thorndike and Robert S. Woodworth, "The Influence of Improvement in One Mental Function upon the Efficiency of Other Functions," *Psychological Review*, VIII (1901), 247–61, 384–95, 553–64.

grounds.[19] But when the issue of what knowledge or training was of the most use, an appeal to Thorndike could be made.

The prevailing doctrine of "social utility" as the criterion for constructing the curriculum fitted superbly into Thorndike's general conception of learning and his analytic method for studying educational problems. Learning was a matter of establishing connections; what to connect was a matter of social utility.[20]

The other major theory that Thorndike demolished was Hall's recapitulation theory. In the first volume of his *Educational Psychology*, Thorndike states the basic problems of educational psychology as follows:

Wisdom and economy in improving man's wants and in making him better able to satisfy them depend upon knowledge—*first, of what his nature is*, [italics ours] and second, of the laws which govern changes in it. It is the province of educational psychology to give such knowledge of the original nature of man and of the laws of modifiability or learning, in the case of intellect, character and skill.[21]

He then devotes the entire first volume to an analysis of the problem of "original tendencies." He refutes the recapitulation theory and the doctrine of catharsis (G. S. Hall), distinguishes between original and "natural" tendencies, and attacks both the doctrine that nature is "right" and the stage theory of instinctual development.

The flavor of his thinking is clearly reflected in the following selection from the concluding statements to this volume:

I have been at some pains to make it clear that the instinctive tendencies of man must often be supplemented, redirected, and even reversed,

---

19. S. A. Courtis, "Contributions of Research to the Individualization of Instruction," *The Scientific Movement in Education*, pp. 201–10. Thirty-seventh Yearbook of the National Society for the Study of Education, Part II. Edited by Guy M. Whipple. Chicago: Distributed by the University of Chicago Press, 1938. In the same volume Frank S. Freeman discusses individual differences (see pp. 405–20). Courtis' point seems substantiated by Freeman's discussion of educational provisions for individual differences (p. 418). The study of individual differences produced facts that supported provisions that either antedated the accumulation of the facts or were simply consistent with them.

20. E. L. Thorndike, "Mental Discipline in High School Studies," *Journal of Educational Psychology*, XV (January, 1924), 1–22; (February, 1924), 83–98; "The Disciplinary Values of Studies: A Census of Opinion," *Education*, XXXV (January, 1915), 278–86; and "The Disciplinary Values of Studies in the Opinion of Students," *Teachers College Record*, XXV (March, 1924), 134–43.

21. Edward L. Thorndike, *Educational Psychology*. Vol. I, *The Original Nature of Man*, p. 1. New York: Teachers College, Columbia University, 1913.

and that in the ordinary sense of the words, original nature is imperfect and untrustworthy. . . . Learning has to remake unlearned tendencies for the better, but the capacity to learn, too, is a part of his nature.[22]

The original "givens" were the material to work with, but to be modified by learning. "They [the apostles and soldiers of truth and justice] are the sufficient miracle: their lives are the proof that human nature itself can change itself for the better—that the human species can teach itself to think for truth alone and to act for the good of all men."[23] Of such statements was the American faith in education made. To understand how well Thorndike's conceptions seemed to fit the spirit of his times, it is necessary to recall that for the progressives the school and education was a major instrument of social reform.

Thorndike's laws of learning were, of course, a major contribution. They spelled out succinctly, buttressed by a mass of evidence, the basic principles that must govern educational procedures. These laws were "the agents by which man acquires connections productive of behavior suitable to the environment in which he lives."[24] They furnish education "with two obvious general rules:—(1) Put together what should go together and keep apart what should not go together. (2) Reward desirable connections and make undesirable connections produce discomfort."[25]

Thorndike's chapter on "Learning by Analysis and Selection"[26] spells out the essence of educational methodology. Methodology is an arrangement of situations to establish connections. The general procedures are designed to elicit comparisons and contrasts in the service of establishing connections between responses and situations.[27] This same chapter also describes adaptation to novel situations, association by similarity, and purposive behavior as special cases of the effects of the exertion of influence by previously established connections.[28]

It seems clear that Thorndike provided cogent analyses of and answers to questions that had plagued educational and psychological

---

22. *Ibid.*, pp. 310–11.   23. *Ibid.*, p. 312.

24. Edward L. Thorndike, *Educational Psychology.* Vol. II, *The Psychology of Learning*, p. 4. New York: Teachers College, Columbia University, 1913.

25. *Ibid.*, p. 20.   27. *Ibid.*, pp. 37–46.

26. *Ibid.*, pp. 32–53.   28. *Ibid.*, pp. 46–53.

thought. His system provided a comprehensive picture of learning that resolved age-old problems. It dealt a death-blow to many educational theories that were unpopular because of their philosophical origins or because their educational implications appeared to be antithetical to education in a democracy.

We ignore in this discussion Thorndike's contributions to the measurement movement and to the study of individual differences. Measurement, for Thorndike, was clearly a means to an end. "We conquer the facts of nature when we observe and experiment upon them. When we measure them we have made them our servants. A little statistical insight trains them for invaluable work."[29] Thorndike's measurement work opened the way for other investigators, and since his time educational research has been statistically oriented.

His study of individual differences seems also to be related to the development of his basic conceptions. The problem of individual variation was a part of the problem of the influence of original tendencies. Individual variation was a stubborn fact that had to be explained. Perhaps Thorndike's major conceptual contribution in this area was his principle that variation in kind could be reduced to variation in amount. Inevitably Thorndike cleared away some old brush, in this case, theories of typologies.[30]

Perhaps one of the most remarkable aspects of Thorndike as a theorist is that he did not ignore competing conceptions or discuss only those that provided convenient strawmen. He did not ignore the influence of hereditary factors as Watson did, nor did he act as if individual variation did not occur or could be eliminated by appropriate educational procedures. He commented on every major psychological conception of his time. He either demonstrated their inadequacies or reduced them to instances of conceptions in his system.

Thorndike's appeal must also be attributed in part to the quantitative character of his system. Buttressed as it was with enormous quantities of data and Thorndike's down-to-earth factualism, it could not but appeal to a generation of educators who believed that sci-

29. Thorndike, *Educational Psychology* (1913), *op. cit.*, p. 164.

30. Edward L. Thorndike, *Educational Psychology.* Vol. III, *Work and Fatigue: Individual Differences,* pp. 372–88. New York: Teachers College, Columbia University, 1913.

ence would solve the problems of education. He was no ivory-tower theorist remote from the everyday problems of education. He showed convincingly what psychology had to offer education.

Finally, *connectionism*, as his system came to be called, provided a learning theory that supported the notion that man was infinitely modifiable (though Thorndike himself probably was not quite so optimistic). Why was his system to fall into disfavor? This question can be answered by a consideration of the influence of John Dewey on educational theory.

The Influence of John Dewey's Psychological Theory

The influence of John Dewey on educational thinking is both well known and indisputable. Yet this influence was only an aspect of the social power he exerted and was, in fact, derivative from it. Dewey, more than any other single thinker or writer, gave American twentieth-century thought its most distinctive characteristics. "He became the guide, the mentor, and the conscience of the American people: it is scarcely an exaggeration to say that for a generation no major issue was clarified until Dewey had spoken."[31] It is relevant, therefore, to ask what Dewey's psychological theory was. Obviously, several generations of American educators have espoused his ideas in whole or in part; their working psychology had its roots in Dewey's philosophy.

DEWEY'S CONCEPTIONS OF THE LEARNING PROCESS

A comprehensive analysis of Dewey's psychology has yet to be accomplished. We present here only those conceptions which appear to be critical for contrasting his position with those of the major learning theorists. These ideas cannot be divorced in any final analysis from Dewey's general philosophical system. Dewey gave American education a philosophy and, in the process, also gave education a psychology of learning.

The most significant of Dewey's psychological conceptions, because it was fundamental to his other ideas, is his analysis of the relation of the person to stimulus events. In a paper now regarded as a psychological classic, he defined this relation:

31. Commager, *op. cit.,* p. 100.

If one is reading a book, if one is hunting, if one is watching in a dark place on a lonely night, if one is performing a chemical experiment, in each case, the noise has a very different psychical value; it is a different experience. In any case, what proceeds the 'stimulus' is a whole act, a sensori-motor coordination. What is more to the point, the 'stimulus' emerges out of this coordination; it is born from it as its matrix; it represents as it were an escape from it.

. . . .

The conscious sensation of sound depends upon the motor response having already taken place; . . . it is the motor response or attention which constitutes that, which finally becomes the stimulus to another act. . . . The motor reaction involved in the running is, once more, into, not merely to, the sound. It occurs to change the sound, to get rid of it. . . . What we have is a circuit, not an arc or broken segment of a circle. This circuit is more truly termed organic than reflex, because the motor response determines the stimulus, just as truly as sensory stimulus determines movement.[32]

Dewey's attack on the reflex arc was significant at the time because it was useful in the battle against structuralism. However, this analysis is central in Dewey's psychological thinking. For Dewey, stimulus and response were not to be sharply distinguished but were always to be viewed as organically related. "Mediated experiences," events in relation to their adjustive function, were the central psychological events.

Contrast the above statements with Thorndike: "Learning is connecting; and teaching is the arrangement of situations which will lead to desirable bonds and make them satisfying."[33] According to Thorndike, stimulus and response are, in principle, distinguished in order that their connection may be achieved. These connections are the central psychological events.

Is it surprising that the two systems came to be described as presenting a picture of an "active" learning organism as opposed to that of a "passive" learning organism? Though this description is grossly oversimplified, it had implications that simply could not be accepted by many educators.

32. John Dewey, "The Reflex Arc Concept in Psychology," *Psychological Review*, III (1896), 357–70. [The reference is to the reprint in *Readings in the History of Psychology*, p. 358–59. Edited by W. Dennis. New York: Appleton-Century-Crofts, 1948.]

33. Thorndike, *Educational Psychology* (1913), *op. cit.*, p. 55.

Thorndike's maxim, "Exercise and reward desirable connections; prevent or punish undesirable connections" means that the teacher is to decide on the particular bonds or connections that are to be established, or in short, to set the stage for the fixing process. The child would be apt to be overlooked as the result of such a procedure, in the eyes of some critics, since by insisting on the analytic and neglecting the synthetic aspects of learning, it would put a premium on skills and habits and come near to denying purposive behavior.[34]

Another major psychological conception of equal importance in Dewey's thinking is that of *interest,* which serves as the basic motivational construct in his system. Interest is, for Dewey, the critical link between the pupil's present stage and where the teacher hopes he will be.[35] "Interest and discipline are connected, not opposed,"[36] and discipline is the power to anticipate consequences, the fruit of mediated experiences.

Anything which intelligence studies represents things in the part which they play in the carrying forward of active lines of interest. . . . This connection of an object and a topic with the promotion of an activity having a purpose is the first and the last word of a genuine theory of interest in education.[37]

For Dewey, "interest" was a quasi-primitive term. He used the simple, common meaning: to be absorbed, engaged, to care about. The relation of the construct to other motivational constructs is not clear. It is clear that he related the concept to intelligent action; interest was not simply unguided or capricious impulse. Yet interest had its roots in the core of the person.

Dewey's third major conception was that of the role of "aims" in action. It is this conception that accounts for the description of his system as "purposive." For Dewey, aims and intelligent action were interrelated. "The net conclusion is that acting with an aim is all one with acting intelligently."[38] Intelligent behavior was foreseeing the terminus of an act; this foresight provided the basis for ordering, selecting, and observing. "To do these things means to have a mind—for mind is precisely intentional purposeful activity con-

---

34. Merle Curti, *The Social Ideas of American Educators,* p. 471. Paterson, New Jersey: Pageant Books, Inc., 1959.

35. John Dewey, *Democracy and Education,* p. 127. New York: Macmillan Co., 1961 (paperback edition).

36. *Ibid.,* p. 129.   37. *Ibid.,* pp. 134–35.   38. *Ibid.,* p. 103.

trolled by perception of facts and their relationships to one another."[39] Mind was not for Dewey one pole of the ancient dualism. It was a convenient label for describing a problem-solving activity in which person and environment are organically related.

Learning is, then, problem-solving or intelligent action in which the person continually evaluates his experience in the light of its foreseen and experienced consequences. The greater the foresight in terms of multiple anticipated consequences, the greater the accumulated experience or "learning." But learning in this sense is not simply an acquisition or achievement but a moment of experience out of which emerges redefined purposes, new evaluations, and action in the service of continued growth.

Aims are in people. The child learns in the light of his own aims. "An educational aim must be founded upon the intrinsic activities and needs (including original instincts and acquired habits) of the given individual to be educated."[40] The teacher also has his aims, necessarily disparate with those of the pupil because their experiences have not been the same.

In learning, the present powers of the pupil are the initial stage; the aim of the teacher represents the remote limit. Between the two lie *means* . . . acts to be performed. . . . These intermediate conditions are of interest precisely because the development of existing activities into the foreseen and desired end depends upon them. To be means for the achieving of present tendencies, to be "between" the agent and his end, to be of interest, are different names for the same thing.[41]

Thus, Dewey interrelates *aim, interest,* and *intelligent action* and, in so doing, provides the essential ideas in what might be called his psychology of learning.

The above discussion and the quotations from Dewey make clear the differences between his theory of the learning process and that of Thorndike. They also suggest why Boring has said:

In his stress on total coordinations Dewey was anticipating the position of Gestalt psychology. In his insistence that the coordination is adaptive or purposeful, being directed toward success, he was also occupying a position in the history of dynamic psychology.[42]

39. *Ibid.* 40. *Ibid.,* pp. 107–8. 41. *Ibid.,* p. 127.

42. Edwin G. Boring, *A History of Experimental Psychology,* p. 554. New York: Appleton-Century-Crofts, 1950.

THE SOCIAL SIGNIFICANCE OF DEWEY'S CONCEPTIONS

Only cursory attention need be given to the social impact of Dewey's ideas since history of it is well known to most readers. Several points in this history deserve emphasis, however.

Dewey was part and parcel of the great intellectual movement in America at the turn of the century to make science a viable force in all aspects of American life and thought. The separation of psychology from its philosophical roots and the science-of-education movement were aspects of this larger trend. In each, Dewey played a significant role, though mainly as guide and mentor.

Thorndike and Dewey in this early period can be seen pitted against the same foes—Dewey providing penetrating analyses, Thorndike his own analyses and overwhelming mounds of data. The unperceptive observer would have seen only the clash with a now outmoded tradition, the demolition of unscientific ideas. But Dewey caught the spirit of the times in a way that Thorndike did not, so that when the differences between them became apparent, Dewey was chosen by educators.

Dewey was chosen because he made sense out of the notion of education for democracy. This idea inevitably had wide appeal to a generation committed to making the world safe for democracy. Democratic education was the hope of all classes, the instrument of social reform.[43] Particularly when democratic education meant or at least was associated with a child-centered school, the idea had enormous appeal to those who wanted to break the power of "big business," to those who saw a new world emerging from science, to those who believed in social progress.

The beginnings of the Progressive era, moreover, coincided with the growth and spread of Dewey's ideas—the same period in which James himself thought he saw the competitive regime "getting wounded to death"; and it is easy to see Dewey's faith in knowledge, experimentation, activity, and control as the counterpart in abstract philosophy of the Progressive faith in democracy and political action.[44]

Dewey was certainly one of the foremost representatives of the progessive movement and one of its leaders. Psychology was not

43. Dewey, *Democracy and Education, op. cit.*, chaps. iii–vi.

44. Hofstadter, *op. cit.*, p. 141

part of that great movement, though individual psychologists were notable for their progressive social ideas. Psychology had become scientific, but the price paid was separation from the larger issues and problems confronting society. The index of Watson's *Behaviorism*, revised in 1930, lists two references to "social experimentation." His discussion emphasizes the blind, nonexperimental character of social changes; his major examples are war and the Eighteenth Amendment.[45] This indifference to social experimentation contrasts markedly with Dewey's public stands on the issues of the day.

Hofstadter notes that the social reformers and progressives turned from biology to psychology during the period from 1890 to 1915. But the psychology which was adopted derived its impetus from James and Dewey.

The new psychology, whose most eminent representatives were Dewey and Veblen, portrayed the organism as a structure of propensities, interests, and habits, not as a mere machine for the reception and registering of pleasure-pain stimuli.[46]

It was the psychology of pragmatism, not the developing scientific psychology, that dominated social and educational thought.

On the issue of the relation of psychology to social problems, Dewey was quite clear but largely ignored by psychologists. In his presidential address to the American Psychological Association, Dewey stated that laboratory results had to be tested "by gradual reapproximation to conditions of life." The school provided an excellent testing ground because it stood midway between life and laboratory.[47]

In a later paper Dewey describes his conception of social psychology and its relation to general psychology.[48] He cites McDougall and Thorndike as the wave of the future in social psychology because they had discredited the imitation and suggestibility theories of social influence. The behavioristic movement is promising be-

45. John B. Watson, *Behaviorism*, pp. 41–43. New York: W. W. Norton & Co., 1930.

46. Hofstadter, *op. cit.*, p. 159.

47. John Dewey, "Psychology and Social Practice," *Psychological Review*, VII (1900), 105–24.

48. John Dewey, "The Need for Social Psychology," *Psychological Review*, XXIV (1917), 266–77.

cause "it transfers attention from vague generalities regarding social consciousness and social mind to the specific processes of interaction which take place among human beings, and to the details of group-behavior."[49] The recurrent theme, already stated in his earlier paper, is that a science of social control had to be developed "for the struggle to gain control of the forces forming society." The theory of the fixed mind, which the new work in psychology made untenable, was being used to preserve the established order. However, "the history of science testifies to a conclusion which may also be arrived at theoretically—the introduction of the experimental method is all one with interest in control—in modification of the future."[50]

Behaviorism became a laboratory science and did not test its ideas under the conditions of life. McDougall was largely rejected by the behaviorists, so it seemed that purposivism was not to be an integral concept in American psychology.[51] Thorndike had his scientific foot in the twentieth century and his moral foot in the nineteenth. He was too conservative for the reformers on the influence of inherited tendencies. Finally, he became preoccupied with efficiency, and long since had provided a rationale for the rivalry motive in education.[52] Thorndike's popular writings seemed to support the prevailing social order, the order that the progressives were determined to change. His ideas on the specificity of learning could be used to support a vocationalism that preserved the masses in their inferior social position. His studies on adult education led him to argue, not long after the child had been removed from the labor market, against compulsory school attendance laws. His work on individual differences seemed to some to favor the status quo. The list becomes endless. Almost every one of Thorndike's major conceptions can be and was interpreted as anti-equalitarian.[53] His data were not discussed; contradictory facts were not introduced. The proponent of scientific objectivity was charged with going beyond his data.[54] The social

49. *Ibid.*, p. 270.　　　　50. *Ibid.*, p. 275.

51. The virtual ignoring of Tolman who assimilated Gestalt concepts and purposive behavior into a behavioristic theory is inexplicable. Educators depend on middlemen for their psychology, and Tolman apparently had no spokesman.

52. Thorndike, *Educational Psychology* (1913). Vol. I, *op. cit.*, pp. 286–89.

53. For a comprehensive discussion of the social implications of Thorndike's ideas, see Curti, *op. cit.*, pp. 459–98.

54. *Ibid.*, pp. 497–98.

implications of his ideas were unacceptable to progressive thought—the major social and intellectual movement in America in the twentieth century.

The Era of Conflicting Psychologies of Learning

Considerable attention has been devoted to Thorndike and Dewey in this discussion because later developments are more easily comprehended from the perspective of the work of these two men. By the time of World War I, Thorndike had produced his major volumes on educational psychology, and Dewey had written *Democracy and Education*. The old theories had been demolished, the scientific study of education had been firmly established, progressive experimentation was under way in the schools.

During World War I the testing movement scored a spectacular success. However, two events occurred which temporarily disrupted this movement in education. The first of these occurred when the results of the Army testing programs were published. A wave of criticism descended on the testers who, unfortunately, had discovered the fact that the average mental age of the American soldier was fourteen years.[55] The test data inevitably reflected ethnic differences, and a dispute on racial superiority ensued. Bagley, among educators, took on the testers. His major point was that their determinism was antidemocratic:

If the determinist is right, the ideal of democracy is wrong; the forces that have resulted in a democratic order are forces of social involution and not of social evolution; the educational aims and ideals that have gone hand in hand with the ideal of insuring a certain kind of equality among human kind, are a tragic, even ghastly, mistake. The determinist talks loudly and frequently about wanting the truth. If he is right, this is the truth and he should not try to evade it.[56]

At the same time the interests of educators had begun to broaden considerably under the influence of progressive social thought. The

---

55. See, for example, Walter Lippman, "The Mental Age of Americans," *New Republic*, XXXII (1922), 213–15; "The Mystery of the 'A' Men," *ibid.*, pp. 246–48; "Reliability of Intelligence Tests," *ibid.*, pp. 275–77; "Abuse of the Tests," *ibid.*, pp. 297–98; "Tests of Hereditary Intelligence," *ibid.*, pp. 328–30; "Future for the Tests," *New Republic*, XXXIII (1922), 9–10.

56. William C. Bagley, *Determinism in Education*, p. 25. Baltimore: Warwick & York, Inc., 1925.

schools were not just simply instruments for teaching the fundamentals and vocational subjects. There were important social problems to solve; attitudes had to be changed. The old tests were too narrow; they were being used to preserve the status quo.[57]

The stage for this period was set, first, by the continuing conflict among psychologists—conflicts which produced a crisis in psychology and led Boring to state that the progress of psychology had been slowed by this internal conflict[58]—and by the publication in 1929 of Bode's influential volume, *Conflicting Psychologies of Learning*.[59]

In this volume Bode analyzes what he regarded as the two main competing psychological theories, Thorndike's connectionism and Watson's behaviorism. It is apparent that the shortcoming of the scientific psychologies, for Bode, was their failure to account for purposive behavior. Bode's objection to Thorndike was that his connections were reflexes and his theory too mechanistic. To discredit the theory, Bode uses an obvious literary device, a description of the Romeo-Juliet relation viewed mechanistically.[60] He then seriously attacks each point in Thorndike's system and concludes:

> The fundamental difficulty with Thorndike, as with the behaviorists, is that he depends too exclusively for explanation upon the nervous system. The environment does nothing except to press the buttons which release the reflexes.[61]

He next proceeds to argue the case for the notion of purposive behavior. In doing so, he introduces Gestalt psychology as a "new approach to the problem of purposive behavior." The following quotation will suggest why Thorndike's influence waned and why Gestalt psychology was to become the preferred psychological theory of educators:

57. Ralph W. Tyler, "The Specific Techniques of Investigation: Examining and Testing Acquired Knowledge, Skill, and Ability," *The Scientific Movement in Education, op. cit.,* pp. 341–55. See also, Guy M. Whipple, "The Contribution of This Society to the Scientific Movement in Education with Special Reference to the Trends in Problems and Methods of Inquiry," *The Scientific Movement in Education, op. cit.* pp. 257–72.

58. Boring, *op. cit.,* p. 742.

59. Boyd Henry Bode, *Conflicting Psychologies of Learning.* New York: D. C. Heath & Co., 1929.

60. *Ibid.,* pp. 178–79.   61. *Ibid.,* p. 190.

There are indications that the tide is turning, and that we are more in the mood to consider the social and spiritual import of the changes which have been wrought by science, *in order that we may achieve a new conception of how intelligence is to function for the betterment of human life* (italics ours). The new conception of the nature of the learning process gives promise of an educational system that will contribute more effectively to the disposition and power to see life steadily and see it whole, in terms of the circumstances and opportunities of the modern age.[62]

The second significant event of this period was the introduction of Gestalt psychology to America. At this point education became acutely concerned about the conflicting psychologies. But, as the preceding discussion has implied, the outcome of the controversy over learning theories in education was already determined.

THE INFLUENCE OF GESTALT PSYCHOLOGY

It is unnecessary to review the substance of Gestalt psychology and field theory, since excellent expositions of the position are readily available[63] and a chapter in this volume is devoted to the subject. The primary question to be answered in this discussion is why Gestalt psychology came to be the preferred psychology of American educators.

The answer to this question is embarrassingly simple. Gestalt psychology and Dewey's conceptions were highly compatible. As Hilgard has stated:

There had already been a rift growing between Thorndike and the more progressive group in education, who, under Dewey's leadership, had made much more than he of the capacity of the individual for setting and solving his own problems. The new insight doctrine fitted nicely their slogan of freeing intelligence for creative activity.[64]

Bode devoted a chapter to an exposition of Gestalt psychology and spelled out how the theory fitted the conception of purposive behavior that prevailed in experimentalist philosophy: "The interesting and important feature of the theory is the fact that it gives an interpretation of purposive behavior which avoids both mental states and outright mechanism."[65] However, he notes that "we are not out

62. *Ibid.*, p. 302.
63. Hilgard, *op. cit.*, chaps. vii and viii; and Boring, *op. cit.*, chap. xxiii.
64. Hilgard, *op. cit.*, p. 224.   65. Bode, *op. cit.*, p. 230.

of the woods," much remains to be done; we have to know more about the relation of stimulus and response and the development of sequences of adaptive behavior.

The point has been made, however; Gestalt psychology was the psychology consistent with the mainstream of American philosophical and educational thought. Ogden had prepared a volume for educators that presented Gestalt psychology as the most viable explanation of the learning process.[66] This early volume of Ogden's is an interesting bridge. Watson appears as a source of data, but his explanations are described as incomplete, "not yet reduced to scientific terms, . . . and lacking in precision."[67] Instincts figure prominently because the need theory and homeostatic equilibrium were to be introduced by Lewin at a later date. Thorndike is dismissed, kindly but firmly, in a few pages.

Ogden's book includes chapters on perception and thinking and reasoning. The cognitive processes were back in psychology, and not just as muscle movements. Cognition provided the ground for adaptive behavior. Reorganization of perceptions, understanding, and insight became the central psychological events.

Gestalt psychology was to merge into field theory, and by 1942, Hartmann and Lewin could spell out the scope of the theory and its educational implications.[68] But the victory had long since been won, so much so that it was now necessary to attempt a reconciliation. Psychology had demonstrated that it could attack social problems experimentally. Lewin's work at the University of Iowa began the development of social psychology, the kind of social psychology that Dewey had called for. Out of this work grew group dynamics, and the American educator had the tool that promised social change.

Behaviorism went down with Thorndike. The distinctions among the behaviorists were too subtle. In any case, Thorndike and the behaviorists were all cut from the same mechanistic, atomistic cloth.

66. Robert Morris Ogden, *Psychology and Education*. New York: Harcourt, Brace & Co., 1926.

67. *Ibid.*, p. 43.

68. George W. Hartmann, "The Field Theory of Learning and Its Educational Consequences," *The Psychology of Learning, op. cit.,* pp. 165–214; and Kurt Lewin, "Field Theory of Learning," *The Psychology of Learning, op. cit.,* pp. 215–42.

They were the laboratory psychologists. By the time that behaviorists turned to larger social problems, the cause was lost.

FREUDIANISM: THE MISSING THEORY

A brief word needs to be said about Freud, whose influence on American education is indeterminate. It may seem cavalier to devote so little attention to a theorist of Freud's stature. Yet even today, when his ideas have been absorbed into our thinking, when his influence in literature and the drama no longer shock, he is barely mentioned in educational psychology texts, a major source of psychological ideas for educators.

Freudianism had a difficult time establishing a base in America from which to exert social influence. Freud's theories were not accepted by American psychologists, with the notable exception of E. B. Holt. A. A. Brill was largely responsible for disseminating his ideas in America, and prior to World War I the Greenwich Village group helped to popularize Freud, at least among intellectuals.

No educational theorist completely adopted Freud and made his ideas the basis for a comprehensive educational theory. Margaret Naumburg and the Walden School were the representatives of Freudianism applied to education, but these applications were outside the public school. Interestingly, this experiment was designed to counteract the prevailing "group-mindedness" of the public school. Naumburg hoped to achieve social change by freeing the individual in the Freudian sense.[69]

Freudianism was eventually absorbed into dynamic psychology. But dynamic psychology is an amorphous theoretical position, and one to which educators are not systematically and consistently exposed. The impact of Freudianism on the conception of the child was great and, perhaps in this way, had a significant though indirect effect on educational theory. Cremin states: "The really pervasive influence of Freudianism on pedagogy came rather indirectly through gradual public acceptance of the psychoanalytic image of the child."[70] To the degree that educators have been exposed to

69. For a discussion of the influence of Freudianism on pedagogy, see Cremin, *op. cit.*, pp. 207–15.

70. *Ibid.*, p. 214.

child psychology, their thinking has been influenced in some undetermined amount by Freud.

Two reasonably direct influences may be found in art education and in the guidance movement. Margaret Naumburg used art as a creative activity to bring the unconscious to conscious life. This approach to art is still a prominent one among art educators.

The guidance movement had its origins before Freudianism was introduced into this country. As the movement, also an amorphous one, absorbed the mental hygiene movement and clinical psychology, it picked up Freudian strains. As late as 1938, however, Trabue, in discussing the guidance movement, makes only a passing reference to developments that presumably were founded in dynamic psychology.[71]

It is perplexing to recognize that Freudian ideas have had a profound effect on American thinking, yet we find so little systematic reference to them in educational theorizing. Several hypotheses may be offered to account for this discrepancy: (*a*) Freudianism influenced the public and popular mind but had no professional spokesman of the stature of Dewey or Thorndike. Freudian ideas did not reach the professional audience of educators in any systematic way. (*b*) Freudianism was gradually absorbed into dynamic psychology and developmental theories and was assimilated, probably unsystematically, by educators who took course work or read in child psychology, mental hygiene, or guidance. (*c*) Freudianism influenced mainly specialists in education, such as guidance personnel. Its larger influence is mediated by individuals who represent no organized group competing in the market place of ideas.

One other factor should be considered. "Lay analysis" never established itself in this country. There has been no easy way for educators to learn "Freudian techniques," nor has there been any translation of these techniques into classroom procedures, as has been the case, for example, with nondirective counseling. This combination of medical associations, lack of readily usable techniques, and recurrent conflict on the therapeutic role of the schools has probably limited the practical influence of Freudian theory.

71. M. R. Trabue, "Contributions of Research to the Development of Guidance in Education," *The Scientific Movement in Education, op. cit.,* p. 231. Since the emphasis in this volume was on research contributions, Trabue may have thought that educational practices growing out of dynamic psychology had not yet been sufficiently or adequately investigated.

FUNCTIONALISM: THE SILENT STREAM

Functionalism must also be regarded as a theory that probably has had the most persistent though disguised effect on educational theory and research. Functionalism as a system has absorbed the major ideas of other systems in one way or another. This tendency to assimilate accounts for its seemingly unorganized but highly pragmatic character. As Hilgard points out, "The difficulty with functionalism is that it does not satisfy the esthetic desire for a neat system."[72] The lack of a sharply defined image has probably made it difficult for educators to identify the position as a worthy competitor against the more clearly identified systems. Its spokesmen have also lacked the strident self-assurance that has characterized some of the major protagonists.

The principal representative of functionalism in American education has been Judd. His *Educational Psychology* amply demonstrates the breadth of ideas that a functionalist was willing to consider seriously.[73] Heredity and the nervous system are there, as are also the cognitive processes. Social influences occupy the most prominent position. Measurement and individual differences receive their due. Unlike comparable presentations, a significant place is given to the psychology of the school subjects and the curriculum. All of this is buttressed by moderate research citation. Here, an educator could find reasonable answers to important practical questions. But the contributions of Judd and other functionalists were probably ignored in the great controversy between purposivism and mechanism.

The greatest influence of this position is probably through the myriad of educational research personnel who have been engaged in curriculum studies. These are the workers who have argued for fairly precise statements of objectives, who have insisted on measurement of effects, and who have asked only that the ideas underlying the proposal make some kind of general theoretical sense. They have not been concerned about the contributions of such studies to the development of a systematic theoretical position. They were in the mainstream of progressive thought but were broader and more eclectic than the progressives.

72. Hilgard, *op. cit.*, p. 479.

73. Charles Hubbard Judd, *Educational Psychology*. Boston: Houghton Mifflin Co., 1939.

The Residue

One of the most striking facts apparent in reviewing the history of education and psychology in the past sixty years is that every major position has left a deposit of ideas and procedure. An obvious example is G. Stanley Hall. His racial heredity and recapitulation ideas were discredited, but child study and developmental notions persist. Transfer of learning in education is hardly advanced beyond Thorndike (and Judd), and Thorndike's conceptions of the influence of reward have been broadened but retained. Gestalt psychology and field theory are with us in the form of continuing concern for cognitive processes and personality as a social phenomenon. Dynamic psychology appears in the concern for adaptation of education to the special needs of the individual, particularly his emotional needs.

Education has needed a science of man, and a science of man is what it has sought from psychology. In the early days when a new science of man was being created, education adopted the "new psychology." When there were competing psychologies, the profession chose that psychology which seemed to offer a more comprehensive science. When a new or more comprehensive psychological theory appears, education will probably assimilate it.

Because education is a moral enterprise, educators have always felt that they needed a philosophy. John Dewey provided one that had enormous appeal and seemed peculiarly adapted to the problem of the school in American society. No viable substitute has been offered for Dewey's philosophy. If one were, it would probably determine the kind of psychological theory educators would prefer.

The history of the past sixty years suggests the kinds of characteristics any psychological theory must have to win a significant place in educational theory.

First, its scientific character must be unimpeachable. Early in this century education turned to science as the solution to its problems and has one of the most persistent trends in this respect of any of the professions. Despite the criticisms of educational research, educators seek the security of research as the ground for their practice. What is regarded as "good science" will vary with the times obviously, as the omnipresence of the computer today suggests. Education will follow that group of scientists who seem to be in the fore-front of the behavioral sciences.

Second, a system to be acceptable must be social in character or must treat social problems in a significant way. Education is a social enterprise, and both theorist and practitioner are painfully aware of the social character of their problems. The comparatively recent interest of education in anthropology reflects this concern with the sociocultural matrix in which the school is embedded. It also accounts for the continued interest in cognitive theory and research in social influence.

Third, the theory must account for developmental phenomena. They simply cannot be ignored. Developmental theories appeal to educators because they think they observe developmental phenomena. The maturing organism is a central concept in educational thinking. Part of the increasing appeal of the emerging social learning theories may be attributed to the fact that they study the phenomena educators assume they observe. They are also unmistakably "social."

Fourth, the theory must promise some form of "control." A recurrent theme in the early part of this century was that science would provide the means to control the educational process, in the service of noble ends, of course. Because "control" has authoritarian connotations, the word "practical" has been substituted. Psychology is criticized because it is not "practical"; educators want practical advice. But whether the word "control" or "practical" is used, what seems to be called for are systems that lead to procedures with predictable effects. The present Skinnerian concepts, in part, satisfy this need.

An important aspect of a system that promises control is that it must have been demonstrated to work under the "conditions of life." This requirement is simply another way of asking for proof of effectiveness.

Fifth, the theory somehow must evidence its concern for the individual. The problem of individuality in education has not been solved. A system of mass education inevitably works with groups, but the needs of individuals press on the practitioner. "Providing for individual differences" may be a shibboleth, but it is a potent one. No single theory has stepped forward to demonstrate how to solve this problem. But a vague, unanalyzed feeling persists that the individual must not be sacrificed.

A theory must probably also treat cognitive processes tenderly. "Subject matter," despite the battles of the progressives, is a controlling force in education. Understanding of and attitudes toward content are critical aspects of educational procedures. Psychologists have been largely responsible for eradicating rote learning in the schools. The residue is the idea that cognitive and attitudinal processes are central concepts in any theory of personality that has educational relevance.

No single psychological theory has all the enumerated characteristics at present. Whether any ever will have remains to be seen. Certainly, psychologists do not create theories to be acceptable to nonpsychologists. On the other hand, there seems no good reason for educational theory to be committed to any single psychological theory short of a comprehensive science of man. Practitioners can afford to be eclectic; even a science of education need not be coterminus with a science of psychology.

These characteristics of the education and psychology relationship will probably be determiners in the foreseeable future. Learning theories, like politicians, will seem to fall out of favor because they have been around too long. But closer analysis will probably reveal that the *Zeitgeist* makes one or more of the above characteristics critical. Each of them is bound up with the profound changes in American thinking that have occurred in this century. Each is enmeshed in the perduring problems education has faced.

CHAPTER II

Contemporary Developments within Stimulus-Response Learning Theory

WINFRED F. HILL

Introduction

AN OVERVIEW OF S-R THEORY

Most of the learning theories within academic psychology have a stimulus-response orientation. This is equally true whether one considers conditioning, animal learning, verbal learning, or thinking. Though in some cases greatly modified and elaborated, the paradigm of stimulus and response remains basic to most theoretical work in learning.

Several factors probably contribute to this primacy of S-R interpretations. For one thing, S-R analysis seems to most theorists (though not to those of a gestaltist persuasion) to fit better with our knowledge of physiology than do the field-theoretical interpretations. For another, the S-R approach focuses attention on observable and measurable events in the external world, a focus many observers consider more compatible with objective research than one that emphasizes the individual's phenomenal experience. This emphasis on the objective environment, in turn, provides a basis for studying the manipulations that produce behavioral change. This makes the S-R approach well suited for studying the conditions under which learning occurs. These various factors help to explain why the S-R approach, despite some limitations, has remained popular with those psychologists interested in the experimental study and theoretical analysis of learning.

Current stimulus-response theories, however, have developed considerably since the days of Thorndike and Watson. In particular, they show many effects of their frequent altercations with cognitive theories. The fact that the S-R approach has continued to flourish in spite of the numerous cogent criticisms that have been directed against it is partly due to its (sometimes grudging) acceptance of cognitive and purposive interpretations from other kinds of theory. Thus, we find within current S-R theory many interpretations that are both cognitive and purposive in all but the name. One of the most striking developments in recent S-R theory is its success in translating what were once considered alien concepts into stimulus-response terms. Two of the chief foci of interest in current S-R theory are the role of mediating responses (the cognitive issue) and the nature of drive and reinforcement (the purposive issue).

Along with this broadening of S-R theory in the cognitive and purposive directions has gone an interest in the formal aspects of theory construction. Tolman's introduction of intervening variables and Hull's espousal of the logical-deductive method have been followed by a marked interest in formal models of learning, most notably those of a statistical sort. Psychologists are becoming more concerned about both the logical basis of their theories and the ways of improving the formal structure of these theories. This trend joins psychology with logic, mathematics, and philosophy of science in an attempt to build better theories of learning.

Neither of the two trends mentioned in the preceding paragraphs is by any means entirely new. Watson, for example, was concerned both with the philosophical implications of his behaviorism and with the ways in which cognitive processes could be described in stimulus-response terms. However, both in terms of the amount of attention they receive and in terms of the sophistication with which they are handled, the emphasis on broadening S-R theory into the cognitive and purposive realms and on making it more precise and formal are two of the most distinctive features of current theoretical work in the psychology of learning.

THREE MAJOR CURRENT APPROACHES IN S-R THEORY

If we survey the developments in the psychology of learning over the past quarter century, three main stimulus-response approaches appear to have taken on the character of traditions. These are associated with the names of Clark L. Hull, B. F. Skinner, and Edwin R. Guthrie. More properly, these three traditions may be said to exemplify general behavior theory within experimental psychology.

Hence the list excludes students of learning whose main interest is in verbal learning and thinking or in physiological processes. The theories considered here are those which attempt to explain a wide variety of behavioral phenomena, particularly those of learning and motivation, in terms of the connections between physical stimuli (or other conditions) and observable responses. They typically have tried to find principles of behavior that apply to all the higher animals as well as to man and that can be used as building blocks in the interpretation of complex forms of behavior.

Of these three men, the one who most clearly has represented a continuing tradition is Hull. In his lifetime he was the center of an active theoretical and experimental group. Since his death in 1952, the dominant figure in the tradition has been Kenneth W. Spence. Spence shared in Hull's work while Hull was alive and, since his death, has carried on the work in much the same way that Hull might have, had he lived. Also noteworthy are the contributions of Neal E. Miller (best known through his collaborations with John Dollard) and, more recently, of Frank Logan. Thus, the tradition has survived its founder by over a decade and is still vigorous in both theory and research. On a wide variety of topics in learning theory, Hull's and Spence's interpretations are the starting point of any discussion. One may accept or reject them, but one can scarcely ignore them. The terminology that Hull introduced has been aptly referred to by Cotton as "the Esperanto of psychology."

With Skinner, it is less exact to speak of a tradition, since Skinner himself continues to be the center of the approach to psychology that he developed. Since the publication of his first book in 1938, he has gradually become less and less a voice crying in the wilderness and more and more the center of an active and influential movement. However, his followers still retain some of the air of a dissident minority. They publish their own journal (*The Journal of the Experimental Analysis of Behavior*), hold some of their own meetings within psychological conventions, and have a touch of messianic zeal about their distinctive approach to psychology. This approach is empirical and practical, so much so that Skinner denies being a theorist at all. Nevertheless, since he certainly has a systematic interpretation of learned behavior, we may consider his approach as one of the traditions in learning theory.

There is also some question about the appropriateness of including

Guthrie's theoretical tradition. There is no question that such a tradition exists, running from Guthrie (who died in 1959) to Fred D. Sheffield, Virginia W. Voeks, and A. A. Lumsdaine. However, it is of much smaller proportions than the Hullian tradition and also, since Skinner's recent boom, considerably smaller than the Skinnerian. A major basis for placing the Guthrian tradition on a par with the two others is the apparent continuity between it and much of statistical learning theory, most notably the work of William K. Estes. It is admittedly an oversimplification to regard Estes as a Guthrian, for he owes much both to Skinner, with whom he studied, and to Hull. Nevertheless, the resemblance between his assumptions about learning and those of Guthrie is so marked that his theory may be considered a continuation of the Guthrian tradition. Guthrie is now most noted for his attempts to reduce learning theory to simple terms of conditioning by contiguity and for his suggestions about the management of practical learning situations. Posterity may well judge, however, that his greatest contribution was in paving the way for the statistical models of learning.

All three of these traditions are developments from the behaviorism of an earlier day. This intellectual ancestry can be analyzed more finely; Guthrie, for example, shares with Watson an emphasis on conditioning by contiguity, while Skinner shares Thorndike's emphasis on reinforcement. For understanding the present situation, however, it is enough to note that all three are modern versions of behaviorism. Like the earlier behaviorism, these three approaches to psychology all emphasize the objective analysis of behavior and the use of conditioning principles in carrying out that analysis. Though the differences among them often seem large to their proponents, in the larger picture of psychological theory their similarities are more striking than their differences.

These three major S-R approaches will be discussed in turn, followed by some general considerations about S-R theory and a brief look at its applications. Due to limitations of space, no attempt will be made to provide complete coverage. Instead, attention will be focused primarily on two areas: (*a*) the currently active topic of reinforcement and its relation to other topics, and (*b*) the ways in which stimulus-response theory is moving closer to cognitive theory.

The Hullian Tradition

HISTORICAL OVERVIEW

The most thorough presentation of Hull's theory in its early form was made in 1943 in *Principles of Behavior*.[1] (A shorter version was included in the Forty-first Yearbook of the National Society for the Study of Education.[2]) Hull's book presented and explained a number of postulates about the nature of behavior and learning, postulates from which theorems could be logically deduced. Hull originally intended the book to be the first volume of a trilogy, in which the second and third volumes would present the derivation of theorems referring to various behavior situations. The second volume appeared in 1952 under the title, *A Behavior System*.[3] It contained 133 theorems referring to mammalian (mostly rat) behavior in complex nonsocial situations. Hull barely succeeded in completing this book before his death, so that the third volume, which was to have dealt with social behavior, remained unwritten.

Even before he wrote the second volume, Hull had begun to revise parts of the system. A revised set of postulates was published in 1951 in his *Essentials of Behavior*[4] and was incorporated in 1952 into *A Behavior System*. These modifications were neither complete enough nor consistent enough to solve all the problems within the system, and if Hull had lived he would probably have made a number of further changes. As it was, the job of modifying the system and continuing the development of the theory was undertaken by Spence, a former student of Hull's and a long-time contributor to his thinking. Spence's general interpretation of learning, less formal than Hull's but otherwise quite similar, was presented in *Behavior Theory and Conditioning*,[5] with a few additions in *Behavior Theory*

1. Clark L. Hull, *Principles of Behavior*. New York: Appleton-Century-Crofts, 1943.

2. Clark L. Hull, "Conditioning: Outline of a Systematic Theory of Learning," in *The Psychology of Learning*, chap. ii. Forty-first Yearbook of the National Society for the Study of Education, Part II. Chicago: Distributed by University of Chicago Press, 1942.

3. Clark L. Hull, *A Behavior System*. New Haven: Yale University Press, 1952.

4. Clark L. Hull, *Essentials of Behavior*. New Haven: Yale University Press, 1951.

5. Kenneth W. Spence, *Behavior Theory and Conditioning*. New Haven: Yale University Press, 1956.

and Learning.[6] A consideration of Spence's interpretation of learning will show the directions in which the Hullian tradition has moved and the similarities that are now apparent between it and other interpretations of learning.

Principal components.—Spence's theory, like Hull's, serves to link independent and dependent variables by way of a number of intervening variables (the concept of intervening variables having been introduced by Tolman). The most basic of these intervening variables is excitatory potential (abbreviated E). It refers to the strength of the tendency to give a certain response to a particular stimulus. This is an intervening variable rather than a dependent variable because it cannot be measured directly, but must be inferred from the latency or amplitude or some other observable characteristic of the response. The theory is designed to make predictions from the values of various independent variables to the value of E, and from this in turn to various dependent variables.

The level of excitatory potential for any given response depends in turn on a number of other intervening variables more closely linked to the independent variables. Three of these are of principal interest: habit strength, drive, and incentive motivation. Habit strength (abbreviated H) is the variable that reflects permanent learning. It depends on the amount of practice—specifically, the number of prior occurrences of the response to the stimulus. Drive (D) and incentive motivation (K) are both motivational variables, with effective motivation equal to D + K. In the case of motivation for food, D represents the internal state of hunger, while K reflects the effect of the external incentive, food. Thus in this case D might be thought of as hunger and K as appetite. In more general terms, D reflects a bodily need and K reflects the availability of some substance that will satisfy the need. In cases where the drive involves noxious stimulation, whether in the form of a primary drive such as pain or a secondary drive such as fear, the relationship is somewhat different, and will not be considered in this section.

The value of E is obtained by multiplying together the values of

6. Kenneth W. Spence, *Behavior Theory and Learning.* Englewood Cliffs, New Jersey: Prentice-Hall, Inc., 1960.

H, D, and K. Thus, the prediction of behavior proceeds from: (*a*) such independent variables as amount of previous reinforced practice, present state of bodily need, and magnitude of reward, through (*b*) the intervening variables H, D, and K, and (*c*) the second-order intervening variable E, to (*d*) such dependent variables as the latency and amplitude of the response. Since two of the three constituents of E are motivational variables, it is clear that this is not merely a learning theory but a general behavior theory.

Treatment of reward.—In Spence's interpretation (which differs from Hull's on this point), the level of H depends exclusively on the number of times that the response has occurred to the stimulus. Reinforcement is not necessary in order for stimulus-response connections to be established and strengthened. Reward operates only by way of K, not of H, and thus becomes a variable in performance rather than in learning as such.

Moreover, K is explained in terms of a more fundamental mechanism, the fractional anticipatory goal response, abbreviated r_G. This is a fractional part of the goal response, which becomes conditioned to the cues of the goal. For example, salivation and small chewing movements become conditioned to the sight of a steak, since salivation and chewing are parts of the behavior involved in eating the steak. The act of eating occurs in the presence of the stimuli from seeing the steak, so that the response of eating is learned to the stimulus of seeing the steak. The complete eating response is not always possible to the visual stimulus (e.g., if only a picture of a steak is presented), but the fractional parts, such as salivation and small chewing movements, can and do occur. These, then, are the fractional anticipatory goal responses.

Whenever a certain kind of reward is consistently found in a given place, r_G appropriate for that reward become conditioned to the stimuli of that place. By stimulus generalization, the stimuli of the path leading to this place also come to elicit r_G, though to a lesser extent. The closer the individual is to the point at which reward has previously been received, the more strongly r_G will occur. These r_G in turn produce stimuli, called s_G, which have motivational effects. The closer the individual gets to the previously rewarded place, the stronger, and hence the more motivating s_G will be. Thus, the gradient of increasing s_G serves to "pull" the individual toward the goal, guiding him in the correct direction and providing a portion of the motivation that keeps him moving.

The r_G, like any other responses, are conditioned to the stimuli of the goal because they occur in the presence of those stimuli, not because of reinforcement. On the other hand, the fact that these particular responses are concerned with the consuming of a reward gives them (or, more precisely, gives the stimuli they produce) special motivational properties. Just how or why these motivational properties of the s_G occur is a question that Spence does not claim to have answered thoroughly. However, since the effects of s_G are motivational, Spence adds together K (produced directly by s_G) and D to obtain a total level of motivation. The formula for E thus becomes (again a departure from Hull) $E = H \times (D + K)$.

RELATION TO OTHER SYSTEMS

Cognitive theories.—The rather technical modifications in the Hullian interpretations of drive and reinforcement that have been described are most interesting because of the cognitive slant that they give to this kind of stimulus-response theory. Even before these changes, many cognitive phenomena were predictable from Hull's postulates, but such prediction has been made easier by the changes. This is primarily because the learning-performance distinction, long emphasized by Tolman, has now been fully incorporated into Hullian theory. The building up of H now depends exclusively on experience, without reference to reinforcement. Latent learning is thus accepted, since habit strength for a given response can be learned to a high level while excitatory potential, and hence performance, remains low. When the appropriate reward is provided, the behavior can then appear quickly at full strength. This reformulation leaves relatively little difference between what Spence calls the habit of making a certain response to a certain stimulus and what Tolman calls the expectancy that making a certain response to a certain stimulus will produce certain effects. Whether it is called a habit or an expectancy, there is a potential for making a given response leading to certain consequences, a potential which may or may not be expressed, depending on conditions. In both cases, this behavioral potential results only from experience of what acts or paths lead to what places or situations, without reference to reinforcement.

The accommodation of Hullian theory to cognitive thinking, begun by Hull himself and carried somewhat further by Spence, has reached its extreme in a recent formulation by O. Hobart Mowrer. In *Learning Theory and Behavior*,[7] Mowrer examines his own attempts and those of others over a period of years to analyze learning and motivation within the S-R framework. At an earlier stage in his thinking, he suggested that visceral responses (corresponding roughly to attitudes and emotions) are learned by sign learning, whereas skeletal (instrumental) responses are learned by solution learning. In sign learning, stimuli are learned as signs of impending events, whereas in solution learning, responses are learned as solutions to problems. Solution learning requires reinforcement by drive reduction, but sign learning does not. He now suggests that sign learning is a broad enough category to include solution learning, so that actually all learning involves discovering the significance of signs. A sound that has often preceded shock will be a sign of danger, and feeling one's self making a response that has previously turned off the shock will likewise be a sign of hope. The usual S-R interpretation (including Mowrer's own, in his earlier theory) would be that the escape or avoidance response is learned because it reduces the drive of pain or fear. Mowrer's new interpretation, however, looks at the sensations produced by the response rather than at the response itself. It is these sensations which become signs of hope, and as a result the response which produces these sensations tends to occur. Although this formulation still does not have all the sign-gestalt properties of Tolman's theory, it is closer to traditional cognitive than connectionist theory. The fact that it, like Spence's formulation, developed out of work within the S-R framework indicates the force of cognitive considerations in current learning theory.

Guthrie's theory.—Spence's reinterpretation of K as equivalent to r_G not only strengthens the cognitive aspect of Hullian theory, it also brings it closer to Guthrie's. For Spence, both instrumental responses (such as running down an alley) and fractional anticipatory

7. O. Hobart Mowrer, *Learning Theory and Behavior*. New York: John Wiley & Sons, 1960.

goal responses (such as chewing and salivating) are conditioned by contiguity. In other words, they are learned as responses to certain stimuli because they occur as responses to those stimuli, without any reference to reinforcement. This is a very Guthrian interpretation, one in which drive reduction disappears from consideration and reinforcement becomes a derived rather than a basic concept. From a practical point of view this does not mean that Spence considers reward unimportant, but that he treats it as a matter of motivation rather than of the reinforcement of learned connections.

Skinner's system.—Finally, Spence's version of Hullian theory also shows resemblances to Skinner's interpretations. Skinner makes reinforcement a crucial variable, without trying to explain reinforcement in terms of any other more basic processes. At first glance, this makes his interest rather different from Spence's. However, the aspect of reinforcement that interests Skinner is the way that changes in reinforcement produce rapid changes in performance, not necessarily in long-term learning. From a practical point of view, therefore, Spence and Skinner agree that current behavior depends on the current reward contingencies. They differ in that Spence treats this generalization as something to be explained, whereas Skinner treats it as something to be used in explaining other phenomena.

The closeness of Hullian and Skinnerian theories is more marked when we look at the work of Spence's former student, Frank Logan, who has brought the two closer together in several ways.[8] One is by his development of micromolar theory, in which different amplitudes of the "same" response are treated as different responses. The micromolar approach makes possible the interpretation of situations in which different amplitudes are selectively reinforced. Such selective reinforcement is a favorite procedure of Skinner's. A second attempt by Logan to incorporate Skinnerian ideas into the Hullian tradition is seen in his elaborate mathematical models for predicting behavior in the free-responding situation, where there are no discrete trials and the subject responds at his own rate. Such free-responding situations are characteristic of Skinner's research. Finally, Logan's research, typically involving many experiments, each on a few subjects and with relatively little use of statistical analysis, has a rather

8. Frank Logan, *Incentive*. New Haven, Connecticut: Yale University Press, 1960.

Skinnerian flavor. Much of Logan's work may be seen as an attempt to apply the theoretical sophistication of Hull to the promising new areas of research that have been opened up by Skinner.

Skinner and His Followers

LAWFULNESS IN THE INDIVIDUAL CASE

Except for Logan's attempts at a *rapprochement,* there is a marked change in approach when we move from the Hullian to the Skinnerian tradition. This is true in spite of the fact that both Hull and Skinner have emphasized precision and rigor, have made great use of the concept of reinforcement, and have served as the inspiration for large amounts of experimental research. The great difference between them is in their orientation toward theory. Hull is the theorist par excellence in the experimental psychology of learning, orienting all of his work toward the elaboration and perfection of his hypothetico-deductive behavior system. Experiments, for Hull, are of value primarily as tests of theorems and hence as bases for confirming or modifying postulates. Skinner, on the other hand, rejects such high-level theorizing, wants nothing to do with intervening variables, and concentrates on experimental research for its own sake. He wants to establish laws of behavior, laws relating independent to dependent variables. Although these laws cannot help being theoretical to an extent, since they involve classification and some degree of generalization, they have none of the deductive structure or the elaborate systems of intervening variables that characterize Hull's theories. They are as close to purely inductive statements as it is practical to get in science. It is on this basis that Skinner claims not to be a theorist at all.

Moreover, Skinner is interested not in statistical lawfulness, which is all to which most Hullians aspire, but in lawfulness of the individual case. Given a powerful independent variable, a reliable dependent variable, and adequate experimental controls, behavior is lawful enough to permit accurate prediction of what an individual organism will do under a given set of conditions. The experimenter's job in Skinner's opinion is to arrange the conditions so that these lawful relations can be determined. Thus, in spite of their vast differences in other respects, Skinner shares with Lewin, Rogers, and

Combs and Snygg an interest in predicting the behavior of single individuals rather than behavior in terms of averages of groups of individuals. This interest may explain in part the appeal that Skinner has had for educators and for various other groups concerned with the applied psychology of learning.

In support of this emphasis on the individual case, Skinnerians have emphasized that the averaging of learning curves can completely distort the typical patterns of the individual curves which are averaged.[9] The most obvious example of this, important to both Guthrians and Gestaltists as well as to Skinnerians, is the case where each individual learner shows a sudden improvement from poor to near-perfect performance in one trial. If different individuals show this one-trial learning after different numbers of trials, an averaged curve will show a gradual improvement from trial to trial. This averaged curve could easily be misinterpreted as showing gradual improvement by each learner, when in fact it is only a statistical artifact of the different stages at which different individuals suddenly achieved mastery.

Skinner's alternative to averaging is the use of individual cumulative response curves. To show the effect of a given experimental manipulation, Skinner usually presents one or two of these curves from "typical" individuals. As his critics have been quick to point out, this approach introduces the dangers of subjective distortion and of confusing individual differences or chance fluctuations with true experimental effects. Actually, these dangers are less serious in the kind of work that Skinner does than might appear at first glance. For the most part, Skinner and his followers have worked with performance variables for which it is practical to test each subject under all experimental conditions and to collect large amounts of data from each subject. This minimizes the danger that either individual differences or accidental fluctuations will be confused with genuine effects of the independent variable. Nevertheless, since this approach does not include statistical analysis, the problem of subjectivity in identifying typical cases and in generalizing from them remains as a drawback of Skinner's approach.

9. Murray Sidman, "A Note on Functional Relations Obtained from Group Data," *Psychological Bulletin*, XLIX (May, 1952), 263–69.

THEORETICAL CONTRIBUTIONS

Skinner's orientation toward research received its first major statement in his *Behavior of Organisms*[10] and has since continued essentially unchanged through his semipopular *Science and Human Behavior*[11] to the present. By his own restricted definition, Skinner has contributed nothing to theory—except negatively, as in his article "Are Theories of Learning Necessary?"[12] In the broader sense, however, his contributions have been by no means negligible. Most noteworthy is his distinction between respondent and operant behavior, with respondent behavior being elicited reflexly by particular stimuli, and operant behavior being emitted by the organism without having any particular identifiable eliciting stimulus. The learning paradigms for these two kinds of behavior correspond to what are conventionally known as classical and instrumental conditioning, respectively. Although the distinction between these two kinds of learning has been made by a number of theorists,[13] Skinner is both one of the first to make it and the only one to make a clear distinction between elicited and emitted behavior. The concept of operant (emitted) behavior represents a theoretically important departure from the traditional paradigm of stimulus and response.

In addition to this major theoretical contribution, Skinner and his followers have made a number of others. Among these are the classification and analysis of reinforcement schedules in the free operant situation,[14] the interpretation of avoidance learning,[15] the analysis of verbal behavior,[16] and the interpretation of a wide varie-

10. B. F. Skinner, *The Behavior of Organisms*. New York: Appleton-Century-Crofts, 1938.

11. B. F. Skinner, *Science and Human Behavior*. New York: Macmillan Co., 1953.

12. B. F. Skinner, "Are Theories of Learning Necessary?" *Psychological Review*, LVII (July, 1950), 193–216.

13. Ernest R. Hilgard and Donald G. Marquis, *Conditioning and Learning*. Revised by Gregory A. Kimble. New York: Appleton-Century-Crofts, 1961 (second edition).

14. Charles B. Ferster and B. F. Skinner, *Schedules of Reinforcement*. New York: Appleton-Century-Crofts, 1957.

15. Murray Sidman, "Two Temporal Parameters of the Maintenance of Avoidance Behavior by the White Rat," *Journal of Comparative and Physiological Psychology*, XLVI (August, 1953), 253–61.

16. B. F. Skinner, *Verbal Behavior*. New York: Appleton-Century-Crofts, 1957.

ty of social phenomena in terms of learning principles.[17] So, although Skinner has kept his theorizing closer to the data than many other psychologists of learning, it is just as appropriate to speak of a Skinnerian system as of a Hullian or Guthrian system.

Unlike most other S-R theorists, Skinner has made no attempt to explain why reinforcers are reinforcing. Rather than deriving the reinforcing relationship from drive reduction (like Hull) or stimulus change (like Guthrie) or consummatory responses (like Spence and Sheffield), he makes the fact that some experiences are reinforcing a central starting point of his system. In Hullian terms, we might say that Skinner first defines the relationship of reinforcement, then postulates that what will reinforce one response will also reinforce others, and goes on from there to derive his theorems. (Skinner would, of course, vigorously reject this way of discussing his work.)

For the most part, the modifications in Skinner's system since 1938 have been extensions rather than actual changes. Research has been extended from rats to other species, particularly to pigeons and also to monkeys and humans. Many complex schedules of reinforcement, both positive and negative, have been studied and interpreted. Language, psychosis, and social organization have all been interpreted within the systematic framework, and the improvement of education through programed learning has recently become a major interest. Through the popularization of these many applications, Skinner's system has threatened to replace Hull's as the one that outsiders most often identify with S-R learning theory in general.

Guthrie and His Influence

GUTHRIE'S LAST STATEMENT OF HIS POSITION

In the 1952 revision of his *Psychology of Learning*,[18] Guthrie reaffirmed his conviction (expressed in the earlier edition of the book and in the Forty-first Yearbook of the National Society for the Study of Education)[19] that association by contiguity is the basic

17. Skinner, *Science and Human Behavior, op. cit.*

18. Edwin R. Guthrie, *The Psychology of Learning.* New York: Harper & Bros., 1952 (revised edition).

19. Edwin R. Guthrie, "Conditioning: A Theory of Learning in Terms of Stimulus, Response, and Association," in *The Psychology of Learning,* chap. ii. Forty-first Yearbook of the National Society for the Study of Education, Part II. Chicago: Distributed by the University of Chicago Press, 1942.

law of learning. He supported this contention by citing his work with Horton, which showed the very stereotyped behavior of cats learning to escape from a puzzle box, and by arguing at length, in reply to a private challenge from Neal Miller, that the concept of reinforcement is not necessary for explaining learning. Noting how little his views have changed in the seventeen years since the first edition, Guthrie expressed the hope that this was because the original ideas were correct rather than because he was growing rigid in his opinions with advancing age.

The likelihood of the latter possibility appears reduced by Guthrie's final statement, his contribution to Volume II of *Psychology: A Study of a Science.*[20] In this volume, while maintaining his basic views, he showed considerable flexibility in extending them to deal with certain phenomena in which there has recently been renewed interest. He placed considerable emphasis on responses that modify subsequent stimuli—in other words, the phenomenon of attention. Movement-produced stimulation had long been a mainstay of Guthrie's system, but it involved the feedback, primarily proprioceptive, produced by the movement. In his more recent analysis, Guthrie put more emphasis on the modification of stimulus reception by changes in receptor orientation. He expanded this concept to include scanning, a systematic variation in receptor orientation serving to discover a given stimulus. This concept of scanning is strikingly reminiscent of Tolman's "search for the stimulus." As a consequence of these considerations, Guthrie suggested that his basic law of learning, "a combination of stimuli that accompanies a movement will, on its recurrence, tend to be followed by that movement,"[21] might alternatively be stated, "what is being noticed becomes a signal for what is being done."[22] Although this does not represent any real change in Guthrie's system, it does point up the trend toward more cognitive interests that pervades much of recent stimulus-response psychology.

20. Edwin R. Guthrie, "Association by Contiguity," in *Psychology: A Study of a Science: II, General Systematic Formulations, Learning, and Special Processes*, pp. 158–95. Edited by Sigmund Koch. New York: McGraw-Hill Book Co., 1959.

21. Guthrie, *The Psychology of Learning, op. cit.,* p. 23.

22. Guthrie, "Association by Contiguity," *op. cit.,* p. 186.

THE CONSUMMATORY RESPONSE AS REINFORCER

Most of Guthrie's contribution to recent psychological theory has come indirectly through his influence on other workers. Although he has not attracted a large following, several people have been markedly influenced by him. Much of their work has involved reformulating certain of Guthrie's ideas in more precise and testable form.

Sheffield.—Noteworthy among these followers of Guthrie in his emphasis on association by contiguity is Fred D. Sheffield. Sheffield's principal interest has been in the effect of rewards. Guthrie avoided the language of reinforcement, and his assumption that rewards influence behavior only by changing the stimulus situation has been subjected to a good deal of criticism.[23] Sheffield proposed a somewhat modified version of Guthrie's formulation. He predicted that whether an individual learned to approach a goal object would depend on how he behaved toward that goal object. If he made a consummatory response to it (eating it, for example), he would tend to learn to approach it. If he did not make a consummatory response, he would not learn the approach response. This hypothesis is Guthrian in that it makes what an individual learns dependent on what he does, but it departs from the simple version of Guthrie's law of learning in that the particular response that is learned (the instrumental reponse) is different from the one that is crucial in the learning situation (the consummatory response).

Sheffield's hypothesis might be seen as following from certain ideas of Guthrie's about the learning of anticipations, where an anticipation is defined as a muscular readiness for a movement in a series. In the present case, the anticipation takes the form of incomplete consummatory responses. Sheffield's view carries the additional idea that the anticipation excites the learner, impelling him to make more vigorously the instrumental response leading to the anticipated goal. This view is strikingly similar to the one that Spence stated several years later, in which the consummatory response is assumed to become conditioned as r_G.

Sheffield, working in the Hullian stronghold at Yale, was particu-

23. Ernest R. Hilgard, *Theories of Learning*, chap. iii. New York: Appleton-Century-Crofts, 1956 (second edition).

larly interested in examining the hypothesis that the occurrence of a consummatory response is a better predictor of learning than is drive reduction. In other words, reinforcement depends on what the individual does (the consummatory response) rather than on what happens to him (drive reduction). One way of demonstrating this was to show that saccharine serves as a reinforcer for rats even though it is completely nonnutritive and, therefore, presumably does not reduce the hunger drive.[24] Since the animal makes a consummatory response to the saccharine, he learns to approach it. Another experiment showed that male rats would learn to run to a female in heat even though they were always interrupted during the copulatory sequence prior to ejaculation.[25] Since presumably sex behavior prior to ejaculation involves increasing rather than decreasing drive, this result suggests that the reinforcement resulted from the copulatory activity, even though it was incomplete, rather than from any reduction in the sex drive.

Premack.—Sheffield's interpretation of reinforcement (which Guthrie would not call by that name) has been extended by Premack.[26] He suggests that any activity is potentially reinforcing, in other words, can serve as a consummatory response in Sheffield's paradigm. Whether a given response will serve to reinforce another response depends not merely on what the given response is but on the relation between the two responses. Every possible response has some rate at which it will be emitted if it is continuously freely available. If it is not freely available but, instead, is available only when some other response has been made first, then it is being used to reinforce the other response. For example, if food is available only if one first opens a package, then the opportunity to eat food is being used to reinforce the response of opening the package. Will it actually be reinforcing? Premack's reply is that it will serve to reinforce the other response if, and only if, the rate of the poten-

24. Fred D. Sheffield and Thornton B. Roby, "Reward Value of a Nonnutritive Sweet Taste," *Journal of Comparative and Physiological Psychology*, XLIII (December, 1950), 471–81.

25. Fred D. Sheffield, J. Jepson Wulff, and Robert Backer, "Reward Value of Copulation without Sex Drive Reduction," *Journal of Comparative and Physiological Psychology*, XLIV (February, 1951), 3–8.

26. David Premack, "Toward Empirical Behavior Laws: I, Positive Reinforcement," *Psychological Review*, LXVI (July, 1959), 219–33.

tially reinforcing response (eating) is greater than the rate of the to-be-reinforced response (opening the package) when both are freely available and independent. In other words, any response can be used to reinforce another less frequent response, but not a more frequent one. This might be paraphrased in everyday speech by saying that individuals will do something they like less in order to be able to do something else that they like better, but not vice versa. However, Premack has made this statement more precise by giving an operational definition of "like better."

Premack has performed a number of experiments providing support for this hypothesis. One of these involved two responses by children—operating a candy dispenser and playing a pinball machine. Premack first ascertained how often each child would operate each of these two machines when they were independent. Some children used one oftener, some the other. He then connected the two machines so that some children could play the pinball machine only if they first operated the dispenser, while for other children these contingencies were reversed. He found that children who preferred the candy dispenser would play more pinball when pinball made candy available, and children who preferred pinball would take more candy when operation of the candy dispenser made pinball available. On the other hand, making the less preferred activity dependent on the more preferred had no effect. Though this result is not particularly surprising, it provides support for an original formulation and shows that it is just as possible for food-getting behavior to be reinforced by something else as for it to serve as a reinforcer.

GUTHRIE'S INFLUENCE ON STATISTICAL LEARNING THEORY

Voeks.—Another of Guthrie's followers, Virginia Voeks, concerned herself with a different aspect of Guthrie's theory. She attempted to convert Guthrie's chatty formulations into a rigorous deductive theory. In doing so, she ignored the problem of reinforcement and stuck strictly to the principle of conditioning by contiguity. Her chief contribution was in formalizing the relationship, important but not overly specific in Guthrie's own work, between the conditioning of stimulus-response connections and the learning of acts.[27]

Voeks' basic system consists of only four postulates (more than Guthrie's one basic principle of learning, but many less than Hull's final twenty-two): Postulate 1, the "Principle of Association," states Guthrie's fundamental law of learning, that stimulus-response connections are formed by contiguous association. Postulate 2, the "Principle of Postremity," clarifies the first by pointing out that a stimulus becomes associated only with the last of the responses that accompanies or immediately follows it. Postulate 3, the "Principle of Response Probability," and Postulate 4, the "Principle of Dynamic Situations," can both be seen as expansions of the words "tend to" in Guthrie's own statement of his law of learning (*supra*). In other words, they convert the exact statements of the first two postulates into probabilistic ones. Postulate 3 does this by stating that the probability of a response is an increasing function of the proportion of the stimuli present that are cues for that response. Postulate 4 does it by noting that the stimuli in a situation are not static but change from time to time because of a variety of factors.

From these four postulates, Voeks deduces eight theorems, her proofs being even more formal than Hull's. The first five deal with the circumstances under which learning will or will not occur, and the last three deal with stability of behavior as a function of stability in the stimulus situation. These theorems help to clarify one of the difficulties with Guthrie's theory: If the response to a certain combination of stimuli is changed by introducing other stimuli, and then the original combination of stimuli is presented alone, will this test situation be enough like the training situation for the new response to occur? Voeks' reply is substantially as follows: All of the stimuli of the original combination are conditioned to the new response. The probability that they will elicit the new response on a test depends on what percentage of the total stimuli on the test trial is made up of these conditioned stimuli. In general, the probability of a given response on a particular trial is an increasing function of the percentage of stimuli present on that trial that are conditioned to the response in question. Thus, Voeks has converted a portion of

27. Virginia W. Voeks, "Formalization and Clarification of a Theory of Learning," *Journal of Psychology*, XXX (October, 1950), 341–62.

Guthrie's work not only into a formal deductive system but also into an explicitly statistical theory.

Estes.—In the same year that Voeks published her postulational system, Estes published an article entitled "Toward a Statistical Theory of Learning."[28] The analysis of learning in terms of stimulus elements that he presented was strikingly like Voeks', but with the mathematical formulation carried further. Estes' article may be regarded as the starting point of the recent marked development in statistical models of learning. Since such models are discussed in chapter v, they need not be considered here. However, a comparison of Estes' article with Voeks' shows how much the statistical learning theorists owe to Guthrie. Their mathematical sophistication and experimental output have now carried the builders of statistical models far beyond Guthrie, but he remains to a considerable extent their intellectual ancestor.

Other Developments

MEDIATIONAL PROCESSES

The preceding discussion has included a number of references to a *rapprochement* between connectionist and cognitive theory. Of particular significance in this connection is the widespread interest within S-R theory in various kinds of mediating response, i.e., responses whose significance is that they produce the stimuli for further responses. This interest is nothing new, as may be seen by noting such well-established concepts as Guthrie's movement-produced stimulation, Hull's pure stimulus act, and Miller and Dollard's response-produced drive stimuli. However, this interest appears to have become especially widespread in recent years. One indication of this is the great prominence given to the fractional anticipatory goal response by Spence, and there are a number of others.

The functions attributed to mediating responses are quite diverse, including motivational functions, cue functions, and combinations of the two. Of greatest current interest are those responses that serve the cue functions in relatively cognitive ways. These are of two main sorts: mediating responses in the narrower sense of the

28. William K. Estes, "Toward a Statistical Theory of Learning," *Psychological Review*, LVII (March, 1950), 94–107.

term, and observing responses, both of which are likely to enter into any complex behavior sequence.[29]

Observing responses are those that orient the sense receptors toward certain stimuli. In other words, they may be considered as responses of paying attention. Wyckoff suggested the term "observing response" and proposed that these responses are reinforced by the more successful instrumental behavior that they make possible.[30] A similar concept is involved in Lawrence's acquired distinctiveness of cues, based on a series of demonstrations that rats can learn to respond to certain cues rather than others independently of what response they learn to make.[31] Actually it is not necessary to assume in these cases that the observing responses are overt, peripheral responses, though theorists have often found it convenient to make such an assumption. Some adjustment in the central nervous system, differentially transmitting sensations of different sorts, would explain the data fully as well. However they are explained, observing responses are of great significance for the topic of learning to learn, which is so important in the applied psychology of education.

Whereas observing responses involve selective responsiveness to different stimuli, mediating responses in the narrow sense involve particular responses to the stimuli, responses which then provide stimuli for further responses. The most obvious example of the use of mediating responses is speech, in which the words we say (or think) provide cues for our subsequent actions. Guthrie's interpretation of purposes as muscular readinesses for certain actions and Hull's and Spence's r_G-s_G sequence are other examples of mediating responses. As with observing responses, there is no need to assume that mediating responses are necessarily overt or peripheral. Also, they may be assumed to be of any required degree of complexity, so that Tolman's sign-gestalt-expectations or even Lewin's life space

29. See, e.g., Howard H. Kendler and Tracy S. Kendler, "Vertical and Horizontal Processes in Problem Solving," *Psychological Review*, LXIX (January, 1962), 1–16.

30. L. Benjamin Wyckoff, Jr., "The Role of Observing Responses in Discrimination Learning, Part I," *Psychological Review*, LIX (November, 1952), 431–42.

31. Douglas H. Lawrence, "Acquired Distinctiveness of Cues: I, Transfer between Discriminations on the Basis of Familiarity with the Stimulus," *Journal of Experimental Psychology*, XXXIX (December, 1949), 770–84; "Acquired Distinctiveness of Cues: II, Selective Association in a Constant Stimulus Situation," *Journal of Experimental Psychology*, XL (April, 1950), 175–88.

can be regarded as patterns of stimulation produced by mediating responses. For both of these reasons, Osgood, Suci, and Tannenbaum (whose analysis of meaning is perhaps the most ambitious application of mediation yet attempted) suggest that the term "mediating process" is preferable to "mediating response."[32] At present, however, "mediating response" seems to be the better-established and more popular term.

EXPANSIONS OF THE DRIVE CONCEPT

Whereas observing and mediating responses have major implications for the cognitive aspects of S-R theory, another current line of interest has equally great implications for its motivational aspects. This is the attempt to determine the range of phenomena to which the terms "drive" and "reinforcer" can properly be applied. More specifically, it deals with a number of situations that have either drive-inducing or reinforcing properties, even though they have not traditionally been included among the primary drives. Among these are exploration, curiosity, activity, and contact-hunger.

Traditionally, the concept of primary drive has been applied only in those situations where survival (or at least normal biological functioning) was threatened, either by deprivation of some essential substance or by injury. Hence, the list of primary drives did not extend much beyond hunger, thirst, heat, cold, asphyxiation, and pain, with sexual and maternal drives occupying a somewhat ambiguous status. All other drives were assumed to be secondary, learned through the pairing of previously neutral stimuli with these few primary drives. Recent evidence strongly suggests, however, that the foregoing list is much too restrictive, and that there are many other innate behavioral tendencies that fit more or less into the usual meaning of a drive.

Harlow demonstrated that monkeys will open a clasp device over and over again (if the obliging experimenter keeps reclosing it for them) for no apparent reinforcement other than the satisfaction of manipulating it.[33] Butler found that monkeys would learn various

32. Charles E. Osgood, George J. Suci, and Percy H. Tannenbaum, *The Measurement of Meaning.* Urbana: University of Illinois Press, 1957.

33. Harry F. Harlow, "Learning and Satiation of Response in Intrinsically Motivated Complex Puzzle Performance by Monkeys," *Journal of Comparative and Physiological Psychology,* XLIII (August, 1950), 289–94.

responses for the reinforcement of being given a brief look out the window of an otherwise opaque cage, and that they would respond at increasingly higher rates after increasing periods away from the window.[34] Montgomery found large amounts of exploratory behavior in rats that apparently could not be explained by any of the traditional primary drives and concluded that the opportunity for exploration can reinforce learning.[35] Hill demonstrated increasing amounts of running by rats in voluntary activity wheels with increasing periods of confinement in very small cages.[36] It is virtually impossible to show conclusively that these findings cannot be explained by the prior learning of secondary drives. However, these studies and many others like them strongly suggest that such motives as curiosity, exploration, manipulation, and activity, the importance of which has long been recognized by educators, should be classified as primary drives.

A particularly interesting example in connection with theories of personality development is Harlow's work on contact-hunger in monkeys.[37] Harlow raised infant monkeys away from their real mothers but with two mechanical "surrogate mothers." One of these surrogate mothers was made of wire and had a nipple that provided the infant with milk, while the other was soft and covered with terry cloth, but had no nipple. According to the more traditional interpretation, the infant should develop love (behaviorally defined) for the wire mother, since it provided reduction of the primary drive of hunger. Instead, the monkeys not only showed a marked preference for the cloth mother but also ran to and clung to the cloth mother in later tests with fear-including stimuli. Apparently access to a soft and cuddly surface was more important to these infant monkeys than was access to food, not only in developing

34. Robert A. Butler, "Incentive Conditions Which Influence Visual Exploration," *Journal of Experimental Psychology*, XLVIII (July, 1954), 19–23.

35. Kay C. Montgomery, "The Effect of the Hunger and Thirst Drives upon Exploratory Behavior," *Journal of Comparative and Physiological Psychology*, XLVI (October, 1953), 315–19; "The Role of the Exploratory Drive in Learning," *Journal of Comparative and Physiological Psychology*, XLVII (February, 1954), 60–64.

36. Winfred F. Hill, "Activity as an Autonomous Drive," *Journal of Comparative and Physiological Psychology*, XLIX (February, 1956), 15–19.

37. Harry F. Harlow, "The Nature of Love," *American Psychologist*, XIII (December, 1958), 673–85.

simple preference but also in developing what can be interpreted as love and trust. This finding suggests that "contact hunger" belongs on any complete list of primary drives.

IMPLICATIONS OF THESE DEVELOPMENTS

There is some question as to what implications these findings have for the general concept of drive. Some interpreters have suggested that the whole concept of drive is now outmoded, that these findings indicate the need for some radically different motivational concept. It appears, however, that the majority of interpreters see these findings as calling only for some minor broadening of the concept of drive. In particular, the assumption that all primary drives reflect biological needs, if it is true at all, is true only in such a broad and vague sense as to have little predictive value. The equating of drive with increase in total stimulation also becomes suspect. However, the motivational tendencies discussed above generally follow the drive paradigm in showing the usual deprivation-satiation-reinforcement relationships. The concept of drive seems likely, therefore, not only to survive but to become increasingly useful.

Applications of S-R Learning Theory

To what extent can stimulus-response theoretical formulations, developed primarily on the basis of laboratory data, be usefully applied to practical problems? This is a topic on which fairly wide differences of opinion can be found, even among men whose theoretical positions are fairly close together.

THE PESSIMISTIC VIEW

The point of view that learning theory has relatively little to contribute at present is argued by Spence as a pure psychologist and by Robert Gagné as one who has worked at applying psychology to military training (each, however, has also had experience in the other's role). Spence argues that learning theorists can achieve their own goal most fully by studying artificially simple situations, thus making their work inapplicable to such complex problems as those of education. He sees some promise in the application of reinforcement theory to teaching machines, and greater hope for the distant future, but he regards most of learning theory as having little present relation to practical issues.[38] Gagné lists some of the suggestions that learning theory seems to make regarding training methods and notes that, in his experience, these suggestions have been of little use. Rather than looking at such traditional variables as reinforcement, distribution of practice, or interresponse generalization, he has found it useful to concentrate on the hierarchical organization of component operations within a larger task.[39] While this conclusion is pessimistic as regards the application of present learning theory to training problems, it also suggests a new approach to learning theory inspired by practical research.

THE OPTIMISTIC VIEW

Representative of the more optimistic view that learning theory can make substantial contributions to education and training are Neal E. Miller, B. F. Skinner, and Fred D. Sheffield. Miller has analyzed the topic of audio-visual aids in terms of the four components in his (modified Hullian) learning theory: drive, cue, response, and reward.[40] He paraphrases the meaning of these to assert that in order for learning to take place the learner must want something, notice something, do something, and get something he wants. From these simple principles, he makes a number of suggestions about ways that audio-visual techniques might be used more effectively. For example, he predicts: "More motivation will be aroused when the actors are similar to people whom the students have been rewarded for copying,"[41] and "The best way to teach a discrimination is to begin with easy extreme cases and gradually work down to finer differences." [42, 43]

38. Kenneth W. Spence, "The Relation of Learning Theory to the Technology of Education," *Harvard Educational Review*, XXIX (Spring, 1959), 84–95.

39. Robert M. Gagné, "Military Training and Principles of Learning," *American Psychologist*, XVII (February, 1962), 83–91.

40. Neal E. Miller, "Scientific Principles for Maximum Learning from Motion Pictures," in *Graphic Communication and the Crisis in Education*, pp. 61–113. Edited by Neal E. Miller. Washington: National Education Association, 1957.

41. *Ibid.*, p. 68.   42. *Ibid.*, p. 86.

43. For a more extensive analysis along similar lines, see J. O. Cook, "Research in Audio-visual Communication," in *Research Principles and Practices in Visual Communication*, pp. 91–106 (Edited by J. Ball and S. C. Byrnes. East Lansing: Michigan State University National Project in Agricultural Communications,

Skinner, who has applied his learning theory (or nontheory) to topics as diverse as animal training and Utopian social organization, has made his most noted application in the field of educational technology. This is in the use of programed learning, most publicized in the form involving the teaching machine[44] but also coming to be widely used in book form. This technique reflects the view of S-R theory that optimal learning requires a response to occur and to be quickly reinforced, plus Skinner's special emphasis on "shaping" desired behavior by successive approximations. From this simple base, Skinner proceeds to his technical recommendations, which are discussed in chapter xv.

Sheffield has also concerned himself with programed learning, though in a somewhat different form. He is one of a group of psychologists working on the programed teaching of skills, particularly through instructional films. His theoretical keynote chapter in a collaborative book on this topic[45] might be taken as an answer to Gagné. Like Gagné, Sheffield is concerned with the hierarchical organization of responses within a sequential task. Unlike Gagné, however, he sees the process of sequential organization as derivable from the principles of contiguous conditioning as discussed by Guthrie. When several responses occur in a sequence, a fractional portion of a later response often occurs earlier in the sequence and thus becomes conditioned to the stimulus for an earlier response (cf. Spence's r_G). This conditioning will occur in those cases where two responses and any others between them in the sequence are compatible and where the contextual cues remain fairly constant from one response to the other. This conditioning of an anticipatory response ties together in a unified sequence the earlier stimulus, the later response, and the other stimuli and responses between them. Those

---

1961). For a somewhat different analysis and further citation of experimental literature, see A. A. Lumsdaine, "Some Conclusions concerning Student Response and a Science of Instruction," in *Student Response in Programmed Instruction*, pp. 471–500 (Edited by A. A. Lumsdaine. Washington: National Academy of Sciences, National Research Council, 1961).

44. B. F. Skinner, "Teaching Machines," *Scientific American*, CCV (November, 1961), 90–102.

45. Fred D. Sheffield, "Theoretical Considerations in the Learning of Complex Sequential Tasks from Demonstration and Practice," in *Student Response in Programmed Instruction*, pp. 13–32. Edited by A. A. Lumsdaine. Washington: National Academy of Sciences, National Research Council, 1961.

portions of a task in which the process can occur readily constitute
"natural units." Such natural units in turn form larger units in the
same way, resulting in a hierarchical arrangement of segments within the task. This analysis of natural units is one of the bases for the
research on training techniques described in the book. Thus, the
same aspect of applied learning that weakens Gagné's confidence in
the applicability of learning theory strengthens Sheffield's confidence in it.

AN ATTEMPT AT RESOLUTION

There may not actually be any deep disagreement between the
optimists and the pessimists regarding the application of learning
theory to education and training. Probably most of both groups
would accept the propositions that: (*a*) the laws of learning are fundamentally the same in the laboratory and in the classroom; (*b*) the
applications so far made from the laboratory to the classroom are
comparatively small in relation both to the amount of knowledge
provided by the laboratory and to the complexity of problems in the
classroom; (*c*) knowledge of learning theory and related laboratory
data provides a worthwhile but also an extremely incomplete background for dealing with the problems of teaching; (*d*) we can look
forward to closer ties between these two areas in the future, representing not only the application of learning theory and laboratory
science to teaching but also the influence of applied work on theory
and pure research; and (*e*) these ties will involve, among other
things, increasing use of the concepts of mediation in relation to the
organization or programing of material to be learned. This is not a
particularly impressive summary, especially in view of the high
hopes that have sometimes been held out to educators, but it is still
basically an optimistic view.

CHAPTER III

The Place of Gestalt Psychology and Field Theories in Contemporary Learning Theory

ERNEST R. HILGARD

The Rise and Fall of Gestalt Psychology

In the late 1920's and early 1930's the Gestalt psychology of Wertheimer, Köhler, and Koffka came like a breath of fresh air upon the American scene, then dominated by a somewhat strident behaviorism. A Cornell educational psychologist, Robert M. Ogden, had much to do with its introduction to America. He translated Koffka's *Growth of the Mind*[1] in 1924 and wrote an educational psychology[2] embodying many of the new ideas in 1926. Koffka lectured widely in this country, visited at Cornell, and spent the rest of the year 1924–25 at the University of Wisconsin; and Köhler came to visit and tour in 1925–26. Both spoke excellent English and were well received. I did not then hear Koffka, but I heard Köhler when he showed his motion pictures of the apes and lectured at Yale; his charming manner captivated the audience, and his points sank in.

Soon there were other representatives of the new viewpoint. Kurt Lewin, an associate and colleague of the original Gestalt group, had a version of his own that came to be called *field* psychology. He was introduced to the American audience by a summary article[3] published in 1929 in the *Psychological Review*, visited at the time of the International Congress at Yale the same year, spent his first year in America at Stanford in 1932–33, and remained in this country in various positions at Cornell, Harvard, Iowa, and the Massachusetts

1. K. Koffka, *The Growth of the Mind.* Translated by Robert Morris Ogden. London: Kegan Paul, Trench, Trubner & Co., Ltd., 1924.

2. Robert Morris Ogden, *Psychology and Education.* New York: Harcourt, Brace & Co., 1926.

3. J. F. Brown, "The Methods of Kurt Lewin in the Psychology of Action and Affection," *Psychological Review*, XXXVI (May, 1929), 220–21.

Institute of Technology. Koffka went to Smith College, and Köhler to Swarthmore; Wertheimer came to the New School for Social Research. Thus, the influence of Gestalt psychology was not only by way of its writings but also through the active participation of its leaders in American psychology. Among other variants, one called organismic psychology, as advocated by R. H. Wheeler, was introduced to the educational profession in 1932 through the influential *Principles of Mental Development* by Wheeler and Perkins.[4] In the same year, Tolman's *Purposive Behavior*[5] appeared. In it he, too, acknowledged some influences from Gestalt psychology, characterizing his behaviorism as molar rather than as molecular, thus sharing the Gestalt preference for wholes over parts. All these developments represented a "new" psychology, which was in general opposition to the atomism and mechanism of Thorndike and the behaviorists.

The excitement created by these new viewpoints lasted into the 1940's, but has now subsided. Various interpretations of this reduced interest have been offered. According to Boring, it was its success that killed it:

The movement has produced much new important research, but it is no longer profitable to label it as Gestalt psychology. Had Gestalt psychology resisted the inclusion of behavioral data in psychology, there might have been a long war over the question whether psychology is or is not principally the study of direct experience. As it was, Köhler's chimpanzees were admitted as data from the start. The result is that Gestalt psychology has already passed its peak and is now dying of success by being absorbed into what is Psychology.[6]

Gardner Murphy sees it this way:

. . . in general Gestalt psychology has been gratefully received and grafted upon existing systems, but it has not, except here and there on a very small scale, been espoused by American psychology as a final or fundamental solution of psychological problems.[7]

4. Raymond Holder Wheeler and Francis Theodore Perkins, *Principles of Mental Development*. New York: Thomas Y. Crowell Co., 1932.

5. Edward Chace Tolman, *Purposive Behavior in Animals and Men*. New York: Century Co., 1932.

6. Edwin G. Boring, *A History of Experimental Psychology*, p. 600. New York: Appleton-Century-Crofts, Inc., 1950 (second edition).

7. Gardner Murphy, *Historical Introduction to Modern Psychology*, p. 294. New York: Harcourt, Brace & Co., 1949 (revised edition).

Perhaps more important than the question of whether or not the systematic positions of Gestalt, field, or organismic psychology have lost their identities is that of their residual influence upon research, for surely the field of the psychology of learning, with which we are here directly concerned, is one of the most active in research. It appears that their residual at present is not large and that Tolman's influence shares the declining interest with the other Gestalt influences. Reviewing the learning literature in 1959, Kendler concluded:

Cognitive learning theory of the sort Tolman espoused, as well as the Gestalt variety, is either asleep or dying. This seems to be the only conclusion to draw from the limited amount of activity each has generated over the past year.[8]

Kendler's statement provides a kind of text for this chapter. What, in fact, can be said about the contemporary influence of the once powerful impact of Gestalt psychology and related viewpoints?

It may be noted, parenthetically, that other viewpoints in psychology have come and gone, without really being disposed of. Functionalism as a system was overshadowed by behaviorism, but I believe that much of contemporary behaviorism is more "functionalistic" than the earlier Watsonian variety. Associationism comes and goes in various guises. Topics in psychology also go out of fashion. Herbart's doctrine of apperception still has a measure of plausibility, but apperception as a topic has disappeared; maturation, once given experimental prominence by such eminent figures as Coghill, Carmichael, Gesell, and Stone, has not kept its place in the laboratory. In other areas, what has become of eidetic images, of chronaxie, of tropisms? Surely the phenomena that were once described are still there to be described. There is a sociology of knowledge, a dynamic history of science; science is not a unidirectional forward march.

Three main hypotheses have to be examined when scientific concepts lose their currency. The hypothetical happenings may be characterized as *disproof*, *neglect*, and *transformation*.

Disproof.—Some ideas are found to be erroneous, and hence are legitimately abandoned. The ether in physics or phlogiston in chemistry are concepts of this kind; they lasted a long time because they

8. Howard H. Kendler, "Learning," *Annual Review of Psychology*, X (1959), 43–88. (Palo Alto: Annual Reviews, Inc.)

were useful, and the crucial experiments and concepts were not yet available to destroy them. Few ideas in psychology have suffered this fate; I believe it is fair to say that the basic ideas of Gestalt or cognitive psychology have not been discarded because crucial experiments destroyed them. Perhaps the sharpest experimental attack was made against latent learning, one of Tolman's ideas. Eventually it became clear that the facts supported his claim, and latent learning became "domesticated" within the opponents' systems.

Another illustration of "disproof" is the subsequent history of the spontaneous changes in the memory trace as originally described by Wulf.[9] Numerous experiments have shown that such changes do not occur as they are supposed to according to Gestalt theory,[10] but the general idea persists, and is said to be still useful, despite these disproofs.[11] Thus, the decline in Gestalt psychology can hardly be attributed to "disproof" if the area in which there is difficulty is one of the areas that is kept alive!

Neglect.—Some rich and plausible conceptions do not lend themselves to the patterns of experimental design and model building that are prominent at any one time in the history of a science; such conceptions suffer temporary neglect. (These are the kinds of ideas that Kendler says may be "sleeping.") At the height of behaviorism, for example, topics that depended upon rich phenomenological study were neglected; hence, for example, there was little study of dreams and hallucinations. Although Tolman called his system a kind of behaviorism (which it really was), it had within it a phenomenological flavor that it shared with Gestalt psychology. Phenomenology is always hard to fit into the canons of quantitative science, whether it is a theory of vision, such as Hering's, or a theory of personality, such as existentialism. What truths there are in phenomenology are convincingly dramatized, then the excitement wears off as nobody is able to go on and make science out of them. To quote Kendler again, the believer may be "lulled into theoretical inactiv-

9. F. Wulf, "Über die Veränderung von Verstellung," *Psychologische Forschung*, I (1922), 333–73.

10. D. O. Hebb and Esme N. Foord, "Errors of Visual Recognition and the Nature of the Trace," *Journal of Experimental Psychology*, XXXV (1945), 335–48.

11. David Krech and Richard S. Crutchfield, *Theory and Problems of Social Psychology*, p. 127 n. New York: McGraw-Hill Book Co., 1948.

ity." The rest of the scientific world neglects what it is not prepared to handle.

When this is the case, appropriate shifts in scientific outlook bring a revival of interest. Thus, Rorschach's inkblots laid around as scientific curiosities for many years until an upsurge of interest in the study of personality, psychoanalysis, and symbolic expression made the investigation of projective products interesting. Hypnotic behavior provides a striking illustration of a body of phenomena occasionally of great scientific interest, then plateauing off into long periods of scientific indifference. It is quite possible that some of the Gestalt and field notions are suffering this neglect until a more favorable *Zeitgeist* will again bring them to the fore.

This, in essence, is what Köhler[12] complained of in his presidential address before the American Psychological Association in 1959. He felt that the logic of behaviorism was so much in the ascendance in America that even problems such as those of perceptual contours were being reduced to atomistic terms; his plea was for experimentation, independent of commitment to schools, that would accept some of the teachings of field physics. In other words, he took the position that Gestalt psychology had *not* been assimilated but, rather, that its major teachings had been neglected.

Transformation.—Important facts are not likely to remain long neglected in an active and vigorous science, though they may crop up in new forms; hence the old knowledge may not have disappeared even though it is no longer indexed under the same terms. Herbart's apperception was for a time displaced by Dewey's concept of interest, and then the ubiquitous notion of "set" more or less took its place in general psychology. Even though the Gestalt term "insight" is not prominent in contemporary research, there is a great upsurge of interest in problem-solving and cognition generally; perhaps, if one looked, one would find that beneath some of the terms such as "display," "feedback," and "structure," there were hidden the basic notions of insight. This is essentially what Boring means when he says that Gestalt psychology died of success. To the extent that these transformations are successful, Gestalt psychology will not need to be revived. Hence, it does make a difference whether the ideas have suffered neglect or transformation.

12. Wolfgang Köhler, "Gestalt Psychology Today," *American Psychologist*, XIV (1958), 727–34.

In order to look at the situation somewhat more accurately, a few of the once-fruitful ideas associated with some of the leaders in the Gestalt-field-cognitive systems will be examined in terms of their contemporary residues.

Köhler and Insight

Köhler was never primarily interested in learning. His early work was in auditory perception, and he made important contributions to the understanding of the time error. Much of his experimental work at Swarthmore, and at the Institute for Advanced Study, before his retirement as an investigator, was devoted to electrophysiological experimentation bearing on his theory of isomorphism, that is, to a correspondence between what happens in perceived phenomena and what goes on in the brain. It was perhaps the chance fact of his isolation on the Island of Tenerife during World War I that led to his extensive work with apes; in any case, it was the experiments on box-stacking and stick-using that reintroduced the concept of *insight* into the psychologist's vocabulary.[13]

Köhler's observations were amply validated in many subsequent studies. Yerkes,[14] independently proposed in 1916 an insight concept based on experiments done during a sabbatical year away from Harvard, which he spent at Santa Barbara, California, because his trip to Tenerife was cancelled on account of the war. Köhler remained at Tenerife *because* of the war, and Yerkes would have been there *except for* the war! Both Yerkes and Köhler were friendly and in close communication; the question of priority is of little moment. When Yerkes set up his Yale Primate Laboratory in 1925, he set Bingham to work quantifying the insight experiments of Köhler.[15] Many other studies were done with apes and monkeys.[16]

13. Wolfgang Köhler, *The Mentality of Apes*. Translated from second revised edition by Ella Winter. New York: Harcourt, Brace & Co., 1925 (original German edition, 1917).

14. Robert M. Yerkes, "The Mental Life of Monkeys and Apes: A Study of Ideational Behavior," *Behavior Monograph*, III (1916), No. 12.

15. Harold C. Bingham, "Chimpanzee Translocation by Means of Boxes," *Comparative Psychological Monographs*, V (1929), No. 25; "Selective Transportation by Chimpanzees," *Comparative Psychological Monographs*, V (1929), No. 26.

16. See H. F. Harlow and P. H. Settlage, "Comparative Behavior of Primates: VII, Capacity of Monkeys To Solve Patterned String Tests," *Journal of Comparative Psychology*, XVIII (1934), 423–35; Theodore A. Jackson, "Use of the

Studies were extended also to children.[17] Tolman and Honzik[18] were able to show insight in the white rat; Perkins and Wheeler,[19] stretching the concept a bit, found configurational learning in the goldfish. It looked, then, as though insight experiments were to become a standard class of laboratory investigations and that insight had demonstrated itself to be a useful concept.

What is the subsequent history of insight? Perhaps it would be well to point out, first, that it had an *earlier* history also. When man was thought of as chiefly rational, insight was probably a usual interpretation of problem-solving, with trial-and-error a somewhat sophisticated later notion. Insight, before Köhler, was a word of the common vocabulary, but it was not considered a scientific word, although it had appeared occasionally in experimental studies.[20] Köhler was not helpful in saving "insight" as a scientific word; in his later *Gestalt Psychology*[21] he has a chapter on insight in which he makes the concept synonymous with the direct awareness of determination, as when one notes that it is the cool drink that quenches one's thirst. This is an interesting issue, but not one which the learning experimenter associates with insight; it has more of a family resemblance with insight into the determination of symptoms that the

---

Stick as a Tool by Young Chimpanzees," *Journal of Comparative Psychology,* XXXIV (1942), 223–35; and Herbert G. Birch, "The Role of Motivational Factors in Insightful Problem-solving," *Journal of Comparative Psychology,* XXXVIII (1945), 295–317.

17. Helen M. Richardson, "The Growth of Adaptive Behavior in Infants: An Experimental Study at Seven Age Levels," *Genetic Psychological Monographs,* XII (1932), 195–359.

18. Edward Chace Tolman and C. H. Honzik, " 'Insight' in Rats," *University of California Publications in Psychology,* IV (1930), 215–32; "Introduction and Removal of Reward and Maze Performance in Rats," *University of California Publications in Psychology,* IV (1930), 257–75.

19. Francis Theodore Perkins and Raymond Holder Wheeler, "Configurational Learning in the Goldfish," *Comparative Psychological Monographs,* VII (1930), No. 31.

20. For example, see Henry A. Ruger, "The Psychology of Efficiency," *Archives of Psychology,* New York, No. 15 (1910). (Reprinted as *Teachers College Educational Reprints,* No. 5. New York: Bureau of Publications, Teachers College, Columbia University, 1926.)

21. Wolfgang Köhler, *Gestalt Psychology.* New York: Liveright Pub. Corp., 1929 (revised, 1947).

psychoanalyst talks about. Hence, it was left to others to indicate what insight means operationally in a laboratory setting.[22, 23]

There were some early protests against the ready acceptance of insight as a competitor to associative learning. Guthrie[24] felt that sudden learning would have to fall in the category of luck, and hence it lay outside science; McGeoch[25] thought of insight as merely an extreme case of transfer of training, hence not in violation of associative laws. Others thought it was useful in a descriptive sense, but care had to be exercised to avoid its explanatory use. Learning could be *with* insight, but not *by* insight. A more recent attack came from Harlow[26] whose studies of learning sets showed that trial-and-error learning could with practice converge upon and become one-trial learning, so that, in essence, insight could be acquired by trial and error!

I have elsewhere pointed out that most of these attacks on insight really missed the main point, which was *not* one trial or sudden learning but, rather, how the manner in which a problem is presented permits the appropriate use of past experience.[27] The issue is not over either the influence of past experience or sudden learning; it is over learning with understanding, in which the components of a problem are so laid out that their natural relations become evident and a sensible solution is possible. The criticism of association theory is not based on the importance assigned to past experience but, rather, on the notion that past experience *guarantees* the solution of a problem, no matter how the problem is presented. The insight point of view is that, *with sufficient past experience*, some problems are more difficult than others owing to their display or structural features; some learners can, to be sure, solve the more difficult prob-

22. Robert M. Yerkes, "The Mind of a Gorilla: I," *Genetic Psychological Monographs*, II (January and March, 1927), 1–193.

23. Ernest R. Hilgard, *Theories of Learning*. New York: Appleton-Century-Crofts, 1948 (second edition, 1956).

24. E. R. Guthrie, *The Psychology of Learning*. New York: Harper & Bros., 1935.

25. John A. McGeoch, *The Psychology of Human Learning*. New York: Longmans, Green & Co., 1942.

26. Harry F. Harlow, "The Formation of Learning Sets," *Psychological Review*, LVI (January, 1949), 51–65.

27. Hilgard, *op. cit.*, p. 234.

lems because of experience with the particular kind of display, others because they are better able to generalize and not be misled by the display. These are empirical problems, important in connection with the psychology of instruction.

As an illustration of how notions close to those essential to an understanding of insight are used by those whose backgrounds do not favor an insight interpretation, I wish to refer to some excellent studies of teaching a practical skill by means of carefully constructed motion pictures, narratives accompanying them, and practice in the actual manipulations. In summarizing these studies, two students of Guthrie (and generally quite favorable to his views) have these principles to offer:

> In the present theoretical framework, the presence of inherent organization in a sequential task makes the serial learning of its parts easier to accomplish. This expected greater ease of serial learning involves two different propositions about the advantages of inherent organization:
>
> 1. A sequential learning task which breaks down into distinctive sub-units simplifies the learning of the total sequence by reducing the task to an easily learned sequence of easily learned sub-sequences.
>
> 2. An organized sequence provides a better perceptual-static-perceptual pattern of the task as a whole, the parts of this static pattern suggesting the separate sequential sub-units.[28]

While this is not Gestalt psychology per se, the emphasis upon inherent organization, upon the meaningfulness of the parts, and upon their perceptual patterning, is exactly the kind of emphasis that one alerted to insight would propose. Note that the emphasis is not upon habits or habit sequences but upon relationships that can make such habits easier to attain. Thus, an association psychology can bring organization into its theoretical formulations, without embracing the Gestalt terminology.

In the field of problem-solving and creative thinking, it is probably true that the Gestalt influence has been accepted but transformed rather than neglected. We shall examine this possibility further in relation to Wertheimer's influence.

28. Fred D. Sheffield and Nathan Maccoby, "Summary and Interpretation of Research on Organizational Principles in Constructing Filmed Demonstrations," *Student Response in Programmed Instruction*, chap. ix. Edited by Arthur A. Lumsdaine. Washington: National Academy of Sciences, National Research Council, Publication 943, 1961.

Wertheimer and Productive Thinking

In this day of renewed interest in thinking, problem-solving, and creativity, references are often found to Wertheimer's posthumous book, *Productive Thinking*.[29] Perhaps, then, the theme of this book represents an aspect of Gestalt psychology that has remained truly contemporary. An earlier monograph on productive thinking, by one of Wertheimer's students, is also widely quoted.[30]

One line of inquiry that has engendered research in the recent past is that having to do with *functional fixedness*, growing out of Duncker's work. The notion as presented is that too much use of an object in its natural way inhibits converting it to original uses. The concept has been shown to be readily demonstrated in the laboratory.[31] Hence, while context is often important for problem-solving, context may interfere as well as help, by producing inflexibility. Two other lines of inquiry growing out of Wertheimer's work have had more recent representations in the literature. One of these came to fruition in a large book by Katona, entitled *Organizing and Memorizing*.[32] In it he carried out the theme that the inherent organization of material would affect both its ease of learning and retention and its transfer to new materials. This thesis has been verified to some extent in later studies.[33] The other line of inquiry was initiated

29. Max Wertheimer, *Productive Thinking*. New York: Harper & Bros., 1945 (revised, 1959).

30. Karl Duncker, "On Problem-solving," *Psychological Monographs*, LVIII (1945), Whole No. 270. (German original, 1935.)

31. See Herbert G. Birch and Herbert S. Rabinowitz, "The Negative Effect of Previous Experience on Productive Thinking," *Journal of Experimental Psychology*, XLI (February, 1951), 121–25; Robert E. Adamson, "Functional Fixedness as Related to Problem-solving: A Repetition of Three Experiments," *Journal of Experimental Psychology*, XLIV (1952), 288–91; and Robert E. Adamson, "Functional Fixedness as Related to Elapsed Time and Set," *Journal of Experimental Psychology*, XLVII (1954), 122–26.

32. George Katona, *Organizing and Memorizing*. New York: Columbia University Press, 1940.

33. For example, see Ernest R. Hilgard, Robert D. Edgren, and Robert P. Irvine, "Errors in Transfer Following Learning with Understanding: Further Studies with Katona's Card-trick Experiments," *Journal of Experimental Psychology*, XLVII (June, 1954), 457–64; and Ernest R. Hilgard, Robert P. Irvine, and James E. Whipple, "Rote Memorization, Understanding, and Transfer: An Extension of Katona's Card-trick Experiments," *Journal of Experimental Psychology*, XLVI (October, 1953), 288–92.

by Luchins,[34] in which he showed that *Einstellung* or "set" could produce rigidity and inhibit the flexibility needed for efficient problem-solving. Experiments along these lines have continued; many of them are reported in a substantial book by Luchins and Luchins,[35] and some suggestions are given in a paper on audio-visual learning.[36]

The studies on reasoning by Maier,[37] who had gone to Berlin for postdoctoral study, were also inspired by the Gestalt group. Thus, there are pertinent ideas that have come from the classical Gestalt group, and they are of service in contemporary psychology.

At the same time, it would be hard to make a case, for the impact of these studies was great in terms of the volume of work they stimulated. Even as friendly a critic as MacLeod (who studied with Wertheimer) has this to say:

> I must confess I have always found Wertheimer's book somewhat disappointing. There is nowhere a richer source of descriptive material, of brilliant insights, of penetrating comments that make one sit up and exclaim "Aha!" It is an exercise in the descriptive analysis of processes of thinking, with only too infrequently a lifting out and a systematic scrutinizing of principles. Were another volume to have been written it might have contained a more formal critique of the psychologist's thinking about thinking, with an examination of alternative assumptions and interpretations. . . . Lacking such a study, however, we must regard his book as essentially a brilliant foray which has revealed all sort of exciting possibilities; but there is still ample room for adventure.[38]

Wheeler's Developmental Organismic Psychology

In the years shortly after Koffka and Köhler came to prominence, a number of educational psychology textbooks showed a strong in-

34. Abraham S. Luchins, "Mechanization in Problem-solving: The Effect of Einstellung," *Psychological Monographs*, LIV, No. 6 (1942), Whole No. 248.

35. Abraham S. Luchins and Edith H. Luchins, *Rigidity of Behavior*. Eugene, Oregon: University of Oregon Books, 1959.

36. Abraham S. Luchins, "Implications of Gestalt Psychology for AV Learning," *AV Communication Review*, Supplement IV (September–October, 1961), 7–31.

37. Norman R. F. Maier, "Reasoning in Humans. I, On Direction," *Journal of Comparative Psychology*, X (1930), 115–43; "Reasoning in Humans. III, The Mechanisms of Equivalent Stimuli and of Reasoning, *Journal of Experimental Psychology*, XXXV (1945), 349–60.

38. Robert Brodie MacLeod, "Retrospect and Prospect, in *Contemporary Approaches to Creative Thinking*, chap. vi. Edited by H. E. Gruber, G. Terrell, and Michael Wertheimer. New York: Atherton Press, 1962.

fluence from the new Gestalt viewpoint.[39] Of these, none was more influential for a time than that of Wheeler and Perkins, espousing a position that came to be known as *organismic psychology*.

This new position added a strong biological and developmental flavor, largely absent from the classical Gestalt teachings despite the word "growth" in the title of Koffka's book. With the authority of Coghill[40] who insisted that the part-actions of the developing embryo always were differentiated out of an integrated whole (rather than combined from part-actions through an act of synthesis), the Gestalt primacy of the whole appeared to have firm biological support. Wheeler and Perkins extended the maturation notion into an all-inclusive educational principle of *pacing*, according to which learning opportunities would be provided to match the inherent growth-potential of the learner. While expressed more through emphatic statement (italics and exclamation points) than through experimental evidence, the notion of pacing was appealing. It was picked up, for example, by Olson, who began measurements of *organismic age* as defining the growth pattern for the individual, and this was then correlated with such matters as self-selection of reading material. It turned out, that, when rich choices were possible, the kinds of books chosen and their number corresponded to the organismic age of the pupil.[41]

All of this appeared to be rather promising. When in 1948 I prepared my *Theories of Learning*,[42] I included a chapter summarizing this position; by 1956, however, when the second edition was prepared, I indicated somewhat regretfully that research on or related to the position was no longer sufficient to call for a new chapter, and the chapter was therefore omitted.

Does this mean that the ideas which seemed so fresh and vital when Wheeler and Perkins presented them in 1932 are valueless in

39. For example, see Ogden, *op. cit.*; Robert Morris Ogden and Frank S. Freeman, *Psychology and Education* (New York: Harcourt, Brace & Co., 1932); Wheeler and Perkins, *op. cit.*; and W. D. Commins, *Principles of Educational Psychology* (New York: Ronald Press Co., 1937).

40. G. E. Coghill, *Anatomy and the Problem of Behavior*. New York: Macmillan Co., 1929.

41. Willard C. Olson and Sarita I. Davis, "The Adaptation of Instruction to the Growth of Children," *Educational Method*, XX (November, 1940), 71–79.

42. Hilgard, *op. cit.*

1964? Not at all; it means only that something was wrong with the manner in which the ideas were developed, so that strong contemporary defenders are not to be found.

Perhaps the pacing notion represents one case in which the failure of experimental evidence to support a primary suggestion had something to do with its abandonment. This notion appeared to gain some support from the work of Snoddy[43] and Doré and Hilgard,[44] but the conjectures were not upheld by Taylor.[45] Even so, the results are not sufficiently devastating to have been responsible for lack of further experimentation had the notion caught on among investigators; a failure or two would not have caused people to give up the idea any more than failures have caused them to abandon such conceptions as reminiscence in rote learning.

It is hard not to fall back upon an *argumentum ad hominem* in this case. Wheeler weakened his influence by going on to somewhat exaggerated claims about the influence of cycles of wet and dry climate;[46] Perkins, while continuing as a respected teacher and a responsible member of the psychological profession, had been but a 23-year-old protégé of Wheeler when their book appeared; although he defended their joint position strongly at first, he possibly became disillusioned with it and yet did not feel ready to do the radical surgery on it that was required. In any case, he has written little about the theory in the intervening years, and the original book was never revised. When a theory loses the support of those central to it, it tends to die of inanition.

The main point, I believe, is that the theories under discussion, even though their influence has weakened, have not been demolished through crushing disproofs; on the contrary, they were often formulated so that either proofs or disproofs would be scarcely possible. A theory so ambiguously formulated, unless kept alive by the

43. George S. Snoddy, *Evidence for Two Opposed Processes in Mental Growth*. Lancaster, Pennsylvania: Science Press Printing Co., 1935.

44. Leon R. Doré and Ernest R. Hilgard, "Spaced Practice and the Maturation Hypothesis," *Journal of Psychology*, IV (1937), 245–59.

45. Susan T. H. Wright and Donald W. Taylor, "Distributed Practice and the Maturation Hypothesis," *Journal of Experimental Psychology*, XXXIX (1949), 527–31.

46. Raymond H. Wheeler, "Climate and Human Behavior," *Encyclopedia of Psychology*, pp. 78–86. Edited by Philip Lawrence Harriman. New York: Philosophical Library, 1946.

commitment of its staunch supporters or reformulated with precision by a new generation, will lose out in the competition for attention.

Lewin and Motivated Learning

Kurt Lewin was an intimate of Köhler, Koffka, and Wertheimer; while he was not one of the core founders of the Gestalt theory, he scarcely counts as a younger generation, for he was only three years younger than Köhler, and was already established in Berlin when Köhler came to that city. His major interest was in motivation, and it was through this interest that his work became relevant to the psychology of learning. The studies by his students of level of aspiration, goal-attractiveness, the dynamics of memory, reward, and punishment are educationally relevant. The one publication in which he expressed himself on these matters in relation to learning is an earlier yearbook of this Society.[47]

Two circumstances, one a logical outcome of his theory, the other a somewhat historical accident, can account for lack of a direct successor to Lewin in the psychology of learning. The first of these, the logical consequence, follows because his theory was essentially ahistorical, that is, concerned with contemporary causation, and was always weak in its historical or development aspects. But a psychology of learning necessarily has its historical aspects; one not interested in them is little likely to remain interested in learning. The historical accident has to do with Lewin's turning to social psychology, in part as a response to Hitler's rise to power and to the pressing problems of World War II. His active disciples tend today to be in that field. Thus, in a recent chapter[48] summarizing his views, very little is said about learning; in a chapter of 83 pages, only six pages are devoted to the studies that might interest a student of learning. This section is devoted to the "evidential grounds" for his system and mentions the early experiments on associative bonds and dy-

47. Kurt Lewin, "Field Theory and Learning," *The Psychology of Learning*, pp. 215-42. Forty-first Yearbook of the National Society for the Study of Education, Part II. Chicago: Distributed by the University of Chicago Press, 1942.

48. D. Cartwright, "Lewinian Theory as a Contemporary Systematic Framework," *Psychology: A Study of a Science*, Vol. II, *General Systematic Formulations Learning and Special Processes*, pp. 7-91. Edited by Sigmund Koch. New York: McGraw-Hill Book Co., 1959.

namic processes, memory, interruption and resumption of tasks, frustration, level of aspiration, and decision. As illustrative of the emphasis, Cartwright does not even list the yearbook chapter on learning in the bibliography that accompanies the chapter. It is not surprising, therefore, that despite a group of loyal supporters of the field-theoretical viewpoint (as they like to call it), none is found in the field of learning. The more direct line might have come through Tolman's students, for Tolman was genuinely interested in learning and he was impressed by Lewin's views. There was a mild controversy between them in the journals, but the discussion ended amicably.[49] Tolman had emphasized cognitions in his book, but he adopted the term *cognitive structure* from Lewin.

Perhaps the most influential impact upon contemporary motivational psychology came by way of the concept of *level of aspiration*, developed by Lewin's student, Hoppe.[50] There has been a moderate amount of literature on this topic for many years, continuing to the present time.[51] Another fertile idea is associated with the name of Zeigarnik[52] who contributed to the study of the dynamics of retention by investigating the recall of finished and unfinished tasks. The "Zeigarnik effect," that the incompleted tasks are recalled better than the completed ones, has many exceptions (as Zeigarnik pointed out), but the framework has proved useful for many subsequent studies.

Lewin's threefold classification of conflicts (approach-approach, avoidance-avoidance, and approach-avoidance) has been so widely adopted that it is now occasionally attributed to secondary sources. This classification influenced a number of the Yale experimenters studying conflict, although the modern form of the conflict theory has been recast by them into S-R terms.[53]

49. Edward Chace Tolman, "Lewin's Concept of Vectors," *Journal of General Psychology,* VII (July, 1932), 3–15; Kurt Lewin, "Vectors, Cognitive Processes, and Mr. Tolman's Criticism," *Journal of General Psychology,* VIII (1933), 318–45.

50. F. Hoppe, "Erfolg und Misserfolg," *Psychologische Forschung,* XIV (1931), 1–62.

51. For example, see William H. Starbuck, "Level of Aspiration," *Psychological Review,* LXX (January, 1963), 51–60.

52. B. Zeigarnik, "Das Behalten erledigter und unerledigter Handlungen," *Psychologische Forschung,* IX (1927), 1–85.

53. For example, see N. E. Miller, "Liberalization of Basic S-R Concepts: Extensions to Conflict Behavior, Motivation, and Social Learning," *Psychology: A Study of a Science,* Vol. II, *op. cit.,* pp. 196–292.

The quite fertile notions of Lewin with respect to reward and punishment—noting particularly the different kinds of policing involved—seem not to have been developed by others, although their pertinence to practical situations has often been pointed out. This may be due to the laboratory orientation of those who compare reward and punishment, in which the total context of conflicting opportunities is limited by mazes with roofs and walls; the "policing" that these provide is not part of the data, although it is well known that if walls or roofs were left off, the rats might do things other than those that the experimenter wished. Lewin would have made these environmental constraints part of the experimental situation to be manipulated.

Estes, assessing Lewin's over-all contributions to learning theory, came out with a quite negative appraisal. To be sure, he was concerned with Lewin's theory in its formal, systematic aspects, not in what its social value may have been nor in how suggestive it might be to someone today. In this he is in agreement with Bergmann, a philosopher of science, who collaborated with Lewin in an attempt to mathematize Lewin's theory, only to find that the task was an impossible one; he found the formulatons of Hull and Spence more congenial.[54]

Leeper,[55] a friendly critic, analyzed Lewin's system painstakingly and found that such quasi-mathematical concepts as distance and direction were left in an unsatisfactory state. He suggested some improvements that would have called for major revisions of Lewin's system.

These negative appraisals of Lewin's theorizing are significant because Lewin was clear about the importance of a "fit" between theory and data. The objections of the critic lie in Lewin's failure to specify more precisely a data language which would permit the actual kind of result that he sought.

Hence the failure of the more systematic aspects of Lewin to be represented in contemporary learning theory rests on these several considerations: (a) The direction of influence is felt especially in

54. William K. Estes, "Kurt Lewin," in William K. Estes *et al., Modern Learning Theory*, pp. 317–44 (New York: Appleton-Century-Crofts, 1954). See also, Gustav Bergmann and Kenneth W. Spence, "Operationism and Theory in Psychology," *Psychological Review*, XLVIII (January, 1941), 1–14.

55. Robert Leeper, *Lewin's Topological and Vector Psychology: A Digest and a Critique.* Eugene, Oregon: University of Oregon Press, 1943.

social psychology and in the psychology of motivation rather than of learning. (*b*) The theorizing was not carried to a stage of precision in which it could be well incorporated into a modern quantitative-experimental-theoretical system of learning. (*c*) With Lewin's early death, his own correctives could not be offered.

Tolman's Cognitive Structure and Latent Learning

Tolman's students have all been closely identified with him, but not with his theory of learning. Again, this does not mean that they have rejected it; rather, in some way it was communicated to them that the details of the theory were not very important; psychology is complex, they should be open-minded, inventive; to be like Tolman, it was not necessary to defend any of the substance of his system.

Although Tolman was really in dead earnest, he always took a somewhat playful and disparaging view toward his own theorizing. We have from him a final chapter prepared not long before his death in 1959.[56] He starts out characteristically:

I would like to begin by letting off steam. If in what follows I have not done a very clear or useful job, I would plead some half-dozen reasons. First, I think the days of such grandiose, all-covering systems in psychology as mine attempted to be are, at least for the present, pretty much passé. I feel, therefore, that it might have been more decent and dignified to let such an instance of the relatively immediate dead past bury its dead. Second, I don't enjoy trying to use my mind in too analytical a way. Hence, I have found it frustrating and difficult to subject my system to the required sorts of analysis. Third, I suppose I am personally antipathetic to the notion that science progresses through intense, self-conscious analysis of where one has got and where one is going. Such analyses are obviously a proper function for the philosopher of science and they may be valuable for many individual scientists. But I myself become frightened and restricted when I begin to worry too much as to what particular logical and methodological canons I should or should not obey. It seems to me that very often major new scientific insights have come when the scientist, like the ape, has been shaken out of his up-until-then approved scientific rules, and discovers, "out of the blue," and perhaps by pure analogy, the new rule of using a stick (or a sign-gestalt). Fourthly, I have an inveterate tendency to make my ideas too complicated and too high-flown, so that they bcome less

56. Edward Chace Tolman, "Principles of Purposive Behavior," *Psychology: A Study of a Science*, Vol. II, *op. cit.*, pp. 92–157.

and less susceptible to empirical test. Fifthly, because of increasing laziness, I have not kept up, as I should, with the more recent theoretical and empirical discussions which bear upon my argument. If I had, the argument would have been different and better and also I would have given credit to those to whom credit is due. Finally, to talk about one's own ideas, and to resort frequently to the use of the first person singular, as one tends to do in such an analysis, brings about a conflict, at least in me, between enjoying my exhibitionism and being made to feel guilty by my superego. However, I am probably merely giving vent to the spleen and had better turn to the argument itself (pp. 94–95).

In the pages that followed, he went on to a sophisticated analysis of his system, despite these preceding disclaimers. He writes of having been much influenced early by Thorndike, particularly because in his "law of effect" he gave a central place to motivation at the very time that Watson was busily defending a frequency-recency theory. Tolman did not like the "law of effect," for in emphasizng the strengthening of a response it did not place goal-seeking in its proper light. He goes on to say that he was also influenced by Köhler's studies of apes, but he suspects that he remained an associationist at heart because he felt that wholes (although they have some primacy over their parts) are acquired by learning. In the remainder of the chapter he reworks his systematic position, with its emphasis upon intervening variables, in a fresh and masterful fashion, but with the very complexity which he recognizes, so that few have troubled to digest it.

In looking for Tolman's influence upon contemporary studies of learning, one could trace out various topics, such as space learning, continuity *vs.* discontinuity, and vicarious trial-and-error. I have selected latent learning, because it represents the system very clearly in both its experimental and theoretical aspects.

Latent learning refers to the fact that what is acquired is a cognitive structure or a cognitive map, that is, knowledge about the environment in the form of what-leads-to-what. This form of learning is contrasted with the learning of movement sequences. In the latent learning experiment the movements have never been made in a smooth-running manner; evidence for learning that has *not* been shown in performance (hence is latent) comes indirectly from the very rapid gains that are made, for example, when food is introduced in a maze that the rat has explored when no food was present.

Stimulus-response or reinforcement theories originally felt that only movements that occurred could be reinforced; there is still this strong emphasis upon learning by doing. Hence, latent learning challenged these positions. The first attack was, therefore, to disprove latent learning experimentally, a disproof that Reynolds[57] and Spence and Lippitt[58] seemed to have succeeded in making. But then a whole host of experiments were done, some favorable to latent learning, some against it; the volume of the experimentation showed that the notion was a fruitful one.[59] In their own review of the literature of latent learning, a field in which they were among the experimental contributors, MacCorquodale and Meehl have this to say:

> . . . it seems safe to say that the current state of the evidence is at least encouraging to the theorist oriented to some form of expectancy theory. We were, frankly, somewhat more impressed by the overall trend of the evidence than we had expected to be.[60]

Once the experimental attack did not succeed in demolishing latent learning, the next step, for those who take another position, is to show that latent learning is actually consonant with that position. This step was taken by Hull,[61] when, in his revised theory, he included a *derivation* of latent learning from his S-R principles, and used the original Tolman and Honzik experiment[62] as evidence that his derivation was correct!

It thus may be true of Tolman's contributions, as of some of the

57. B. Reynolds, "A Repetition of the Blodgett Experiment on 'Latent Learning,'" *Journal of Experimental Psychology*, XXXV (1945), 504–16.

58. Kenneth W. Spence and Ronald Lippitt, "An Experimental Test of the Sign-Gestalt Theory of Trial and Error Learning," *Journal of Experimental Psychology*, XXXVI (1946), 491–502.

59. See reviews by D. L. Thistlethwaite, "A Critical Review of Latent Learning and Related Experiments," *Psychological Bulletin*, XLVIII (1951), 97–129; and Hilgard, *op. cit.*

60. K. MacCorquodale and P. E. Meehl, "Edward C. Tolman," in William K. Estes *et al.*, *op. cit.*, p. 213.

61. Clark Leonard Hull, *A Behavior System: An Introduction to Behavior Theory concerning the Individual Organism*. New Haven, Connecticut: Yale University Press, 1952.

62. Tolman and Honzik, *op. cit.*

others, that their very success has made them "anonymous," as they become part of the general body of psychological knowledge.

The Conservation of Knowledge through Transformation

As indicated earlier, some promising and plausible ideas do not pan out and are, therefore, discarded as false or misleading; this does not seem to have been the case with the concepts under discussion. Some ideas just stagnate as scientific curiosities, because in the structure of contemporary science they lead no farther. Perhaps the most fertile ideas of science lose their identities because they are successful in generating new ideas that replace them. It is this last disposition of ideas coming from Gestalt, field, and related viewpoints that we wish to look into.

CRITIQUES OF STIMULUS-RESPONSE ASSOCIATIONISM

A strong role was played by Gestalt theorists and by Tolman in their persistent criticism of stimulus-response associationism. They criticized atomism, mechanism, and failure to introduce organizational or structural concepts. When these criticisms continue today, are we to associate them with the earlier critics?

Consider the book by Miller, Galanter, and Pribram.[63] It is definitely critical of S-R psychology and attempts to introduce a new unit into psychology, the TOTE (Test-Operate-Test-Exist) schema. If one looks for historical antecedents, the earliest clear one would be Dewey's criticism of the reflex-arc concept, in which he, too, made a point about the response operating on the environment.[64] A nearer relative would be Muenzinger's S-E unit (from starting-phase to end-phase) as introduced some years later.[65] Muenzinger assigns influences upon himself to George Herbert Mead (who was a Dewey associate at Chicago) and to Tolman. Hence one might infer that there is some Dewey-Tolman influence in the background of this new book, but it can hardly be said to have guided it.

63. George Armitage Miller, Eugene Galanter, and Karl Pribram, *Plans and the Structure of Behavior*. New York: Henry Holt & Co., 1960.

64. John Dewey, "The Reflex-arc Concept in Psychology," *Psychological Review*, III (July, 1896), 357-70.

65. Karl Friedrich Muenzinger, *Psychology, the Science of Behavior*. Denver, Colorado: World Press, 1942 (revised edition).

Consider another book, that by Deutsch.[66] It, too, is critical of stimulus-response psychology. It is a highly original book. The word "structure" is used in a somewhat Gestalt-like sense (not in the sense of structure of the nervous system). Some of the experiments are modified from Tolman. Hence this might be viewed as in some sense in the same tradition; yet it is by no means summarized as contemporary Gestalt or cognitive theory.

Criticism is thus likely to bring together many different lines of influence, and unless there is internal evidence of direct influence, the similarities between criticisms that arise at different times are no guarantee of historical continuity between the earlier and the later critics.

PROBLEM-SOLVING AND CREATIVITY

As cognitive processes have come to the fore, in the establishment of "Centers for Cognitive Studies" (under various names), whether at Colorado, Harvard, or Wayne, surely those who were arguing for increasing attention to cognitive processes many years ago deserve some credit, and we think naturally of the Gestalt psychologists in this connection.

It is often difficult to be fair to history, because there are many threads that can be followed through time. It was not the Gestalt psychologists who first got S-R psychologists interested in concept formation, problem-solving, and thinking. Woodworth was responsible for the early work on concept formation, thinking, and the atmosphere effect, as carried on by his students Heidbreder[67] and Sells.[68] Hull's doctoral dissertation was on the evolution of concepts,[69] and his very first papers deriving behavior from conditioning considerations had to do with knowledge, purpose, and directing

66. Jaraslav Antonin Deutsch, *The Structural Basis of Behavior*. Chicago: University of Chicago Press, 1960.

67. Edna Heidbreder, "An Experimental Study of Thinking," *Archives of Psychology*, No. 58 (1924); "Toward a Dynamic Psychology of Cognition," *Psychological Review*, LII (1945), 1–22.

68. Saul B. Sells, "The Atmosphere Effect: An Experimental Study of Reasoning," *Archives of Psychology*, No. 200 (1936).

69. Clark L. Hull, "Quantitative Aspects of the Evolution of Concepts," *Psychological Monographs*, XXVIII (1920), Whole No. 123.

ideas.[70] To be sure, by that time Koffka had already been at Wisconsin, where Hull was at the time these papers were incubated, and his well-known distaste for Koffka's approach may well have motivated him to work on an alternative approach.

The present cognitive centers are staffed by people with miscellaneous backgrounds, with the influences not primarily S-R learning theory or Gestalt; there are many other influences, such as information theory, cybernetics, modern mathematics, symbolic logic, computer simulation, Piaget, psychoanalysis, and the new intellectualism of the Zeitgeist. Some lines can be traced to past influences from Gestalt. Thus, the editors of the Colorado symposium on creative thinking[71] include Max Wertheimer's son, and among the eight other authors are two trained as Gestalt psychologists and one who took his degree with Tolman; hence, in this group at least, some historical lines can be discerned.

STRUCTURE AS A FACTOR IN LEARNING

The word *structure* recurs from time to time with somewhat different meanings. In Wertheimer it meant that problems could be solved if they could be structured in such a way that the natural or organic solution would be forthcoming, as opposed to an unnatural solution by some kind of formula which, though correct, did not exhibit its true meaning. A notion very similar to this has gained currency in education through Bruner[72] who has employed the word *structure* to mean that the knowledge or substance to be taught has an inherent relatedness that should be followed in its presentation to the learner. The structure determines the appropriate sequencing of materials, as well as the appropriate presentation at any level of progress. The earlier cited quotation from Sheffield and Maccoby is in the same spirit.

70. Clark L. Hull, "Knowledge and Purpose as Habit Mechanisms," *Psychological Review*, XXXVII (1930), 511–25; "Goal-Attraction and Directing Ideas Conceived as Habit Phenomena," *Psychological Review*, XXXVIII (1931), 487–506.

71. *Contemporary Approaches to Creative Thinking.* Edited by Howard E. Gruber, Glenn Terrell, and Michael Wertheimer. New York: Atherton Press, 1962.

72. J. S. Bruner, *The Process of Education.* Cambridge, Massachusetts: Harvard University Press, 1960.

The two modes of problem-solving that have been promulgated by those using computer simulation of thinking are the *algorithmic* method and the *heuristic* method.[73] When an algorithm is used in solving a problem it corresponds to what Wertheimer meant when he talked of using a formula. It is correct that, to divide by a fraction, you invert and multiply; you don't have to understand the procedure to use it. In the heuristic method[74] you take advantage of short cuts by trying to guess the answer, or following a line that seems plausible. The answer is not guaranteed, as it is when you use an algorithm, but it may lead to a great saving of time. Machines can be programed to use heuristic methods as well as algorithms. To some extent this, too, is related to what Wertheimer taught: if you can restructure a problem, you can often find the way to a shorter solution. All one can say in this connection is that Wertheimer was on the right path but that those programing machines do not find it necessary to refer to his book.

MOTIVATIONAL CONCEPTS DERIVED FROM LEVEL OF ASPIRATION

Three of the present emphases within motivational theory have strong affiliations with Lewin's level of aspiration and yet go by different names. One of these is *achievement motivation*, brought to prominent attention by McClelland and his associates.[75] Another is *cognitive dissonance*, associated with the name of Festinger,[76] who was one of the early investigators of level of aspiration under Lewin. The third is *cognitive balance*, a theory developed by Heider,[77] one who was also associated closely with Lewin. Here we have the clearest illustrations of the conservation of a basic idea through transformations that permit it to be enriched. In this case, the original form (level of aspiration) continues alongside its transformations.

73. A. Newell, J. C. Shaw, and H. A. Simon, "The Process of Creative Thinking," in *Contemporary Approaches to Creative Thinking, op. cit.,* pp. 63–119.

74. George Polya, *How To Solve It.* New York: Doubleday & Co., 1957.

75. David C. McClelland, J. W. Atkinson, R. A. Clark, and E. L. Lowell, *The Achievement Motive.* New York: Appleton-Century-Crofts, 1953.

76. Leon Festinger, *A Theory of Cognitive Dissonance.* Evanston, Illinois: Row, Peterson & Co., 1957.

77. Fritz Heider, *The Psychology of Interpersonal Relations.* New York: John Wiley & Sons, 1958.

HISTORICAL CONTINUITY AND CULTURAL LAG

While it is a good thing to keep ideas in their historical contexts, we may occasionally do a disservice by keeping alive distinctions that no longer have any force. Textbooks, both in general psychology and in educational psychology, tend to falsify the state of psychology by keeping alive certain issues that no longer excite investigators. In part, this is due to a very natural sort of cultural lag, for the textbook writer is helpless in the face of the many developments going on around him to select those that are not passing fads. He is more comfortable with issues that are still recognizable, even though they were more exciting twenty-five years ago.

Should a contemporary student be taught about the issue between functionalism and structuralism that took place early in this century? Probably not, unless there is some special historical purpose. The question can now well be put as to whether or not he needs to be taught about Gestalt psychology. The dilemmas of the textbook-writer and the teacher are well illustrated by the problems faced in this chapter, of discovering to what extent Gestalt psychology is still viable, to what extent it has been transformed and absorbed into the kind of psychology that needs no label. Perhaps the answer depends somewhat upon the field of inquiry; in a recent book collecting papers on Gestalt psychology, most of which have appeared since 1950,[78] there is no section devoted to learning; and under the rubric "cognitive processes," nothing on either problem-solving or learning, except for one chapter on the perceptual condition of association.

Whether or not the Gestalt system remains identifiable, the historian of psychology must recognize its impact whenever there are references to wholes as different from their parts, to structures as evolved from figure-ground relationships, and to cognitive processes (insight and understanding) as deserving prominence in any discussion of learning.

78. Mary Henle, *Documents of Gestalt Psychology*. Berkeley and Los Angeles: University of California Press, 1961.

CHAPTER IV

Neurological Notes on the Art of Educating

KARL H. PRIBRAM

We know an object when we know how it is made, and we know how it is made in the degree in which we ourselves make it. Old tradition compels us to call thinking "mental." But "mental" thought is but partial experimentation, terminating in preliminary readjustments, confined within the organism. As long as thinking remained at this stage, it protected itself by regarding this introverted truncation as evidence of an immaterial reason superior to and independent of body. As long as thought was thus cooped up, overt action in the "outer" natural scene was inevitably shorn of its full meed of meaning; it was to that extent arbitrary and routine. When "outer" and "inner" activity came together in a single experimental operation, used as the only adequate method of discovery and proof, effective criticism, consistent and ordered valuation, emerged. Thought aligned itself with other arts that shape objects by informing things with meaning [Italics mine].[1]

When asked to contribute to this yearbook I was delighted—problems of education are my daily fare, and I have developed some prides and some prejudices on how one goes about learning and teaching. Second consideration, however, led to hesitancy—for I was to say something of physiological import to educators. What on earth could a neuropsychologist have to contribute? And third, a still more considerate question emerged—since when does the neurologist *not* have something to say in these matters? Was it really so very long ago (1913) that Thorndike[2] discussed the neurology of the capacity to learn and of readiness?

It has been a half century—a fruitful half century of functionalism and progressivism; of positivism and behaviorism; of Gestalt and

1. John Dewey, *Experience and Nature*, p. 346. LaSalle, Illinois: Open Court Publishing Co., 1958 (revised edition).

2. E. L. Thorndike, *Educational Psychology*. Vol. I, *The Original Nature of Man;* Vol. II, *The Psychology of Learning*. New York: Teachers College, Columbia University (Mason-Henry Press), 1913.

field; of conditioning and learning. Amazingly, Carmichael's 1940 yearbook chapter is the only one on the central nervous system in all these fifty years.[3]

Yet, neurological science has not been dormant in this interim. Why then the hiatus? Most likely because those working with cerebra produced little of relevance to those working with curricula. Meanwhile, those engaged in building a purely behavioral science did give answers to old questions.

So why *now* the nervous system? First, because recent results of neurochemical, neurophysiological, and neuropsychological experiments bear directly on problems of education. Second, because the answers given to these problems by the purely behavioral scientist have been so multiform and often conflicting and, yes I will say it, wrong—that education must be given some basis for choice among answers. A return to neuropsychological fundamentals can clarify issues and, on occasion, resolve them.

The issues are these. Behavioral science has, up to now, been overly concerned with externally placed guides on behavior. Lip service to organismic states has been rendered through reference to physiological needs, the so-called primary sources of satisfaction, of drive and reinforcement. This emphasis, in turn, did a misservice to education by placing external guides on the material to be taught. The view proposed here, a view derived from neurobehavioral research, is that the reinforcing process, basic to education, has an intrinsic organic, i.e., neurological, structure which respects the intrinsic structure of the materials to be taught. The job of education is to facilitate the matching of these two intrinsic structures, much as a sculptor matches his intrinsic vision to the intrinsic properties of stone. In this endeavor lies the art of educating.

On Readiness[4]

In the old scheme, knowledge, as science, signified precisely and exclusively turning away from change to the changeless. In the new experi-

3. Leonard Carmichael, "The Physiological Correlates of Intelligence," in *Intelligence: Its Nature and Nurture*, pp. 93–155. Thirty-ninth Yearbook of the National Society for the Study of Education, Part I. Chicago: Distributed by the University of Chicago Press, 1940.

4. Readiness is here used in the sense of immediate readiness to learn as implied in Thorndike's "law of readiness." It is related to, but not identical with, the readiness based on developmental level, as discussed in chap. ix (E.R.H.).

mental science, knowledge is obtained in exactly the opposite way, namely, through deliberate institution of a definite and specified course of change. *The* method of . . . inquiry is to introduce some change in order to see what other change ensues; the correlation between these changes . . . constitutes the definite and desired object of knowledge.[5]

The first question an educator must ask is how can an individual be readied to engage in the educational process? The question so stated is in many respects similar to that faced by the scientist who must devise an experiment to engage his subject matter. And the results of neurological investigations suggest that the nervous system also goes about the first steps of *its* task in much this same way.

When a person or animal is placed in a situation where the same tone is repeatedly "beeped" at irregular intervals, a sequence of events is observed. At first an orienting reaction can be recorded. Often the subject will turn head and eyes to locate the source of the sound. A galvanic skin response is recorded. Blood flow to the head is increased while that to the finger tips diminishes. Electrical activity of the parts of the brain connected to the internal ear show a choppy "activation" pattern characteristic of alerting. Other parts of the brain also give altered electrical records typically found when changes of state are taking place (e.g., theta rhythms are recorded from the hippocampal formation).

After about five to ten minutes in the repetitious environment, these behavioral and physiological indexes of orientation can no longer be observed. Habituation has occurred. The person (or animal) is apparently no longer reacting to the stimulus situation.

But this appearance is deceptive. Diminish the intensity of the tone slightly, and immediately the orienting reaction recurs. Or, after habituation is in full force, shorten the tone beep: orienting is again observed—but now to the "unexpected" silent period caused by the earlier termination of each beep. Obviously habituation reflects not a passive, "fatigued," inactivity of the organism, but, rather, a state of expectancy delicately tuned to recurrences in the situation. Any slight departure from prior conformations—any nuances—produce the orienting reaction.

The central nervous system is the repository of this state of ex-

5. John Dewey, *The Quest for Certainty*, p. 84. New York: Minton, Balch & Co., 1929.

pectancy. For instance, in the frog, nerve cells ("newness neurons") have been identified (in the optic tectum) which react with a burst of discharges whenever some novelty (such as a fly) is introduced into its visual field. These bursts rapidly diminish if the novel object remains in the field or after repeated presentations; other cells maintain an increased firing rate over longer periods "following" the presence of the object as long as it remains within the field.

Reaction to novelty thus appears to be one built-in feature of the central nervous system. The problem remains to identify the way in which neurons are organized so that the editing function of redundancy reduction, i.e., information enhancement, occurs. Repeatedly these aggregates of nerve cells must pose the question, "Is this news?" Already, some mechanisms are known. For instance, in the retina, contrast is enhanced by a process of "surround inhibition"— i.e., by a mechanism which shuts down on the activity of receptors that are neighbors of those directly excited. A similar mechanism has been shown operative in the cerebral cortex. Physiologists and psychologists of the Pavlovian persuasion refer to this process as external inhibition because it is induced by excitations derived from outside the organism. They contrast external with internal inhibition which builds up within the organism, especially during frustration. Internal inhibition is identified by its electrical concomitants and, in the extreme, is accompanied by behavioral sleep. Recently, Magoun has suggested that the various inhibitory mechanisms—all active neural processes—be thought of as arranged in a continuum. There is merit in this suggestion, though it poses some interesting problems.

Surround or external inhibition is observed to take place when microelectrode recordings are made from single strands of neurons. Neurons are known to have a spontaneous beat—i.e., they discharge rhythmically, much as does the heart, provided only that the tissue fluids in their surround remain physiological in their concentration of nutrients, respirants, and salts. When neurons are excited either by other neurons or by receptor events, their rate of "beating" or "firing" increases. As already noted, when this happens, records made from neighboring nerve cells show a diminution in the frequency of firing. And this is correlated behaviorally with an enhancement of the contrast between excited and nonexcited fields (e.g., vision). More of this in a moment.

Internal inhibition, on the other hand, is said to take place when gross electrical recordings from brain tissue show changes correlated with behavioral drowsiness or sleep. It is not known whether these gross electrical changes indicate an increase or decrease in the firing of individual nerve cells—techniques are not yet sufficiently far along to sample a large enough population of neurons at any one time to answer this question easily. Preliminary evidence indicates, however, that the activity recorded with gross electrodes is only partially correlated with the firing patterns obtained from neurons —that the gross electrodes record what are called changes in local graded responses of neural tissue, while microelectrodes record nerve impulses that are transmitted along the entire extent of the neuron. It is perfectly possible, though not yet established, that on certain occasions local, graded potentials of neural tissue increase, while the frequency of nerve impulse discharges of the same tissue decreases. The local graded response activity is recorded primarily from the dendrites of neurons and from the junctions between neurons (synapses) and between neurons and glia (gliapses). Nerve impulse transmission is, of course, largely a function of the axons of nerves. It is now well known that what happens in one part of the neuron does not necessarily reflect what is going on elsewhere in that same nerve cell.

To sum up, if neural inhibitory processes are, indeed, to be thought of in some unitary way, the suggestion must be seriously entertained that changes in the frequency of nerve impulses and changes in local graded neural potential can vary reciprocally. If this is so, the active neural process, which is called "inhibition" and observed to take place in the enhancement of contrast, could be expected to spread, i.e., involve more and more neighboring tissue. This organized, spreading, and gradually more-and-more-internalized inhibitory process would thus be called on to account for the phenomenon of habituation and, as already noted, is correlated with behavioral drowsiness and sleep. The suggested model does have appeal to those of us who have fought off this spread of "internal inhibition" while some speaker drones on and on and on. . . .

Return for a moment to the retina. There are other interesting phenomena. Place a mirror onto the sclera and arrange a slit of light so that it is reflected from the mirror onto a black background. Arrange also that the beam reflects accurately the angle of movement of the mirror. Now, whenever the eye moves, the arc described by the light on the black background is such that the identical retinal element is continuously excited. Within a half minute or a minute, the slit of light fades and disappears. Or put on sun glasses, and soon the relative brightness of objects will appear as before. These phenomena are traced to the rapid adaptation of retinal receptors. Each receptor element responds to change only briefly— then adaptation supervenes, and the frequency of firing returns to its prior basal rate. The reason we are able to see anything at all is that the eye is in continuous *movement*. Through movement, different receptors are momentarily brought into play with respect to an exciting stimulus. Thus, *movement provides an override on the process of adaptation so that perception can take place*. But adaptation, nonetheless, plays a role in making up, with surround inhibition, a mechanism for redundancy reduction. Convergence of the input from a group of receptors upon a single nerve cell in the central nervous system, a cell with the same property of adaptation, will result in a "newness neuron," sensitive only to "averages" of the changes in frequency of firing of the receptor pool from which it draws its input. And through surround inhibition among such centrally placed neurons, *this* "average" would be enhanced. A still more central neuron, drawing input from a population of these first-order neurons, again by simple convergence, would, by repeating the process again, reduce redundancy—i.e., react only to differences among differences.

But readiness is not all encompassed by the notion of newness. As already noted, movement provides an override on the mechanism of redundancy reduction. Try this experiment. Look at this book and move your eyes about it from corner to corner. The book and this page remain in place—they do not move, though your eye did. Now push your eyeball with a finger. Immediately the page goes shooting off in the direction opposite to the push you gave the eye. Somehow, active movement and passive movement of the eye give different results in perception. Many experiments involving different sensory modes have taken off from this simple observation, and it is now clear that active movement is accompanied by a pre-setting of the perceptual mechanism so that constancy of perception of the environment can be achieved. For our purposes here, what is important is that the override on the adaptation-habituation process is itself governed. If it were not, the world would go rushing by as an incomprehensible flux. This central control over active movement and, thus, perception is a story in itself—but, first, a few words about what these experimental results can say about the readiness of a person to become engaged in the educational process.

Neuropsychological experiment has demonstrated that an organism orients (attends) when, after exposure to recurrent events, these events *change*. *Novelty rises out of variations on the familiar.* And *everyone* must be familiar with something. The question is, how is the educator to ascertain what is familiar to his pupils. He cannot simply ask, for they will not be aware—they are habituated; by definition they cannot respond explicitly to that which is *most familiar*. The educator can, by knowing the background of his pupils, make heuristic probes—ask questions and give answers which, if they catch the attention of his pupils, will uncover the boundaries of the familiar. He may ask the students—once they become engaged, pupils have become students—to participate in the questions and especially the answers so that they may help in this uncovering of their own boundaries. In this way the students themselves immediately begin to exert some control on the override of the habituation mechanism—they move their "eyes" and do not have them moved from without. This is at least one safeguard that can be established so that the material presented does not go rushing by in an incomprehensible flux.

Once engaged, how is engagement maintained? Obviously repetitiousness carried to an extreme will lead to habituation and even to internal inhibition, drowsiness. But so will its opposite. If too many contrasting novelties are presented in too rapid succession, surround inhibition is, according to our model, apt to spread and become internal inhibition—the result, frustration and sleep. The good teacher, therefore, watches (much as an experimentalist watches for deflections of the indicators of *his* measuring instruments) these signs of alerting and dozing—the brightness of eyes, the expectant postures, and their converse—among students and paces himself accordingly.

There need be no guesswork involved in ascertaining "readiness." The neuropsychological laboratory has not only given first glimpses of the mechanisms involved—sufficient to demonstrate their importance as preparation for a learning experience. In addition, this work has also indicated the method that can be applied in evaluating readiness, viz., the observation of orienting reactions. That such application is feasible has already been demonstrated: an important technique regularly used in psychotherapy to "uncover unconscious processes" relies exactly on this procedure. The therapist notes and, in graded doses, points out to the patient excessive strengths (or lacks) of response that ordinarily would not be expected were the patient fully aware of what is the familiar to him —i.e., his "unconscious." As an educator, the teacher out of necessity watches the orienting reactions of his students. He might also fruitfully watch his own reactions during teaching as a means of self education. He does this by exploring in the same fashion his own familiarities, the nonexplicit assumptions with which he approaches his subject matter and which, on occasion, are brought "uncomfortably" to light by the "naïve" queries of his students. Thus, he himself becomes engaged in education—this turn, the pupils teach; the teacher learns.

The Capacity To Learn and To Remember

There is little scientific writing which does not introduce at some point or other the idea of tendency. The idea of tendency unites in itself exclusion of prior design and inclusion of movement in a particular direction, a direction that may be either furthered or counteracted and frustrated, but which is intrinsic. Direction involves a limiting position, a point or goal of culminating stoppage, as well as an initial starting point. . . . [But this goal may be] an end-in-view and is [a] constant and cumulative re-enactment at each stage of forward movement. It is no longer a terminal point, external to the conditions that have led up to it; it is the continually developing meaning of present tendencies— the very things which as directed we call "means." The process is art and its product, no matter at what stage it be taken, is a work of art.[6]

Capacity calls to mind a fixity, a basic moiety of equipment which is subject to measurement, as by tests of intelligence. Yet, in his chapter on the anatomy and physiology of original tendencies,

6. Dewey, *Experience and Nature, op. cit.,* p. 302.

Thorndike discusses the changes presumed to occur at the synapse which might account for the capability to learn. If some such process is indeed involved in learning, capacity to learn could as well involve some changeable, changing baseline that needs recurrent reassessment to be meaningful. What is the evidence?

Great strides have recently been made in taking questions of memory storage into the laboratory. For over a century neurohistologists have asked whether neural growth can take place in the central nervous system after the initial period of development. Only within the last few years has an affirmative answer been obtained.

Rabbits were irradiated in a cyclotron so that one layer of the brain cortex was selectively damaged. This could be accomplished because the radiation is rapidly absorbed in soft tissue and so gives off its energy in a remarkably restricted range. Thus, a cell layer could be "excised" without damage to more superficial or to deeper layers. The studies were undertaken to determine some precise relations in the connections between deep-lying brain structures and the cortex. The investigators were, therefore, astounded to find that, after an initial period when destruction was evident, neural new growth had occurred in the area of the lesion. Nerve cells do not divide in the mature brain—nor did they in these rabbit preparations. What did happen was an orderly growth of fibers, probably branches from undamaged nerve fibers.

Of course, students are not rabbits, nor have they been exposed to the cyclotron's fury. But there is more. Another group of investigators, in following certain chemical changes produced in rat brains by differential amounts and kinds of experience, found that their results were correlated with changes in the thickness of the brain cortex involved. Rats given visual experience showed a differential thickening of the visual cortex; in blinded rats the differential thickening favored the somesthetic areas of the brain. Again the increase in tissue is not attributable to an increase in the number of nerve cells—the assumption must be that the increase is due to increased branching of the nerve-fiber network and an increase in the nonneural (e.g., glial) elements (which do continue to reproduce throughout life).

There is much more. Biochemists have shown that nerve cells secrete a greater abundance of ribonucleic acid than any other cells in the body. And ribonucleic acid, RNA, is a sister substance to DNA, the material from which genetic memory is fashioned. Glia are also involved in a longer-term process, which might reflect the fact that experienced events must go through a period of consolidation before they are memorized.

Some further distinctions are becoming clear. The mechanisms in the brain that serve learning and those that serve retention have been separately involved: lesions of the brain cortex (made with aluminum hydroxide cream), which cause marked disturbance of the electrical record, *impede learning* some five-fold but *leave intact retention* of solutions to problems. Conversely, removals of that same cortical tissue have little effect on the acquisition of new but related problem-solutions during any one training session; however, recall of the previous day's performances is severely restricted.

All this and more—but I have reviewed this material elsewhere in detail and there presented a model to suggest how the memory mechanism might be viewed.[7] Here it is sufficient to point out that inroads are being made—and they are of considerable proportion—on the age-old problem of organic changes occurring as a function of experience. The locus of that change is in the brain, and more specifically in the ramifications of finely branching nerve fibers and their relations with each other and with the glia in which they are embedded.

Thus educators, aware of these facts, can take seriously the experiments which show that an excessive "massing" of experiences leads to poor acquisition. Consolidation of the memory trace appears to be a two-fold process. The first part takes, at the most, an hour. During this hour the neural (probably neurochemical) traces set up by the experience are fragile. Not only will a blow on the head completely wipe them out—and cause a retrograde amnesia for immediately prior events—but in addition, these early traces are subject to "inhibition" through retroactive influences upon them by exposure to new and related material. The rate with which different persons consolidate their memory appears to differ. In one study some retarded children were found to perform as well as controls when their exposure to test trials in a problem was spaced sufficient-

7. Rather than cite the research studies in the body of the chapter, references can be found in the bibliography at the end.

ly far apart. In general, the old adage that "in a lecture few souls are saved after the first fifteen minutes" can be used as a rule of thumb—very few experiences per hour can be consolidated as far as we now know the physiological and behavioral evidence.

At this point the reader may well be saying to himself "My, but this fellow sounds old fashioned. Hasn't he heard of the marvels of teaching machines, or programed texts, of the process of reinforcement by which behavior is so gradually 'shaped' that in painless fashion mountains of facts can be acquired?" Yes, your author has heard of these methods and was privileged to be on the same program when Skinner initially reported these innovations. They are, indeed, powerful tools. What has neurobehavioral science to say about them?

The proper use of teaching machines and programed texts hinges on the more basic question of the nature of what constitutes reinforcement for an organism. And about reinforcement neuropsychologists have found out a great deal.

Teaching machines are direct descendants of Thorndike's second and third laws (the first was the Law of Readiness). The second is the Law of Exercise or Use, which states that "when a modifiable connection is made between a situation and a response, that connection's strength is, other things being equal, increased. By the strength of a connection is meant roughly the probability that the connection will be made when the situation recurs." The third law is, of course, the most famous—the Law of Effect: "When a modifiable connection between a situation and a response is made and is accompanied or followed by a satisfying state of affairs, that connection's strength is increased." The converse of these two laws in terms of "disuse" and an "annoying state of affairs" was also given. And psychologists have been busy since, in an attempt to give experimentally based substance to these laws.

The issues are: (a) what is meant by "a connection," (b) by its "strength" and (c) by "a satisfying (or annoying) state of affairs." The body of knowledge that has grown around these issues is called learning theory, and, as already mentioned, centers on the problem of what constitutes reinforcement for an organism. For the most part, laboratory analysis has involved animals, and this almost necessarily has led to some misconceptions which are only now beginning to be remedied.

What is meant by a "connection"? Thorndike and many who followed him thought of the memory-storage mechanism simply in terms of the association between situation and response—contiguous events becoming associated solely by virtue of the contiguity of their effects in the central nervous system. There is, of course, some merit in this conception which has guided the thinking of empiricists for centuries. Yet, today, we can spell out in much greater detail just what contiguity involves. The alert reader will already have anticipated——contiguity implies readiness. The processes discussed in the first section *are* those involved in bringing together within the organism, i.e., within the brain, events and situations experienced on separate occasions—and events not so brought together fail to influence.

The mechanisms discussed in the last section are, of course, not the only ones known to function in readiness. Bruner has reviewed the earlier evidence, which has been added to in many ways. For instance, a great deal of work has been done to show that the activity of all receptors, or at least the input channels from them, is directly controlled by the central nervous system. These "gates" allow the organism to be sensitive only to certain excitations—the gates in turn are self-adapting mechanisms, i.e., they are subject to gradual alteration by the very inputs they control. This is true in the case of control over muscle receptors as it is for others, thus actions are guided much as are perceptions: responses to situations do not become simply associated; readiness is necessary as well.

In line with these facts, the fundamental neural organization in control of the association between stimulus and response can no longer be conceived as a reflex arc. On the basis of many new neurological facts, the suggestion has been made that the reflex arc be replaced by a feedback unit which involves (*a*) a *Test* of readiness with regard to the input, (*b*) an *Operation* that seeks to match the test, (*c*) a re-*Test* to see whether match has been accomplished, before (*d*) *Exit* from control is effected. This TOTE mechanism is ubiquitous—and, as will become clear in the last section of this presentation, it is essentially a modified homeostat, a mechanism which can control the very input to which it is sensitive. TOTEs are conceived to be arranged hierarchically into Plans, the antecedents of actions. And structurally Plans are nothing more than programs, similar to those that guide the operation of computers—well-worked-out outlines such as those used in programed texts and teaching machines. George Miller, Eugene Galanter, and I have already detailed the importance of this new structural view for dealing with some of the persistent problems in psychology. There will be more to say about homeostats, TOTEs, Plans, and programs later on—here the point is that contiguity (association) has *structure*.

This structure is first of all the structure of readiness, of expectancy—of processes such as habituation and redundancy reduction. The problem of association, then, is the problem of readiness which was outlined in the last section. There is no reason at this juncture of our knowledge to treat Thorndike's "connection" separately from his "readiness." The two can no longer be usefully distinguished.

What then can be meant by the "strength of a connection"? Thorndike defines this in terms of the probability of recurrence of a response in a situation—a definition adopted by Skinner to describe the effect of reinforcement. Operationally, therefore, strength of a "connection" is strength of a response in a situation. And response strength has recently become an important focus for learning theory.

Animal experimenters are beset by the difficulty that their subjects have a limited repertoire of "the familiar" to engage in the experimental procedure. Reinforcement in animal experiments has, therefore, been largely in terms of food reward or mild electric-shock punishment. A large body of evidence on the usefulness of these reinforcers was accumulated to the point where learning theorists believed that all behavior modification rests, in the final analysis, on the use of such rewards and punishments. More of this in a moment. But recently this simple notion was found to be inadequate to handle the results of even these same animal experiments. Learning theory faced an impasse. The impasse was this: response strength, i.e., the probability that a response should recur in a situation, ought, according to learning theory, to be proportional to the occurrence and immediacy of appropriate reward and inversely related to the effort expended to obtain that reward. But experimental evidence had accumulated to show that "common assumptions underlying learning theory failed to give an adequate description of changes in response strength." In fact, this evidence suggested "that the variables of reward, temporal delay, and effort may have just the opposite effects from those predicted by the assumptions. . . ." The quotations are taken from a recently published monograph by Lawrence and Festinger. The authors present their evidence that under conditions of *non*-reward, in situations where reward had on earlier occasions been experienced, the strength of response is greater when the experienced rewards had been few, delayed, and obtained with considerable effort. Festinger had already found these same relationships effective in guiding the behavior of human subjects and had proposed that a state of cognitive dissonance (between expected and realized rewards) is set up in the organism when expectations are not met. The organism tries, under the new circumstances, to reduce dissonance "by converting the consequences of his actions into something that justifies the action or he can change his behavior so that it becomes consonant with the consequences experienced." In other words, he can try to alter his expectations or his behavior in such a way that the two again become consonant.

It was of interest to me that the increase in response strength described to occur in these circumstances showed similarities to that observed in addiction. It is common knowledge among morphine addicts that very often the strength of the addiction is proportional to the amount of endeavor required to obtain the drug. (In fact most patients who have had morphine therapy and go through withdrawal symptoms when treatment terminates have an understandable aversion to the drug.)

The question raised by the experiments and observations of dissonance and addictionance is the central one for education: what is the nature of the process of reinforcement? Clearly, rewards external to the materials explored during learning are effective. Grades have their place in school, just as do food rewards in animal learning experiments. But the same impasse is reached in education as is reached in learning theory. Effort, delay, and spacing of reward are known to improve performance. The suspicion is therefore raised that grades and other extrinsic rewards signify something; i.e., give information to the rewarded about something else, something more basic.

There is an example which points up the signifying role of extrinsic reward in an unforgettable manner. My own work has proceeded in large part with the aid of monkeys. These animals are endowed with large pouches in their cheeks into which stores of food can be put for use at a more convenient time. When, in a problem-solving situation, some monkeys make a correct response signified by a reward, they pop the peanut into their food pouch. When, on the other hand, they make an error and there is no reward, they will very often put their hand to cheek, push, and munch with relish their earlier-gotten gain. This never interferes with learning (by comparisons in scores achieved by these monkeys and others with other habits).

Further, a monkey who is doing well in learning a task bounces with zest into the testing apparatus; one whose mastery is failing for the moment droops and is difficult to transfer from his colony cage. Nor can food-reward alter this demeanor. Conversely, I have given as many as fifty trials at a time to monkeys whose food pouches are filled, who are holding peanuts with both feet and one hand, and who are sated. These animals literally will throw peanuts over their shoulder and so free one hand to get on with the problem. And we have, of course, all observed many, many students who "eat up" course material rather than good grades.

There is also no question that teaching machines and programed learning, by their step-wise guides to achievement, have provided a technique for maintaining performance in a problem-solving situation. Whether this will amount to more than an "addiction" probably depends on the way in which these teaching aids are used, not on the technique itself. However, there is a most important fundamental contribution to education in the technique which must not be missed. Programed texts and teaching machines implicitly recognize the significant aspect of reward: reinforcement is constructed through rewards intrinsic in the material to be learned. Each item of information gained values the next step in the sequence of operations.

But this is ahead of the story. The relation of information and value is taken up in the next section. Here, the point is that rewards signify something, something basic and intrinsic in the learning process. Thorndike called this something "a satisfying state."

What, then, constitutes satisfaction? For a time, neuropsychologists thought they had found the answer. And a partial answer it is, for the experimental results give some important clues to the solution of the puzzle. The experimental findings were that animals would work to turn on a minute electric current delivered to certain parts of their brains. This was immediately hailed as a discovery of "the pleasure center"—conservative physiologists suddenly found themselves to be hedonists. But further consideration showed that the problem had only been pushed back a step—to be sure, the brain was involved, and only parts of the brain at that. But through what mechanism was the self-stimulation effect produced? Why was electrical self-stimulation reinforcing? Just what is the nature of reinforcement? And we are back to the initial question.

Nonetheless, these discoveries did leave a clue and provided a handle to the problem: the locations in which these self-stimulations were effective were systematically explored—they are all within the core of the brain substance. Of special interest is the fact that the forebrain placements of the self-stimulation electrodes fall within a system of structures known as the limbic formations. And much work has been done toward finding out what these limbic structures do. The most recent findings supplement earlier ones to the effect that, when parts of the limbic brain are removed, animals have trouble learning to execute behavior sequences. For instance, a monkey is asked to solve the problem of pushing on windows in which numerals are displayed. Normal monkeys can be taught to push first a 4, then a 6; or first a 3, then a 5, then a 7, even though these numerals appear in random order in as many as sixteen different windows. Monkeys who have had part of their limbic brain (the hippocampus) removed on both sides experience great difficulty with such a task. (Control operations that remove other parts of the forebrain do not have this effect—with one exception: i.e., when the anterior part of the frontal lobe is injured, the part made infamous by the lobotomy procedure.)

Somehow, therefore, the problem of reinforcement and the problem of behavior sequences are tied together—if in no other fashion than that both depend on some common neural mechanism, and that is a great deal. But there is more. As already noted, Skinner in his definition of reinforcement, adopted Thorndike's "increased proba- bility of *recurrence* of a response." *Recurrences* occur in sequence. Further, in animal experiments all events that increase the probabil- ity of recurrence of a response are *not* called reinforcers. Cues, events that antecede and guide action, share this property. Only those events *consequent* on action, the consequences of actions, are called reinforcers. And such events have been shown by Skinner and his collaborators to exert their control over behavior not so much singly but by the schedules of their appearance—i.e., reinforcers oc- cur as *sequences*. The organism must be ready (i.e., shaped) to re- spond to the reinforcing events.

These sequences have their effect on behavior by appearing con- tiguously with that behavior. This is contiguity, but contiguity as we have now come to understand it. Events reinforce only when they occur contiguously—i.e., in context—when the organism is ready to respond to them. Reinforcers are, therefore, truly the *con- sequences* of actions—sequences of events occurring in context.

For another occasion I spelled out in detail the experimental foun- dations that led to this view and its ramifications throughout the problems of motivation. The scope of the issues involved can be sensed from the section headings of this other work, which read: I. "A structuralist looks at operant conditioning"; II. "The structure of contiguity—some psychophysiological facts"; III. "Drive struc- tures and the real CNS"; IV. "Performance theory: addictionance and effectance"; V. "Perceptual performances: reinforcement as in- formation processing"; and VI. "The anatomy of happiness." All of what is said there is of relevance here and I am sorely put to the task of selection: perhaps you will find in this presentation a sufficient sample to engage your interest to pursue the full manuscript.

My answer to the questions of what produces response strength, what is satisfying, stems thus directly from the observations we have been pursuing. Learning theorists using animals were led to believe that the "goads" to behavior (to use George Miller's term) were the drive stimuli which originate in an organism's physiological need states. But effort and hustling, delay and sparseness of reward, are also found to increase response strength under certain circumstances.

Could it be that under these circumstances activity per se is rewarding? This makes little sense, for it would not account for the difference between, say, hustling and unordered, random hyperactivity. And here we may have a clue: could it be that ordered activity per se is rewarding? And further, what can be meant by "ordered activity"—certainly not patterned muscular contractions, since these are equally manifest when we observe random activity. No, clearly when the *consequences* of action become orderly (consonant), i.e., sequences of events appearing *in context*, then and only then is activity ("judged") rewarding, i.e., reinforcing.

The suggestion is that reinforcement is the expression of an organism's tendency toward orderliness; that satisfaction results when a degree of orderliness has been achieved. There is good reason to suspect that the central nervous system is so constructed that order is imposed on its inputs if this is at all possible; if it is not, search continues. Mathematical models that simulate the neural process have given a variety of related and precise expressions to this mechanism. These need now to be put to test in the neurophysiological laboratory. Techniques are available, and data should be in hand during the next few years.

At the moment, the analysis of reinforcement here pursued has shown that the process of satisfaction is to be conceived as *intrinsic* to the material ordered and *intrinsic* to the construction of the nervous system. Education so conceived is truly a process of *e-ducere*, the art of bringing out this tendency to orderliness.

At what points is orderliness sufficient to satisfy? This question is intimately related to another: how is learned material remembered? Earlier the evidence was presented to show that the neural mechanisms, those important to learning and those involved in retention, differ. Perhaps satisfaction results when learned material is not just retained but is remembered in the sense opposite to "dismembered," and therefore as a remaking into context—when acquired information places a value on new inputs. But before these conceptions of the intrinsic nature of reinforcement and satisfaction can come clear, we must more fully explore what is meant by "the tendency to become orderly." And so we turn to the important topic of structure.

Transfer and the Problem of Structure

It goes without saying that man begins as a part of physical and animal nature. In as far as he reacts to physical things on a strictly physical level, he is pulled and pushed about, overwhelmed, broken to pieces, lifted on the crest of the wave of things, like anything else. . . . That appetite is blind, is notorious; it may push us into a comfortable result instead of into disaster; but we are pushed just the same. *When appetite is perceived in its meanings, in the consequences it induces, and these consequences are experimented with in reflective imagination, some being seen to be consistent with one another, and hence capable of co-existence and of serially ordered achievement, others being incompatible, forbidding conjunction at one time, and getting in one another's way serially—when this estate is attained, we live on the human plane, responding to things in their meanings. A relationship of cause-effect has been transformed into one of means-consequence.* Then consequences belong *integrally* to the conditions which may produce them, and the latter possess character and distinction. The meaning of causal conditions is carried over also into the consequence, so that the latter is no longer a mere end, a last and closing term of arrest. . . . Its value as fulfilling and consummatory is measurable by *subsequent* fulfillments and frustrations to which it is contributory in virtue of the causal means which compose it [italics and underscoring mine].[8]

The question of how to teach is intimately interwoven with the problems of the transfer of training. How can education be conducted so that transfer is maximized? Just how is transfer accomplished? Thorndike in his chapter on the "Influence of Improvement" focused on the identification of "similar elements" between the material learned and the new situation. Where do we stand today?

Return for a moment to the effect of brain operations on problem-solving behavior. Compare two lesions, both of the temporal lobe of the cerebral hemispheres. One lesion involves the limbic formations of the temporal lobe (a part of the brain already discussed in the last section); the other ablation involves the cerebral mantle, the newer cortex of temporal lobe in portions of what is usually called the "association" area. The problem is the following: the animals, monkeys, are asked to choose between two small doors hung on a black background. The doors are painted grey and are identical except that one is darker than the other. These doors are easily inter-

8. Dewey, *Experience and Nature, op. cit.*, pp. 300–301.

changed and exchanged from trial to trial in random order between the two placements. On each trial the monkey is allowed to open only one door. When he chooses the darker grey he finds a peanut in the opening; when he opens the other door he is faced with an empty tray. Unoperated monkeys learn to choose the darker door after a couple of hundred trials or so. The monkeys with the limbic system lesions learn with equal facility. Those with the lesions of the newer "association" cortex have great difficulty, however. As already noted in the last section, this difficulty is more related to remembering what they had learned in previous session than to learning per se. However, finally they do perform the task as well as the others. Now the problem is changed. Every fifth trial two new doors are hung in place of the others. One of these new doors is the same dark grey as the previously rewarded one; the other is darker yet. Placement is again random. This time a peanut is put behind both doors. Note that only every fifth trial is set up this way—for the other four, the lighter pair of doors continues to be used, and only the one dark door has a peanut behind it.

The expectation is that normal monkeys will transfer their choice of "push the darker door" to the new situation, the fifth trial in every series. And normals do just this. So do the animals with the "association" cortex ablations. Only the monkeys with the limbic lesions fail to transfer. They choose the test doors on a fifty-fifty basis; they treat the test trials as a completely new situation.

This failure to transfer is not related to a change in the way these animals generalize among the stimulus aspects of a situation. A test of stimulus generalization shows these monkeys to perform as do their controls. It is the "association" cortex ablation that produces greater generalization—i.e., a wider range of physically related stimuli is now treated as identical. In other words, retention and transfer have been clearly dissociated. And the brain systems involved in transfer are those already shown to be importantly concerned in the process of reinforcement.

So once again, it is necessary to turn to reinforcement, consequences of behavior. As suggested in the last section and detailed in the presentation already mentioned, reinforcement results when events subsequent to behavior become contextually related to the behavior, i.e., become con-sequent. Context, that is to say, readiness, can be supplied by a variety of stimulus events. In animal experiments the subject is usually deprived of food or water for a period of time so that the drive-stimuli, excitations that accompany physiological needs, provide context, readiness, for food pellets or sips of water which are scheduled to become available when the "correct" action has been performed. Only recently has it become apparent to practically all experimenters (some had been saying this for a long time) that, to the animal, such reinforcers give information about the correctness or incorrectness of the action in the stimulation: i.e., that reinforcers instruct. *During learning, reinforcers act as instructions; they are informative.*

But animals, even rats, are smart: after a period of isolation, put a rat in a T-maze with one alley of the T painted white, the other black, with a mate placed at the end of the white alley. No normal rat runs down that black alley more than once or twice. He has learned to find the female in one trial. She has acted as information to guide correct choice. However, her role as reinforcer is not finished. Repeat trials and allow mating to occur, but not every time. Measure his running speed. You will find it to be directly proportional to the number of times mating has taken place. In technical language, *she*, the reinforcer, has, in addition to giving information, *placed a value on his* running speed. *Reinforcers* are thus shown to be *valuative in performance.*

But values indicate readiness, context. How can reinforcement be both informative and valuative? How can they be both context and content? Or better, how do event sequences that are content during learning become context during performance; how is information transformed into value?

The example chosen deals with drive stimuli. In the first section, readiness was discussed in perceptual terms. Needless to say, information is usually thought of as perceived. The information-value problem is, therefore, not limited to cases where drive stimuli are concerned. In fact, the problem is an even more general one. In the last section, the ordering of consequences of actions was found to constitute reinforcement in situations where addiction and dissonance were observed. In that case the consequences of actions had to provide their own order; they themselves had to become the context within which subsequent events would become consequent—

i.e., reinforcing. The question raised was just what is involved in this ordering of consequence: (*a*) When does it occur? (*b*) What constitutes its composition?

As to when it occurs, the following statement by Mace is relevant:

What happens when a man, or for that matter an animal, has no need to work for a living? . . . the simplest case is that of the domesticated cat—a paradigm of affluent living more extreme than that of the horse or the cow. All the basic needs of a domesticated cat are provided for almost before they are expressed. It is protected against danger and inclement weather. Its food is there before it is hungry or thirsty. What then does it do? How does it pass its time?

We might expect that having taken its food in a perfunctory way it would curl up on its cushion and sleep until faint internal stimulation gave some information of the need for another perfunctory meal. But no, it does not just sleep. It prowls the garden and the woods killing young birds and mice. It *enjoys* life in its own way. The fact that life can be enjoyed, and is most enjoyed, by many living beings in the state of affluence (as defined) draws attention to the dramatic change that occurs in the working of the organic machinery at a certain stage of the evolutionary process. *This is the reversal of the means-end relation in behaviour.* In the state of nature the cat must kill to live. In the state of affluence it lives to kill. This happens with men. When men have no need to work for a living there are broadly only two things left to them to do. They can "play" and they can cultivate the arts. These are their two ways of enjoying life. It is true that many men work because they enjoy it, but in this case "work" has changed its meaning. It has become a form of "play." "Play" is characteristically an activity which is engaged in for its own sake—without concern for utility or any further end. "Work" is characteristically activity in which effort is directed to the production of some utility in the simplest and easiest way. Hence the importance of ergonomics and work study—the objective of which is to reduce difficulty and save time. In play the activity is often directed to attaining a pointless objective in a difficult way, as when a golfer, using curious instruments, guides a small ball into a not much larger hole from remote distances and in the face of obstructions deliberately designed to make the operation as difficult as may be. This involves the reversal of the means-end relation. The "end"—getting the ball into the hole—is set up as a *means* to the new end, the real end, the enjoyment of difficult activity for its own sake.[9]

9. C. A. Mace, "Psychology and Aesthetics," *British Journal of Aesthetics,* II, No. 1 (January, 1962), 10–11.

A somewhat similar statement by White of the role of progressive achievement of competence as an important guide to behavior is encompassed in the idea of effectance.

Effectance is to be conceived as a neurogenic motive, in contrast to a viscerogenic one. It can be informally described as what the sensory-neuro-muscular system wants to do when it is not occupied with homeostatic business. Its adaptive significance lies in its promotion of spare-time behavior that leads to an extensive growth of competence, well beyond what could be learned in connection with drive-reduction.[10]

There is, then, no question of the importance of this reversal of means-end, of content and context, of information and value. It occurs at some stage when order achieved among consequences overrides prior contextual orders.

How is this accomplished? What constitutes the composition of order? That is the problem to which an analysis of the structure of the reinforcing process must be addressed. Bruner, in his influential report of the conference on the process of education, describes the act of learning as follows:

Learning a subject seems to involve three almost simultaneous processes. First there is acquisition of new information—often information that runs counter to or is a replacement for what the person has previously known implicitly or explicitly. At the very least it is a refinement of previous knowledge. . . .

A second aspect of learning may be called *transformation*—the process of manipulating knowledge to make it fit new tasks. We learn to "unmask" or analyze information, to order it in a way that permits extrapolation or interpolation or conversion into another form. Transformation comprises the ways we deal with information in order to go beyond it.

A third aspect of learning is *evaluation*: checking whether the way we have manipulated information is adequate to the task.[11]

Interestingly, these three stages mirror roughly three stages that can be distinguished in the intellectual development of the child. Preschool children are mostly occupied with acquiring information —their concern is to "manipulate the world through action" and thus

10. R. W. White, "Competence and the Psychosexual Stages of Development," in *Nebraska Symposium on Motivation, 1960*, p. 103. Edited by M. R. Jones. Lincoln: University of Nebraska Press, 1960.

11. J. S. Bruner, *The Process of Education*, p. 48. Cambridge: Harvard University Press, 1962.

to establish "a relationship between experience and action."[12] Experiences, the consequences of actions, are placed into the context of the actions that brought them about or into the context of drives and perceptions. "What is principally lacking in this stage of development is what the Geneva school (Piaget, Inhelder, *et al.*) has called the concept of reversibility."[13]

The second stage involves this concept of reversibility. The child is now able to grasp the idea that quantity can be conserved even when things are partitioned.

If marbles, for example, are divided into subgroups, the child can grasp intuitively that the original collection of marbles can be restored by being added back together again. The child tips a balance scale too far with a weight and then searches systematically for a lighter weight or for something with which to get the scale rebalanced. He may carry reversibility too far by assuming that a piece of paper, once burned, can be restored.

. . . the child develops an internalized structure with which to operate [on his experience]. In the example of the balance scale, the structure is a serial order of weights. . . . Such internal structures are of the essence.[14]

Finally, the child develops the ability to evaluate, to operate on hypothetical propositions, to value values, often by returning to testing and checking, i.e., by again gathering new information.

The second stage of the act of learning, the stage when the child is using to the maximum this capacity for reversibility, is of interest here. What is the internalized structure that allows this reversibility to occur and with it the ability to transfer, thus providing an organism the grasp of constancy, of invariance? (Inhelder: "The most elementary forms of reasoning—whether logical, arithmetical, geometrical, or physical—rest on the principle of the invariance of quantities: that the whole remains, whatever may be the arrangement of its parts, the change of its form, or its displacement in space or time."[15]) What internalized structure allows transfer among palpably different experiences to take place?

In the last section a hint was given about the nature of this structure: the suggestion was made that it is constructed as a hierarchically nested series of test-operate-retest-exit units, a plan, a

12. *Ibid.*, p. 34.   14. *Ibid.*, pp. 36–37.
13. *Ibid.*, pp. 34–35.   15. *Ibid.*, p. 41.

program; homeostats set in the context of other homeostats and, thus, contextually biased by them and, in turn, biasing. What is the evidence?

The idea of homeostats was proposed by Cannon to account for the exquisite control exercised by the hypothalamus in the core of the brain over the internal environment of the organism. Since Cannon's time the structure of this homeostat—or better, of the several homeostats that make up the regulating mechanism—has been clearly established. Each homeostat is composed much as is the thermostat that regulates the temperature of our homes. There is a sensitive element, a receptor (e.g., the thermostat's thermocouple), there is a connection with an apparatus that can produce the substance to which the sensitive element is sensitive (e.g., the furnace produces the heat which is sensed by the thermocouple) and these are so arranged that the producing device is switched off when the amount of the substance rises above a certain point and switched on when the amount of the substance falls below the point. A great deal of detail is known about the homeostatic devices that control respiration, temperature, eating, drinking, and sexual behavior.

These physiological mechanisms provided the model for engineers who wanted to build devices that could regulate the input to which they were sensitive. As long as these inputs were conceived as substances, the applications of the model were limited. During the past world war, however, several of Cannon's pupils (e.g., Wiener and Rosenblueth) extended the model to bands of the energy spectrum other than heat; cybernetics and information theory were the result.

As already indicated, in the organism as well, the homeostat model applies more generally. The TOTE was made necessary when the central control over muscle receptor function became an established fact. And its applicability to sensory as well as to motor function has been well documented.

So why has this homeostatic model not taken hold completely— what is wrong with it? The model was designed (both with respect to the organism and in engineering) to track and to maintain equilibria. The very problems that concern educators and psychologists are not touched by such a "static" structure, wonderful though it may be. Psychologists have been concerned with learning, with drive, with motivation; educators with how to teach, to guide, to motivate. Change, not complacency, is at stake.

An almost forgotten device comes to their aid. Every thermostat is equipped with a gadget, usually a little wheel, by which the thermostat's set point can be altered. This is the thermostat's *bias*. With it, wonderful, and horrible, things can be accomplished. Make a sudden change on the setting and the stable system that was a temperature-controlled environment begins to fluctuate and oscillate for a period around a new set point. Or, make a continuous small change of the setting and one can, unless other safeguards have been built in, blow up the furnace through continually accruing heat production. Manipulate the bias and the homeostat becomes anything but a purely equilibrial device. Complacency is gone.

Is there any evidence that is consistent with the view that the body's homeostats are biased? I have suggested elsewhere that the results of electrical self-stimulation can be so conceived. Certain predictions followed: self-stimulation should be obtainable not only when drive systems are biased by the excitation but also when the electrodes are placed in motor systems. This has been experimentally demonstrated. The suggestion is that the organization of action resembles the biased homeostat, the structure of drives. It follows that the bias of the neural mechanism in control of action should be resettable, much as is the bias of the drive homeostats, to produce the phenomenon of self-stimulation. This has been accomplished by John Lilly. Prolonged trains of excitation (subliminal to those that would produce movement) were delivered to the precentral motor cortex whenever the lever was depressed by the subject (a monkey). Lever pressing had to be placed so that the on-off nature of the excitation could be maintained. The monkey learned to do this, however, and spent many (may I say "happy"?) hours at this occupation.

There is, thus, good reason to believe that biological homeostats, just as mechanical ones, are settable, that they are equipped with the mechanisms that can bias them. The biasing operation is conceived to take place as follows:

Homeostats can be hierarchically arranged. The blower on the home-furnace of a hot air system is controlled by a thermostat separate from, but subordinate to, the main thermostat. There is some evidence that the food-appetitive and general activity mechanisms of the organism are both contained within the larger regulation of basal temperature. But, I believe this simple statement of a hierarchical relationship does not give a full account of the process which is of concern here. What seems to happen is that there is a true reversal of means and ends, of context and content, of bias and the mechanism biased. Differentiation can take place in the biases placed on the mechanism—the temperature of a home will be controlled by several thermostats, each of which biases the main mechanism but is in turn biased by it. This complex yet orderly interrelation among subsystems and system achieves stabilities beyond those possible for the simpler systems. The suggestion is that the biased homeostat becomes differentiated, mainly through differentiation of its bias, perhaps because of inherent imperfections. These imperfections must be in the control the mechanism has over the variables to which it is sensitive. This poses a paradox—for differentiation occurs most readily when such control appears to be accomplished. But just at these junctures, increased sensitivity is also achieved: viz., the thermostatic system that has allowed temperature to vary between 65° and 75° F. is insensitive to temperature changes of one or two degrees. When the system is sufficiently stable to control temperature at 70° it becomes exquisitely sensitive to a two-degree change. And these new sensitivities cause the system to react where it would not have done so on prior occasions. Thus, though this is a structural, even a homeostatic, view of the behavioral process, its design certainly does not lead to stagnation.

What operations lead to the differentiation of biases? As already noted, one of the conditions for differentiation is the achievement of a stable level of control over input. Here may be a clue. The same limbic systems that play such an important role in electrical self-stimulation and in the learning of sequential tasks may be involved in the following manner: Specifiable electrical changes have been recorded in the limbic systems (the amygdaloid complex) whenever the organism has been exposed to a novel event or one that has meaning in terms of reward and punishment. These electrical changes subside once the organism is familiar with the event, unless another part of the limbic systems (the hippocampal formation) has been ablated, in which case the electrical changes continue to occur when this or any other event takes place. In addition, the amygdaloid complex of the limbic systems has been shown necessary to the establishment of electrocortical conditioned responses. The suggestion has been made that the hippocampal formation inhibits (perhaps by way of the reticular core of the brain stem) the succession of unrelated inputs to the amygdala that might occur and so allows this structure to maintain the neural activity necessary to the conditioning process. In a conditioning or learning situation, electrical changes are recorded from the hippocampal formation during the initial trials. Later, no such changes accompany successful action; they occur only when errors are made.

Very careful but complicated analysis of the electrical activity recorded during learning of a visual discrimination has led Adey to venture that phase relations between wave patterns recorded from the deeper and more superficial portions of the hippocampal cortex change as a function of task performance. Early, while many errors are made, the activity recorded from the deeper layers of the hippocampal cortex precedes that from the more superficial layers; later, when performance contains many error-free runs, the reverse is the case. Input to the deeper layers is from other core structures of the brain; input to the more superficial layers is from the adjacent entorhinal and cingulate cortex.

Despite the preliminary nature which these data must have because of the state of the computing art in neurobiological science, it nonetheless strikes a responsive chord. This is especially so since Flynn, MacLean, and Kim concluded in their pioneering work on the effects on behavior of afterdischarges produced by electrical stimulation of the hippocampus:

Is it possible that the neural perturbations remaining in these structures after sensory stimulation allow a more ready association of two temporally separated events than is possible in the neocortex, where one does not see a comparable phenomenon?[16]

In addition, Freeman, using an entirely different technique, has reported a somewhat similar "comparator" process to account for electrical phenomena recorded from the pyriform cortex (cats) just prior to the performance of a conditioned response.

16. J. P. Flynn, P. D. MacLean, and C. Kim, "Effects of Hippocampal Afterdischarges on Conditioned Responses," in *Electrical Stimulation of the Brain*, p. 386. Edited by D. E. Sheer. Austin: University of Texas Press, 1961.

The proposal is that the limbic systems serve in reversing, as a function of experience, the context-content relationship between drive stimuli and other reinforcing events. There is some evidence that other than drive stimuli are involved in this limbic system function. The stimuli in question may perhaps be only those close relatives of drive stimuli, such as olfaction and taste; but behavioral evidence (deficits on alternation tasks that follow hippocampal and cingulate resections) suggest that the stimuli affected are of a still wider range.

If, indeed, this evidence holds, a first step will have been accomplished in unraveling the mechanism by which bias differentiates. The hippocampus, by inhibiting the succession of unrelated inputs, allows continuing activity of the amygdala to stabilize the system. The stable system is then sensitive to alterations in context-content relationships. In the experiments mentioned, context is initially provided by drive stimuli, content by the consequences of action; after these consequences compose a structure of their own they vie for the context position and finally win out—perhaps on a simple event-rate basis. Or it may be that reversal takes place when more order is achieved among the consequences of action than exists among drive stimuli. In any case, the reversal has been observed to occur.

This is as far as the analysis based on neuropsychological experiment can now be pushed. It tells us that a mechanism exists by which reversals of content and context can occur in at least one and perhaps two locations in the brain (Adey and Freeman). Because of the similarities to this process encountered in the development of perceptual and motor skills, precise questions can be put to the laboratory with the aim to identify, in other locations, this mechanism for reversal. For it is clear that reversal—of content-context, of means with end, of information and value—is the fundamental transformation necessary for serial ordering of achievement.

As noted in the last section, the efficacy of *in*-struction by teaching machines and programed texts may, in large part, be attributed to the limits placed on the sequences of operations that must be endured before the information gained at one step comes to place a value on that gained in the next. The danger is that programs poorly constructed will determine meaning "in terms of consequences hastily snatched at and torn loose from their connections"—and so "the formation of wider and more enduring ideas" will be prevented. At the moment, the only safeguard against this that might be suggested is that the reinforcing structure intrinsic to the material in some way match the intrinsic reinforcing structure of the organism. Continuous differentiation of the context, the valuative process, must be the aim. This is accomplished through the test-operate-retest-exit process, guided by inputs (information) administered in such a way that exit is achieved only after many sub-TOTEs have been brought into operation. To prevent runaway operation, however, temporary stabilities must be achievable—only when a certain information pool has been brought under control can new sensitivities be engaged. Successful programs are, of course, constructed in just this manner by intuitive teachers. Research is sorely needed, however, to make explicit the "natural" locations of equilibria in subject matters as well as in the subjects to be exposed to them.

Given these precautions, and thus keeping the whole structure that has been developed at any moment clearly in focus, there is little merit in the accusation that because of their routine character, teaching aids (programs) fail to meet the most urgent requirement of education: to produce *creative* people. We harbor many misconceptions about creativity. According to the most prevalent misconception, discoveries and inventions arise out of the blue. But the contrary is the case. In reality, discoverers make their discoveries through what they already know: they match the unfamiliar against a thoroughly incorporated body of fact. Columbus, for example, knew a great deal about navigation. He knew the assumed boundaries of the flat world and what could be expected if, as some people suspected, the world were really round. But other explorers had to repeat Columbus' feat before the discovery of America was admitted (should we say as context?) to the thinking of all sailors.

The inventor achieves novelty within the bounds of certainty. He comes upon, finds, only when properly prepared for the finding. The term "inventor" derives from the same root as "inventory." Edison expended his "ninety-nine percent perspiration" by taking stock of the boundaries of known electrical science. Only then, at those boundaries, did the new procedures strike him as plausible. The inventor innovates, as when, like Edison, he substitutes tungsten for iron to make an electric light bulb from an electric heating element.

The construction of a great symphony follows familiar lines: the rules of theme and subthemes, beat and counterpoint, form and movement, must all be thoroughly mastered before creative composition can begin. Beethoven created music by taking discipline even farther than its already complex structured limits. He sensed nuances where none had been sensed before. He prepared musical programs more complicated than seemed possible.

And what of the poet, supposedly the freest of free souls? Perhaps more than any creator, he is constrained by the known rules within which novelty can be expressed. Shall he choose iambic pentameter, rhyme or alliteration, couplet or sonnet? He must carefully tend the meaning of a word so that where several meanings are possible each is enhanced by the context in which the word appears. In such a wealth of rules and orderliness lies the creativity of the poet as well as his freedom. For freedom is not anarchy. Real freedom is intelligent, knowledgeable choice and rises out of order when order achieves sufficient complexity.

Thus, man's brain shapes freedom. Through ever more effective innovations in the rules for social interaction, man's brain frees him from fear. Through ever improving methods of production and distribution, man's brain frees him from want. Through ever growing powers to perceive and plan, man's brain frees him for love and fun.

Man's brain does all this and always has. We share the promise that it always will: though slowly and by steps with pain. For that is how we learn.

Thus to be conscious of meanings or to have an idea, marks a fruition, an enjoyed or suffered arrest of the flux of events. But there are all kinds of ways of perceiving meanings, all kinds of ideas. Meaning may be determined in terms of consequences hastily snatched at and torn loose from their connections; then is prevented the formation of wider and more enduring ideas. Or, we may be aware of meanings, may achieve ideas, that unite wide and enduring scope with richness of distinctions. The latter sort of consciousness is more than a passing and superficial consummation or end: it takes up into itself meanings covering stretches of existence *wrought into consistency*. It marks the conclusion of long continued endeavor; of patient and indefatigable search and test. *The idea is, in short, art and a work of art. As a work of art, it directly lib-*

erates subsequent action and makes it more fruitful in a creation of more meanings and more perception [italics and underscoring mine].[17]

Bibliography

This manuscript has pulled together work that, in the author's opinion, has direct bearing on education. He has detailed the explicit references to this work in other contexts. Here, therefore, these other manuscripts are suggested as key primary references, together with some others that would serve in a similar fashion. The assumption is that a program of reading initiated in this fashion would acquaint the reader pretty well with all primary sources of current ferment and endeavor on this important and exciting frontier of knowledge.

ON READINESS

BRUNER, JEROME S. "On Perceptual Readiness," *Psychological Review,* LXIV (1959), 123–52.

MAGOUN, H. W. Presentation to be published in *Nebraska Symposium on Motivation, 1963.* Edited by M. R. Jones. Lincoln: University of Nebraska Press (in press).

Sensory Communication. (Contributions to the Symposium on Principles of Sensory Communication, Massachusetts Institute of Technology, 1959. Edited by W. A. Rosenblith.) New York: M.I.T. Press and John Wiley & Sons, 1961. See especially: H. B. BARLOW, "Possible Principles Underlying the Transformations of Sensory Messages," chap. xiii, pp. 217–34; J. Y. LETTVIN, H. R. MATURANA, W. H. PITTS, and W. S. McCULLOCH, "Two Remarks on the Visual System of the Frog," chap. xi, pp. 757–76; and F. RATLIFF, "Inhibitory Interaction and the Detection and Enhancement of Contours," chap. xi, pp. 183–204.

SOKOLOV, E. N. Presentation in *The Central Nervous System and Behavior.* (Transactions of the Third Conference. Edited by M. A. B. Brazier.) New York: Josiah Macy, Jr., Foundation Publications, 1960.

ON CAPACITY TO LEARN AND REMEMBER

LAWRENCE, D. H., and FESTINGER, L. *Deterrents and Reinforcement: The Psychology of Insufficient Reward.* Stanford, California: Stanford University Press, 1962.

PRIBRAM, KARL H. "A Review of Theory in Physiological Pyschology," *Annual Review of Psychology,* pp. 1–40. Palo Alto, California: Annual Reviews, Inc., 1960.

———. "The New Neurology: Memory, Novelty, Thought, and Choice," in *EEG and Behavior.* Edited by G. H. Glaser. New York: Basic Books, 1963.

17. Dewey, *Experience and Nature, op. cit.,* p. 301.

PRIBRAM, KARL H. "Reinforcement Revisited." Presentation to be published in *Nebraska Symposium on Motivation, 1963.* Edited by M. R. Jones. Lincoln: University of Nebraska Press (in press).

ON TRANSFER AND STRUCTURE

BRUNER, JEROME S. *The Process of Education.* Cambridge: Harvard University Press, 1962.

———. *On Knowing—Essays for the Left Hand.* Cambridge: Harvard University Press (Belknap Press), 1962.

MILLER, G. A.; GALANTER, E.; and PRIBRAM, KARL H. *Plans and the Structure of Behavior.* New York: Henry Holt & Co., 1960.

PRIBRAM, KARL H. "Proposal for a Structural Pragmatism: Some Neuropsychological Considerations of Problems in Philosophy," in *Psychology and the Philosophy of Science.* Edited by B. B. Wolman and E. Nagel. New York: Basic Books (in press).

GENERAL

Handbook of Physiology. Vol. III, *Neurophysiology.* Edited by John Field *et al.* Prepared by the American Physiological Society. Baltimore, Maryland: Williams & Wilkins Co., 1960.

MILLER, G. A. *Psychology: The Science of Mental Life.* New York: Harper & Row, Publishers, 1962.

CHAPTER V

The Relevance of Mathematical Models for Education

FRANK RESTLE

An educator may ask why certain parts of a course are difficult and how the difficulty can be overcome. He may ask how much it would help to increase teacher-time for the teaching of an item which has been difficult to learn. He wonders how fast an accelerated course could be pushed without losing the children. He may ask whether expensive teaching devices will be worth their cost to his students.

The final answer to any such question must be found by experimentation done in the classroom under classroom conditions. However, the classroom is an expensive, inconvenient, and inflexible laboratory. The one final way to decide whether a bridge will stand is to build the bridge and see; but it is not sensible to build twenty bridges of various weights and types of construction to see which ones stand. Instead, laboratory studies and theoretical analyses are used to calculate what constitutes the best bridge, and then a large safety factor is introduced in actual construction. The application of experimental psychology to education follows a similar pattern. Psychological experiments are not like classrooms, but they represent more efficient means of getting information. Combined with suitable mathematical theory, laboratory data can be used to answer questions about educational practice and to plan reasonable educational programs. It is only sensible to distrust the predictions and to introduce large safety factors, at least until it is known from practice that the psychologist's predictions actually work in the classroom.

In practice, the engineer does not calculate "the bridge." First, he invents a general idea or scheme for the whole project. When it comes to carrying out his general idea, many small decisions must be made: how deep the footings, how thick the pilings, what size the beams, what strength the cables, what width of roadway should be chosen? In order to compute the amount of needed piling, the engineer begins by considering the rest of the bridge as a very simple system—he is only interested in the weight and the stresses the bridge throws on *this* piling. He then obtains measurements of the strengths of pilings of various sizes, calculates the size and weight of the bridge, and (hoping he has not overlooked an important variable) calculates the thickness of piling needed. Then he applies his large safety factor before ordering the pilings. Each decision is about a detail; each decision requires a gross oversimplification of the remainder of the problem; each decision requires specific information and measurements; each is calculated from knowledge of the detail; each is subject to error if an important variable is not taken into account; and each is, anyway, subject to the skepticism reflected in the safety factor.

These remarks are made because the reader will soon see that the mathematical models of learning to be discussed are concerned with details, not the broad structure of the curriculum or educational philosophy; the whole educational process (except the detail) is summarized in a very simplified way; the conclusion depends upon measurements of ability of students, difficulty of material, and the like; and the conclusions, when formulated, are put forward in a spirit of humility, with the assumption that they will not be correct.

In fact, of course, there is no such thing as educational engineering as I have described it. Yet, some of the necessary ingredients are available, and it is possible to solve some educational problems in an approximate way. The remainder of this chapter consists of the statement of an extremely simple theory and an exposition of how it can be used to solve two problems of educational practice.

In this paper I shall state a theory of learning and work out its consequences. The developments of the theory are written as simply as possible so that a reader with only a little mathematics can follow the discussion by working through the equations. Readers with no mathematics should be able to follow the general direction of the argument, though of course they must lose the detail.

In the second part of the paper the theory is applied to solve two complicated problems. First, suppose there is a very large population of students (as in a state university or a large consolidated school district) and one must divide them into classes for instruction in some subject. How large should the classes be? If classes are too large, students waste a great deal of time; but if classes are too small, teachers give the same material over and over, and the teachers' time is wasted. What is the optimal compromise? The theory discussed above permits us to calculate an answer to this problem. Second, consider a long cumulative course like algebra, in which mastery of one part depends upon mastery of earlier parts of the course. If the teacher goes too fast, he soon loses most of his students and teaches nothing. If he goes too slowly, he never even tries to teach enough. What is the best compromise pace for a cumulative course, and how effective is it? This question can also be answered by the theory.

Theory

The theory is that learning of a single, unitary item is an all-or-nothing event. Before learning occurs, no partial progress is made; after learning has occurred, performance on the problem stabilizes. This theory has been found to fit some simple paired-associate learning and other verbal-learning tasks in the laboratory,[1] and also to fit discrimination-learning and concept-formation experiments.[2]

1. Gordon H. Bower, "Application of a Model to Paired-Associate Learning," *Psychometrika*, XXVI (1961), 255–80.
Gordon H. Bower, "An Association Model for Response and Training Variables in Paired-Associate Learning," *Psychological Review*, LXIX (1962), 34–53.
W. K. Estes, B. L. Hopkins, and E. J. Crothers, "All-or-None and Conservation Effects in the Learning and Retention of Paired-Associates," *Journal of Experimental Psychology*, LX (1960), 329–39.
Frank Restle, "Sources of Difficulty in Learning Paired-Associates," *Studies in Mathematical Psychology*, I (1963) (in press).
Irvin Rock, "The Role of Repetition in Associative Learning," *American Journal of Psychology*, LXX (1957), 186–93.

2. Gordon H. Bower and T. R. Trabasso, "Concept Identification," *Studies in Mathematical Psychology*, I (1963) (in press).
Frank Restle, "Statistical Methods for a Theory of Cue-learning," *Psychometrika*, XXVI (1961), 291–306.
Frank Restle, "The Selection of Strategies in Cue-learning," *Psychological Review*, LXIX (1962), 329–43.
Patrick Suppes and Rose Ginsberg, "A Fundamental Property of All-or-None Models, Binomial Distribution of Responses Prior to Conditioning with Application to Concept Formation in Children." Technical Report No. 39, "Psychology Series, Institute for Mathematical Studies in the Social Sciences," Stanford University, 1961.
T. R. Trabasso, "The Effect of Stimulus Emphasis on the Learning and Transfer of Concepts." Unpublished Doctor's dissertation, Michigan State University, 1961.

The implications of "all-or-nothing" learning are mathematical and strong. For the purposes at hand I shall assume that, before learning, the subject cannot pass a test on the item; and after learning, he can. (A true-false or multiple-choice item might permit passing the item by "guessing," without learning; a difficult essay question might be failed or only partly credited after learning. Hence, more detailed theory is needed to apply the theory directly to test data, but the present simplification shows the direction, if not the full detail, of the analysis.)

DISCRETE TIME

Now suppose that the student is instructed on the item at regular intervals, trials, 1, 2, . . . , n, . . . until mastery. Even if the students

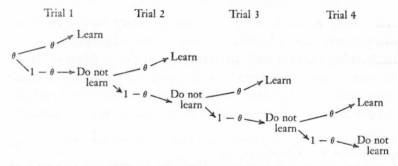

FIG. 1

in an experiment (or classroom) are of about the same ability, we know that they will not all learn at exactly the same time, particularly if the thing to be learned is simple. Suppose that the probability of learning on the first trial is θ. The remaining proportion, $1 - \theta$, do not learn on trial 1. The theory of all-or-nothing learning says that there was no partial learning on trial 1, hence the students who did not learn on trial 1 have not progressed at all. From this, we conclude that the probability of learning on trial 2, given that the item is not learned on trial 1, must be θ.

Consider a large (hypothetical) group of learners all of the same ability and all trained the same way. On each trial, some of the non-learners will learn, and (with all-or-nothing learning) the probability of learning is always the same number, θ. The tree diagram in Figure 1 shows the progress of the group.

Now if we trace the probability of learning on trial 3 (and not before) we find that to do this, the subject must follow the lower branch at trial 1 with probability $1 - \theta$, then the lower branch at trial 2 with probability $1 - \theta$, then the upper branch at trial 3 with probability θ. The probability of this combination is $(1 - \theta)$ $(1 - \theta)\theta = (1 - \theta)^2\theta$. To learn at trial 4 and not before, the subject must follow a branch with probability $(1 - \theta)^3\theta$. Now we see that to learn on trial n (and not before), for any trial n, the subject would follow a branch with probability $(1 - \theta)^{n-1}\theta$. This we write as

$$P \text{ (learning on trial } n) = (1 - \theta)^{n-1}\theta . \qquad [1]$$

This probability will be called $p(n)$. Equation [1] is called a "geometric distribution" since the probabilities of learning on the various trials n form a geometric sequence.

If we now ask the probability of learning *by* trial n, designated by $P(n)$ with capital P, this is

$$
\begin{aligned}
P(n) &= p(1) + p(2) + \ldots + p(n) \\
&= \theta + (1 - \theta)\theta + (1 - \theta)^2\theta + \ldots + (1 - \theta)^{n-1}\theta \qquad [2] \\
&= \theta \cdot S_n ,
\end{aligned}
$$

where S_n is the partial sum,

$$S_n = 1 + (1 - \theta) + (1 - \theta)^2 + \ldots + (1 - \theta)^{n-1} .$$

S_n can be evaluated in a simple way by the following algebraic manipulations:

$$S_n = 1 + (1 - \theta) + (1 - \theta)^2 + \ldots + (1 - \theta)^{n-1}. \qquad [3]$$
$$(1 - \theta)S_n = (1 - \theta) + (1 - \theta)^2 + (1 - \theta)^3 + \ldots$$
$$+ (1 - \theta)^{n-1} + (1 - \theta)^n. \qquad [4]$$

Subtracting [4] from [3] term by term, most of the terms on the right cancel and

$$[1 - (1 - \theta)]S_n = 1 - (1 - \theta)^n .$$
$$= \theta S_n = 1 - (1 - \theta)^n .$$

Now $P(n)$, the probability of learning by trial n, is θS_n from Eq. [2]. Hence we conclude,

$$P(n) = 1 - (1 - \theta)^n . \qquad [5]$$

The expectation or "true mean" of a distribution is the sum of the various possible scores each weighted by its probability of occurrence. Let $E(n)$ be the expected trial of learning; then

$$E(n) = 1p(1) + 2p(2) + 3p(3) + \ldots \qquad [6]$$

an infinite series. Substituting the formula in Eq. [1] for each $p(n)$ we have

$$E(n) = \theta + 2(1 - \theta)\theta + 3(1 - \theta)^2\theta + \ldots$$
$$+ n(1 - \theta)^{n-1}\theta + \ldots . \qquad [7]$$
$$(1 - \theta)E(n) = (1 - \theta)\theta + 2(1 - \theta)^2\theta + \ldots$$
$$+ (n - 1)(1 - \theta)^{n-1}\theta + \ldots . \qquad [8]$$

Subtracting [8] from [7] gives

$$\theta E(n) = \theta + (1 - \theta)\theta + (1 - \theta)^2\theta + \ldots ,$$

or, canceling the common factor, θ,

$$E(n) = 1 + (1 - \theta) + (1 - \theta)^2 + \ldots . \qquad [9]$$
$$(1 - \theta)E(n) = (1 - \theta) + (1 - \theta)^2 + \ldots . \qquad [10]$$

Subtracting [10] from [9], and noting that since each is an infinite series, there is no last term to be left over,

$$[1 - (1 - \theta)]E(n) = \theta E(n) = 1$$

and

$$E(n) = 1/\theta . \qquad [11]$$

From the equation that the variance of a distribution is

$$\mathrm{Var}(n) = E(n^2) - [E(n)]^2$$

the same method of calculation can be used to obtain the true variance. The answer is somewhat tedious to calculate in the simple method used here, but it is

$$\mathrm{Var}(n) = \frac{1}{\theta^2}(1 - \theta) . \qquad [12]$$

Notice that $\sigma = \sqrt{\mathrm{Var}(n)}$ will be

$$\sigma = \frac{1}{\theta}\sqrt{1 - \theta} ,$$

which will be slightly less than the mean. Since the standard deviation is almost as large as the mean, the data are highly variable. Notice that the model says that all subjects are alike, in that they have
the same probability of learning, θ.

The model presented above supposes that learning occurs only at
certain trials, $1, 2, 3, \ldots, n, \ldots$, but not between. In the classroom
situation it may be that learning can occur at any time, t, that is, in
continuous time. The assumption of all-or-nothing learning yields a
model for continuous time which is not difficult, though complete
understanding of it requires a slight knowledge of the calculus. To
approach the theory, begin with the cumulative distribution function $F(t)$, the probability that learning occurs *by* time t. Let the
beginning of the learning period be $t = 0$.

The probability of learning within any interval $(t, t + h)$ may be
written as $F(t + h) - F(t)$, the probability of learning by $t + h$
minus the probability of learning by time t. Suppose there is some
probability k_h that the subject will learn in the interval (o, h), i.e.,
within the first h time intervals. Now consider those subjects who
have not learned by time t. By the all-or-nothing assumption, they
have made no partial progress, so the probability that they will
learn within the interval $(t, t + h)$ should also be the same constant
k_h. That is, the conditional probability of learning within the interval
$(t, t + h)$, given no learning by time t, is equal to k_h and does not
depend on t.

P(learning in the interval $[t, t + h]$ given no learning by t) $= k_h$.
This conditional probability is

$$\frac{F(t + h) - F(t)}{1 - F(t)} = k_h. \qquad [13]$$

A simple algebraic rearrangement of [13], and dividing both sides by
h, gives

$$\frac{F(t + h) - F(t)}{h} = \frac{k_h}{h}[1 - F(t)]. \qquad [14]$$

Now it should be evident that as the time interval h is taken smaller
and smaller, the probability of learning in an interval of length h,
namely k_h, also gets smaller and smaller. To progress to continuous

time, take the limits of both sides of Eq. [14] as h gets smaller. Let the limit of k_h/h, as h approaches zero, be called λ. Then,

$$\lim_{h \to 0} \frac{F(t+h) - F(t)}{h} = \lambda [1 - F(t)] . \qquad [15]$$

Students of the calculus will recognize the left-hand side of [15] as the derivative of $F(t)$ with respect to t, which we shall write $f(t)$. Then [15] is a differential equation,

$$f(t) = \lambda[1 - F(t)] , \qquad [16]$$

which has the solution

$$F(t) = 1 - e^{-\lambda t} \qquad [17]$$

and

$$f(t) = \lambda e^{-\lambda t} . \qquad [18]$$

From this it is possible to compute the expectation of the time of learning,

$$E(t) = \int_0^\infty t\lambda \, e^{-\lambda t} dt = 1/\lambda , \qquad [19]$$

and the variance, which turns out to be

$$\mathrm{Var}(t) = 1/\lambda^2 . \qquad [20]$$

In this model, the standard deviation σ is exactly equal to the true mean.

Generally speaking, the consequences of the two models, that for discrete trials and that for continuous time, are about the same. They cannot be used interchangeably, since some data are collected by trials and require the trial-model, others are collected as measurements of time on a clock and naturally lead to continuous-time analysis. For general purposes, such as application to the classroom, there is little reason to prefer one or the other. For the derivations which follow, the continuous-time model is slightly more convenient.

This is not the place to attempt a detailed evaluation of this theory. For present purposes it is enough to show that it is not a mere conceptual curiosity—that data from learning experiments may follow the all-or-none rule. The essential procedure in the experiment is, of course, to purify the task until it contains only a single source of difficulty of any significance. For our purposes, the all-or-nothing theory says that the distribution of trial-of-learning will be the geometric distribution. In experiments, we often cannot determine the trial-of-learning exactly because the subject may guess on trials before learning. In such experiments, we use either total errors or trial-of-last-error as variables which have geometric or related distributions, corresponding roughly to trial-of-learning. Figure 2 shows

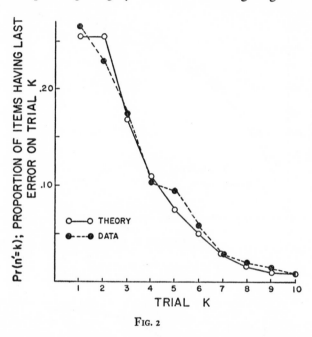

FIG. 2

such a distribution for paired associates learning by college students, in a study by Bower.[3] Figure 3 shows such a distribution (in cumulative form) for concept-identification learning by college students.[4] Figure 4 shows a distribution of total errors in solving a verbal puzzle.[5] Of course, the reader cannot evaluate the theory from these examples; they merely demonstrate that theoretical distributions from an all-or-none theory sometimes coincide closely with empirical dis-

3. Bower in *Psychometrika*, XXVI (1961), 255–80.

4. Bower and Trabasso in *Studies in Mathematical Psychology*, I (1963) (in press).

5. Frank Restle and James H. Davis, "Success and Speed of Problem-solving by Individuals and Groups." *Psychological Review*, XLIX (1962), 520–36.

tributions. There is no adequate proof that simple problems always give rise to all-or-none distributions, or that more complex problems can always be dissected into all-or-none components. However, there is enough evidence to justify an exploratory extension of the all-or-none idea to educational problems.

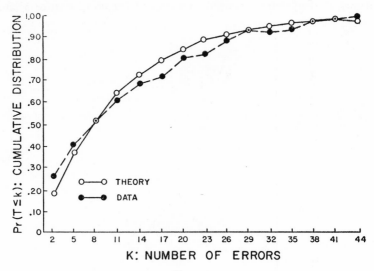

FIG. 3

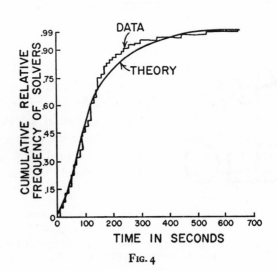

FIG. 4

Applications

The all-or-none theory, in continuous time, is now used to calculate two optima: the optimal class size as a function of teacher cost plus student cost and the optimal speed of teaching a cumulative course. The reader will recognize that the conditions imposed are somewhat artificial and arranged to permit relatively simple and intelligible calculations.

OPTIMAL CLASS SIZE

Consider a large number N of students of equal ability who are to be taught a unitary item, and suppose that training is to continue until all N have learned. Suppose that for each student, the probability of learning by time t is $F(t) = 1 - e^{-\lambda t}$. The group may all be trained at once, held in class until the last learns, or may be divided into smaller classes of, say, size r. If the group is divided, each subclass can be held until the last student in *it* learns.

The most efficient procedure can be calculated with some further information. First, note that if the whole class of N is taught at once, a great many students will waste a lot of time waiting until the last student learns. If the classes are smaller, less student time is wasted. However, with smaller classes more instructor-time is needed, since the instructor now must wait, separately, for the completion of learning in each class. [Dividing the class will save student time but increase the expenditure of instructor time.] Suppose that the cost of student time is taken to be one unit per hour, and instructor time costs I units per hour. The number N of students is very large, and we consider dividing the N students into classes of size r, of which there will be N/r. Suppose that N is so large that there are relatively few "left-over students" after a division, so that any class-size can be used.

Now let M_r be the mean time until all members of a class of size r finish solving the problem. The average cost of student time (rated at one unit per unit time) in each class of size r will be rM_r, and, since there are N/r classes, the mean cost of student time is

$$C_s = N \cdot M_r . \qquad [21]$$

An instructor must be engaged for an average time of M_r for each of the N/r classes. At a rate of I per unit time, the instructor cost is

$$C_I = I \frac{N}{r} M_r,$$ [22]

whence the total cost, from Eqs. [21] and [22], is

$$C = NM_r + \frac{I N M_r}{r}$$ [23]

$$= [1 + (I/r)] NM_r.$$

The problem now reduces to finding the minimum of Eq. [23] with respect to the class-size, r. To do this, we first must calculate M_r, the mean time until the last of a class of r students solves the problem. One approach is to note that the probability that any one student learns by time t is $F(t) = 1 - e^{-\lambda t}$. The probability that all of r students have learned by time t is $[1 - e^{-\lambda t}]^r$, which is the cumulative distribution function for the group. The derivative of this is the density function, and from that density function we can calculate the mean. A neater derivation was shown to the author by Professor Herman Rubin.

The time until the rth student learns can be considered to be sum of the time until the first learns, plus the time from the first to the second learning, and so on. At the beginning there are r students, any of whom may learn at any time. The probability that at least one learns, per unit time, is $r\lambda$, and the time until the first student learns has the density function $r\lambda e^{-r\lambda t}$. Therefore, the mean time to the first solution is $1/r\lambda$. When the first subject learns, there are $r - 1$ subjects left, none of whom has learned. Therefore, at that time, the situation is just like it was at the beginning of the class work, except that there is one less subject to learn. Hence, the mean time from first to second learner is $1/(r - 1)\lambda$. Continuing the argument shows that

$$M_r = \frac{1}{\lambda}\left[\frac{1}{r} + \frac{1}{r-1} + \ldots + \frac{1}{2} + 1\right]$$ [24]

$$= \frac{1}{\lambda}\sum_{i=1}^{r}\left(\frac{1}{i}\right).$$

Bush[6] gives

$$\sum_{i=1}^{r}\frac{1}{i} \cong 0.577215665 + \ln\ r + \frac{1}{2\,r} - \frac{1}{12\,r^2}, \qquad [25]$$

where ln r is the natural logarithm of r, or $\log_e r$, so the cost of teaching the N students in classes of size r is

$$C \cong \left[1 + \frac{I}{r}\right]\frac{N}{\lambda}\left[0.577215665 + \ln(\,r\,) + \frac{1}{2\,r} - \frac{1}{12\,r^2}\right]. \qquad [26]$$

To get a maximum, we seek a class size r such that, if the class size is increased to $r+1$; the total cost neither increases (showing that cost is increasing with r) nor decreases (showing that cost decreases with increasing r). This equilibrium r will either be a maximum or minimum. Using the maximizing equation,

$$C_{r+1} = C_r$$

$$N\left[1 + \frac{I}{r+1}\right]M_{r+1} = N\left[1 + \frac{I}{r}\right]M_r. \qquad [27]$$

Note that from Eq. [24],

$$M_{r+1} = M_r + \frac{1}{(\,r+1\,)\lambda}.$$

Then Eq. [27] turns into

$$M_r + \frac{1}{(\,r+1\,)\lambda} + \frac{IM_r}{r+1} + \frac{I}{(\,r+1\,)^2\lambda} = M_r + \frac{IM_r}{r}$$

$$I\left[\frac{M_r}{r} - \frac{M_r}{r+1} - \frac{1}{(\,r+1\,)^2\lambda}\right] = \frac{1}{(\,r+1\,)\lambda}.$$

Let

$$\Sigma_r = 1 + \tfrac{1}{2} + \ldots + \frac{1}{r} = M_r\lambda$$

from Eq. [24]. Then multiplying through by λ,

$$I\left[\frac{\Sigma_r}{r(\,r+1\,)} - \frac{1}{(\,r+1\,)^2}\right] = \frac{1}{r+1},$$

whence

$$I = \frac{r(\,r+1\,)}{r(\Sigma_r - 1) + \Sigma_r} = \frac{r}{\tfrac{1}{2} + \tfrac{1}{3} + \ldots + \frac{1}{r+1}}. \qquad [28]$$

6. R. R. Bush, "A Short Table of Sums: Memorandum for the 1957 Summer Institute on Applications of Mathematics in the Social Sciences." New York: Social Science Research Council, August, 1956.

In effect, Eq. [28] tells how valuable a teacher's time must be, relative to student time, for a class of size r to be optimal. Figure 5 shows a plot of I (teacher cost) and r (optimal class size). Notice that for $I = 2$, teacher twice as expensive as student, the solution is a small tutorial class ($r = 1$). The ordinary class size of about 30 is optimal if $I = 10$.

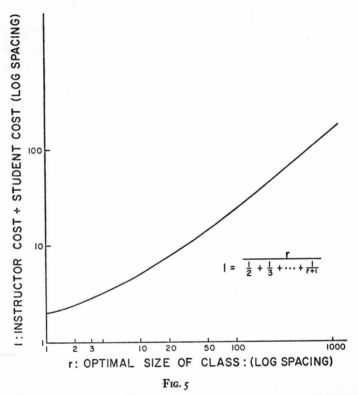

FIG. 5

It is unlikely that administrative decisions can or should be based on this analysis. Actual class size is fixed by the number of students and teachers available, by the size of rooms available, and by disciplinary difficulties. Furthermore, the teacher does not continue teaching until the whole class has learned a particular unitary item, so the basic assumption is unreasonable. However, the analysis does point to a few factors relevant to decisions about class size. First, the theory is that the limitation on class size comes from variability in time of learning. If all students learned at the same time, one would want to teach them all for that fixed time. Since (theoretically, for no reason at all except the intrinsic variability of individual learning times) students are actually very variable in learning time, it is wise to divide the class into smaller groups so that one does not have too many students waiting too long. The other factor is the relative cost of teachers versus students. A great teacher might usefully address the whole population by television, but when one is teaching graduate students or public leaders, classes are very small because the student's time is almost as valuable as that of the teacher. I think these considerations have generally been taken into account in education, and the analysis above merely serves to clarify some of the decisions which have been made by rule of thumb or by tradition in the past.

It should also be mentioned that programed learning, or the use of teaching machines, is an extreme case of the model given above—class size is one, and there is no wasted student time. The argument above says that teaching machines are efficient if, and only if, their cost can be reduced so that their cost, per hour, is only a fraction of teacher costs and is, in fact, almost as low as our basic unit, student time.

THE OPTIMAL RATE FOR A STRICTLY CUMULATIVE COURSE

In a cumulative course like mathematics, the learner must master one stage of instruction before he can learn the next. This can be contrasted with a type of survey course, in which each item of information can be acquired separately, and there is no particular prerequisite. For the purpose of analysis, imagine a strictly cumulative course; if the student misses any point, he has zero probability of learning any successive points.

Consider the dilemma of a teacher of such a course, who has a lengthy textbook and a certain amount of time (perhaps a few hours, perhaps a whole semester) to teach. If he goes very slowly, he may cover only one or two points in the time allowed. Perhaps all of his class will have mastered the material, but what they know will be very little. On the other hand, if the teacher speeds up, he will lose more and more students. If he starts off at a breakneck pace, he may have no one with him after a short time, and teach almost nothing at all. Hence, it appears that one can go either too slow or too fast and that there may be an optimal pace.

As in the first example on class size, the all-or-nothing theory gives a handhold for solving this problem. The difficulty in finding a good rate of presentation again arises from the variability of the time-to-learn, for, if everyone learned the first point at about the same time, the only sensible pace would be to teach until the critical time, then progress to the next point. The all-or-nothing theory says that individual solution-time is highly variable, hence presents the problem with its full complexity.

The only example presented in the following paragraphs has a sequence of items all of the same difficulty and assumes that the teacher's decision is merely to divide his total available teaching time (T) into equal fractions or segments. He may divide instruction into any number n of segments, each of which will be of length $t = T/n$.

Suppose, from the all-or-nothing theory, that in a segment of length t the probability that a subject will learn the item is $1 - e^{-\lambda t}$. However, assuming a strictly cumulative course, let this probability of learning in interval t be zero if any earlier segment was failed. To have a fairly realistic and well-defined problem, maximize the expected total items mastered by a student.

The problem is attacked in two phases. Suppose the teacher selects some n and t such that $nt = T$. There is a probability P_t that a student will master the first segment. Given that the first segment is mastered, the student has probability P_t (again) of mastering the second. The probability that he masters exactly m segments is

$$P(m) = \begin{vmatrix} (P_t)^m(1-P_t) & (\text{for } m < n) \\ (P_t)^n & (\text{for } m = n) \end{vmatrix} \qquad [29]$$

Equation [29] arises because, to master exactly m segments, the student must master the first m, an event with probability $(P_t)^m$ and then fail the next, with probability $1 - P_t$. The only exception is if he masters all n, in which case no failure is implied.

Now, the expected (or mean) number of segments mastered is

$$E(m) = \sum_{i=1}^{n} iP(i) = P_t(1-P_t) + 2P_t^2(1-P_t) + \cdots \qquad [30]$$
$$+ (n-1)P_t^{n-1}(1-P_t)nP_t^n,$$

as in Eq. [6]. Following the method given in Eqs. [7–11], the solution is followed by an extended sequence of steps. To keep the notation simpler, let P_t be called a. Then,

$$E(m) = a(1 - a) + 2a^2(1 - a) + \ldots + (n - 1)a^{n-1}(1 - a) + na^n .$$

Subtracting na^n from both sides,

$$[E(m) - na^n] = a(1 - a) + 2a^2(1 + a) + \ldots$$
$$+ (n - 1)a^{n-1}(1 - a) . \qquad [31]$$

$$a[E(m) - na^n] = a^2(1 - a) + \ldots + (n - 2)a^{n-1}(1 - a)$$
$$+ (n - 1)a^n(1 - a) . \qquad [32]$$

Subtracting [31] from [32] term by term,

$$(1 - a)[E(m) - na^n] = a(1 - a) + a^2(1 - a) + \ldots$$
$$+ a^{n-1}(1 - a) - (n - 1)a^n(1 - a) . \qquad [33]$$

Canceling $(1 = a)$, which is a common factor of both sides,

$$[E(m) - na^n] = a + a^2 + \ldots + a^{n-1} - (n - 1)a^n . \qquad [34]$$

$$a[E(m) - na^n] = a^2 + \ldots + a^{n-1} + a^n - (n - 1)a^{n+1} . \qquad [35]$$

Subtracting [35] from [34],

$$(1 - a)[E(m) - na^n] = a - na^n + (n - 1)a^{n+1} . \qquad [36]$$

Dividing both sides by $(1 - a)$,

$$E(m) - na^n = \frac{a - na^n + (n - 1)a^{n+1}}{1 - a} . \qquad [37]$$

Adding na^n to both sides,

$$E(m) = \frac{a - na^n + (n - 1)a^{n+1}}{1 - a} + na^n . \qquad [38]$$

Finding a common denominator for the right side of [38],

$$E(m) = \frac{a - na^n + (n - 1)a^{n+1} + na^n - na^{n+1}}{1 - a} . \qquad [39]$$

Simplifying the numerator of the right side of Eq. [39] yields

$$E(m) = \frac{a - a^{n+1}}{1 - a} . \qquad [40]$$

Returning to the original notation, substitute P_t (the probability of mastering an item in time t) for a, and the mean of the items mastered is

$$E(m) = \frac{P_t - (P_t)^{n+1}}{1 - P_t}.$$ [41]

From the all-or-nothing theory, $P_t = 1 - e^{-\lambda t}$. Substituting this value into [41] yields

$$E(m) = \frac{1 - e^{-\lambda t} - (1 - e^{-\lambda t})^{n+1}}{e^{-\lambda t}}.$$ [42]

We now wish to maximize $E(m)$ with respect to t, under the restriction that $nt = T$, where T is the fixed total instruction time available. Thus we can write $n = T/t$, and

$$E(m) = \frac{1 - e^{-\lambda t} - (1 - e^{-\lambda t})^{[(T/t)+1]}}{e^{-\lambda t}}.$$ [43]

It is possible to maximize Eq. [43], but the calculation is very messy. Instead, it seems more interesting to calculate the consequences of various divisions of typical courses. The course can be described adequately by the rate-of-learning, λ, and the total course-length, T. Consider, for example, that a single student is taught the first item until he learns it, then the second, etc., as by a tutor or teaching-machine. The mean time per item would be $1/\lambda$ from Eq. [19]. The mean number of items finished in such a tailor-made course is the total time T divided by the mean time per item, or $T/(1/\lambda) = T\lambda$.

Figure 6 shows the expected mean items mastered per subject as a function of how finely the program is divided. The inner panel shows the theoretical result for a very short program with $T\lambda = 3$, that is, a course in which an individually tutored student would master an average of about three items. Notice that the optimal program is one which divides the total available time T into one-half or one-third and that, with such a short course, the ordinary lock-step course (with optimal speed of progression) gives .46 (almost half) as much learning as does individual tutoring. The upper panel shows a similar calculation for a longer course in which a tutored student would master an average of 12 items. Here the optimal pace is to give about one-fourth of the total time to an individual item.

The efficiency of this optimal speed of progression, compared with individual tutoring, now drops to .35. In the bottom panel are shown calculations for a very long course, in which the tutored subject can master an average of 144 items. The optimal rate is to divide this long course into about 30 segments, of which somewhat over 26 can be mastered. However, with so long a course, even the optimal speed of progression leaves the lock-step course much inferior to individual tutoring; the course can only teach about 19 per cent as much as taught by the theoretical tutor.

Several comments about the calculations may indicate the general significance of the results and their application. With a very short course (only 3 items) the optimal time-per-segment is enough to

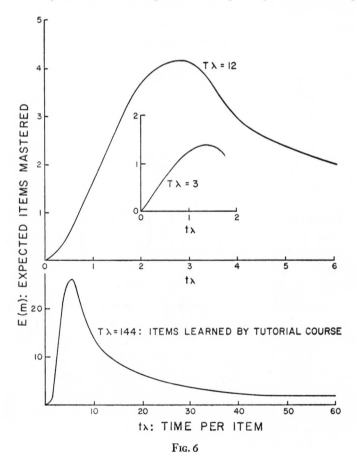

Fig. 6

bring the class to about 75 per cent learners. With a short course one does well to progress quite rapidly, dropping students by the wayside in fairly large numbers so as to give some opportunity to faster learners. In the moderate-length course, with 12 segments learned with a tutor, the optimal time-per-segment is one which produces about 95 per cent solvers. With the longer course the teacher should slow down, otherwise he will lose his whole class (or most of it) for the whole last part of the course. For the very long course, with a tutored-mean of 144 items, the optimal time-per-segment is one which produces 98 per cent solvers per item. Here, with a very long program, the teacher goes quite slowly and tries to keep most of the class with him.

Another point is readily apparent from Figure 6; with a short program, it really does not much matter how fast the teacher goes, just so he is not very much too fast. With a medium-length program, there is a fair range of speeds which are about equally good, though it is now possible to go too slowly. But with a very long, strictly cumulative course, the teacher must try for an optimal pace, and a relatively small deviation from the optimum can have a severe effect on the average amount learned.

In practice, teachers naturally try to avoid strictly cumulative courses. One device is to provide frequent review for students who may have failed an item. Another is to supplement classroom lock-step teaching with individual study, tutoring, and homework. Alternative developments of the same step are often provided so that a student may get through the course one way if not another (as, for example, when both geometrical and algebraic methods are used in a mathematics course; or the same point in comparative anatomy is taught, using several different structures). The redundancy of most scientific and mathematical courses is, no doubt, a reflection of the attempt to avoid the severe difficulties and dangers of the strictly cumulative course.

Another device is testing—the teacher may be able to find out, at frequent intervals, how many students are keeping pace in a particular program of teaching. He can, accordingly, linger and review or move ahead, depending on the momentary state of the class. An informal device used by most teachers is simply to watch the class, to note signs of enlightenment or bewilderment, and to adjust the pace of instruction to obtain an optimal balance. However, teachers with a trait of orderly behavior are inclined to postpone examinations until a given cumulative block of instruction is completed. This analysis suggests that such end-of-block examinations, while perhaps best for evaluation, are inefficient as devices for directing the teacher's decisions. One needs a test in the middle of the block, to find out if most of the students are "coasting" or if too many have already lost the thread of the course.

Discussion

It should be evident to any experienced teacher that the models discussed in this chapter are not ready for application in the classroom. The assumption of all-or-nothing learning is doubtful for many kinds of instructional material. The implicit assumption that there are no individual differences within the class is certainly inadequate. In calculating optimal class size, it was assumed that the teacher would teach the whole class until the last member learned, although such a procedure is both inefficient and (without an unusual testing program) impossible in practice. In calculating optimal pacing of a cumulative course, it was assumed that all segments of the course are equally difficult, that a student who misses one point must miss all following points, and that the teacher works with a strict program of progression and without any feedback from the class. It would be unwise to gloss over these theoretical inadequacies.

The point of the chapter has been to show how, with some effort, a practical educational problem can be analyzed mathematically through application of elementary probability theory. The actual mathematical steps are shown because the models used are inadequate but can be made more adequate. The very simple and artificial restraints on teacher and student, imposed in the examples, can be replaced by more accurate descriptions of the situation. The parameters of learning can be estimated directly from classroom experience merely by finding the proportion of items learned by students with various amounts and kinds of teaching. The informational feedback used by the teacher can be estimated either by investigating his testing procedures or by noticing his variation in practice and deducing what information he is using.

The purposes of this chapter will be achieved if it has been shown that interesting, nontrivial problems of teaching practice can be formulated in mathematical terms and that sensible (if very inexact) conclusions can be drawn from such analyses. Only by the hard work of collecting information, trying various procedures, and expanding the models can a quantitative theory of classroom teaching be developed. However, the position taken in this chapter is that the actual conditions of the classroom, the restraints imposed by the situation and the intrinsic variability of the learning process, can all be taken into account and that the problems are capable of being solved. The answers will not all be simple—engineers have found many of their problems to be so complicated that high-speed digital computers must be used to solve them. However, before plunging into such detailed analysis, it is useful and instructive to consider a few simplified problems, so as to gain an idea of what kind of variables and what kinds of analyses are likely to be useful. The examples in this chapter should be thought of as analogous to the problems in the first chapters of a high-school physics text—somewhat unrealistic, and certainly inadequate to building a skyscraper or a rocket ship, yet a modest and perhaps necessary step toward those more glamorous technical triumphs.

CHAPTER VI

Laboratory Studies of Verbal Learning

BENTON J. UNDERWOOD

Introduction

SPECIALIZATION OF RESEARCH EFFORTS

An examination of reports in two journals (*Journal of Experimental Psychology; American Journal of Psychology*) for the twelve-year period, 1950-61, shows that slightly more than one thousand dealt with experiments in human learning. Many of these reports involved several different experiments. The number of such articles published annually in the two journals and in others does not appear to have decreased since 1961. Thus, an estimate of the total number of experiments on human learning published in the last decade in all journals would certainly number several thousand. One of the inevitable correlates of this vast flow of energy into research on human learning is specialization. "Learning" as an identifying label on a man's research interest has little descriptive value; rather, he must be identified with a particular area of learning, the areas being identified by particular tasks or procedures. Five of the major areas may be identified.

Conditioning.—Pavlovian conditioning (and variants thereof) remains an active area of study, with the eyelid reflex and psychogalvanic response being the primary agents of study. It is this area of research in human learning which, more than any other, can be said to be concerned with the analysis of variables and phenomena in terms of their relevance to modern extensions and revisions of the theories originating in the 1930's, e.g., Hullian theory.

Probability learning.—In a situation used to study simple probability learning, the subject may have before him a red and a green light, and two response keys, one for each light. On a given trial the subject is asked to predict which of the two lights will come on, this prediction being made by pressing the appropriate key. A fundamental variable is the relative frequency with which the lights do in fact come on, e.g., 50:50, 40:60, 30:70, and so on. These proportions are related to the frequency with which each key is pressed over a long series of trials. Work in this area of human learning is relatively new. Almost all of the studies have been published since 1950, and yet they number in the scores. That such studies would "catch on" may seem puzzling to an outsider. Two factors seem responsible. First, some investigators have viewed this procedure as another way of studying Pavlovian conditioning. Second, the apparent simplicity of the situation has made it seem highly suitable for making initial tests of various mathematical models of learning (see chap. v).

Perceptual-motor learning.—In the immediate postwar years, perceptual-motor learning was identified with the pursuit rotor, reversed alphabet printing, and block turning. This is no longer true; very few studies appear in the current literature in which these tasks are used. The area might better now be identified as the study of display-control relationships. Tasks may simulate that of a pilot of a high-speed plane, of the operator of a control tower at an airport, or any situation resulting from increased automation where complex signals are "fed in" and various responses to these signals studied. That this is "true" perceptual-motor learning is suggested by the fact that investigators often find it necessary to study the perceptual problems in learning to identify signals or patterns of signals. So, also, response factors are given special attention. For example, the study of reaction time has been revived since further knowledge of the factors influencing reaction time seemed necessary before the higher-order response capacities and their relationships to complex stimulus situations could be meaningfully assessed.

Problem-solving.—Included in this area are concept learning and utilization, thinking, creativity, and all other forms of tasks which emphasize the "higher" mental processes. Analytical investigators in the field would not, however, lump all of these together. Rather, they may draw distinctions among the tasks, depending upon the various processes believed emphasized or de-emphasized by the tasks. Specialty areas are clearly developing within this broad field.

Verbal learning.—In the count of reports in various topical areas noted above, studies of verbal learning led all others, accounting for about one-third of all studies on human learning. It is also very probable that this classical area of research will develop specialty areas as the output of research continues.

The area of "human learning" has ceased to exist as a meaningful theoretical or experimental entity. If communality exists across the broad areas of research, it is in the analytical approaches being carried on (see later). There are no general theories of human learning which relate an appreciable proportion of the phenomena at the level at which they are currently being studied.

THE AGE OF ANALYSIS

Ours is an age of analysis. The fragmentation of laboratory studies of human learning into subareas is symptomatic of extensive conceptual and experimental analysis of limited phenomena as exhibited in particular tasks. Attempts to understand gross phenomena by experimental research inevitably lead to finer and finer analysis whereby the gross phenomena are broken down into subphenomena. Across the whole area of human learning the vast flow of research can only be characterized as representing finer and finer analysis carried on at an almost feverish pace. It is as if there is some end in sight, and there may be. At some point this trend will stop, and synthesis will begin with the emergence of its general principles, its integrating theories, and predictions relative to new situations.

The foregoing assessment is believed to hold for most areas of human learning, although the level of analysis may vary considerably from one area to another. Of course, in one form or another, analysis has and will always constitute a fundamental part of any experimental discipline. That this phase is emphasized by the writer comes from a belief that perhaps at no other time in the history of psychology have changes taken place so rapidly as a consequence of analysis as they are taking place at the moment in human learning. Changes are occuring so rapidly that it is difficult to stop them long enough to assess them. If the word "ferment" is ever appropriate for the current state of a scholarly endeavor, it is certainly appropriate for research on human learning at the moment.

Implications for the present chapter.—The present chapter will attempt to reflect some of the problems which are currently engaging research workers in verbal learning. It is not a survey; space limitations have forced elimination of certain topics (e.g., transfer). As a further space-saving measure, no attempt has been made to fully document all assertions. The assumption of such freedom was necessary lest the reference list become as long as the text.

The editors of the *Yearbook* requested that some consideration be given the relationship between laboratory learning and school learning. While some comments in this direction have been made, they have produced no genuine feeling of satisfaction that the bridges between the schoolroom and the laboratory are substantial. The present writer is not restrained in attempting these bridges by theoretical boundary conditions, but he is restrained by analytical boundary conditions. To refuse persistently to "go out on a limb" in suggesting applications of laboratory principles, and at the same time offer hope that the time will come when genuine applications are possible, is both "old hat" and frustrating to those who continue to wait for the time to come. Nevertheless, a true technology of learning will only come when a certain level of experimental analysis is achieved and is paralleled by a logical analysis of the tasks to which the laboratory principles are to be applied. As suggested earlier, the experimental analysis of verbal-learning tasks may be rapidly approaching the "lowest" level possible with available techniques. If the task to which laboratory knowledge is to be applied can be logically analyzed into the same components or into components similar to those possessed by laboratory tasks, application should be direct. A field test under such circumstances has a reasonable chance of success. The conservative nature of any suggested applications which appear later reflects this position.

Association Formation

THE CONCEPT OF AN ASSOCIATION

Any theory of learning which pretends to be complete must include assumptions about the critical factor or factors involved in establishing a new association. Indeed, such a focus is the core of any theory. Historically, the verbal-learning laboratory has not been a fertile source of such assumptions, probably because of its association with the functionalist tradition. At present, however, the thinking, questioning, and theorizing developing around learning, if not hitting directly at critical factors for associative formation, are coming very close. Several issues must be discussed.

A new association is said to have been formed between two verbal units when, following some training procedure, one will elicit the other with a probability greater than the zero probability which obtained before training. This seemingly neutral specification points up many of the conceptual problems present in contemporary thinking. No investigator takes the position that the association develops between two units in the form they are mechanically presented to the subject. Obviously, each must have some form of representation in the subject's mind, so to speak, and the association is developed between these two representations. But, these representations allow several conceptions. They may be thought of as stimuli, and the association may then be said to have developed between stimuli. Or each representation may be thought of as a stimulus which elicits "internal" responses, and the association is formed between responses. Or, of course, the association may be said to be formed between a stimulus and a response. That one term as presented mechanically to the subject is called a stimulus term and the other a response term need not bias in any way the constructual association which the theorist may wish to erect to suit his own predilections.

Although the mechanical presentation of the paired-associate task (in which the subject is asked to produce a response term when the stimulus term is shown) may lead to the notion that an association has directionality—from stimulus to response—this may not be proper. Much recent work has shown that although during training the subject only reproduces the response term, he may, if called upon to do so, reproduce the stimulus term when the response term is given. This may be conceptualized in either of two ways. First, a single associative process may be said to be bidirectional, or, second, two associative processes may be said to have been formed, each with different directional properties.

Lack of space precludes the extended presentation of data necessary to evaluate the differences in and implications of these forward and backward associations, as they are usually called. Any language teacher can vouch for the presence of forward and backward associations. If a student learns the French equivalents of ten English words, he very likely can produce a high proportion of the English words when the French words become the stimulus terms. At the same time, in many serial-like tasks, backward associations appear to be nonexistent or at least nonfunctional. To recite the alphabet backward is far from easy; to recite a well-learned sentence backward or spell a word backward is very difficult, and to play a well-memorized piano composition backward may be impossible. However, the nature of the associations involved in serial tasks is quite obscure, and the lack of generality of backward associations across learning tasks may not be as severe as it would seem on the surface.

In the definition of an association it was stated that there is a change in the probability of one item evoking another. The use of the term "probability" encompasses two very diverse conceptions which have recently confronted each other. The classical notion is that the process or processes which constitute an association have an *incremental* characteristic; that is, there is a gradual accretion of something which constitutes an association and the probabilities of one term eliciting another is some direct function of the amount of accretion. Thus, with successive trials there is a gradual increase in the probabilities that the stimulus term will elicit the response term; probabilities may vary continuously from zero to one. In 1957, Rock suggested that the formation of a verbal association might not be incremental in nature but, rather, may be an all-or-none process.[1] Of course, such notions of one-trial learning have a precedent in theories based on animal studies, notably in the Guthrian theory, but investigators in the field of human verbal learning have been loath to accept the notion. Now in fact, Rock actually attained some *rapprochement* with the incremental notion. Subsequently, however, Estes took a completely uncompromising position, and it is this position that will be outlined here.[2]

The all-or-none position asserts that all trials before an association is formed are irrelevant to the formation of the association. An association is either formed or not formed on a given trial; there is no gradual increase in an associative process. Once an association *is* formed, its "strength reflects a probability of one. Furthermore, rep-

1. Irving Rock, "The Role of Repetition in Associative Learning," *American Journal of Psychology*, LXX (June, 1957), 186–93.

2. William K. Estes, "Learning Theory and the New 'Mental Chemistry,'" *Psychological Review*, LXVII (July, 1960), 207–23. [It may be noted that a derivative of this position has been used by Restle in his models (chap. v).]

etition of the response in the presence of the stimulus has no influence of any kind. This is to say that the classical notion that overlearning facilitates retention is denied.

There is already a rather large literature which has developed
around the controversy of incremental versus all-or-none learning.
The most thoughtful evaluation of the broader implications of the
all-or-none position may be found in Postman.[3] In this chapter, two
points will be discussed. First, it should be noted that one can hold
to either an incremental conception or an all-or-none conception
without having to say how learning per se occurred. That is, one
can say that associations, by whatever mechanisms they are formed,
develop gradually. Likewise, one could hold that associations are
formed in an all-or-none manner without specifying the factors responsible for the formation. Thus, the controversy does not directly
involve the mechanisms responsible for learning, only the characteristics of the product of the mechanisms.

The second point that seems particularly relevant here is the assertion in the Estes version of the all-or-none law that continued
repetition of an association has no influence. The position asserts
that once an association is formed—as evidenced by its being given
correctly once—further repetition is senseless. If this is in fact true,
the implications for educational practices are obvious and far-reaching. If Estes is correct, all rote repetition should be removed from
simple associative learning situations in the classroom. While such a
move might provide solace for those who dislike the whole idea of
rote learning in school situations, the issue here is whether or not
Estes' notion should be taken seriously in application (Professor Estes has *not* suggested that it should).

The present writer believes Estes to be dead wrong on this aspect
of his theory. This decision is made entirely on the basis of available
evidence, since Estes, while accepting the fact that forgetting may
occur, has presented no theoretical conception of how it occurs. It
is quite possible to amass a large number of studies which will show
that repetition of an association beyond the point at which it is first
given correctly will at least enhance the *performance* of that asso-

3. Leo Postman, "One-Trial Learning," in *Verbal Behavior and Learning:
Problems and Processes*. Edited by Charles N. Cofer. New York: McGraw-Hill
Book Co., 1963.

ciation on retention tests. Whether or not the continued repetition strengthens the association per se is beside the point for evaluation of whether or not overlearning influences retention in the applied situation. The evidence that such continued repetition does influence retention performance is so strong that it cannot be dismissed.

THE CONDITIONS OF AN ASSOCIATION

In the definition of an association presented earlier, the phrase, "some training procedure," was used. What are the *critical* training procedures for the development of an association? This is a most difficult question. The fact is that, if the usual college-student subject is in some way induced into the verbal-learning laboratory and told to learn a task, he will do so, even under an extraordinarily wide range of conditions as far as presenting the material is concerned. He even learns if he is not told to do so. Of course, different conditions are related to the rate at which he learns, but the question of the moment is what conditions must be met before *any* learning occurs.

Giving this question to an experiment for a decision is made especially difficult by the fact that much of the learning observed appears to be a transfer learning. Such learning involves the transfer and strengthening of associations which have already been formed in the past so that learning from "scratch" may not occur. Thus, "new" associations may be formed by associational aids, mnemonic devices, or other coding habits. Other than that such habits are widely used, little of a systematic nature is known about them. The fact that many subjects will use such habits does not necessarily mean that this is the most efficient way to learn, although it is a compelling hypothesis. If associational aids were classified and evaluated experimentally as to their efficacy in various situations, teaching the use of them in the school situation could follow.

The foregoing comments point to a strong need for systematic work on verbal learning with children, thus assessing critical factors involved in association formation prior to the learning of a heavy overlay of second-order associational skills. Because of the interpretative cloudiness produced by associational aids used by college students the investigator must devise situations in which the subject will not "use" these associational aids. Thus, as in the incidental-learning procedure, the subject is exposed to material without being told to learn it. Under such conditions the second-order associational habits are probably not elicited. Most of the incidental learning studies have used free learning in which an association between a particular stimulus term and a particular response term is not required so that some analytical power is lost. Nevertheless, it is a fact that learning does occur and sometimes the amount is nearly as great as under conditions in which learning is intentional.[4] Thus, the mere perception of a verbal unit produces a representation of it which, under appropriate instructions, can be translated into the instrumental response.

Referring now to the development of an association between a particular stimulus term and a particular response term, bits of evidence are appearing which suggest that simple contiguity of events may be a sufficient condition for the formation of an association. In various forms, theories of conditioning are tending in this direction as exemplified by Spence[5] and by Brogden.[6] There is also direct evidence of the role of contiguity in verbal learning.[7] The fact that Thorndike[8] reached an opposite conclusion will, of course, have to be rationalized if the role of contiguity per se is to be given fundamental status as a principle of learning. No attempt will be made to do so in this chapter. It is sufficient to say that the future may see greater emphasis placed on the classical principles of association, last systematically presented by Robinson in 1932.[9]

Variables

TASK VARIABLES

Of the variables which can be manipulated in the laboratory, only those which constitute some characteristic of the verbal task to be

4. Leo Postman and Pauline A. Adams, "Studies in Incidental Learning. VIII, The Effects of Contextual Determination," *Journal of Experimental Psychology,* LIX (March, 1960), 153–64.

5. Kenneth W. Spence, *Behavior Theory and Conditioning.* New Haven, Connecticut: Yale University Press, 1956.

6. W. J. Brogden, "Contiguous Conditioning," *Journal of Experimental Psychology,* LXIV (August, 1962), 172–76.

7. Charles Osgood and Lois Anderson, "Certain Relations among Experienced Contingencies, Associative Structure, and Contingencies in Encoded Messages," *American Journal of Psychology,* LXX (September, 1957), 411–20.

8. Edward L. Thorndike, *The Fundamentals of Learning.* New York: Bureau of Publications, Columbia University, 1932.

9. Edward S. Robinson, *Association Theory Today.* New York: Century Co., 1932.

learned can be said to be related in a substantial way to the rate at which learning occurs. Two of the most powerful variables will be discussed.

Meaningfulness.—The higher the meaningfulness, the more rapid the learning; this principle holds across all types of verbal learning tasks. In paired-associate learning, when response terms are manipulated throughout the full range of meaningfulness, the effect is great, and much greater than for corresponding variations in the meaningfulness of stimulus terms. Just how this variable produces its effect will be understood in terms of degree of utilization of habits already formed. Unfortunately, the analytical problem is a difficult one because several variables reflecting this habit-transfer tend to vary together. Thus, while meaningfulness may be specified as differences in the number of verbal units which are evoked by other verbal units in a limited period of time, it can be shown that correlated with this measure are other characteristics of the materials such as frequency, level of letter integration, and ease of telescoping the unit into a unitary sound. Which of these characteristics (or others) is responsible for the effect? Or, do they all play roles? Or, is one characteristic most important for response learning (learning response terms so they are readily available) and another for associative learning in which a response term must be connected to a particular stimulus term? Research reports relevant to answers to such questions are appearing at a rapid rate. Their effect thus far is that of causing frequent shifts in the various possible and yet reasonable positions which might be taken on the issues. Of the high importance of the gross variable of meaningfulness there can be no doubt; concerning the precise mechanisms of interpretation, there is.

Intratask similarity.—The analytical problems associated with intratask similarity are more complicated (or so it appears at the present time) than those associated with meaningfulness. There are two basic reasons for this. First, there are several different ways by which similarity among verbal units may be varied. Second, the moment similarity is varied in a paired-associate list, several subphenomena are differentially affected. For example, in a case of high similarity among stimulus terms, as compared with a case of low similarity, the discrimination between the group of items which are response terms and those which are stimulus terms is enhanced.

Thus, a positive influence would be present with high similarity that would not be present with low similarity. Yet, generally speaking, high similarity among terms in a task requiring acquisition of specific associations will produce an over-all negative effect in learning, and under appropriate conditions, the effect is large. It is clear that the major deterrent to learning resulting from high similarity is associative interference. To learn such a task requires the acquisition of differentiating responses to the similar units where differentiating responses are not initially elicited.

Even a momentary consideration of the two variables (meaningfulness and intratask similarity) will suggest that there are schoolroom counterparts. Can anything substantial be said by way of engineering learning in the school so as to minimize the difficulty in learning initially meaningless symbols or to minimize the difficulty in learning terms or concepts which have high similarity? It does not seem so. To repeat a theme, the heavily analytical stage in which laboratory studies find themselves is rapidly tearing phenomena apart. Putting them back together again still has to be accomplished. Actually, the critical question for the school situation very frequently resolves itself into the classical whole-part problem, with a somewhat different emphasis than given to this problem in the past. Even a so-called simple learning task, it has been shown, consists of several sublearnings. It is an important applied question to ask whether, for over-all learning efficiency, it is better to master these sublearnings before combining them into the over-all task, or is it better to learn the complete task from the beginning?

The importance of analyzing a gross task into its constituents is probably pointed up by the history of the whole-part problem. Why did this problem die out as an active research topic? Probably because the contradictory results gave no satisfactory resolution. And why the contradictory results? Probably because manipulations of a whole-part kind produced differential effects on the various constituent learnings of the over-all tasks. Until the constituents are understood to some degree through independent study, the whole-part variable applied indiscriminately could very well lead to contradictory results with different tasks. This is not to be taken to indicate that the earlier studies on the whole-part variable were done without some notions as to constituent parts, but, generally speaking, the part learnings were not in themselves objects of study. Contradictory results for a variable across tasks usually indicates a lack of understanding of the task constituents, and no substantial principles to be applied can emerge from such a situation. For example, it might be reasoned that, to master a task in which highly similar terms are involved, it would be best to present the similar terms contiguously so that the subject may, so to speak, examine them for possible differentiating cues. Yet, data on such manipulations are contradictory for different tasks. It is a reasonable guess that such contradictions will be resolved only when the constituent learnings are better understood. Indeed, task analysis has been strongly recommended by Gagné as a result of his experimental analysis of the formation of mathematical concepts.[10]

There is every reason to believe that in the near future the whole-part problem will be reopened. The level of analysis is attaining a point in verbal learning where it would appear profitable to start trying to see how the part learnings may combine to produce an over-all skill. These laws will tell how part skills combine into broader skills. Such research will result in evidence bearing on the engineering of efficient learning procedures.

There are, of course, certain obvious translations of the laboratory knowledge into the classroom. For example, if the language skill to be developed is only that of translating a foreign language into English, the instructional program should be quite different than if the reverse were true. Translating from the foreign language into English requires little if any time for response learning. That is, the subject need not be able to reproduce the foreign word. The major learning is that of associating the foreign word (as the stimulus term) with the response term (the English word). These associations, plus grammatical knowledge, allow translation. The reverse situation, translating English to a foreign language, requires an enormous amount of time for response learning in addition to the associative learning; the subject must be able to reproduce the foreign word in addition to associating it with the English equivalent.

10. Robert M. Gagné, "The Acquisition of Knowledge," *Psychological Review.* LXIX (July, 1962), 355–65.

MOTIVATION

Laboratory studies of verbal learning in which incentives have been manipulated have shown no consistent effect on rate of learning of the college-student subject. In so far as incentives may be said to influence motivation, it must be concluded that the laboratory studies of verbal learning give little information on the role motivation plays in learning. Just how learning and motivation interact is a most complex problem, which has tried theorists for years. No attempt will be made here to treat the various points of view since they will be covered in part in other chapters. However, certain observations will be made relative to the lack of a consistent relationship between incentive variation and verbal learning.

The fact that learning occurs without intent to learn indicates a clear limitation of the role played by motivation in the associative processes. Indeed, such evidence may indicate that motivation is not involved at all in the formation of associations. Motivation to learn may cause the subject to attend to the appropriate aspects of the situation (as designated by the instructions), and motivation to learn may cause him to use associational aids. It may also cause him to emit responses which may in turn facilitate learning. Yet, this does not mean that motivation is involved in the formation of associations per se. Thus, if it were possible to get the subject to do all of the above without intent to learn, learning may occur just as rapidly as in the intent-to-learn situation. This Guthrian-like position is a defensible one. Yet, if it be admitted that motivation may indirectly influence learning, why have motivational studies in verbal learning not shown greater and more consistent results? There are a number of possibilities. Increases in motivation may add negative as well as positive factors, and the balance between these factors may vary as a function of the task. It is sometimes said that the relationship between motivation and performance is curvilinear because the negative influences of motivation increase more rapidly than do the positive influences beyond a certain level of motivation. The optimum level of motivation may vary with the nature of the task. "Trying too hard" may be detrimental in learning one task but not another.

If there is one universal benefit of motivation, it comes from keeping the subject working. With few if any exceptions, all laboratory studies of learning would support the notion that the longer the subject works at learning, the more he will learn. Motivation in this broad sense, then, is of utmost importance to learning. It squares with the common-sense notion of the influence of motivation. But, of course (to repeat), this does not mean that motivation influences directly the process of forming associations; motivation may simply maintain the subject in a situation so that factors which are responsible for learning can operate. How the teacher may aid in sustaining motivation is the topic of another chapter.

Forgetting

THEORY

If a college-student subject learns a single paired-associate list until all responses can be correctly anticipated on a single trial, recall after twenty-four hours will show 75–90 per cent of the items will be given correctly. Theories, devised to account for the 10–25 per cent forgetting which occurs, still rely heavily on interference from other tasks as a critical factor.[11] This is true despite the fact that difficulty is being met in trying to demonstrate experimentally the detailed mechanisms by which the interference operates. At a general level, the interference is said to stem from the learning of other tasks following the learning of the task to be recalled (retroactive inhibition) and from tasks acquired prior to the learning of the task to be recalled (proactive inhibition). There has been a shift in the importance assigned these two scores of interference. In earlier years, retroactive inhibition was assumed to be the major source of interference in producing forgetting in the natural course of events. Now, proactive inhibition is assigned the major role. The reason for this switch in emphasis comes not only from laboratory data, which show the heavy influence of proactive inhibition, but also from a consideration of the logic of the situation. This latter may be illustrated. Assume that a student, ten years of age, learns a given task and the retention of this task is tested one month later. The fact that proactive inhibition is assigned a major role in causing the observed forgetting is based on the assumption that, during the first ten years

11. Leo Postman, "The Present Status of Interference Theory," in *Verbal Learning and Verbal Behavior*, pp. 152–78. Edited by Charles N. Cofer. New York: McGraw-Hill Book Co., 1961.

of the student's life, he will have acquired more habits that will interfere with the task to be recalled than he will acquire during the one-month interval between learning and the retention test. Of course, the logic which favors the greater emphasis on proactive inhibition than on retroactive inhibition must be tempered by certain modifying variables. For example, conflicting habits learned during the one-month interval may be stronger than habits learned earlier; they may also be based on more nearly similar material. Nevertheless, the strong role played by proaction is demonstrated in the laboratory.

An ingenious procedure worked out by Peterson and Peterson has developed an entirely new area of study in that retention of single verbal units is being examined over very short intervals of time.[12] These investigators showed that a single item, presented for a brief exposure, will show very heavy forgetting over a period of twenty seconds. The potential of the technique is enormous. Whether viewed from a theoretical or an applied point of view, it is of importance to understand the laws of forgetting which obtain for various materials over intervals of months and years. For obvious reasons, such studies, conceived of in the form of the techniques of the classical retention studies, are difficult to carry out. If the laws of forgetting obtained by the Peterson-Peterson technique for the retention of single items over very short intervals can be shown to parallel the laws obtained by the classical technique, then very long-term retention studies may be simulated in a single laboratory session. By the Peterson-Peterson technique, seconds may become days, minutes become months. The single-item technique may become to classical studies of retention what computers have become to the desk calculator. The big "if," of course, concerns the parallelism of the laws obtained by single-item and by the classical techniques. At this time it may be said only that the evidence is very encouraging.

VARIABLES OF FORGETTING

There are many misconceptions concerning the influence of certain variables on forgetting. It will be worthwhile to attempt a clarification of the issues. Retention measurements are usually distin-

12. Lloyd R. Peterson and Margaret Jean Peterson, "Short-Term Retention of Individual Verbal Items," *Journal of Experimental Psychology*, LVIII (September, 1959), 193–98.

guished from learning measurements in terms of the length of the interval separating acquisition trials. If the interval is longer between two trials than the interval which prevailed between earlier trials, retention is arbitrarily said to be involved. Of course, the performance on each so-called learning trial involves retention processes; the performance measure on any learning trial is a composite of amount learned on previous exposures and amount remembered of that amount. These two processes are inextricably confounded. At any time, however, such a composite measure may be determined without allowing further learning. Retention may then be measured after varying intervals of time using the earlier composite measure as a base. Using this base, the issue concerns the variables which may influence the rate of forgetting as determined by the retention measurements taken after varying intervals of time.

Degree of learning.—This variable was discussed earlier in conjunction with the all-or-none conception of association formation. The evidence shows that the higher the degree of learning, the better the retention (the slower the rate of forgetting). Furthermore, the position can be strongly defended that there are only two major factors involved in a substantial way in influencing forgetting over time. These are, first, the degree of learning of the task to be recalled and, second, the number and strength (degree of learning) of interfering associations. With these two factors in mind, the alleged influence of other variables may be examined.

Task variables.—Supposing one group of subjects is given ten acquisition trials on a task consisting of units of high meaningfulness and another group ten trials on a task made up of units of low meaningfulness. Supposing further that retention for the tasks is measured after twenty-four hours. Most assuredly, the group given the task of high meaningfulness would show the higher retention scores. From such data it has sometimes been concluded that low-meaningful material is forgotten more rapidly than high-meaningful material. Yet, the fact is that the differences in retention are probably due entirely to differences in degree of learning attained in the ten acquisition trials. Indeed, if level of learning is equivalent before a retention interval is introduced, there is no evidence that *any* task variable (meaningfulness, intralist similarity, and so on) is associated with appreciable differences in rate of forgetting. Enormous differences in learning may be produced by task variables, but they produce small if any differences in rate of forgetting.

Individual differences.—That there are large individual differences in rate of learning tasks is apparent. Even among a supposed homogeneous population of college students, the differences in time to attain mastery of relatively simple verbal-learning tasks produce pesky statistical problems resulting from the wide range of scores. But, as in the case of task variables, if slow learners and fast learners achieve the same degree of learning before a retention interval is introduced, there is no evidence that the rate of forgetting differs. A slow learner may appear to show more rapid forgetting than a fast learner in uncontrolled observations because the level of learning is higher for the fast learner.

Individuals differ on an indefinite number of traits or characteristics. Do these play any substantial role in rate of forgetting? The evidence, while by no means conclusive, indicates that in the formal laboratory setting they play at best a minor role. This may be illustrated by the following procedure. Give a heterogeneous group of subjects a fairly difficult verbal-learning task, presenting this task for a constant number of trials so that a wide range of scores is obtained in terms of total correct responses given during the constant number of trials. Retention by recall is then measured, say, after twenty-four hours. The final step is to correlate the recall and learning scores. These correlations will be found to be high. This implies that the recall measurements are to a large extent dependent upon the level of learning attained; individual-difference variables do not appear to throw much "chaff" into the system.

The convergence of such facts as those presented has made degree of learning emerge as the critical variable involved in retention. Such a conclusion, with its corresponding relegation of individual-difference variables to a very minor role, will be resisted. Indeed, it is resisted by those of us who have been investigating forgetting within the framework of an interference theory. Certain implications of an interference theory not only point up the relevance of certain task variables to forgetting but also point to the relevance of certain individual-difference variables. Studies determining the influence of task variables have not supported the sizable effect on retention expected by the theory. Little work has been done on the role of particular individual-difference variables, but certain expectations may be pointed out. Very young children, according to theory, would show less rapid forgetting of a verbal task than would, say, college students. This follows from the notion of interference and the assumption that the young children would have fewer conflicting associations in their repertoire to cause proactive interference. Another expectation would be that if an imbecile were given enough trials on a verbal task to reach the same degree of learning as that attained by a genius, the genius would show more rapid forgetting. This would be predicted on the grounds that the genius has learned and will subsequently learn (before the retention test) more interfering associations than the imbecile. When such predictions are carefully tested they may be supported, but the character which other evidence is assuming does not give cause for optimism. One confounding individual-difference variable about which little is known could be called "resistance to interference." Individuals may differ in their susceptibility to interference from conflicting associations. Such a characteristic might be correlated with, indeed, may be partly responsible for, differences in rate of learning. Such a factor would counteract the greater interference expected for a fast learner (as compared with a slow learner) at the time of recall. The hypothetical balance of such factors, however, is too delicate to "push" without supporting data, and such data are not available.

To assert that present evidence gives no basis for expecting appreciable individual differences in rate of forgetting, if level of learning is equal, should not be misinterpreted. Given an assortment of facts or concepts, equal in availability for a group of subjects, there still will likely be great individual differences in the manipulation of these facts and concepts, in ability to interrelate them, and so on. The lack of individual differences in rate of forgetting rote-learned material should, at the present time, be taken as just that and no more.

Massed versus spaced practice.—The evidence on massed versus spaced practice in *learning* verbal tasks indicates that spaced practice facilitates learning only under a highly specialized set of conditions, and even then the magnitude of the effect is so small as to have no applied consequence. That is, it would be horribly inefficient to use spaced practice if total time (learning time plus spaced time) is the criterion of efficiency. Massed practice is far superior by this criterion.

In certain situations of high interference between tasks, spaced practice may actually impede learning. However, under such situations, spaced practice may facilitate retention. The qualifier "may" must be included since there appear to be certain forms of interference between tasks for which spaced practice does not produce the facilitation. It is known that for interference produced by the classical paradigm of negative transfer in which the subject learns two different responses to the same stimulus, spaced practice on the transfer list will result in facilitating retention. In fact, evidence now being collected in the writer's laboratory, in which the spaced interval is one day, shows that learning is seriously impeded in the initial stages of learning but that retention is enormously facilitated after eight days (as compared with massed learning). The effect is so marked that there is reason to believe that such long spacing in any learning task in which interference is present will result in better retention than learning the same task by massed practice.

The above facts have a fairly close analogy with certain observations made of school learning and retention. One observation is that, while cramming for an examination may result in good performance immediately, forgetting will be very rapid. The use of reviews and tests of other forms of spaced learning might, being analogous to spaced practice, be recommended by the laboratory relationship between spacing and retention. However, certain cautions must be introduced until the better understanding of the mechanisms producing the effect is achieved. Present thinking would strongly recommend the spaced practice if the interference is produced by associations which are "unwanted"; that is, if they are *not* produced by interference from other school tasks, the retention of which is also at stake. The reason for this is that certain evidence indicates that the spacing procedures produce their effect by eliminating or extinguishing the conflicting associations, or at least the term involved in the associations. Thus, extreme spacing in acquiring a Spanish vocabulary may extinguish the French vocabulary learned the previous year. Or, the interference may arise from another school subject being taken concurrently, and at the present time there is little evidence on the simultaneous acquisition of interfering habits or on the role of distributed practice in their retention. All factors considered, however, there is little hesitancy in recommending the use of spaced practice if high retention of the particular task being learned is the end product to be achieved.

CHAPTER VII

Implications of Training Research for Education*

ROBERT GLASER

During the past fifteen years, an increasing number of experimental psychologists have been engaged in work on training research problems. This involvement of psychological scientists in the research and development aspects of training has taken place to a great extent in the military services and to a lesser extent in industry. A look at the numbers involved shows a unique peacetime involvement of experimental psychologists with problems of military training.[1] The purpose of this chapter is to survey the contributions and implications of this activity for education, educational psychology, and the psychology of learning as it relates to a technology of instruction and teaching practices. Guiding an examination of the results of this work are questions such as the following: Has it been possible to translate the academic knowledge of the psychologist into training practices and into an instructional technology? What are the implications of military training research for educational psychology and educational practices? What are its implications for the science of learning? What implications does the research and development process in other technological areas have for education? In general, these questions relate to the continuum from pure science, through applied science and technological development, to practical implementation.

A multitude of publications has been produced by all the military services which, while not as generally accessible as psychological journals, has been available to interested individuals and has

* Many of the ideas expressed in this chapter have evolved in the course of research supported by the Office of Naval Research, Personnel and Training Branch, and by the American Institute for Research.

1. Arthur W. Melton, "Military Psychology in the United States of America," *American Psychologist*, XII (December, 1957), 740–46.

been deposited in libraries throughout the country and in the Armed Services Technical Information Agency (ASTIA).[2] Some of this work in the military has been published in psychological and educational journals, and recently a number of books have appeared to report work and thinking in this area to psychologists and educational researchers.[3] Less writing has appeared which is directly oriented toward the practicing educator and teacher. In general, in a note on current trends in the literature on training, Saul estimates that while the literature on industrial training is sketchy the annual output of published material pertinent to training is about five hundred journal articles and books a year.

This estimate explicitly excludes a large part of the literature on human learning and also on education. . . . Our experience indicates that government and government-sponsored agencies are the most productive of systematic research and application in this area: in the U.S. especial mention may be made of the U.S.A.F. Personnel and Training Research Center, Lackland Air Force Base, Texas; the Human Resources Research Office, Washington University, D.C. [sic], the U.S.N. Office of Naval Research, Washington, D.C., and the U.S. Naval Training Devices Center, Port Washington, Long Island.[4]

Instructional Objectives

A first step in designing an instructional system is the specification of its purposes and the objectives to be achieved. When the literature reflecting work in the military is examined, it is evident that a concern of experimental psychologists who have turned their attention to training research is the lack of explicit specification of the behavior under consideration. Many reports express a concern with the problem of and techniques for defining training objectives. As a result of this attention to the actual behavior that is the concern of

2. For information regarding the availability of these documents and report series, the reader is referred to "Availability of Documents," in *Teaching Machines and Programmed Learning*, pp. 578–79. Edited by A. A. Lumsdaine and Robert Glaser. Washington: National Education Association, 1960.

3. *Psychological Principles in System Development* (Edited by Robert M. Gagné. New York: Holt, Rinehart & Winston, 1962); *Training Research and Education* (Edited by Robert Glaser. Pittsburgh: University of Pittsburgh Press, 1962); *Student Response in Programmed Instruction* (Edited by A. A. Lumsdaine. Washington: National Academy of Sciences, National Research Council, 1961).

4. E. V. Saul, "Note on Current Trends in Literature on Training," *Ergonomics*, II (February, 1959), 180–82.

training, specific procedures have been developed and large sums of money allocated for collecting and recording human behavior data on military tasks so that these specifications could be used in designing selection and training procedures. The methods employed are crude in the eyes of many psychologists but the materials collected represent a substantial improvement over more vague and general information which previously supplied the basis for the development of a course of instruction.

Task analysis and task taxonomy.—A primary example of the analysis of instructional goals is the notions of task analysis developed in the military context by Miller.[5] Such procedures should provide information to assist the designer of a course of instruction in making design decisions. Furthermore, factual data of this kind can combat prejudices and ritualistic practices about what is relevant or nonrelevant to criterion performance. In both military training and civilian education there has been the need, constantly expressed by psychologists and educators, to analyze and classify the behavior with which they deal. It seems that once the properties of student performance can be described in language that is uniformly acceptable and relatively unambiguous to most people, then the real job of discovering how these classes of behavior are learned and should be taught can proceed.

In considering the analysis and specification of instructional objectives, a problem that arises is the development of a schema and set of categories for describing and classifying behavior in a way that is meaningful for instruction. The assumption underlying the importance of task taxonomy and the identification of the kinds of tasks that are being dealt with in a training situation is that the conditions of efficient learning are different for different tasks and a broad answer to the question of learning efficiency will not be very useful. After some years of familiarity with Air Force training, a very general classification of tasks that attempts to consider factors producing efficient learning in a variety of military jobs has been

5. Robert B. Miller, "Analysis and Specification of Behavior for Training," in *Training Research and Education, op. cit.,* pp. 31–62; Robert B. Miller, *A Method for Man-Machine Task Analysis* (WADC-TR-53-137. Wright Air Development Center, 1953); and Robert B. Miller, "Task Description and Analysis," in *Psychological Principles in System Development, op. cit.,* pp. 187–228.

presented by Gagné and Bolles.[6] Gagné has elaborated this approach with respect to education in general.[7]

The concern with task analysis and task taxonomy as basic requirements for the specification of educational objectives has been a major theme in military training research even though procedures for carrying out this endeavor are primitive and require much developmental effort. Over and over again the psychologist's attempt to behaviorally define what he is working with, at least as far as he can, has been a major factor in providing a basis for improving military training programs. By virtue of his training, the psychologist cannot operate unless he can identify his dependent variables in some tangible fashion and unless he can specify possible relationships between the manipulation of training variables and these dependent behaviors. He asks, "What is being trained for that can be observed in the actions of men and that can be manipulated by instructor performance or the instructional environment?" This attitude alone has forced behavioral specification into many training situations in which the personnel involved have not previously asked questions with a behavioral orientation. Crawford[8] has stated that ". . . perhaps the most important single contribution to the development of training through research has been the determination of methods for the formulation of objectives of instruction."

The important implication for educational practice is the need for the development of techniques for the analysis of what the student needs to achieve. On the basis of the behavioral specification of the end results of the school environment, achievement tests can be constructed, teaching and research in instruction can proceed, and curricula can be designed. An approach that might underlie such a development has been described in a recent booklet by Mager,[9]

6. Robert M. Gagné and R. C. Bolles, "A Review of Factors in Learning Efficiency," in *Automatic Teaching: The State of the Art*, pp. 13–53. Edited by Eugene Galanter. New York: John Wiley & Sons, 1959.

7. Robert M. Gagné, "The Analysis of Instructional Objectives for the Design of Instruction," in *Teaching Machines and Programmed Learning: II, Data and Directions*. Edited by Robert Glaser. Washington: National Education Association, 1964 (in press).

8. Meredith P. Crawford, "Concepts of Training," in *Psychological Principles in System Development, op. cit.*, p. 326.

9. Robert F. Mager, *Preparing Objectives for Programmed Instruction*. San Francisco: Fearon Publishers, 1961.

who was originally schooled in the analysis of military tasks and has thought widely about its application to more general subject matter.

When confronted with the problem of task classification, the psychologist had to face up to the fact that a definitive terminology for behavioral description was not available nor forthcoming from the science of psychology in the foreseeable future. Melton has described this basic lack as follows:

> . . . I can see the problem but I cannot see the solution for it! My statement means that psychology does not have a satisfactory classification scheme in terms of which specific tasks engaged in by human beings can be described, identified, and placed in a dimensional matrix in relation to other tasks. Without this taxonomy we are forced to use such crude descriptive categories as we referred to previously—discrimination learning, selective learning, tracking, concept formation, paired-associate learning—with the implication that we believe in a typology of learning, when, in fact, most of us do not, and when, in fact, it is known that all instances within these classes are not functionally equivalent.
> So, the psychologist, in addition to being plagued with a wealth of variety in human tasks, faces this universe of tasks without even the crutch that would be provided by a systematic taxonomy. This lack of taxonomy places substantial limitations on the ordering of our knowledge about learning and on the feasibility of communicating that knowledge. It therefore stands in the way of the identifications of isomorphisms between learning tasks about which there is information from the laboratories of psychologists and knowledges and skills in which individuals need to be educated. Even tentative refinements in our present crude descriptive classification of tasks would, if combined with an agreement to standardize, greatly improve the communication between, and integration of, the science of learning and each of the education and training technologies that relate to it.[10]

Relationships between Objectives, Aptitudes, and Training

In the military services and in industry, increasing attention has been paid to the determination of the best combination of instructional objectives, entering-behavior (aptitude, achievement, and background) requirements, and instructional procedures in order to achieve over-all organizational goals with maximum utility. Depending upon their characteristics at a particular time, different aspects,

10. Arthur W. Melton, "The Science of Learning and the Technology of Educational Methods," *Harvard Educational Review*, XXIX (Spring, 1959), 101. (Also in *Teaching Machines and Programmed Learning, op. cit.,* pp. 658–60.)

such as the nature of the job for which men are to be trained, test selection standards, and the time, cost, and characteristics of instruction, can be varied to permit optimal functioning of the organization. For example, in the military services, the reorganization of task structure and of the tasks assigned to various personnel can permit the more intensive training of specialists on particular job aspects while certain portions of their former jobs can be assigned to persons who have less time available for training and a lower-level entering behavior. In civilian life, while shortage in certain professions might benefit from such task rearrangement, it is less easy to accomplish.

Work in this context has prompted consideration of the relationships among aptitude measurement, training, and achievement, and embryonic models have been considered to relate the aspects involved. Travers,[11] for example, as a first step toward the development of a theoretical structure for use in the development of research on aptitudes, attempts to classify and inventory the variables that must be considered in the prediction of achievement. The categorization he suggests is one designed to permit some integration of aptitude measurement with stimulus-response learning theory. While recognizing that the major determinant of achievement in any training program is the training program itself, he considers classes of variables which can be studied when training is assumed to be constant for a group of individuals. The classes of variables described are previous achievement, prerequisites for learning, learning sets, ability to make necessary discriminations, and motivation. Travers attempts to write a general equation in which achievement is a function of previous achievement plus a multiplicative function of motivation and entering behavior, including aptitude variables.

Carroll,[12] in a review of research on the prediction of success in intensive foreign-language training in military and government agencies, developed a model to interpret some of the results of this program which are applicable to the study of the prediction of achieve-

11. Robert M. W. Travers, *An Inquiry into the Problem of Predicting Achievement.* AFPTRC-TR-54-93. Lackland Air Force Base, Texas: Air Force Personnel and Training Research Center, 1954.

12. John B. Carroll, "The Prediction of Success in Intensive Foreign Language Training," in *Training Research and Education, op. cit.*, pp. 87–136.

ment in complex learning tasks. The model considers variation in both individual differences and instructional variables. The instructional variables are adequacy of instructional presentation and time allowed for learning. The individual-difference variables are general or verbal intelligence (the extent to which the individual will be able to understand or infer appropriate directions and explanations given in the course of instruction), aptitude (the time needed by the individual to learn the task to a specified criterion of achievement), and motivation (the maximum amount of time the individual applies himself to learning the task). Certain simplified relationships between these variables are considered under varying assumptions of conditions of instruction and motivation.

The postulation and examination of such formal relationships of the function of instructional and individual-difference variables can serve to generate the investigation of relationships between entering behavior and subsequent training and achievement. This kind of thinking has to a large extent been fostered by the over-all requirements for the efficient use of manpower in military and industrial training and by the military notions of "personnel systems." The implications of similar integrated approaches for general education are extremely provocative.

The Design of Training

HumRRO.—The Human Resources Research Office is essentially the training research and development arm of the Chief of Army Research and Development and it has been in operation since 1951. In 1963 this organization employed one hundred psychologists (sixty-five Ph.D's) and consisted of a headquarters and seven major laboratories. HumRRO's concepts of the "engineering of training" are reflected in a recent chapter by Meredith P. Crawford, its director.[13] He outlines the following sequence as the principal activities required in the orderly development of a training program:

(1) Analysis of the operational subsystem. This is essentially an analysis of the hardware and human components required by a system. From this information, judgments can be made about the relative contribution that human performance can make to the system with appropriate se-

13. Crawford, *op. cit.*, 301-41.

lection and classification, human engineering of the equipment, and training.

(2) Analysis of the particular job. Out of this analysis of the whole system comes a particular job or jobs which is subjected to detailed task analysis in terms of the inputs to the job from the rest of the system (the stimulus situation which the human must learn to handle) and the outputs that must be made to the system (the responses that the human must produce, e.g., control movements, decisions, and so on).

(3) Specification of knowledge and skills. On the basis of the information assembled in (2), the behavioral processes by which the individual transforms input into output are identified. This step provides an assessment of the probable content of the behavioral repertoire required of the person to be trained.

(4) Determination of training objectives. On the basis of the specification of knowledges and skills required by the job analysis of possible career patterns, the objectives of the training program are specified.

(5) Construction of the training program. This step involves selection and development of the specific subject matter and instructional materials, devices, and procedures to be used in the training course.

(6) Development of measures of job proficiency. A proficiency test of the job as a whole is developed on the basis of the information obtained from step (2). These measures are developed independently of the work accomplished in steps (3), (4) and (5).

(7) Evaluation of the training program. The proficiency test is used to evaluate the training program and its development. This evaluation step supplies information on the adequacy of training and information for future research and development efforts.

Implicit in Crawford's discussion is the notion that the design of a training program is a joint function of subject-matter delineation and administrative-managerial arrangements which permits the use of certain instructional procedures and testing and evaluation. Where does the application of the psychology of learning come in? It is actually part of curriculum specification and managerial arrangements and is not explicitly made apart from these aspects. For example, knowledge of results, if found to facilitate learning in experimental study, is implemented by appropriate administrative arrangements for the testing of appropriate knowledge; a particular hierarchical arrangement of responses based on a discrimination-training sequence used in laboratory studies may suggest a particular subject-matter arrangement or a newly designed training device. It is in this way that psychological knowledge is applied, sometimes on the basis of more or less evidence, but its application is subject to empirical check.

AFPTRC.—The Air Force Personnel and Training Research Center was in operation from 1949 to 1958. In 1956 the organization, directed by Arthur W. Melton, employed approximately 168 psychologists (one hundred Ph.D.'s) and consisted of a headquarters and nine major laboratories plus a network of field units. The work of this large concentration of psychologists is available primarily in the voluminous report series produced by the Center.[14] For the most part, these are reports of research and to a lesser extent of training operations. For example, in 1954, of the 132 major reports published by AFPTRC, 22 related directly to operational problems, 108 reported supporting research, and two were research reviews. Unfortunately, a compendium of the work of the Center is not available as is the work of the World War II Aviation Psychology Program, directed by John C. Flanagan, in the nineteen-volume series published by the U. S. Government Printing Office in 1947–48.

Some idea of the program of AFPTRC is given by the work of its laboratories. The Aircraft Observer Research Laboratory developed training aids and techniques to perfect skills in high-altitude bombing and navigation as well as techniques for the measurement of these skills. Two Pilot Research Laboratories investigated improved training techniques, developed methods for measuring proficiency in flying and techniques for establishing standards of skill. Of special interest was research on the stages of proficiency at which training aids and simulators were optimally effective. The Crew Research Laboratory studied factors in effective team and group interaction both in the field and in the laboratory; this laboratory also investigated morale factors and techniques for the training and measurement of group performance. The Personnel Research Laboratory, primarily concerned with selection and classification, also carried out research and development on the measurement of job knowledge and proficiency. The Skill Components Research Laboratory carried out laboratory studies of the acquisition and retention of motor skills and studied the design and utility of training devices. The Officer Education Research Laboratory was concerned with the education of personnel for command and administrative positions.

14. See footnote 2.

The Training Aids Research Laboratory developed sound films, audio-visual displays, and guides to assist in complex training; in general, this laboratory worked on the development of principles of instruction and the design of instructional media. The Armament Systems Personnel Research Laboratory was concerned with training men in armament equipment, e.g., missile and bombing controls; this laboratory concerned itself with techniques for forecasting training requirements, the development of training principles, techniques of proficiency measurement, analysis and development of training equipment, and the application of systems concepts to training.

Training Research

Taking the AFPTRC program as a significant illustration, one notes that a good proportion of the research performed was reported in the professional literature, primarily in the form of journal articles or in collected volumes of research.[15] These research articles in large measure represent investigations which study independent variables with which the psychologist is familiar from his past training and, since they were accepted by current journal editors, are competitive in terms of quality and acceptable research problems with research published from academic laboratories. What differs very frequently is the task that the experimental subjects perform, e.g., it may be learning code names rather than nonsense syllables, or it may be problem-solving with electronic troubleshooting materials rather than a string problem or card-sorting task. As a result of a general perusal of these publications, the writer has the impression that many of the early articles represented efforts which were beginning steps for psychologists working in a training context. Psychologists applied their standard ways of proceeding and used variables they knew about; they had not yet enough time to learn about the successes of their methods and whether their variables and approaches were significant in a training research situation.

15. *Symposium on Air Force Human Engineering, Personnel, and Training Research* (Edited by Glen Finch and Frank Cameron. Washington: National Academy of Sciences, National Research Council, 1956, 1958); *Symposium on Air Force Human Engineering, Personnel, and Training Research* (Edited by Glen Finch. Washington: National Academy of Sciences, National Research Council, 1960); *Student Response in Programmed Instruction, op. cit.*

However, as time passed, the existence of a research and development group in a training research environment influenced both basic and applied research, the one being shaped by the other because of the nature of the enterprise. The assumption can be made, then, that the initial published work of the psychologists represents things the academic psychologist thought were relevant for training research in one way or another. Later efforts or reflections upon these earlier efforts should represent the psychologist's judgment of how his initial approaches fared and what new directions and new variables seem most significant in making differences in training. From this aspect, perhaps one of the most significant changes in the tone of these articles is an emphasis on the characteristics of task variables and the implications of task characteristics for the effectiveness of different learning variables, a point which will be elaborated later in this chapter.

Another facet of these journal articles is that they generally represent attempts to check out particular hypotheses or values of a variable in order to determine their functional relationships. Obviously this is a legitimate and worthwhile enterprise contributing to psychological knowledge and, oftentimes less directly, to instruction. Less frequent are reports of attempts to produce particular kinds and levels of proficiency in a subject by arrangement of the learning environment, as is done in operant conditioning studies or in the development of programed instructional sequences. It is perhaps this distinction between the hypothesis-testing enterprise as a scientific endeavor and the production of a learning environment and task sequences as an endeavor which is one distinction between a psychology of learning and research leading to a technology of instruction.

Recently, under the sponsorship of the Office of Naval Research, an attempt has been made to review certain areas of military training and training research and to examine their implications for education.[16] Some of the areas reviewed in this volume will be briefly mentioned.

Perceptual motor-skill training.—Extensive programs on motor-skills learning were begun with special vigor after World War II. Much of the impetus for this came from World War II programs

16. *Training Research and Education, op. cit.*

of training research concerned with the training of pilots and of gunners. Motor skills appeared to be an important factor in many military tasks and were emphasized in both selection and training. As a result, motor skills probably received much more attention than in civilian education where verbal skills represent the primary behaviors of concern. Unique in the history of in-service research was the program of the Perceptual and Motor Skills Research Laboratory of AFPTRC, although other motor-skill research was performed and sponsored by other laboratories and other services. A detailed review of much of this research, published between 1945 and 1959, and its implications for further research in the field are presented by Bilodeau and Bilodeau.[17] Exemplary research programs on motor skills where the investigators also kept an eye on training implications are described by Fleishman[18] and Fitts.[19]

Simulators, training aids, and instructional devices.—The military has placed much emphasis on the development of technological aids for instruction. Much effort and money have gone into research and development programs concerned with the design and use of training aids and simulators. These consist of slides, technical manuals, films and TV, teaching machines, and complex system simulators, e.g., aircraft and submarine training simulators. The variety of research, development, and practical use of these technological aids has been described in detail by Lumsdaine.[20] In particular, teaching-machine devices developed in the military, government agencies, and industry have been described by Lumsdaine and Glaser,[21] Bryan

17. Edward A. Bilodeau and Ina McD. Bilodeau, "Motor Skills Learning," in *Annual Review of Psychology*, pp. 243–80. Palo Alto, California: Annual Reviews, Inc., 1961.

18. Edwin A. Fleishman, "The Description and Prediction of Perceptual-Motor Skill Learning," in *Training Research and Education, op. cit.*, 137–75.

19. Paul M. Fitts, "Factors in Complex Skill Training," in *Training Research and Education, op. cit.*, pp. 177–97.

20. A. A. Lumsdaine, "Design of Training Aids and Devices," *Human Factors Methods for System Design*, pp. 217–90 (Pittsburgh: American Institute for Research, 1960); A. A. Lumsdaine, "Experimental Research on Instructional Devices and Materials," in *Training Research and Education, op. cit.*, pp. 247–94; A. A. Lumsdaine, "Instruments and Media of Instruction," in *Handbook of Research on Teaching*, pp. 583–682 (Edited by N. L. Gage. Chicago: Rand McNally Co., 1963).

21. *Teaching Machines and Programmed Learning, op. cit.*

and Nagay,[22] and Holt and Shoemaker.[23] In the present volume, such technological aids are considered by Pressey in chapter xv and Lumsdaine in chapter xvi. A significant aspect of technological aids in the military is the use of simulators and the notion of simulation. A recent analysis and review of simulators has been made by Gagné.[24] Simulation techniques for the analysis of large-scale industrial systems are being employed in modern technological development and might also be applied to the analysis of the large-scale operation of a school system. Simulation has also been developed as a procedure in teacher education. Kersh[25] discusses the development of a device which provides a simulated classroom environment for practice teaching.

The training of electronics maintenance technicians.—Because of its very great importance in modern warfare, much training research and development effort has been undertaken to improve the quality and efficiency of the training of electronics technicians. A summary of this work is reported by Bryan.[26] He considers such issues as the content of school training, advanced training, on-the-job training, and the training of technicians for high-level problem-solving (i.e., trouble-shooting of electronic equipment). The most challenging aspect of electronic training is the trouble-shooting of electronic equipment. This essentially is a diagnostic problem-solving process which is required to detect and analyze the trouble symptom in electronic equipment, investigate its cause, and then prescribe appropriate repair or remedial procedures. This kind of problem-solving has been of interest to experimental psychologists, and this interest is reflected in reviews of problem-solving and thinking.[27] From a review of military studies and his extensive experience

22. G. L. Bryan and J. A. Nagay, "Use in Federal Government Agencies," in *Teaching Machines and Programmed Learning*: II, *Data and Directions, op. cit.*

23. H. O. Holt and H. A. Shoemaker, "Use in Industry," in *Teaching Machines and Programmed Learning*: II, *Data and Directions, op. cit.*

24. Gagné, "Simulators," in *Training Research and Education, op. cit.*, pp. 223–46.

25. B. Y. Kersh, "The Classroom Simulator," *Audiovisual Instruction*, VI (November, 1961), 447–48.

26. Glenn L. Bryan, "The Training of Electronics Maintenance Technicians," in *Training Research and Education, op. cit.*, pp. 295–321.

27. Robert M. Gagné, "Problem Solving and Thinking," in *Annual Review of Psychology*, Vol. X, pp. 147–72. Palo Alto, California: Annual Reviews, Inc., 1959.

in the field, Bryan[28] presents a formal descriptive analysis of trouble-shooting behavior and suggests some of the training problems involved.

Group behavior and multi-man systems.—In military and industrial research, the training has been focused on small working groups (teams) and large-scale organizations. With special reference to the training of groups, reviews have been prepared on team learning and large-system training.[29] In the standard psychological literature on groups, most of the work has been directed at the problems of motivation and organization. Recent work, especially that stimulated by military problems, has directed attention to the mechanics of team training.[30] The importance of appropriate feedback in very large-scale systems training has been discussed by Carter.[31]

Performance assessment.—Major emphasis in military training programs has been placed on the construction of evaluative measures for assessing the outcomes of training, and advances in the methodology of the construction of achievement tests have been more rapid than have been advances in instructional practice. This effort has been stimulated by the need for an answer to the question, "Does training produce the goals that it is established to produce?" This is essentially a question of quality control of the products of the training enterprise. Summaries of the work and thinking on performance measurement are contained in several review articles.[32]

28. Bryan, *op. cit.*

29. R. Boguslaw and E. H. Porter, "Team Functions and Training," in *Psychological Principles in System Development, op. cit.*, pp. 387–416; Launor F. Carter, "Exercising the Executive Decision-making Function in Large Systems," in *Training Research and Education, op. cit.*, pp. 409–27; Murray Glanzer, "Experimental Study of Team Training and Team Functioning," in *Training Research and Education, op. cit.*, pp. 379–407; Murray Glanzer and Robert Glaser, "Techniques for the Study of Group Structure and Behavior: II, Empirical Studies of the Effects of Structure in Small Groups," *Psychological Bulletin,* LVIII (January, 1961), 1–27.

30. Glanzer, *op. cit.*; D. J. Klaus and Robert Glaser, *Increasing Team Proficiency through Training: I, A Program of Research* (Pittsburgh: American Institute for Research, 1960).

31. Carter, *op. cit.*

32. Norman L. Frederiksen, "Proficiency Tests for Training Evaluation," in *Training Research and Education, op. cit.*, pp. 323–46; Robert Glaser and D. J. Klaus, "Proficiency Measurement: Assessing Human Performance," in *Psychological Principles in System Development, op. cit.*, pp. 419–74; Clark L. Wilson, "On-the-Job and Operational Criteria," in *Training Research and Education, op. cit.*, pp. 347–77.

The guiding-principles and relevant-factors approach.—In concluding this section it is necessary to point out that an extremely
prevalent approach by psychologists in practical training is the one
typically found in most educational psychology texts. In them the
authors compile and organize appropriate literature and attempt to
formulate from it a list of principles of learning on which there is
some kind of apparent consensus; also frequently included is a list of
independent variables which psychologists have investigated for
many years as important factors influencing learning. Hilgard,[33] in
a symposium on the psychology of learning basic to military training programs, listed fourteen points which represented his opinion
of relevant empirical knowledge on which he suspected a poll of
learning theorists would find widespread, albeit at times grudging,
agreement. Concerning his list and the relationships between theories
of learning and practical problems of training, Hilgard indicates
that much of the debate over theoretical distinctions, laboratory exi-
gencies, and quantification requirements, while important, has prevented the examination of consensus on relevant research findings.
Glaser[34] takes a similar approach in attempting to discuss factors
relevant to research leading to instructional technology. Other lists
of factors influencing learning efficiency and the conduct of instruction have been presented by Gagné and Bolles,[35] by Glaser,[36] and by
Crawford.[37] A recent survey of learning and industrial training by
McGehee and Thayer[38] presents a detailed listing and discussion of
learning factors and principles.

33. Ernest R. Hilgard, "Theories of Human Learning and Problems of
Training," in *Symposium on Psychology of Learning Basic to Military Training
Problems*, pp. 3–13 (Washington: Department of Defense, Panel on Training
and Training Devices, Committee on Human Resources, Research and Development Board, 1953); Ernest R. Hilgard, *Theories of Learning* (New York: Appleton-Century-Crofts, 1956).

34. Robert Glaser, "Learning and the Technology of Instruction," *Audiovisual
Communication Review*, IX (Supplement IV, 1961), 42–55; Robert Glaser, "Psychology and Instructional Technology," in *Training Research and Education*,
op. cit., pp. 1–30.

35. Gagné and Bolles, *op. cit.*

36. Robert Glaser, "Research and Development Issues in Programed Instruction," in *Perspectives in Programing*. Edited by Robert T. Filep. New York:
Macmillan Co., 1963.

37. Crawford, *op. cit.*

38. William McGehee and P. W. Thayer, *Training in Business and Industry*.
New York: John Wiley & Sons, 1961.

Advocates of this approach profess to summarize principles and rules of thumb for managing the learning process which are derived primarily from laboratory learning research. The principles listed (and "principles" is usually put in quotes) are stated as guides to practices which must be validated in real training and educational situations. This statement is followed by the cautions required because of the differences between laboratory research and real-life education, e.g., type of subject, duration of learning, complexity of the task, and so on. Following this is a statement of the necessity for programatic research to bridge the gap between the science of learning and the management of training and education.

Approaches and Attitudes of Psychologists Working in Military Training and Training Research

This section examines the attitudes and actions of a number of eminent experimental psychologists who have directed training research organizations in the military.

Webb.—While directing training research in the Navy, Webb wrote the following in a letter published in the *American Psychologist:* "Simply stated, I am having a tough time getting research and the market place together. Stated otherwise, can research be used to solve practical problems? Whether these difficulties stem from the nature of things or from my own inadequacies, I, of course, cannot judge." He points out that there are two classical directions for solving a problem, once it is identified: (*a*) go to the laboratory or previous laboratory findings, and (*b*) conduct a situational experiment. The results of laboratory experiments leave the investigator with ". . . broad generalizations drawn from highly specific conditions which will hold true if controls may be introduced to meet those highly specific conditions—which they can't." If experiments are conducted in the field then ". . . you aren't sure where the effect you obtained in the operational context came from, and the conditions were so complex that you couldn't really describe them." Webb indicates that as a result of his experience, he is aware that situationally centered research pays off, for example, work in aviation has saved millions of dollars and many lives. However, he is concerned about an easier translation of laboratory findings to his task of application.[39]

Melton.—As is known, AFPTRC succumbed after nine years for lack of support. Some of the lessons learned in this enterprise have been expressed by Melton in commenting on automated education as follows:

Perhaps I am a "worry wart," but I can see the managers of resources in our society, as well as some starry-eyed educators and psychologists, being carried away by the imaginativeness and insightfulness of the concept of automated education, and forgetting our counsel that contemporary psychology is able to give only first approximations as answers to questions about the processes and programming of human learning which are quite critical in the engineering of education. As a consequence, I can publicly cringe at the thought that millions may well be appropriated for such technological efforts, with the usual 1 per cent, or onetenth of 1 per cent, for fundamental research in psychology in support of the improvement of the technology. Why am I gun shy on this point? Those of you who know the history of psychological research in the Air Force personnel and training effort over the past ten years will understand. In the context of the Personnel and Training Systems of the Air Force, it was recognized about 1950 that a technology was needed, *and feasible,* for anticipating the tasks that human beings would perform in new weapon systems, like the ballistic missile systems, and for specifying, far in advance of even the prototype model, what the specific selection, training, and on-the-job management techniques for the production and maintenance of these human components should be. . . .

After a period of confusion and poor communication, the very simple *idea* of extracting information about human tasks from the *designs* of future weapon systems and using such information to establish the special procedures for selection and training of men to perform those anticipated tasks finally caught on, and was properly recognized as an essential step in the production of an operational weapon-system. Consequently, millions of dollars are now being spent annually by the Air Force in implementing this procedure for defining what is now appropriately called the Personnel Subsystem of each new weapon system. But somewhere along the line a warning of the psychologists who devised this technology was forgotten. Lost somewhere along the line was their warning that the technology that could be supported by contemporary psychological science was primitive—only a first approximation—and that substantial support of certain critical areas of fundamental psychological science should proceed concurrently with the initial implementations of the technology,

39. W. B. Webb, "Applied Research: Variations on a Theme," *American Psychologist,* XII (April, 1957), 225-26.

if the technology were to become reliable and effective. Such support was not only not increased within the Air Force; it was drastically decreased. Now we are witnessing the elaborate employment of a technology by the Air Force, but with the scientific underpinning on starvation rations. One is reminded of the disembodied grin of the Cheshire cat, and the whole affair would be the source of some sardonic humor if the consequences were not so serious for our long-range security, for the viability of the important technology which was introduced into the Air Force, and for our science.

Now, this is not the only case where enthusiasm for a psycho-technology has been coupled with relative apathy for its scientific foundations. I think here again of mental testing, progressive education, guidance, visual education. My concern is that this not be the history of the next ten years in the automation of teaching. . . . It is important to note, however, that psychologists and educators are currently joining forces in thinking about the objectives of education and about the developments in basic knowledge and theory of learning that are necessary to support these objectives. These efforts will come to naught if the resources for the development of basic knowledge do not represent some substantial and continuing proportion of the total resources applied to the application of engineering technology to education.[40]

Travers.—In discussing the relationship of psychological research to educational practice, Travers writes as follows:

Small scale research efforts in separate school systems are hardly likely to have the impact on education that is really needed. The problems of education are probably such that a large-scale programmatic research effort is required to provide the body of knowledge needed to effect educational change and the responsible organization would have to have stability over a period of many years in order for it to come to the point of being productive. The experience provided by the Air Force Personnel and Training Research Center indicates that within a decade such an organization can begin to yield highly significant research findings. The organization would have to be both led and manned by scientists whose status is well-established and most of these would have to come from outside of the educational field. This follows successful research practice in other fields. Engineering problems are typically investigated by teams which include chemists, physicists, mathematicians, and other non-engineering specialists. Such an organization serving the civilian economy

40. A. W. Melton, "Some Comments on 'The Impact of Advancing Technology on Methods of Education' by Dr. Simon Ramo," in *Teaching Machines and Programmed Learning, op. cit.*, pp. 662–63.

might well have a much better opportunity of survival than one serving the military.[41]

Gagné.—The most analytical discussion of the relationship of principles of learning to military training has been presented by Gagné.[42] The question of how scientific knowledge of learning is used to improve training for military tasks is asked. The question is not, "How can a scientific approach be applied to the study of training?" but rather, "How can what is known about learning be put to use in designing maximally effective training procedures?" Gagné lists as best-known psychological principles such things as the importance of practicing a response, reinforcement, distribution of practice, meaningfulness, increasing the distinctiveness of the elements of a task, and response availability. For this list of principles he leans to some extent upon the article by Underwood.[43] The point is made that when one seriously attempts to apply these principles to designing effective training situations, one does not fare particularly well. For example, the importance of practice on a task to be learned sometimes leads one astray when verbal instructions are more effective in improving performance than sheer practice. Sometimes in the application of the principles of learning there is frequently no way to manipulate them in the training situation and, at other times, evidence fails to support the principle. Gagné cautions that the principles are not invalid, but "strikingly inadequate to handle the job of designing effective training situations."[44]

To substantiate this opinion, Gagné discusses the results of training research with respect to the three representative military tasks. (*a*) In teaching a gunnery task, Gagné asserts that the finding of military training research is that practice is not particularly effective. The responses required for the task, turning knobs and moving the gun sight up and down with a handle, are highly familiar ones that need not be learned or that can be learned in every few practice

41. Robert M. W. Travers, "A Study of the Relationship of Psychological Research to Educational Practice," in *Training Research and Education, op. cit.,* p. 556.

42. Robert M. Gagné, "Military Training and Principles of Learning," *American Psychologist,* XVII (February, 1962), 83–91.

43. Benton J. Underwood, "Verbal Learning in the Educative Process," *Harvard Educational Review,* XXIX (Spring, 1959), 107–17.

44. Gagné, "Military Training and Principles of Learning," *op. cit.,* p. 85.

trials. Instruction about what one is to look for in sighting the gun is much more effective in improving performance than practice of these specific motor responses. (b) With respect to a procedural task, it is not practicing the switch-pressing responses which contributes most to learning, but it is learning a list of what needs to be done. (c) In trouble-shooting complex equipment, one cannot identify a single task that needs to be practiced but, rather, what needs to be learned is classes of tasks or generalizations.

It seems that in presenting his case, Gagné takes the definition of response too literally (almost in terms of terminal overt motor repetitive responses) and concludes that there are aspects other than these which are more important in doing a particular job. They include such things as sighting (framing) in the gunnery task, memorizing a list in the procedural task, and learning to generalize or conceptualize in the trouble-shooting task. However, these, too, can be interpreted as manipulable responses, albeit of a different order than the final repetitive motor task. Gagné sometimes ignores concepts that have been applied in producing learning in the psychological laboratory. In pointing out that the enhancement of reinforcement was ineffective in learning the gunnery task, he ignores the fact that the effect of a reinforcing stimulus may be more permanent if its control is gradually withdrawn than if it is withdrawn abruptly. In attempting to apply the notions of discrimination to memorizing a list of procedures by putting distinctive markings on the switches to be used, Gagné considers that the change was made in the task rather than in the conditions of learning. Indeed, in programed instruction, for example, the use of supportive or auxiliary tasks which are different from final tasks facilitates discrimination learning and is quite useful in performing the desired terminal tasks. In his trouble-shooting example, Gagné ignores, to some extent, the established notion of generalization in concept formation which occurs as a result of responses to a variety of instances of a response class. Gage[45] cites an article by Glaser[46] to suggest that learning theory can be reinterpreted in more subtle ways than is indicated by Gagné.

Nevertheless, Gagné's analysis of the apparent inadequacy of

45. N. L. Gage, "Paradigms for Research on Teaching," in *Handbook of Research on Teaching, op. cit.,* p. 136.

46. Glaser, "Learning and the Technology of Instruction," *op. cit.*

merely applying learning principles leads him to the statement of important principles which are required in addition to the more usual ones cited by psychologists. To these principles he attaches such names as: task analysis, intro-task transfer, component task achievement, and the sequencing of tasks.[47] These principles imply the following activities with respect to the management of learning: (1) A task to be learned should be analyzed into component tasks which may be learned in different ways and which require different instructional practices. (2) The successful achievement of the component tasks is required for performance of a final task. (3) The component tasks may have a hierarchical relationship to each other so that successful achievement of one component task is required for successful achievement of the subsequent component task. (4) This suggests that, in designing a training program, the following steps must be taken: "(a) identifying the component tasks of final performance; (b) insuring that each of these component tasks is fully achieved; and (c) arranging the total learning situation in a sequence which will insure optimal mediational effects from one component to another."[48] The message Gagné wishes to transmit is that, faced with the problem of improving training, one should look for much less help from well-known learning principles than from the implications of the techniques of task analysis and component task sequencing. For example, in providing trouble-shooting training that was demonstrably successful in military work, it was the identification of the subordinate tasks involved and their sequencing which was the key to training improvement. Gagné has followed up his notions of task analysis and instructional sequencing by attempting to carry out their implications in general education, namely, mathematics instruction. Student achievement in mathematics is analyzed in terms of hierarchies of knowledge and component task achievement in the course of the acquisition of knowledge.[49]

It seems to this writer that there is an important explanatory factor to Gagné's discussion which is related to the question of why the

47. Following the lead of Miller (see footnote 5).

48. Gagné, "Military Training and Principles of Learning," *op. cit.,* p. 88.

49. Robert M. Gagné, "The Acquisition of Knowledge," *Psychological Review,* LXIX (July, 1962), 355–65; Robert M. Gagné and Noel E. Paradise, "Abilities and Learning Sets in Knowledge Acquisition," *Psychological Monographs,* LXXV, No. 14, 1961.

problem of task analysis has not appeared as a significant factor to the experimenter in the laboratory. In the laboratory an investigator decides upon and constructs an experimental task pertinent to his particular purposes. He has preselected this task to fit his problem and in a sense has analyzed its stimulus and response characteristics so that he can work with it. In the practical training situation, however, when the experimental psychologist attempted to apply his knowledge of the science of learning, he was not in a position to predesign an experimental task or to employ a standard experimental task. He was, on the other hand, faced with the problem of identifying the kind of task and behavior he was working with so that he could proceed to operate in his usual way. He was used to working with specified behavior and needed to do so in the training situation. Gagné's reaction, then, appears to be the result of this necessity for analysis of the task on which one is working; this is a necessity in real life but not required with standard simplified laboratory tasks. Once a complex task is analyzed into component tasks, the question arises about the characteristics of certain subtask arrangements which can facilitate learning. Some ways of learning things are more efficient than others and contribute to different ends, i.e., longer retention, broader generalization, and the like. There is also the truism that some things must be learned before others, and the analysis of even this simple problem of ordering that which is to be learned has not proceeded very far in influencing much of educational practice; for example, the question of "readiness" can be reinterpreted in terms of a hierarchy of component task achievements. In order to state his case, Gagné overemphasizes the nonutility of existing learning principles. However, he frequently talks about their relative contribution to learning, because, indeed, it seems that a synthesis of the implications of task analysis and the application of learning variables, such as reinforcement, discrimination training, and so forth, is what must take place in the future.

Lumsdaine.—A series of research studies relevant to the sequenced reproducible instructional programs presented by films and also relevant to teaching machines and related devices was initiated by Lumsdaine in the Air Force and reported in a recent publication.[50] In general, the program of research was concerned with the experi-

50. Lumsdaine, *Student Response in Programmed Instruction, op. cit.*

mental study of procedures for guiding the responses of learners in order to increase the effectiveness of instruction. The studies paid particular attention to the manipulation of the responses made by the learner and techniques for eliciting and guiding his responses during the course of instruction. The summary of these studies indicates the classes of variables that are considered: (1) Cue factors. This includes the use of prompting and discriminative cues for response guidance and for controlling response through the manipulation of stimulus variables. (2) Transfer factors and "vanishing." This concerns the transfer from conditions of practice to those of actual performance and includes problems of the withdrawal of prompts and mediating transfer from practice to terminal performance situations. (3) Response factors. This concerns questions of the form of response, such as overt versus covert responding; response feedback, e.g., knowledge of results, confirmation and reinforcement; and motivational effects of student response. (4) Organizational and progression factors. Involved here are task organization features, patterns of repetition, and placement of review.

The basic conviction underlying the papers included in this volume is that ". . . an important characteristic of successful instructional theory (and theory-based experimentation) is that it is conceived with particular reference to the role of student response —implicit or explicit—and to the control of stimulus conditions that govern such response."[51] The final chapter by Lumsdaine emphasizes the necessity for research in this context for the development of a "science of instruction" and suggests conceptual and experimental problems in the field of programed instruction in particular (see also chap. xvi by Lumsdaine).

A major implication of this chapter: the synthesis of task analysis and learning variables.—The experiences described immediately above and earlier in this chapter lead to the conclusion that a promising approach to research and development in instructional technology is a synthesis of the concepts of task analysis and task sequencing, on the one hand, and instructional variables for guiding the learner's response on the other. An example of a study which approaches a synthesis of these two ingredients is one reported by

51. *Ibid.,* p. 471.

Wulff and Emeson.[52] Their approach and methodology points a direction for future work in instructional research and development. Further illustration of this dual concern with task characteristics and learning variables is a series of studies by Sheffield, Maccoby, and collaborators[53] and the studies carried out by Stolurow and associates.[54] The work of Gilbert, developed to a large extent with reference to practical job situations, is directly concerned with the co-ordination of task characteristics, the behavioral properties of classes of tasks, and relevant instructional techniques.[55]

The Logistics of Integrating Research, Development, and Practice

When psychologists have committed themselves to research and development in a military or industrial setting, it is of interest to examine the kind of organizational and functional entities they have sought to establish to implement the process of changing instructional practices. Several fundamental notions underlying successful educational innovation based upon scientific research appear to have been recognized by those attempting to implement educational change. These notions are:

(1) A rejection of the assumption that teaching practices will change if teachers are shown by research that their teaching can be

52. J. Jepson Wulff and David L. Emeson, "The Relationship between 'What Is Learned' and 'How It's Taught,' " in *Student Response in Programmed Instruction, op. cit.*, pp. 457–70.

53. Nathan Maccoby and Fred D. Sheffield, "Combining Practice with Demonstration in Teaching Complex Sequences: Summary and Interpretation," in *Student Response in Programmed Instruction, op. cit.*, pp. 77–85; Garry J. Margolius, Fred D. Sheffield, and Nathan Maccoby, "Timing of Demonstration and Overt Practice as a Function of Task Organization," in *Student Response in Programmed Instruction, op. cit.*, pp. 101–5.

54. Marvin H. Detambel and Lawrence M. Stolurow, "Stimulus Sequence and Concept Learning," *Journal of Experimental Psychology*, LI (January, 1956), 34–40; Lawrence M. Stolurow, "The Utilization of Class-descriptive Cues in the Learning of Technical Information—Studies in Task Engineering," in *Symposium on Air Force Human Engineering, Personnel, and Training Research* (1956), pp. 248–66; Lawrence M. Stolurow, Thomas F. Hodgson, and John Silva, "Transfer and Retroaction Effects of 'Association Reversal' and 'Familiarization' Training in Trouble Shooting," *Psychological Monographs*, LXX, No. 12, Whole No. 419 (Washington: American Psychological Association).

55. T. F. Gilbert, "Mathetics: The Technology of Education," *Journal of Mathetics*, I (January, 1962), 7–73; "Mathetics, II, The Design of Teaching Exercises," *Journal of Mathetics*, I (April, 1962), 7–56.

more efficient; and recognition of the complementary assumption that the behavior of the instructor is the aspect of an instructional system that is least amenable to change and innovation.

(2) Recognition that there exists no agency charged with the practical necessity for making technological applications to instruction on the basis of available knowledge and techniques. The absence of such a technological entity is a general attribute of our society. While for example, medical and engineering schools and institutes exist as agencies functioning between fundamental research and professional practice, no counterpart has been available for the development of a technology relevant to educational practice. A historical and cultural analysis of some reasons for this state of affairs has been cogently presented by Travers.[56]

(3) As a consequence of (1) and (2), agencies need to be established to serve as technological centers committed to the production of tangible tools, materials, and methods that can be used to produce changes in instructional practices and to monitor their use and integration into an educational system. These agencies should function over the range of activities from fundamental research to the development and introduction of instructional innovation. Under the dictates of practical pressures and persuasive personalities, an organization may swing primarily to one side or the other of the research and development (R & D) continuum. However, in the absence of a broad base of research findings waiting to be implemented, such an agency can contribute best to the development of psychological science and to educational practice by setting up a situation in which each aspect can fruitfully interact with and feed back to the other.

An organization in support of a training system.—Vallance and Crawford[57] and Crawford[58] describe the philosophy and functional organization of the Army's Human Resources Research Office, which has established a formal pattern for training research and development to assist a large training system. These authors describe

56. Travers, "A Study of the Relationship of Psychological Research to Educational Practice," *op. cit.*

57. Theodore R. Vallence and Meredith P. Crawford, "Identifying Training Needs and Translating Them into Research Requirements," in *Training Research and Education, op. cit.*, pp. 497–523.

58. Crawford, *op. cit.*

how training problems of a using agency are translated into the content of training research. Four conditions are listed as necessary for the conduct of training research in a practical operating system. These are the following: (*a*) *A problem-posing agency* (an agency that has and can pose a problem whose solution would result in increased proficiency of human performance on the job, or increased efficiency of training). (*b*) *An R & D facility* (an agency that can perform the required research and development activities). (*c*) *A logistical support agency* (an agency that can support the R & D activities with funds, matériel, and nonresearch manpower). (*d*) *An implementing agency* (an agency that can act to implement a successful solution to the problem initially proposed). HumRRO is described as a practical example of an organization which is conducted under these conditions.

A hypothesized structure for a co-ordinated research and development endeavor.—Gilbert[59] has described a pattern for research and development in education based upon the research and development pattern of an industrial organization. In classifying the separate and independent functions in an R & D organization, it is assumed that the various skills required can be exemplified by observing the course of the development of a scientific product, whether it be a transistor or a new method of teaching arithmetic. The components of such an organization are the following:

(1) *Exploratory research.* This is the function that the scientist calls theoretical, basic research; it is characterized by questioning attitudes and relative independence with respect to the application or further development of existing procedures or knowledge. In a co-ordinated research and development setting, the exploratory research operation serves as a channel which is in contact with significant developments in science, and may be the determining factor in whether or not exploratory scientists work on problems relevant to practical innovation.

(2) *Fundamental development.* This research function, fundamental development, gives necessary continuity to carrying knowledge from theory to practice. Its work consists of the laboratory investigation of variables potentially relevant to the findings and discoveries made in exploratory investigations. For example, following

59. Thomas F. Gilbert, "A Structure for a Coordinated Research and Development Laboratory," in *Training Research and Education, op. cit.*, pp. 559–78.

the development of transistor theory, much experimental work was required to understand the properties of materials relevant to the construction of a transistor. The fundamental development function results in much productive, scientific research and can be a very fruitful stage in a field of science. It is, however, not the responsibility of fundamental development to produce a product such as a transistor but, rather, to produce the further knowledge necessary for its production.

(3) *Specific development.* When new principles and techniques in a science are discovered and the relevant variables described, the next task is the development of prototype models of the engineered products and procedures made possible by this scientific knowledge. For example, after Bell Telephone scientists had created the theory of the transistor and established relevant knowledge about it, a transistor still had to be produced. This involved the building of a model utilizing the available knowledge with an eye toward future field use. The construction of this model serves as a test of the utility of the preceding research and also feeds problems back to the more basic laboratory. In this stage the development of a prototype model involves much laboratory experimentation and is still not ready for more general use.

With respect to the specific development function, Gilbert writes as follows:

Whereas the laboratory of more fundamental research represents the natural world in highly stylized and abstract ways, the specific development laboratory may represent this world in more contemporaneous detail; for example, it may be designed as a model classroom or clinic. It must, however, have some access to the more stylized laboratory for the simple reason that specific development must go on regardless of the stage of fundamental development. In producing a program to teach arithmetic, the specific development people will need to make decisions concerning behavior about which there is no reliable research knowledge. Rather crudely fashioned experimentation can provide some practical answers to pressing questions, permitting the program to continue. Naturally, the value of coordinated research is that specific development has easy access to the fundamental laboratory personnel who should be able to supply information if it exists—and further, the specific development program is simultaneously providing problems to the fundamental laboratory.[60]

60. *Ibid.*, pp. 574–75.

(4) *Design and proving.* When a transistor or a teaching machine for arithmetic has been developed into a working prototype model, it is not yet ready for introduction into field communication systems or classrooms. The prototype model must undergo many detailed modifications before it becomes a practically designed device. The design and proving function, in addition to producing a consumable product, is also charged with engineering testing and with demonstrating the effectiveness of the product under a wide sample of realistic field conditions. Such field testing involves the development of criterion standards on the basis of which the performance of a product can be evaluated. Again the field tests by design and proving engineers can provide many problems which must be fed back to the exploratory and developmental scientist.

(5) *Training and follow-through.* The research organization should not yet detach itself from the enterprise, once an efficient method or product has been successfully engineered and installed in the field. Careful monitoring of the use of the new method in different situations is quite necessary for the successful translation of scientific findings into practical accomplishments. In the course of accomplishing this phase, the research organization receives much information about practical field usage, which dictates further design refinement and indicates further problems for experiment. The R & D organization must also be required at this time to provide training for key administrators and teachers who will be using the new development. Special training groups can insure the proper training of field personnel and can also serve as a channel through which information is fed back to the R & D staff. Industry has very frequently employed extensive groups of technical field representatives who accomplish this function for newly installed hardware equipment.

A major implication of this chapter: centers for educational research and development.—The pattern of military training research described in this chapter and the pattern of successful research and development in industry suggest that some adaptation of functional arrangements like those proposed by Gilbert for co-ordinated R & D centers seems to represent an important lesson that education can learn from industry and the military. Such organizations would undertake to incorporate the findings of science into educational practice and to permit the requirements of educational practice to influence the work of science. Left alone, the experience in education to date indicates that the progress of behavioral science does not insure systematic and fruitful interplay between basic knowledge, applied research, and subsequent technology. Unless someone or some organization specifically works at it, there seems little reason to expect direct transfer of laboratory findings and direct application of theoretical findings to educational practice.

The establishment of research-based, technologically oriented centers would be a significant undertaking for the advancement of educational practice.[61] Major concern would be the development of prototype model instructional systems which sample the educational range. These models would grow out of and feed back into behavioral science and would be the result of collaboration between the research laboratory and on-going educational practice. Behavioral scientists, scientists and subject-matter scholars, and educators would produce research and development products in the same way Cape Canaveral produces a workable booster. At times the researcher would ask for a practical test, and at times the engineer must inquire about basic knowledge. Practicing educators would work with such centers to bring innovations into daily practice; researchers would bring findings from their laboratories to the center and take problems for behavior theory back to their laboratories.

Involved in this process is the development of a theory of instruction which is fundamental to specifiable teaching practices. Modification of educational programs based upon research and dictated by carefully established educational objectives can improve the efficiency and effectiveness of instruction and correct its underlying scientific basis. A two-way process is set up in which the science of behavior is enriched and the technology of teaching is developed.

61. Robert Glaser, "Research and Development Issues in Programmed Instruction," in *Perspectives in Programing*. Edited by Robert T. Filep. New York: Macmillan Co., 1963 (in press).

CHAPTER VIII

The Teacher's Role in the Motivation of the Learner

PAULINE S. SEARS and ERNEST R. HILGARD

The significance of motivation for learning is usually assumed without question. On the one hand, the promise of reward or the threat of punishment provides means by which the teacher can keep the pupil at work; on the other hand, interest, curiosity, and self-selected goals keep the learner at work without pressure from the teacher. The teacher has a choice between using specific goads or enlisting self-activating motives, or perhaps employing some combination of these. The considerations that bear on what can or should be done are the concern of this chapter.

Motivation in Learning Theory

The straightforward relationship between motivation and learning is not supported by experimental studies of learning as these are carried out and described by psychologists. One obstacle to experimentation is the uncertain distinction between learning and performance as they relate to motivation: It may be that learning (habit formation) arises through simple contiguous association, independent of motivation, while motivation affects the utilization of habit, that is, performance. For purposes, such as those of instruction, the distinction between learning and performance becomes somewhat less important, since what keeps the pupil performing is also likely to keep him learning. Still, if the distinction is important in theory it may also have some importance in practice. For example, some relatively low-pressure learning, such as browsing in a library, may be quite important, even though it goes on at a low level of motivation. When motivation is aroused, the results of this browsing may be capitalized on, thus providing an illustration in practice of the distinction that the experimentalists make in theory.

There is considerable turmoil within learning theory at the present time, as other chapters of this yearbook indicate. The once dominant need-drive-incentive theory, interpreting reinforcement as drive-reduction, has been undergoing searching re-examination. The drives usually studied (hunger, thirst, pain) were always treated as aversive drives, from which relief was sought; now the "neglected drives" of curiosity, manipulation, activity, and achievement, which emphasize the positive side of something sought rather than the negative of something to be escaped, have come to the fore.[1]

Secondary reinforcements, that is reinforcing situations supposed to have been derived from primary ones based on primitive drives, turn out not always to be secondary at all, and their properties are quite complex. Lawrence and Festinger[2] have shown in a series of provocative experiments that small or intermittent rewards, if they are sufficient to keep an organism at the task, tend to yield responses more resistant to extinction than large and regular rewards; they attribute this to the "extra attractions" that have to be adduced to justify the amount of work expended for the slight reward obtained.

The drive theory itself has been subjected to criticism by those who see learning becoming attached to cue-stimuli, whether these cues are internal or external.[3] Thus we do not need a "doorbell-answering-drive" to make us respond to a ringing doorbell: the ringing bell is both cue and drive.

The literature on motivation has been summarized in a large number of recent books, many of which have little to say about human motivation. One of the broader studies is that of Rethlingshafer,[4] which includes animal studies but is more particularly concerned with human motives.

1. Ernest R. Hilgard, "Motivation in Learning Theory," in *Psychology: A Study of a Science*, Vol. V. Edited by S. Koch. New York: McGraw-Hill Book Co., 1963.

2. Douglas H. Lawrence and Leon Festinger, *Deterrents and Reinforcement: The Psychology of Insufficient Reward*. Stanford, California: Stanford University Press, 1962.

3. For example, see William K. Estes, "Stimulus Response Theory of Drive," in *Nebraska Symposium on Motivation*, pp. 114–68 (Edited by Marshall R. Jones. Lincoln, Nebraska: University of Nebraska Press, 1958); and Evan R. Keislar, "A Descriptive Approach to Classroom Motivation," *Journal of Teacher Education*, XI (June, 1960), 310–15.

4. Dorothy Rethlingshafer, *Motivation as Related to Personality*. New York: McGraw-Hill Book Co., 1963.

Despite the uncertainty about the precise relationship between motivation and learning, the general importance of motivation in relation to the learner's absorption in his task, his resistance to distraction, his favorable attitudes toward school, can scarcely be denied. Thus, some problems of detail (e.g., that excessive motivation may in some cases hinder learning) need not confuse us or prevent our paying confident attention to motivation as important in classroom learning.

Motives Which Teachers Can Utilize or Arouse

A distinction has to be made between a motivational disposition and an aroused motive. A motivational disposition is a relatively enduring tendency to be prone to certain forms of motivational arousal, although at any one time that motive may be dormant. Thus, a person might be characterized as having a voracious appetite, which means that he is easily aroused by food; yet at any one time he may be satiated. Hunger is an aroused motive; the enduring characteristic of having a good appetite is a motivational disposition. In the same way some children are easily aroused to aggression, easily become dependent, or anxious. When so characterized, their motivational dispositions are being described.

SOCIAL MOTIVES: WARMTH AND NURTURANCE

Social motives have to do with one's relationships to other people. The desire to affiliate with others is one class of dependable human motivational dispositions found in parent-child relations, friendships, and as an important aspect of sex and marriage. Because the teacher is an adult, the affiliative motive often takes the form of dependency, that is, the child is the welcome recipient of the warmth and nurturance of the adult. There is evidence that such warmth and nurturance clearly relate to performances by young children on concept formation, memory, and maze performance, and affect the imitation of irrelevant behavior performed by adults. A nurturant adult, who then withdraws that nurturance, leads the child to make great efforts to restore the warm interaction. Most of the experimental evidence comes from tests made over short periods of time, and it would be valuable to know how these relationships endure through time.

These conclusions are supported by the studies of Hartup,[5] Rosenblith,[6] Bandura and Huston,[7] Gewirtz,[8] and Gewirtz and Baer.[9]

The investigations just mentioned are chiefly laboratory-type studies designed to examine the effect of manipulation of nurturant variables upon child behavior. That their conclusions have implications for the classroom can be documented by studies of teacher warmth and pupil behavior. For example, Cogan[10] found that warm and considerate teachers got an unusual amount of original poetry and art from their high-school students. Reed[11] found that teachers higher in warmth favorably affected pupils' interest in science. He found that the utilization of intrinsic interest by the teacher and the teacher's personal warmth were highly correlated; this would seem to justify some emphasis upon warmth of personality in the selection of teachers who are to be trained to make use of pupils' intrinsic motivation.

EGO-INTEGRATIVE MOTIVES: THE ACHIEVEMENT MOTIVE

A group of motives that serve to maintain self-confidence and self-esteem have sometimes been referred to as ego-integrative motives. These have been variously characterized as motives of self-actualiza-

5. Willard W. Hartup, "Nurturance and Nurturance-Withdrawal in Relation to the Dependency Behavior of Preschool Children," *Child Development*, XXIX June, 1958), 191–203.

6. Judy F. Rosenblith, "Learning by Imitation in Kindergarten Children," *Child Development*, XXX (1959), 69–80.

7. Albert Bandura and Aletha C. Huston, "Identification as a Process of Incidental Learning," *Journal of Abnormal and Social Psychology*, LXIII (1961), 311–18.

8. Jacob L. Gewirtz, "A Program of Research on the Dimensions and Antecedents of Emotional Dependence," *Child Development*, XXVII (1956), 206–21.

9. Jacob L. Gewirtz and Donald M. Baer, "The Effect of Brief Social Deprivation on Behaviors for a Social Reinforcer," *Journal of Abnormal and Social Psychology*, LVI (1958), 49–56; Jacob L. Gewirtz and Donald M. Baer, "Deprivation and Satiation of Social Reinforcers as Drive Conditions," *Journal of Abnormal and Social Psychology*, LVII (1958), 165–72; Jacob L. Gewirtz, Donald M. Baer, and Chaya H. Roth, "A Note on the Similar Effects of Low Social Deprivation on Young Children's Behavior," *Child Development*, XXIX (1958), 149–52.

10. Morris L. Cogan, "The Behavior of Teachers and the Productive Behavior of Their Pupils," *Journal of Experimental Education*, XXVII (December, 1958), 89–124.

11. Horace B. Reed, "Implications for Science Education of a Teacher Competence Research," *Science Education*, XLVI (December, 1962), 473–86.

tion[12] or of competence.[13] The achievement motive may be taken as a convenient representative of this group of motives, for it has been the subject of numerous investigations.

Our society is achievement-oriented, and it is not surprising that the desire to meet standards of excellence motivates some students. Any such motivational disposition is, however, quite complex, and without some clarification we confuse motives of social competition (the desire for prestige or power) with those of meeting standards of excellence in a skill or in scientific or artistic production. The earlier studies on level of aspiration, concerned more with aroused motives, have been supplemented by studies of persistent achievement motives, initiated by McClelland and his associates,[14] and since carried on by many others.[15]

Because the achievement motive is so obviously related to classroom behavior, we shall return to it in other contexts.

CURIOSITY AND OTHER COGNITIVE MOTIVES

Among the "neglected drives" that have more lately come to prominence we may recognize a group that can be called cognitive because they are concerned with "knowing" the environment or the relationships among things and ideas. Pavlov long ago recognized what he called a "What-is-it reflex," by which he referred to curiosity in animals. The exploratory motives have been reintroduced by Harlow;[16] Berlyne[17] has brought out his own work and that of others in book form. This group of motives also includes manipula-

12. A. H. Maslow, *Motivation and Personality*. New York: Harper & Bros., 1954.

13. R. W. White, "Motivation Reconsidered: The Concept of Competence," *Psychological Review*, LXVI (1959), 297–333.

14. David C. McClelland, John W. Atkinson, Russell A. Clark, and Edgar L. Lowell, *The Achievement Motive*. New York: Appleton-Century-Crofts, 1953.

15. For example, *Motives in Fantasy, Action, and Society* (Edited by John W. Atkinson. Princeton, New Jersey: Van Nostrand Co., 1958); and V. J. Crandall, "Achievement," in *Child Psychology*, pp. 416–59 (Sixty-second Yearbook of the National Society for the Study of Education, Part I. Edited by Harold W. Stevenson. Chicago: Distributed by University of Chicago Press, 1963).

16. H. F. Harlow, Learning and Satiation of Response in Intrinsically Motivated Complex Puzzle Performance by Monkeys," *Journal of Comparative and Physiological Psychology*, XLIII (1950), 289–94.

17. D. E. Berlyne, *Conflict, Arousal, and Curiosity*. New York: McGraw-Hill Book Co., 1960.

tive motives[18] and activity motives.[19] These are related to what in the past have been called *intrinsic* motives, that is, motives that reside in the task itself rather than external to it (i.e., *extrinsic* motives, such as rewards or prizes).

These motives, too, are so important in school learning that further attention will be paid to them. All of these motives—social, ego-integrative, and cognitive—are open to manipulation in one way or another by the teacher. We turn now to how this may be done and what consequences can be expected.

The School Environment and Instructional Procedures as They Bear upon Motivation

The general atmosphere of the school may determine which motives are aroused and, hence, which children will profit most from the school. This follows if some children respond more to one kind of motivation than to another; if all are to be served, some flexibility is essential. Within the general atmosphere the particular instructional methods and emphases also affect the utilization of motivational potential for learning (see chap xi).

THE SCHOOL ENVIRONMENT AND ATMOSPHERE

It is well known that the socioeconomic backgrounds of the pupils affect their school motivation, particularly achievement motivation. This is well attested in numerous studies of subcultures within America, such as those of Rosen[20] and Strodtbeck.[21] To the extent that school success (and continuing in school) is associated with higher occupational level, vocational aspiration can often be taken as a measure of achievement motivation. While the father's occupation has little relation to school success in the early grades, by the time the pupil reaches junior high school, his achievement is likely

18. H. F. Harlow and G. E. McClearn, "Object Discrimination Learned by Monkeys on the Basis of Manipulation Motives," *Journal of Comparative and Physiological Psychology*, XLVII (1954), 73–76.

19. W. F. Hill, "Activity as an Autonomous Drive," *Journal of Comparative and Physiological Psychology*, XLIX (1956), 15–19.

20. Bernard C. Rosen, "Race, Ethnicity, and the Achievement Syndrome," *American Sociological Review*, XXIV (1959), 47–60.

21. Fred L. Strodtbeck, "Family Interaction, Values, and Achievement," in *Talent and Society: New Perspectives in the Identification of Talent.* Edited by David C. McClelland *et al.* Princeton, New Jersey: D. Van Nostrand Co., 1958.

to be more related to his father's occupation than to his intelligence level.[22] These facts need to be recognized by the teacher; the inevitability of poor motivation on the part of those from lower occupational groups need not be accepted, but the need for special motivational efforts is obvious.

Let us suppose that a school wishes to stress problem-solving and creativity, in line with the current emphasis upon cognitive motives. How, then, can an atmosphere be created in which such motives will be aroused? The question has been studied by Shaftel, Crabtree, and Rushworth,[23] who point out that the teacher in dealing with the young child must do the following things: (a) make sure that the emotional climate of the classroom is suitable for the development of a healthy self-concept, (b) evoke problems when they are not immediately apparent to the children, (c) stimulate a problem-solving climate, which involves the process of search, rather than focusing on one right answer, and (d) plan a curriculum which stimulates problem-solving, by the use of experience units, construction activities, science experiments, group work, dramatic play, and role-playing.

A book by Taba[24] goes into specifics on the development of curricula and teaching methods which will release cognition and serve to satisfy cognitive needs. She makes use of some of the reflections about intelligence and experience recounted by Hunt,[25] and some of the observations of Piaget.[26] (The new interest in Piaget is evidenced in many places; a very able summary of his work has appeared.[27])

The old concept of ability grouping, as simplifying the task of the

22. Joseph A. Kahl, *The American Class Structure*. New York: Rinehart & Co., 1957.

23. Fannie R. Shaftel, Charlotte Crabtree, and Vivian Rushworth, "Problem-solving in the Elementary School," in *Problems-approach in the Social Studies*, pp. 25–47. Edited by Richard E. Gross. Washington: National Education Assn., 1960.

24. Hilda Taba, *Curriculum Development: Theory and Practice*. New York: Harcourt, Brace & World, 1962.

25. J. McV. Hunt, *Intelligence and Experience*. New York: Ronald Press, 1961.

26. Jean Piaget, *The Psychology of Intelligence* (London: Routledge & Kegan Paul, 1950); Jean Piaget, *The Origins of Intelligence in Children* (Translated by Margaret Cook. New York: International University Press, 1952).

27. John H. Flavell, *The Developmental Psychology of Jean Piaget*. Princeton, New Jersey: D. Van Nostrand Co., 1963.

teacher, has been examined in a new light by Thelen.[28] He proposes that some teachers find given students, selected on the basis of the teacher's purposes, more "teachable" than others. When pupils are grouped in accordance with this criterion, the teacher tends to be more satisfied with his class, to like the pupils better, and to give them higher grades. The pupils, in turn, tend to be more orderly and more manageable, more co-operative, and more satisfied with the activities. They like each other better, and the class appears to be more cohesive than classes not selected on this basis. The achievement gains in these classes depended on the purposes of the teacher. When achievement was central among the teacher's purposes, these teachable groups did better. For some teachers achievement was not a central goal; their students did not do as well by achievement criteria.

ACTIVITIES CAPITALIZING ON COGNITIVE MOTIVATION

It is difficult to unravel those aspects of instruction that should be called motivational from those that are merely successful for whatever reason. It can be assumed that a kind of program that leads to spontaneous effort, to absorption in learning, and to results that yield the self-esteem that comes from reaching goals that are self-set by the learner must be well-grounded in appropriate motivation. In part, these results come about without direct concern for motivation through a kind of contagion of interest when problems are well set up, so that search leads to creative answers. Much of modern curriculum-planning concerns itself with the structure of knowledge and with the kind of thinking that is divergent rather than convergent; when conditions are appropriate, motivation appears to take care of itself.

Thus, major curricular studies in specific fields, such as the Biological Sciences Study Group[29] and the Physical Sciences Study Group,[30] try to get the student to learn not only content but also the

28. Herbert A. Thelen, "Development of Educational Methods for Different Types of Students." Chicago: Department of Education, University of Chicago, 1960 (duplicated).

29. Bentley Glass, "Renascent Biology: A Report on the AIBS Biological Curriculum Study," *School Review*, LXX (Spring, 1962), 16–43.

30. Gilbert C. Finlay, "The Physical Science Study Committee," *School Review*, LXX (Spring, 1962), 63–81.

strategy and approaches of the scientist. In so doing, it is anticipated that as a by-product the student will wish to adopt a pattern of behavior conducive to productive thinking.

Suchman[31] has developed a program for training in inquiry skills with reference to science instruction. He conceives that some dissonance is necessary for development of such skills: a puzzling problem, a lack of structure. However, induction of relational constructs or discovery depends on existing conceptual systems in the child. Hunt[32] has suggested that controlling intrinsic motivation is a matter of providing an organism with circumstances that provide a proper level of incongruity with the residues of previous encounters with such circumstances that the organism has stored in his memory—the "problem of the match" between incoming information and that already stored.

Some experiments have been directed specifically to the problem of the conditions under which new ideas are freely developed. Torrance[33] divided all pupils in a university experimental school from the first to the sixth grade into four experimental groups at each grade level. Four conditions were created by two conditions of training and two sets of verbal instructions regarding output. The training conditions consisted in teaching two groups the principles for developing new ideas as suggested by Osborn,[34] while the other two groups, not taught any principles, were told that they would receive prizes for the best performance. The two sets of verbal instructions, combined with the two training conditions, were, first, a motivation to produce as many ideas as possible; second, a motivation to produce clever, original, and unusual ideas. In general, the results were in the expected direction: the special training in principles produced desired results beyond those produced by the promise of prizes, and the specific instructions to produce clever and unusual responses yielded more of them than the request for mere quantity of ideas. However, this was a short-range experiment and

31. J. Richard Suchman, "Inquiry Training: Building Skills for Autonomous Discovery," *Merrill Palmer Quarterly*, VII (1961), 147–69.

32. Hunt, *op. cit.*

33. *Guiding Creative Talent*. Edited by E. Paul Torrance. Englewood Cliffs, New Jersey: Prentice-Hall, Inc., 1962.

34. Alex F. Osborn, *Applied Imagination: Principles and Procedures of Creative Thinking*. New York: Charles Scribner's Sons, 1957.

leaves unanswered the question: Would a series or pattern of exercises or training produce a permanent change in thinking abilities or cognitive style of a student?

How a teacher can produce divergent rather than convergent thinking is well illustrated by some studies by Gallagher.[35] There appears to be a correspondence between the sorts of statements the teacher makes and those the students make, as these are studied at the junior high school level. Thus, the profile of divergent ideas produced by the students corresponds rather closely to the pattern set by the teacher. In those sessions during which the teacher asks for more divergent production, the percentages of student responses in this direction are correspondingly high. Only a slight increase in the teacher's percentage of divergent questions brings forth a large increase in divergent production by the student. A single question, such as "What would have happened were the United States colonized from the west coast to the east instead of vice versa?" can bring forth as many as 15 or 20 responses, each related to a divergent idea. This illustration points again to the close relationship between content and motivation: The motivation here is to keep curiosity alive, and the only motivational device needed is to ask the right questions, and not to stifle curiosity by sticking too closely to facts that are to be memorized.

The introduction of mechanical aids to instruction, such as audiovisual aids and teaching machines, raises interesting motivational questions. Part of the appeal of the teaching machine is to the manipulative motives, and at the least an active process is substituted for a passive one. Smedslund[36] analyzes the orienting response, the overt response, and the reinforcement, and decides that the teaching machine relies entirely on extrinsic motivation. His analysis is, however, incomplete, for the program of a teaching machine need by no means be cut-and-dried, and sustained only by the reward of "right." A well-designed teaching program brings out cognitive motivation, and provides the intrinsic satisfactions that come with competence. At least the learner knows that he is learning, a result, alas, that is

35. *A Report on a Conference of Research on Gifted Children.* Edited by James J. Gallagher. Washington: U.S. Department of Health, Education, and Welfare, U.S. Office of Education, Cooperative Research Branch, 1963.

36. J. Smedslund, personal communication, 1961.

often not yielded for some pupils in the same classrooms. The chief criticism of too general reliance on teaching machines is that the learning process is essentially sedentary and isolated, even though the learner is active in finding his way through the program. Much of creative search involves moving about and active interchange with others (see chaps. xv and xvi).

OBSERVED TEACHER INTERACTION WITH CHILDREN

Teacher behavior has such a strong effect upon pupil motivation that it is worthwhile to review some of the observational studies that show how this comes about. For purposes of this review, these interactions will be grouped under three topics: (*a*) *affective* interaction, in which emotional-attitudinal variables, those most often considered in connection with positive mental health, will be in the foreground; (*b*) *evaluative* interaction, in which the teacher judges and criticizes rewards, and punishes; and (*c*) *cognitive* interaction in which emphasis is essentially nonaffective and nonevaluative of achievement but encourages problem-solving, intellectual ferment, originality, and creativity.

Affective interaction between teacher and pupils.—The teacher's responsibility for maintaining discipline in the classroom brings to the fore the affective consequences of various rewarding and punishing techniques, though these are by no means the only sources of affective influence of teachers upon students. Other aspects include the general warmth of the atmosphere that is created, the tolerance of some release of feeling on the part of the child, the protection of the individual egos, the satisfaction of individual needs. The techniques of control are, however, readily open to observation, and a number of studies have been directed toward them.

In an experiment in regular classrooms with eighth- and ninth-grade children, Kounin, Gump, and Ryan[37] studied the effects of three "desist techniques." Under one condition the teacher was punitive and intense. When a pretrained male student got up while slides were being shown and sharpened his pencil the teacher stalked toward him, saying, "Hey you, who do you think you are?" in a firm, irritated voice; put her arm on his shoulders in a gesture of pushing him into his seat and said, "Now sit down! If you ever do that again,

37. Jacob S. Kounin, Paul V. Gump, and James J. Ryan, "Explorations in Classroom Management," *Journal of Teacher Education*, XII (June, 1961), 235–46.

I'll really make trouble for you."[38] A second condition involved a matter-of-fact reprimand—i.e., "Don't do that again. Please sit down in your seat now." Under the third condition the teacher indicated her awareness of the behavior but did nothing about it. When the effects on the audience children were compared under the three conditions, the punitive technique was found to result in "the subjects' rating the *deviancy* as 'most serious,' the degree of *interference* with attention to the task as 'greatest,' the *teacher* as 'making too much of an issue' over the event, the experience 'most discomforting,' and the *teacher* 'best able to maintain order in a class of tough kids.' "[39] The simple reprimand resulted in the students reporting the highest ratings for teacher fairness and paying more attention to the lesson after witnessing the event. Under the "ignoring" condition, pupils rated the teacher highest in her liking for children but thought the misbehavior most likely to recur.

In another study,[40] three pairs of punitive versus nonpunitive first-grade teachers were selected from three elementary schools. The 174 children in these teachers' classrooms were individually interviewed about what they thought was "the worst thing to do in school" and were asked for their explanations of why these misconducts were bad. Regarding their responses as expressions of their preoccupations, it was concluded that children who have punitive teachers, as compared with children who have nonpunitive teachers, manifest more aggression in their misconducts; are more unsettled and conflicted about misconduct in school; are less concerned with learning and school-unique values; and show some, but not consistent, indication of a reduction in rationality pertaining to school misconduct. A theory that children with punitive teachers develop less trust of school than do children with nonpunitive teachers was also presented to explain some of the findings.

Some hypotheses concerning the types of social power that are exercised in classrooms were tested in a correlational study by Rosenfeld and Zander.[41] Among other findings were the following:

38. *Ibid.*, p. 237. 39. *Ibid.*

40. Jacob S. Kounin and Paul V. Gump, "The Comparative Influence of Punitive and Nonpunitive Teachers upon Children's Concepts of School Misconduct," *Journal of Educational Psychology*, LII (February, 1961), 44–49.

41. Howard Rosenfeld and Alvin Zander, "The Influence of Teachers on Aspirations of Students," *Journal of Educational Psychology*, LII (February, 1961), 1–11.

1. Two forms of coercion by teachers are discriminated by students: disapproval of inadequate performance, and disapproval when the performance is as good as the student feels he can do. The first type has little effect on future aspiration or performance, while the second has a deleterious effect on both aspiration and future performance.

2. Two forms of reward are also discriminated by students. When rewards are showered indiscriminately, tendencies to accept the teacher's influence are lowered; when rewards are limited to adequate performances, the teacher's influence is increased.

The ways in which teachers exercise power, as indicated by these types of reward and punishment, have additional consequences in affecting the favorableness or negativeness of student attitudes toward the teacher and toward course content.

While rewarding and punishing behavior affect teacher influence, there are many other affective interactions between teachers and pupils. Della Piana and Gage[42] found, for example, that some pupils are more concerned about feelings and personal relationships, while others are mainly achievement-oriented. Classes made up predominantly of pupils of the first type tend to accept the teacher whom they like, and to reject the teacher whom they dislike, on personal grounds; classes composed of pupils of the second type pay less attention to teacher warmth in estimating their acceptance or rejection of particular teachers. It often turns out that what is important for one pupil is not important for another; this is one reason why cookbook formulas for good teaching are of so little use and why teaching is inevitably something of an art.

Another subtle influence of affective responsiveness of teachers has to do with creativity. A rather plausible principle from psychoanalysis is that creativity involves some freedom in the use of unconscious or preconscious processes. These processes tend to be less critical and more impulsive than the more rational and analytical processes, and hence are likely to call for some tolerance on the teacher's part. The process of partial or limited regression has been

42. G. M. Della Piana and N. L. Gage, "Pupils' Values and the Validity of the Minnesota Teacher Attitude Inventory," *Journal of Educational Psychology*, XLVI (March, 1955), 167–78.

called "regression in the service of the ego" by Kris;[43] the importance of something similar has been stressed by Kubie,[44] who believes that too much emphasis upon convergent thinking in the early years leads to a neurotic distortion of the creative process. That is, the child becomes frightened or anxious over that part of the normal play of his own fantasy life which does not follow the "rules" of evidence and logic.

Thus Spaulding[45] found strong negative relations between the expression of creativity in elementary-aged children and teacher behavior characterized as formal group instruction, using shame as a punishment technique. Sears[46] has shown that there are positive correlations between creativity and teachers' rewarding by personal interest in the child's ideas, accompanied by a high frequency of listening to the child. Such teaching techniques probably provide an atmosphere in which the child can permit himself more leeway in expression of unconventional ideas without threat of devastating criticism. Torrance[47] has emphasized the pressures toward conformity, away from creativity, exerted by the peer group of classmates. Competition may increase such pressures. Teachers may be able to provide an atmosphere which reduces these pressures somewhat. It is interesting that, in the aforementioned Sears study, much the same teacher behavior which tended to be related to creativity in the children was also positively related to the degree in which children in the classroom liked one another. A peer group in which there are good feelings between the children probably is more tolerant of nonconformist behavior than one in which the children like each other less.

The competitive situation of the classroom is almost inevitably

43. Ernst Kris, *Psychoanalytic Explorations in Art*. New York: International University Press, 1952.

44. L. S. Kubie, *Neurotic Distortions of the Creative Process*. New York: Noonday Press, 1952.

45. R. Spaulding, "Achievement, Creativity, and Self-concept Correlates of Teacher-Pupil Transactions in Elementary Schools." Urbana, Illinois: University of Illinois (U.S. Office of Education Cooperative Research Project No. 1352), 1963 (mimeographed).

46. Pauline S. Sears, "The Effect of Classroom Conditions on Strength of Achievement Motive and Work Output of Elementary-School Children." In press, 1963.

47. Torrance, *op. cit.*

anxiety-provoking for some children, and the handling of this anxiety in one form or another becomes an important task for the teacher. There is a large literature on this topic, concerned both with anxiety in general and with the special anxieties arising in the test situation so often confronted in school.[48] The results are complex and, in some cases, contradictory. The subtlety of the relationships involved is well illustrated by a study by Sarason, Mandler, and Craighill[49] in which it was found that (a) low-anxious college students did better, in general, on a laboratory task than high-anxious subjects, and (b) pressure to complete the task improved the performance for low-anxious subjects, but did not do so for high-anxious ones. It appears that anxiety is interfering enough, without adding new components to it through pressure; low-anxious subjects, working without interference, can accept the exhortation to do better.

The interplay between anxiety and achievement has been studied by Flanders[50] in experimentally produced climates, characterized on the one hand as "learner-centered" and on the other as "teacher-centered." In the learner-centered climate the teacher was acceptant and supportive of the student and problem-centered in approach; in the teacher-centered climate the teacher was directive and demanding, often deprecating, in his behavior toward the individual. Anxiety was estimated from physiological measures (pulse rate, galvanic skin responses) and by the direction and intensity of movements of a lever operated by the students to indicate positive and negative feelings. The major conclusions were:

1. When a conflict arises, student behavior oriented to the handling of interpersonal anxiety takes precedence over behavior oriented toward achievement.

48. Seymour B. Sarason *et al., Anxiety in Elementary-School Children* (New York: John Wiley & Sons, 1960); Britton K. Ruebush, "Anxiety," in *Child Psychology*, pp. 460–516 (Sixty-second Yearbook of the National Society for the Study of Education, Part I. Edited by Harold W. Stevenson. Chicago: Distributed by the University of Chicago Press, 1963).

49. Seymour B. Sarason, George Mandler, and Peyton G. Craighill, "The Effect of Differential Instructions on Anxiety and Learning," *Journal of Abnormal and Social Psychology*, XLVII (April, 1952), 561–65.

50. Ned A. Flanders, "Personal-Social Anxiety as a Factor in Experimental Learning Situations," *Journal of Educational Research*, XLV (October, 1951), 100–110.

2. The "teacher-centered" behavior of directing, demanding, and using private criteria in deprecating a student leads to hostility to the self or the teacher, aggressiveness, or occasionally withdrawal, apathy, and even emotional disintegration.

3. The "learner-centered" behavior of accepting the student, being evaluative or critical only by public criteria, and being usually supportive, elicited problem orientation, decreased interpersonal anxiety, and led to emotionally readjusting and integrative behavior.

In these days of emphasis upon cognitive processes, it is quite possible for the pendulum to swing too far, and hence to defeat the attainment of the very cognitive goals that are being sought. If cognition is made synonymous with achievement and competition for excellence, the concomitantly aroused anxiety may defeat the development of the very creativity and problem-solving orientation that is being sought. Hence the teacher's awareness of the affective interaction with pupils is as important in a curriculum directed toward cognition as one with other goals, such as those of social competence or personal adjustment. Much of the abstract discussion of educational goals overlooks the essential interrelatedness of low anxiety and high performance, and the need for teacher warmth if the climate to create is to be provided.

Evaluative interaction between teacher and pupils.—As indicated in the foregoing section, teacher evaluation can be by private criteria or by public criteria; in the one case the evaluation is likely to be punitive and to arouse hostility; in the other case it is likely to be informative and hence lead to better learning.

A very interesting experiment was done by Page[51] with high-school and junior high school students and a large number of teachers. The teachers graded objective tests of their students and then randomly assigned each paper to one of three groups. The group-one pupil was given back his paper with no comment except the mark. Each group-two pupil was given a stereotyped comment from excellent if his score was high to "let's raise this grade." Every C student, for example, received his mark with the notation, "perhaps try to do still better?" For group three, the teacher wrote a personal comment on every paper, saying whatever she felt would encourage

51. E. B. Page, "Teacher Comments and Student Performance," *Journal of Educational Psychology*, XLIX (1958), 173–81.

that particular pupil. On the next objective test, groups two and three out-performed group one. The personalized comments seemed to have a greater effect than the standardized comments, but even a very short standard comment written on the paper produced measurable improvement. The greatest improvement was found in the failing students in group three, who received an encouraging personal note.

This study points up the motivational significance of evaluative practices that go beyond the indication of right or wrong answers. Personal interest of the teacher in the student's progress is shown to be effective.

A good deal of teacher evaluation is of nonacademic or non-achievement types of behavior, particularly evaluation of conduct. That teachers tended to disagree with clinicians about the severity of different kinds of behavior problems was a conclusion reached a number of years ago by Wickman.[52] Teachers, for example, were more disturbed by defiant and aggressive behavior than by withdrawn behavior, while the clinicians reversed the order of behavior. A number of similar studies have been made since, and these have been reviewed by Beilin.[53] New studies have found that there has been a shift in the hierarchy of teachers' attitudes since 1927 to approximate more closely those of clinicians. These shifts are more prominent in elementary-school teachers than in secondary-school teachers. The differences in attitudes between teachers and clinicians are interpreted in the framework of role theory. The attitudinal hierarchy of teachers and clinicians is seen as reflecting their respective roles and the way these roles influence the organization of their respective experiences. Wickman's findings of 1928 are interpreted as indicative of the role of the teacher of that era. The role expectations of teachers have changed since then in the direction of the teacher's attention to emotional problems of children and particularly to withdrawal tendencies in children.

Without reviewing further studies at this point, it is perhaps suffi-

52. E. K. Wickman, *Children's Behavior and Teachers' Attitudes.* New York: Commonwealth Fund, 1928.

53. Harry Beilin, "Teachers' and Clinicians' Attitudes toward the Behavior Problems of Children: A Reappraisal," in *The Causes of Behavior: Readings in Child Development and Educational Psychology.* Edited by Judy F. Rosenblith and Wesley Allinsmith. Boston: Allyn & Bacon, Inc., 1962.

cient to point out that a teacher's evaluative activities go far beyond marking papers; they include attention to many experiences of success and failure, of expanded or restricted autonomy, of immediate and long-term goal-setting, of recognition of individual progress, and of attitudinal response to divergent behavior. These evaluative behaviors have the characteristics of positive and negative reinforcers, and, as such, are motivationally relevant to learning.

Cognitive interaction between teacher and pupils.—To the extent that the teacher imparts skill and knowledge and teaches the approaches to solving problems and creating products that are both novel and valuable, he is having a cognitive interaction with pupils. This is the most readily understood purpose of teaching, but it is by no means easy to categorize the processes that are involved. They include methods, such as lecture, discussion, individual projects; they include content-related matters, such as structuring the problem and developing content-relevant understandings. Attempts at categorizing, such as those of Medley and Mitzel,[54] Smith,[55] and Wright and Proctor[56] are none too satisfactory, being either very general or at such a commonsense level as to have no element of newness in them. Thus, Wright and Proctor[57] classify the content of what teachers of mathematics say to their pupils as promoting (*a*) ability to think, (*b*) appreciation of mathematics, and (*c*) curiosity and initiative. The effort to devise such categories has value, however, in that it calls attention to the fact that what the teacher says to the pupil goes beyond the exposition of subject matter.[58]

54. Donald M. Medley and Harold E. Mitzel, "Measuring Classroom Behavior by Systematic Observation," in *Handbook of Research on Teaching*, pp. 247–328. Edited by N. L. Gage. Chicago: Rand McNally & Co., 1963.

55. B. Othanel Smith, "A Study of the Logic of Teaching: A Report on the First Phase of a Five-Year Research Project." Washington: U.S. Office of Education, 1959 (duplicated).

56. E. Muriel J. Wright and Virginia H. Proctor, *Systematic Observations of Verbal Interaction as a Method of Comparing Mathematics Lessons*. St. Louis, Missouri: Washington University (U.S. Office of Education Cooperative Research Project No. 816), 1961.

57. *Ibid.*

58. For problems of cognitive interactions as related to particular subject matters, see the chapters in this yearbook by Bruner on mathematics and by Carroll on reading. *The Handbook of Research on Teaching* (*op. cit.*) contains excellent comprehensive reviews of significant studies.

Spaulding,[59] using tape recordings from 21 elementary teachers, identified empirically components of teacher behavior similar to the more global behavior syndromes discussed by Anderson,[60] Withall,[61] and Lewin, Lippitt, and White.[62] Support was given to the prediction that self-concepts of children would be higher in classrooms in which the teacher was "socially integrative" and "learner supportive." Spaulding's description of the behavior found to be positively related to self-concept was as follows: "calm, acceptant transactions in general with private, individualized instruction and a concern for divergency, attention to task, and the use of task-appropriate procedures and resources."

However, a test of the predictions involving "democratic" teacher behavior[63] failed to gain support. Neither pupil self-concepts, achievement, nor creativity was found to be related to this pattern of behavior.

All of these pupil outcomes were positively correlated to a modest degree with the component described as follows: "business-like lecture method with insistence upon attention to task and conformity to rules of procedure."[64] In the case of scores on reading achievement, this correlation was strongly significant. Ryans[65] also found businesslike methods and warmth related to students' behavior. For elementary-school classes, high positive relationships were noted between observers' assessments of "productive pupil behavior" (e.g., assessments presumed to reflect pupil alertness, participation, confidence, responsibility and self-control, initiating behavior, and so on) and observers' assessments of previously identified patterns of teacher behavior which seemed to refer to understanding, friendly

59. Spaulding, *op. cit.*

60. Harold H. Anderson, "Domination and Socially Integrative Behavior," in *Child Behavior and Development*, pp. 459–84. Edited by Roger G. Barker, Jacob S. Kounin, and Herbert F. Wright. New York: McGraw-Hill Book Co., 1943.

61. John Withall, "Development of a Technique for the Measurement of Socioemotional Climate in Classrooms," *Journal of Experimental Education*, XVII (March, 1949), 347–61.

62. Kurt Lewin, Ronald Lippitt, and R. K. White, "Patterns of Aggressive Behavior in Experimentally Created 'Social Climates,'" *Journal of Social Psychology*, X (1939), 271–99.

63. *Ibid.*　　　　　　　　　　64. *Ibid.*, p. 119.

65. David G. Ryans, "Some Relationships between Pupil Behavior and Certain Teacher Characteristics," *Journal of Educational Psychology*, LII (April, 1961), 82–90.

classroom behavior; organized, businesslike classroom behavior; and stimulating, original classroom behavior.

For secondary-school classes, low positive relationships appeared to obtain between productive pupil behavior and the above-named categories of teacher behavior, with a tendency for the stimulating, original teacher classroom-behavior pattern to show a slightly higher correlation with pupil behavior than the understanding, friendly or the organized, businesslike teacher behavior patterns.

A narrower definition of pupil task-oriented behavior was used by Sears.[66] Time samples of the percentage of time elementary-school children were attentive to the assigned task were found strongly related to teacher behavior. If children work steadily during a large proportion of class time, their teachers tend to give rewards in evaluative terms, to the group rather than to the individual, without show of interest in individual personalities. They tend to teach by statement and by giving of information. Thus the teacher behavior related to task-oriented work is very different from that associated with children's production of creative responses. It was also found that high frequencies of task-oriented behavior, as defined here, did not relate to achievement as reflected in test scores. The quiet, apparently industrious groups did not achieve more.

The teaching methods just described could be characterized as directive on the part of the teacher. Stern[67] has reviewed 34 studies (largely of colleges classes) comparing nondirective with directive instruction in influencing two types of learning outcome: (a) gain in achievement of cognitive knowledge and understanding, and (b) attitude change toward self or others. The following quotation summarizes the findings:

In general, it would appear that amount of cognitive gain is largely unaffected by the autocratic or democratic tendencies of the instructor. The majority of investigators who have attempted to measure differences in achievement report no particular advantage for either approach. . . . Regardless of whether the investigator was concerned with attitudes toward the cultural outgroup, toward other participants in the class, or toward the self, the results generally have indicated that non-directive instruction facilitates a shift in a more favorable, acceptant direction.[68]

66. Sears, *op. cit.*

67. George G. Stern, "Measuring Non-cognitive Variables in Research on Teaching," in *Handbook of Research on Teaching, op. cit.*, p. 427.

68. *Ibid.*, p. 428.

However, in connection with student reactions to nondirective instruction, "at least as many students feel dissatisfied, frustrated, or anxious in a nondirective classroom as consider it valuable." Nondirective instruction, as practiced by some instructors, may be more laissez faire than learner-centered, and may arouse latent anxieties in students with precarious ego-strength. The next section considers the interaction of student predisposition and teaching method.

Child Personality, Teacher Personality, and Their Consequences for the Motivation of the Learner

It has not been possible, in attempting to indicate some of the influences of teachers upon pupils, to avoid occasional mention of differences in pupils (and teachers) that affect the results, not entirely related to the specific classroom behavior of the teacher or specific instructional techniques. In this section we shall call attention more specifically to some of the personality factors that influence the acceptability of different methods of teaching.

PUPIL PERSONALITY AND THE CONDITIONS FAVORING ACHIEVEMENT

As one illustration, consider the differences between the independent, autonomous student and the one who is dependent-prone, that is, is likely to turn for support to adult authority. These relationships among students of eighth-grade geometry have been studied by Amidon and Flanders.[69]

The primary purpose of this study was to determine the effects of direct versus indirect teacher behavior and of clear versus unclear student perception of the learning goal on the achievement of eighth-grade geometry students. A specially trained teacher role-played both a very direct and a very indirect teacher in a laboratory situation involving 140 eighth-grade pupils, chosen from a larger population on the basis of high scores on a test of dependency proneness. All students were randomly assigned to one of the following four experimental treatments: direct teacher influence with clear goals, direct teacher influence with unclear goals, indirect teacher influence with clear goals, and indirect teacher influence with unclear goals.

69. Edmund Amidon and Ned A. Flanders, "The Effects of Direct and Indirect Teacher Influence on Dependent-prone Students Learning Geometry," *Journal of Educational Psychology*, LII (December, 1961), 286–91.

Students in the various classifications were then compared on the basis of pre- and postachievement tests in geometry. No differences were found between the clear-goal and unclear-goal treatments, indicating that in this study, at least, achievement of dependent-prone students was not affected by perception of the learning goal. An analysis of the direct and indirect treatments indicated that the children taught by the indirect teacher learned more than did the children taught by the direct teacher.

The results of this study take on additional meaning when compared with the results of Flanders[70] using the same experimental design. Flanders found no differences (among the four experimental conditions) in the total group of 560 students who ranged from very high to very low on the dependence scale. Apparently, dependent-prone students are more sensitive to types of teacher influence than are independent-prone students as measured by scores on the test for dependence proneness.

Whether or not a particular type of student can learn when he is exposed to a particular style of teaching has interested a number of researchers. Smith[71] and Wispe[72] have both shown that when students are classified by the use of personality test data, they respond differently to highly organized (versus loosely organized) classroom activities in a college remedial reading course[73] and to college lecturing (versus group discussion) techniques[74] in Freshman sociology.

Asch,[75] Kagen and Mussen,[76] and Livson and Mussen[77] have stud-

70. Ned A. Flanders, "Teacher Influence, Pupil Attitudes, and Achievement." Minneapolis: University of Minnesota (U.S. Office of Education Cooperative Research Project No. 397), 1960 (mimeographed).

71. Donald E. P. Smith, "Fit Teaching Methods to Personality Structure," *High School Journal*, XXXIX (December, 1955), 167–71.

72. Lauren G. Wispe, "Evaluating Section Teaching Methods in the Introductory Course," *Journal of Educational Research*, XLV (November, 1951), 161–86.

73. Donald E. P. Smith, *op. cit.*   74. Wispe, *op. cit.*

75. Solomon E. Asch, "Effects of Group Pressure upon the Modification and Distortion of Judgments," in *Groups, Leadership, and Men.* Edited by H. Guetzkow. Pittsburgh: Carnegie Press, 1951.

76. Jerome Kagan and Paul H. Mussen, "Dependency Themes on the TAT and Group Conformity," *Journal of Consulting Psychology*, XX (1956), 19–27.

77. Norman Livson and Paul H. Mussen, "The Relation of Control to Overt Aggression and Dependency," *Journal of Abnormal and Social Psychology*, LV (1957), 66–71.

ied the reactions of dependent-prone persons in various kinds of experimental situations. They concluded that dependent-prone individuals are more likely to comply with authority figures and conform to group pressures than the less dependent-prone. Their results suggest that a dependent-prone student might become overly concerned with following the suggestions and directions of a teacher and more dependent on support and encouragement.

Kagan, Sontag, Baker, and Nelson,[78] working from the Fels Institute longitudinal data, studied the 35 subjects who had gained the most on I.Q. retest, and the 35 who had lost the most. The ascending I.Q. group was characterized by independence, mastery, high need achievement, and curiosity. The descending I.Q. group showed dependence and an attitude that competition was not emotionally comforting. Thus, there seems to be a relation between motivational dispositions and the production represented by scores on an intelligence test. The more active and achievement-motivated subjects, the data suggest, interact more effectively with their environment in ways which provide for increase in I.Q. Much of the teacher's interaction with pupils must be directed toward arousal of such motivation.

Gains in achievement for children of superior mental ability were found related, in Sears' study,[79] to various teacher behaviors which may provide such arousal. These included the frequency with which the teacher emphasizes the expanding and amplifying of ideas, giving of alternatives and possibilities rather than of straight statements of facts, and also the amount of listening to the child done by the teacher. These methods essentially stimulate but do not direct, and for bright children they seem to be effective in connection with achievement.

Another illustration of pupil personality as affecting responsiveness to teaching is that of Grimes and Allinsmith[80] concerned with compulsivity and anxiety. They tested the hypothesis that there

78. Jerome Kagan, Lester W. Sontag, Charles T. Baker, and Virginia L. Nelson, "Personality and I.Q. Change," *Journal of Abnormal and Social Psychology*, LVI (1958), 261–66.

79. Sears, *op. cit.*

80. Jesse W. Grimes and Wesley Allinsmith, "Compulsivity, Anxiety, and School Achievement," *Merrill-Palmer Quarterly*, VII (October, 1961), 247–72.

would be an interaction between teaching method and pupils' personality characteristics in the determination of school achievement. It was conjectured that in the early years of schooling both highly anxious and highly compulsive children would respond to structured methods of teaching, such as the teaching of reading by phonics. In agreement with this conjecture, they found differences by the third grade favoring phonics over word recognition for such children.

When teaching method is held constant, there are differences correlated with the personality characteristics. The results can be summarized as follows:

1. Compulsive children do better than less compulsive children under structured conditions.
2. Compulsive children are neither favored nor disfavored when teaching is unstructured.
3. Anxious children do as well as nonanxious children under structured conditions.
4. Anxious children have their achievement impeded in unstructured settings.

Although anxiety and compulsivity were not correlated, they were shown to interact. Those children who are both anxious and compulsive do very well in the structured setting; those who are highly anxious, but low in compulsivity, do poorly in the unstructured setting, becoming "underachievers."

It appears that instructional methods make a difference for certain kinds of pupils, and a search for the preferred method of teaching can succeed only when consideration is given to the personality of the learner. On the other hand, many of the relationships cited are of only moderate size and based on selected samples of teachers. Definitive answers to questions of results of different instructional techniques await replication of new samples.

TEACHING PERSONALITY AND TEACHING EFFECTIVENESS

Heil, Powell, and Feifer[81] have related pupil achievement to interaction between teacher and pupil personalities. Three teacher and

81. L. M. Heil, Marion Powell, and I. Feifer, *Characteristics of Teacher Behavior Related to the Achievement of Children in Several Elementary Grades.* Washington: U.S. Department of Health, Education, and Welfare, Office of Education, Cooperative Research Branch, 1960.

four pupil personality types were identified. The various teacher-pupil combinations were compared in terms of measures of pupil achievement, teacher knowledge, and classroom ratings. The well-integrated (self-controlling) teachers were the most effective with all types of students, whereas the weakly integrated (fearful) teachers were ineffective with everyone except the children identified as "strivers." The third type of teacher (turbulent) indentified by these investigators is similar to a defensively intellectual person in using intellectualization as a mechanism of defense. The turbulent teachers were found to be effective with children who had been categorized as "conformers" or "strivers," particularly in mathematics and science achievement. They were ineffective with "opposers" and "waverers," two classroom-problem types requiring interpersonal skills to which these teachers were totally indifferent. The behavior of the "self-controlled teacher" suggests the importance of consistency, structure, routine activities, and orderliness—especially for "opposing" or "wavering" (anxious) children. The criterion measure in this study was simply scores on achievement tests.

It was earlier pointed out that teacher warmth tends to be associated with the encouragement of creativity. Sears[82] found that teachers who like pupils tend to have pupils who like each other. Other aspects of teacher behavior related to the pupils' liking of each other include the manner in which such teachers use rewards and punishments. Rewards tend to be individualized, directed to the person, rather than to the group; punishments, however, are more often group-directed, hence reducing the sting of individual criticism. Children perhaps show liking for each other under these circumstances because the teaching techniques allow for social interchange without tension engendered by personal evaluation.

Thus, the teacher as a motivating agent operates in two interrelated ways. First, teacher personality and behavior act through a kind of contagion, in which the teacher becomes a model for appropriate behavior. The principles at work here are those of imitation and identification. Second, the teacher, as an administrator of rewards and punishments, wields power and creates a structure in which learning occurs. Here the principles are the more usual ones of positive and negative reinforcement. In addition, and in subtle

82. Sears, *op. cit.*

ways, the child becomes an independent seeker and learner, satisfying his curiosity in his own ways and at his own pace.

The consequence of displaying interest in the individual child and his ideas, of acting in a warmly encouraging manner rather than in a critically evaluative one, is to produce a creative child, with a liking for the other children. The consequence of "efficient" teaching, in which the quiet industrious classroom is the goal, comes about through group methods and frequent evaluation, with a product neither high in conventional subject-matter achievement nor characterized particularly by new ideas or child-to-child affiliation. However, businesslike, well-organized teaching together with individualized attention to the student is associated with favorable learning outcomes, and structure appears to be favorable, at least on a short-term basis, for more anxious or dependent students. There are suggestions, however, that dependent students tend to become more dependent on authority figures with directive teaching, and that their achievement may be better in certain situations with less directive teaching.

Summary and Conclusions

The turmoil in learning theory at the present time is reflected also in the uncertainty about the relationship between motivation and learning. Some extreme positions assert that motivation affects only performance, not learning; another viewpoint is that motivation is an irrelevant category, and that all learning is eventually under the control of the stimulus. These uncertainties within the more abstract discussions of learning theory need not detract from the practical importance of motivation in applied settings, where the distinction between learning and performance becomes less important, and where motivational dispositions are as relevant as motivational arousal.

The kinds of motives that the teacher can utilize and arouse are not the ones most often studied in the animal laboratory (hunger, thirst, and pain), but have more to do with personal and social motives that characterize children growing up in a particular culture. Even in the laboratory there is a turn away from deprived states to positive motives, such as activity, curiosity, and manipulation, to "hope" rather than "fear" as fundamental. Among the motives that the teacher necessarily uses in one way or another are the social (illustrated by warmth and nurturance), the ego-integrative (illustrated by the achievement motive), and the cognitive (illustrated by curiosity).

The school environment and atmosphere contribute to the arousal and support of particular motives. Various socioeconomic backgrounds bring children to school with different expectations of achievement. The ways in which pupils are grouped may affect their teachableness by given teachers. The ways in which the school is set up will determine whether or not creativity will be encouraged.

The current interest in making schools more intellectually exciting can be described as an effort to enhance and capitalize upon cognitive motivation. Most of the new curricula more or less take for granted that if students are free to work out their own solutions to problems, if they have an opportunity for divergent rather than merely convergent thinking, intrinsic motivation appears to be readily aroused.

Efforts to see how, in fact, teachers affect students have led to extensive observations of teacher behavior, to attempts to relate this behavior to certain consequences in the behavior, attitudes, and achievements of pupils. These interactions are conveniently classified as affective, evaluative, and cognitive. Affective consequences arise through teacher efforts to maintain control by way of reward and punishment; many other affective consequences are related to the anxieties created by the competitive situation in classrooms. Evaluation can be done individually in such a manner as to threaten self-esteem, or it can be done according to group standards and thus be less threatening. The nonacademic behavior of students is of course evaluated, particularly in the effort to maintain discipline; the judgment of severity of pupil problems tends today to conform more nearly to that of clinicians than formerly. Cognitive interaction of teachers and pupils lies at the heart of instruction. Some plausible conjectures about autocratic and democratic atmospheres do not appear to be supported by some recent studies; businesslike and matter-of-fact approaches tend to yield achievement as well as creativity. At the same time, support is given to nondirective approaches, apparently because they keep alive the searching behavior important to divergent thinking. Teachers who are insistent on quiet, orderly behavior, who teach by informative statements, produce task-oriented behavior favorable to convergent thinking; teachers who show personal interest and who avoid critical individual evaluation tend to favor the more creative products of divergent thinking.

Child personality affects the ability to profit from particular kinds of teaching. Compulsive and anxious children respond differently from those less compulsive and less anxious; for example, those high in these characteristics do very well ("overachieve") in structured situations; those who are highly anxious, but low in compulsivity, do poorly ("underachieve") in an unstructured setting. Dependency tendencies also affect the profit from particular kinds of teaching. Hence, teachers must know their pupils and must be flexible in their approaches if they are to have the most favorable results.

Teacher personality also has an influence on teaching effectiveness. This is to be expected because of the importance of the teacher as a "model" for pupil behavior. In some comparisons of self-controlling, fearful, and turbulent teachers, best results, by achievement measures, were obtained by the self-controlled teachers. Another dimension—that of warmth—appears to affect creativity, the warmer teachers encouraging divergent behavior. While perhaps there is little the teacher can do about his own personality, some self-awareness is no doubt helpful in avoiding extremes of unfavorable influence. Those responsible for teacher selection may be helped to make wiser choices when the results of some of these studies become better established.

The problems of motivation are so intertwined with problems of personality that an adequate account of motivation in relation to learning cannot rest solely on the findings of the learning laboratory. A classroom is a social situation, with a power structure, including peer relationships, and adult-child relationships; hence the most favorable motivational conditions need to take all of these factors into account, recognizing that the teacher is both model and reinforcer and, in ways not fully understood, a releaser of intrinsic motives.

CHAPTER IX

Issues Related to Readiness To Learn

FRED. T. TYLER

Comprehensive curriculum-planning must take into account questions dealing with the *what*, the *how*, and the *when* to teach. Today, these topics are receiving considerable attention, and from diverse, interested parties—physicists, mathematicians, biologists, chemists, mathematical logicians, psychologists, educators, the National Academy of Sciences, and the National Science Foundation. The Woods Hole Conference was planned because of "new progress in, and concern for, creating curricula and ways of teaching science. . . ."[1] In this chapter we deal with readiness—"the when to teach." Here is an issue that is far from settled; and today's answers are often in marked contrast to some of those proposed forty years ago.

Introduction

In this chapter, then, we shall be dealing with the general problem of readiness for school learning—what readiness is, and how it comes about; and we shall be in an area of considerable controversy. To give point to this statement, consider the following two quotations from recent literature. Bruner devoted one chapter to the proposition that "the foundations of any subject may be taught to anybody at any age in some form."[2] For Bruner, readiness is practically an unnecessary concept; children are always ready. Hymes, on the other hand, wrote: "As surely as the baby sat and crawled and stood and walked, always in his own good time, the power on which reading instruction can build will also develop. Maturation and living make

1. Jerome S. Bruner, *The Process of Education*, p. vii. Cambridge: Harvard University Press, 1960.

2. *Ibid.*, p. 12.

this inevitable."[3] Two positions could hardly be more at odds with each other. Hymes is even at odds with himself, for later he wrote, "Readiness means that children are always ready to learn" (p. 81).

Before analyzing these different positions regarding readiness, it may be well to note that the notion of readiness, by whatever name, has long had a place in educational writing. In his *Linguarum Methodus Novissima*, Comenius includes among his axioms, or didactic principles, these which are relevant to our discussion: "Doceri immaturum aegre docebis" and "Imparatum doceri docere ne occipias." Rousseau advises us: "Observez la nature, et suivez la route qu'elle vous trace." James, too, follows "nature." "*Feed* the growing human being, feed him with the sort of experience for which from year to year he shows a natural craving."[4]

Questions about "when to teach" have been a matter of special controversy for the past forty years. A brief summary of the nature of the debate will serve as an introduction to the later discussion.

COMPLEXITY OF THE CONCEPT OF READINESS

For some of the early writers, the concept seemed relatively simple. For instance, the Committee of Seven[5] listed two components: (*a*) mental age and (*b*) knowledge of requisite subskills. Harrison's chart showing the factors which foster readiness[6] represents the appearance of a multidimensional conception of readiness. Harrison also introduces a new term, "inner maturation," which led to further ambiguities, since sometimes it was used to denote a state of readiness and other times it was a factor making for readiness.

THE CONCEPT OF MATURATION

The term "maturity" appeared in the first edition of Woodworth's *Psychology:* "In fact, what does maturity mean, except that

3. James L. Hymes, Jr., *Before the Child Reads*, p. 28. Evanston, Illinois: Row, Peterson & Co., 1958.

4. William James, *Talks to Teachers*, p. 104. New York: Norton & Co., Inc., 1958.

5. Carleton W. Washburne, "The Grade Placement of Arithmetic Topics: A 'Committee of Seven' Investigation," *Report of the Society's Committee on Arithmetic*, p. 641. Twenty-ninth Yearbook of the National Society for the Study of Education, Part II. Chicago: Distributed by University of Chicago Press, 1930.

6. M. Lucile Harrison, *Reading Readiness*, between pp. 6–7. New York: Houghton-Mifflin Co., 1939.

the natural characteristics have finally reached their complete development? And it is as true of internal structure as of external, that natural development, far from being complete at birth, keeps on till maturity. The neurones continue to grow, and their synapses in the nerve centers to become closer knit, just by virtue of natural growth; . . . The native intelligence of the child gradually unfolds. . . ."[7] Current writers apparently use the term in a similar sense (see below). It should be noted that the concept of maturation seems to be applied by some writers to cognitive functioning, following Woodworth's suggestion that intelligence unfolds, as well as to neural changes.

Thus, Washburne seemingly accepted some such idea of maturation when he wrote that numerous conditions, including mental age, "physical readiness of the eyes," experimental background, specific reading readiness, "must be taken into account if we are not to force open a bud not yet ready to bloom."[8] He urged that when a child is not happily successful, we should ask "whether, perhaps, we have not given him something to do for which he has not the necessary ripeness. After all, what is the hurry?"[9]

In contrast, as we shall see, we sometimes get the impression that the educator's question in the 1960's has become, like that of the traffic officer to the dawdling motorist on the freeway, "What's the delay?"

AMBIGUITY OF MATURATION

There was a hint of ambiguity in the concepts of readiness, maturity, and maturation in Washburne's writing. The hint is reinforced by the numerous adjectives that are attached to maturity, including mental, emotional, social, language, physical, experimental, physiological, skeletal, and anatomical.

However, there are further ambiguities inherent in the term, for it may connote the end of a process, or the beginning, or a relative, continuing, normative process. Cessation of change in height denotes height maturity. Puberty is the beginning of sexual maturity. (Also, maturation may be a matter of deterioration, as in the appearance of

7. R. S. Woodworth, *Psychology*, p. 92. New York: Henry Holt & Co., 1921.
8. Carleton Washburne, "Ripeness," *Progressive Education*, XIII (1936), 127.
9. *Ibid.*, p. 130.

farsightedness in adulthood and in changes in other organs and glands.) There are many who would agree with Meyer: "Is not all maturity relative and an ever-progressive attainment even in the adult? Does not all maturity have to be maturity *for something?* And when does it become maturity in general?"[10] Jersild points up the notion of relativity when he suggests that a three-year-old may be more mature than a thirteen-year-old in terms of what can be expected at each age level even though the latter can achieve more than the former. Frank observes that maturation "has no terminal point or fixed norms but is continuously and progressively at work" and that to evaluate maturation we must use criteria "appropriate to each stage and to each unique organism personality."[11]

There is some justification for Krogman's suggestion that the terms "maturity" and "maturation" are all things to all people.[12]

The complexity and ambiguity of the concept of maturation means that it can only with difficulty be applied in practical situations because, from our knowledge of intraindividual differences, we should expect that an individual will show irregular patterning of his various maturities. What, then, can be the practical significance of the maturity in general, that is, average maturity? "Organismic age" is one such attempt to arrive at an index of general maturity, but to compute it, one has to average a heterogeneity of maturities. Averages representing disparate maturities are likely to be more concealing than revealing.[13] Further, even any one component, as for instance mental (age) "maturity," is likely itself to be a composite rather than a unitary matter.

READINESS BY WAY OF POSTPONEMENT

If we agree that maturation, as the term is often used, implies a gradual, biological unfolding independent of practice, then there is

10. A. Meyer, "The Meaning of Maturity," in *Our Children: A Handbook for Parents*, p. 159. Edited by D. C. Fisher and S. M. Gruenberg. New York: Viking Press, 1932.

11. Lawrence K. Frank, "Introduction: The Concept of Maturity," *Child Development*, XXI (March, 1950), 21–24.

12. Wilton Marion Krogman, "The Concept of Maturity from a Morphological Viewpoint," *Child Development*, XXI (March, 1950), 25.

13. Fred. T. Tyler, "Concepts of Organismic Growth: A Critique," *Journal of Educational Psychology*, XLIV (October, 1953), 321–42.

little à teacher can do other than await the appearence of some outward manifestation which presumably signifies that the pupil has attained some hoped-for stage. Of course, this idea has its advocates among those who would "postpone" reading or arithmetic until some proposed maturity level has been attained.

This idea, supported, it was often assumed, by evidence from the child study movement, probably formed the foundation for one of the recommendations proposed by the Committee for the Twenty-fourth Yearbook of the National Society for the Study of Education: "A clear recognition of the vital contribution of wide experience to good interpretation, with special emphasis on pre-reading experiences and temporary postponement, if necessary, of formal instruction in reading."[14] We have here an early statement of the doctrine of educational postponement which came to play such an important part in much thinking in the following years.

Extensive investigations of "grade placement of topics" in arithmetic were initiated in 1926 by Washburne and his "Committee of Seven," and were reported to be continuing in 1938.[15] In general, these investigators interpreted their results to mean that much arithmetic was being taught too soon—before the pupils were "ready." "Delay" became a rallying point—at least for some educators.

However, even in the 1930's there were those who were critical of the evidence and questioned some of these proposed practices.[16] Buswell,[17] for instance, attached little significance to work of the "Committee of Seven" because it investigated the "program of arithmetic as it was," to the neglect of what it might be with different

14. *Report of the National Committee on Reading*, p. 305. Twenty-fourth Yearbook of the National Society for the Study of Education, Part I. Chicago: Distributed by the University of Chicago Press, 1925.

15. Carleton W. Washburne, "The Work of the Committee of Seven on Grade-Placement in Arithmetic," *Child Development and the Curriculum*, p. 299. Thirty-eighth Yearbook of the National Society for the Study of Education, Part I. Chicago: Distributed by the University of Chicago Press, 1939.

16. William A. Brownell, "A Critique of the Committee of Seven's Investigations on the Grade Placement of Arithmetic Topics," *Elementary School Journal*, XXXVIII (March, 1938), 495–508; Louis E. Raths, "Grade-Placement of Addition and Subtraction of Fractions," *Educational Research Bulletin*, XI (January 20, 1932), 29–38.

17. G. T. Buswell, "Deferred Arithmetic," *Mathematics Teacher*, XXXI (May, 1938), 195–200.

materials, purposes, and methods. Brownell, for one, agreed that there might be sound reasons for postponing certain topics in arithmetic—but he argued that they were not to be found in an appeal to lack of intellectual readiness. Even at that time there was empirical evidence (as in MacGregor's study) that children could learn arithmetic at younger ages than were proposed by Washburne's committee. In 1960, Brownell was still of his earlier opinion, telling us that young children in English schools are learning arithmetic which we in America know they cannot learn.[18]

From the outset, Brownell was seeking to advance some reasonable antidote to the doctrine of postponement. He was not discarding all notions about the necessity for readiness in learning, although it almost seems as if some recent writers are doing just that. Thus, while Brownell is saying, "We can expect children to learn much more in arithmetic than we are now asking them to learn," Bruner is asserting, as we have seen, that "the foundations of any subject may be taught to anybody at any age in some form."[19] The issue of postponement will be treated in more detail in the next section.

Factors in Readiness

In the previous section we pointed out that readiness and maturity are complex and ambiguous terms, and we drew attention to the doctrine of postponement. Next we deal in more detail with the origins and implications of the concept of maturation; secondly, with one specific type of maturation, viz., mental; and, thirdly, with what may be designated by the term, "learning sets."

MATURATION

Definitions.—Sperry, in his discussion of neural maturation, concluded that intrinsic forces of development, unaided by learning, produce the basic patterns of synaptic association of the nervous system.[20] It is not clear whether or not he considers that some types

18. William A. Brownell, "Observations of Instruction in Lower-Grade Arithmetic in English and Scottish Schools," *Arithmetic Teacher*, VII (April, 1960), 174.

19. Bruner, *op. cit.*, p. 12.

20. R. W. Sperry, "Mechanisms of Neural Maturation," in *Handbook of Experimental Psychology*, p. 237. Edited by S. S. Stevens. New York: John Wiley & Sons, Inc., 1951.

of behavior also are produced by intrinsic forces inasmuch as he specifically avoided questions about the maturation of behavior.[21] Johnson expresses a similar idea, that maturation is a process which occurs practically independent of outside stimulation.[22] Maturation, according to McCandless, refers to "neuro-physiological-biochemical changes from conception to death" and is development that occurs as a *"function of time, or age."*[23] Eichorn and Jones, in their discussion of maturation, observe that it has long been accepted that intrinsic growth is a necessary complement to the learning process.[24]

As far as we can tell, all these writers are thinking of maturation as a process which depends upon biological rather than experiential factors. The question is whether the term is equally as applicable to behavior as to structure and physiological processes. It is worth noting, however, that function may modify structure—i.e., "the laying down of myelin is stimulated and accelerated by function."[25] In other words, even such a process as myelinization, which one might think of as an example of maturation, can be affected by processes other than those of a biological unfolding.

Gesell, who gave a good deal of attention to the concept of maturation, conceived of maturation as a matter of inner forces rather than of external stimulation. Further, he apparently thought of these forces as affecting both structure and function. For example, he wrote that he applied the term maturation to the "intrinsic and prospective aspect of ontogenetic patterning."[26] It was his opinion that the environment, internal or external, was not responsible for developmental sequences: "Environmental factors," he maintained,

21. *Ibid.*, p. 275.

22. D. M. Johnson, *Psychology: A Problem-solving Approach*, p. 12. New York: Harper & Bros., 1961.

23. Boyd R. McCandless, *Children and Adolescents*, p. 118. New York: Holt, Rinehart & Winston, 1961.

24. Dorothy H. Eichorn and Harold E. Jones, "Maturation and Behavior," in *Current Psychological Issues*, p. 211. Edited by G. H. Seward and J. P. Seward. New York: Henry Holt & Co., 1958.

25. Sperry, *op. cit.*, p. 267.

26. Arnold Gesell, "The Ontogenesis of Infant Behavior," in *Manual of Child Psychology*, pp. 355–56. Edited by Leonard Carmichael. New York: John Wiley & Sons, Inc., 1954.

"support, inflect, and specify; but they do not engender the basic forms and sequences of ontogenesis."[27]

Maturation and postponement.—Gesell and Thompson,[28] on the basis of their co-twin control studies, stressed the importance of the added maturity that comes about from the passage of time, and of the ineffectiveness of "early" practice. They pointed out that their conclusion, deriving from the stair-climbing investigations, might well be limited to gross motor functions. However, their general notion about "maturity" and their doctrine of delaying the introduction of exercise were soon adapted to educational theory and practice with respect to both motor skills and cognitive processes. However, analogies between motor and ideational activity may be misleading. In any case, the control twin in the co-twin studies was not completely inactive during the "maturating" period, with the result that he may have been developing skills useful in stair-climbing while he was engaged in other activities.

Gradients.—Gesell's studies of maturation led him to formulate the ideas of "developmental trends" and "gradients (electrochemical and otherwise)," which governed the course of both somatic and behavioral organization.[29] These two ideas soon were extended by others to encompass cognitive activities of significance to school learning. Ilg and Ames, for instance, published gradients for arithmetic, handwriting, and reading—and they related their gradients, which they presented by ages, to the Gesellian concept of maturation.[30]

Ilg and Ames assure us that "checking any one child's abilities with this gradient will not only tell us whether or not he is ready for certain levels of instruction in arithmetic but, perhaps more important, if he is *not* ready, it can tell us how far he has come, just what stage he *is* functioning at, and relatively how long it will be

27. *Ibid.,* p. 354.

28. Arnold Gesell and Helen Thompson, "Learning and Maturation in Identical Infant Twins: An Experimental Analysis by the Method of Co-Twin Control," in *Child Behavior and Development,* p. 216. New York: McGraw-Hill Book Co., Inc., 1943.

29. Gesell, *op. cit.,* p. 339.

30. Frances Ilg and Louise B. Ames, "Developmental Trends in Arithmetic," *Journal of Genetic Psychology,* LXXIX (September, 1951), 3.

before we might expect him to function at a desired level."[31] Their proposal sounds very efficient—if very fatalistic; and it sounds like maturation in the sense of unfolding produced by inner forces and independently of cognitive experiences. Are we justified in conceiving of behavioral gradients in arithmetic, or reading,[32] or handwriting[33] that are analogous with, comparable to, or derivable from, the concept of a biochemical gradient?

The data on arithmetic, reading, and writing gradients reveal something about the competencies of the children observed, but they do not mean that we would get identical gradients for pupils who lived, played, worked, and studied under other conditions. Observational, naturalistic studies of the type Ilg and Ames report tell us "what is," but they do not reval "what might be"—unless, as seems unlikely, such gradients are indeed predetermined by inner forces apart from cultural and social effects.

The concepts of maturation and gradients were soon adapted to educational practices—without justification. After all, the subjects in "deprivation" studies were not in cold storage so that they may have been having experiences which through transfer speeded up the appearance of rather skilled responses in stair-climbing or in formal arithmetic in Grade VI;[34] in which case, the advanced skill at the later age without specific practice was not due simply to maturation. Nonetheless, Hymes adopts the maturational concept: "All the evidence says: Readiness comes as a healthy child grows and matures. Time is the answer—not special drills or special practice."[35] Harris, too, recently defined reading readiness as a state of *general* maturity.[36]

We see, then, that the terms "maturity" and "maturation" still appear in educational writing, but in fact, as we suggested earlier,

31. *Ibid.*, p. 24.

32. Frances Ilg and Louise B. Ames, "Developmental Trends in Reading Behavior," *Journal of Genetic Psychology*, LXXVI (June, 1950), 291–312.

33. Ilg and Ames, "Developmental Trends in Arithmetic," *op. cit.*

34. L. P. Benezet, "The Story of an Experiment," *National Education Association Journal*, XXIV (November, 1935), 241–44; XXIV (December, 1935), 301–3; and XXV (January, 1936), 7–8.

35. Hymes, *op. cit.*, p. 10.

36. Albert J. Harris, *How To Increase Reading Ability*, p. 26. New York: Longmans, Green & Co., 1961 (4th ed., rev.).

the idea of "general maturity" is vague and not very helpful. If, on the other hand, we should think of readiness in terms of specific kinds of maturity, then we must recognize that "(1) There are no known structures which are specialized to the achievement of success in subjectmatter learning (the eye functions in reading, but it functions also in many other types of behavior). (2) Progress in the subjectmatter areas is, therefore, not produced by the maturing of specialized structures (it does not come as the inevitable result of some kind of 'unfolding')."[37]

Stages and mental structures.—In his chapter on "Readiness for Learning," Bruner makes considerable use of concepts attributed to Piaget and his colleagues, and especially as they were interpreted by Inhelder at the Woods Hole Conference.[38] Now it is not always easy to determine the sense in which the term "stage" is being used by Piaget and others. For instance, are the stages, which are said to appear sequentially in a stable order, continuous or discontinuous in nature?[39] Sometimes it seems as if the sequence, which is predetermined, is a biological unfolding without reference to the child's surroundings.[40] At one point Bruner seems to credit the school with considerable influence,[41] but almost immediately he seems to play down its role when he says that instruction in scientific ideas need not follow natural development *slavishly*.

"Mental structure" is another important concept in Piaget's thinking. Mental structures, as "systems of rules of logic,"[42] appear to be related to a theory of knowledge. It almost seems as if Piaget considers that cognitions appear in a specific sequence because of the nature of knowledge. Again, we are faced with questions about the reasons for the sequence. Inhelder tells us that "the genesis of the mechanisms of knowledge" cannot be explained in terms of maturation, learning from experience, or social transmission. Rather, Piaget

37. William A. Brownell, "Readiness for Subjectmatter Learning," *National Education Association Journal*, XL (October, 1951), 445–46.

38. Bruner, *op. cit.*

39. Barbel Inhelder, "Some Aspects of Piaget's Genetic Approach to Cognition," in "Thought in the Young Child," *Monographs of the Society for Research in Child Development*, XXVII, No. 2 (1962), 23–24.

40. See *ibid.*, p. 23, and W. Kessen, in *ibid.*, p. 69.

41. Bruner, *op. cit.*, p. 39.   42. Kessen, *op. cit.*, p. 81.

proposed "equilibration" as the explanatory concept—that is, adaptation is a matter of sequential changes which occur because "each organism is an open, active, self-regulating system."[43] The discussions of the concepts of "mental structure" and "equilibration" do not enable this writer to see their practical significance for readiness for learning.

According to Inhelder, "The order of succession of the stages is constant,"[44] which implies a law of development or a set of invariances. How are we to interpret invariances located by observational methods in "naturalistic" settings? Rosenblith, for example, raised just such a question when she wondered whether the observed stages are due to biological conditions or to culture and learning experiences, and when she asked whether it might be possible to arrange an environment in which some specific sequence did not appear.[45] The implications of Piaget's concepts may be better understood when Piaget and his colleagues provide concrete evidence derived from their own *operational* activities in assessing readiness, i.e., the validity of the generalizations must be tested through practice.

Bruner seemingly accepts Piaget's position on intellectual development and its educational significance. It is, therefore, difficult to understand how he can maintain "that any subject can be taught effectively in some intellectually honest form to any child at any stage of development,"[46] and at the same time say, first, that the "pre-operational" child cannot grasp the idea of "reversibility," and second, "because of this fundamental lack the child cannot understand certain fundamental ideas that lie at the basis of mathematics and physics. . . . It goes without saying that teachers are severely limited in transmitting concepts to a child at this stage, even in a highly intuitive manner."[47] The notion of "effective teaching" in the first quotations seems inconsistent with the ideas of the second. (Another recent interpretation of Piaget's theories of development may be found in Hunt.[48])

The Critical period.—The notions of "critical periods" and timing

43. Inhelder, *op. cit.*, p. 28.

44. *Ibid.*, p. 23.

45. Kessen, *op. cit.*, p. 86.

46. Bruner, *op. cit.*, p. 33.

47. *Ibid.*, p. 35.

48. J. McV. Hunt, *Intelligence and Experience.* New York: Ronald Press Co., 1961.

are well stated by Goodenough and Tyler: "The idea of developmental stages appears in another guise in the work educators have done with regard to 'readiness' for different kinds of school learning. . . . There seems to be a period in which a child is ripe for reading, intellectually and emotionally. . . . The popular notion of 'the psychological moment' takes on new meaning with regard to development."[49] It is almost as if Brutus were admonishing today's teacher:

> There is a tide in the affairs of men,
> Which, taken at the flood, leads on to fortune;
> Omitted, all the voyage of their life
> Is bound in shallows and in miseries.

The experimental basis for the idea of "critical periods" is found in various embryological studies. For instance, Goodenough and Tyler report the appearance of quite different structural defects depending upon the precise time in the developmental sequence that certain influences come into play.[50] More extended discussions may be found in Stockard[51] and Gates.[52]

Another phenomenon that is currently attracting considerable interest, that of "imprinting," is related to the concept of critical periods. According to the notion of imprinting, animals which do not live with others of their own species at an appropriate time in the developmental sequence do not learn to behave in ways that characterize their species. The early research on imprinting dealt with social behavior of geese, ducklings, and puppies.[53] In his paper on this subject, Scott points out that there are three kinds of critical-period phenomena—one of which involves optimal time for learning. Scott recognizes that we know little about optimal periods as they relate to intellectual skills, partly because, in his opinion, they are based upon both age and the relative rate of maturation of various

49. Florence L. Goodenough and Leona E. Tyler, *Developmental Psychology*, p. 13. New York: Appleton-Century-Crofts, 1959.

50. *Ibid.*, p. 82.

51. C. R. Stockard, *The Physical Basis of Personality*. New York: Norton & Co., 1931.

52. R. R. Gates, *Human Genetics*. New York: Macmillan Co., 1946.

53. F. A. Beach and J. Jaynes, "Effects of Early Experience upon the Behavior of Animals," *Psychological Bulletin*, LI (1954), 239–63.

organs. In discussing the importance of timing, he says, "Any attempt to teach a child or animal at too early a period of development may result in his learning bad habits, or simply in his learning 'not to learn,' either of which results may greatly handicap him in later life."[54]

Numerous writers have summarized and evaluated many of the studies which have influenced educational thinking about timing as a part of the readiness problem;[55] Some educators and psychologists have been considerably influenced by the concept, but McCandless sensibly warns us that the evidence about the importance of timing is incomplete, and practical decisions concerning it should be taken with caution. He advises care about accepting the idea that we can minimize opportunities for children's learning on the assumption that maturation will take care of development. Such an idea, he says, "ignores the fact that more subtle results of early and late teaching have been neglected in studies such as those cited."[56] Possibly, for education, Lowell's statement that there is truly "a tide in the affairs of men, but there is no gulf-stream setting forever in one direction" represents a more realistic notion than was Shakespeare's—at least it is more optimistic and forward looking. Effective and economical learning is probably more than a matter of moving in on the child at some maturationally defined point in time.

Reactions against postponement.—It is not surprising that there have been reactions against the doctrine of postponement. Brownell was convinced as early as 1938 that much arithmetic was being unduly postponed, and that children are capable of dealing with many topics long before they appear in the curriculum—if we think it desirable to introduce them earlier. An even greater departure from the concept of postponement is proposed by Bruner: "We begin with the hypothesis that any subject can be taught effectively in some intellectually honest form to any child at any stage of development. It is a bold hypothesis and an essential one in thinking about the na-

54. J. P. Scott, "Critical Periods in Behavioral Development," *Science,* CXXXVIII (1962), 947.

55. See: W. Fowler, "Cognitive Learning in Infancy and Childhood," *Psychological Bulletin,* LIX (1962), 116–52; Goodenough and Tyler, *op. cit.*; and McCandless, *op. cit.*

56. McCandless, *op. cit.,* p. 121.

ture of the curriculum. No evidence exists to contradict it; considerable evidence is being amassed that supports it."[57] The hypothesis is indeed bold, but one wonders whether it is essential for curriculm-planning. The phrase "in some intellectually honest form" may provide an escape hatch; but is there in fact no evidence that contradicts the hypothesis? Do common experience and observation not convince us of the impossibility of teaching such a class of responses as "solving linear equations" to a neonate? (If Bruner says "any," his reader is surely free to select *any* child, *any* subject matter, *any* age, and *any* stage of development.) His assertion, if he intended that it be taken seriously, can be as harmful as the earlier question, "After all, what's the hurry?" On the other hand, his statement can serve a useful purpose if it leads us to question the desirability of, or the necessity for, the delay found in some school curricula. Apparently Bruner was overstating the case in order to emphasize the weakness in the doctrine of delay, because two pages later he quotes Inhelder: "Grasping the idea of invariance is beset with difficulties for the child, often unsuspected by teachers."[58] Such being the case, there are limitations upon what the "child" can learn.

Possibly this is as good a time as any to refer to some current attempts to teach certain processes and skills to children at earlier ages than has been the custom. Moore is reported to be teaching children, aged two to five, to type, read, write, and take dictation.[59] Suppes is teaching geometric concepts in the lower primary grades.[60] Some English children, aged seven, can manipulate numbers in several bases other than the decimal systems, and some eight-year-olds can simplify quadratic expressions.[61]

Too little is known about these attempts to teach young children more "complex" ideas and skills for us to be able to assess them in any realistic sense. However, even if it be demonstrated that young children can learn this or that "advanced" process, we should still need to decide whether it is desirable and appropriate for them to do so. Sociologically, we may ask whether this is the best way for

57. Bruner, *op. cit.,* p. 33.   58. *Ibid.,* p. 41.

59. *Carnegie Corporation of New York Quarterly,* IX (1961), 1–3.

60. Bruner, *op. cit.*

61. Brownell, "Observations of Instruction in Lower-Grade Arithmetic in English and Scottish Schools," *op. cit.,* pp. 170–71.

children to spend their time and energy. Intellectually, we may ask whether this is the most suitable preparation for future intellectual activities. Emotionally, we may ask whether "early" systematic instruction in reading, mathematics, or what have you, will have a harmful effect upon motivation, or upon personal and social behavior. The effects of intellectual activities on personality (non-cognitive functioning) will depend upon what is taught, but possibly even more upon how it is taught and by whom and for what purposes. Appropriate instruction with suitable materials may be important factors in motivations for later intellectual activities. However, instruction can be introduced prematurely; it can as truly be delayed unduly. Soft sentimentality may be damaging to the personality; so, too, may excessively high expectations and requirements.

The point we are trying to make here is simply this: Just the fact that children can learn this or that does not by itself mean that we, therefore, must require them to do so at some young age or in some early grade. A whole network of related philosophical, sociological, psychological, and educational questions must be tackled before we can come to a practical judgment as expressed in questions like: Why should we introduce the material? What is the intended purpose? Is the objective feasible?

MENTAL MATURITY

Mental age and reading.—One specific type of maturation, "mental," has often been selected for special attention in many studies of readiness for school learning. An example is found in Washburne's question: "At what stage of a child's mental growth, as measured by intelligence tests, can he most effectively learn" this or that topic in arithmetic?[62] Harrison, too, considered that "mental maturity and rate of mental maturing constitute the most important factors in reading readiness."[63]

"The M.A. is a measure of the level of mental maturity achieved at a particular time,"[64] i.e., mental maturity is identified with the

62. Washburne, "The Grade Placement of Arithmetic Topics," *op. cit.*, p. 641.

63. Harrison, *op. cit.*, p. 61.

64. Albert J. Harris, "Reading and Human Development," in *Development in and through Reading*, p. 23. Sixtieth Yearbook of the National Society for the Study of Education, Part I. Chicago: Distributed by the University of Chicago Press, 1961.

concept of mental age and, hence, is measured by means of intelligence tests. If mental age is, indeed, a measure of mental *"maturity,"* then we are faced, according to the previous discussion, with the prospect of considering mental age to be a matter of intrinsic, inner growth. Yet such an idea is hardly likely to be entertained by those familiar with the methods used to determine mental age.

A few examples will illustrate how mental age has been used as an estimate of readiness. Dolch and Bloomster[65] propose, on the basis of their research, that "a mental age of seven years seems to be the lowest at which a child can be expected to use phonetics, even in the simple situations provided by these two tests." Their conclusion was widely quoted and probably had an important influence on the teaching of phonics, even though some educators may have questioned the feasibility of stating such a specific criterion for readiness for phonics, and especially without giving due consideration to instructional materials and methods. Recourse to the M.A. ignores the fact that scores on intelligence tests are only slightly related to structural changes, auditory perception, and so on—conditions that are important in phonetic competence.

Harrison claimed that "to make any progress in reading a child must have attained a mental age of at least six years and that a mental age of six and one-half years more nearly insures success."[66] Morphett and Washburne[67] agreed, and indeed, Washburne's confidence in this criterion increased, for later he wrote, "Nowadays each first-grade teacher in Winnetka has a chart showing when each of her children will be mentally six-and-a-half, and is careful to avoid any effort to get a child to read before he has reached this stage of mental growth."[68]

However, doubts soon began to be expressed. Gates, for instance, was early convinced that "statements concerning the necessary mental age at which a pupil can be intrusted to learn to read are essentially meaningless. The age for learning to read under one

65. E. W. Dolch and Maurine Bloomster, "Phonic Readiness," *Elementary School Journal*, XXXVIII (November, 1937), 201–5.

66. Harrison, *op. cit.*, p. 61.

67. Mabel Vogel Morphett and Carleton Washburne, "When Should Children Begin To Read?" *Elementary School Journal*, XXXI (March, 1931), 496–503.

68. Washburne, "Ripeness," *op. cit.*, p. 127.

program or with the method employed by one teacher may be entirely different from that required under other circumstances."[69] A similar position has been taken by numerous writers, but old myths neither die nor fade away: we find the early papers by Morphett and Washburne produced in *Readings in Educational Psychology* by Noll and Noll.[70] Also, according to a recent textbook, "research indicates that a mental age of $6\frac{1}{2}$ is required to read."[71]

The weaknesses of relying upon mental age as the criterion for readiness for specific types of learning should be apparent from our knowledge about the validity, reliability, and predictability of intelligence tests and about the variability in an individual's performance on subtests of an intelligence test. Some doubts about the possibility of expressing readiness in terms of a precise mental age should have occurred even to the early investigators. Thus, for instance, Morphett and Washburne reported two different mental ages in their study of reading readiness—viz., six and one-half years if measured by the Detroit First-Grade Intelligence Test, seven and one-half if measured by the Stanford-Binet Intelligence Scale.

Mental age and arithmetic.—Educators and psychologists have not confined their interest to reading, for they also assigned arithmetical topics to specific mental ages. The most extensive research on placement is that by Washburne and his Committee of Seven. In an early report Washburne wrote: "This much, at least, can be said with certainty: Multiplication facts should not be taught below a mental age level of 8 years, 4 months, nor to children who have not attained virtual mastery of the addition facts."[72] Their recommendations received considerable attention, favorable and critical, and undoubtedly they affected the arithmetic curriculum over a period of many years. And yet, the same author writes: "It is entirely possible that the degree of effective mastery could be raised and that the mental level at which it can be attained could be lowered if the teaching conditions as a whole were improved."[73]

69. Arthur I. Gates, "The Necessary Mental Age for Beginning Reading," *Elementary School Journal*, XXXVII (March, 1937), 507.

70. Victor H. Noll and Rachel P. Noll, *Readings in Educational Psychology*, pp. 83–91. New York: Macmillan Co., 1962.

71. Ira J. Gordon, *Human Development*, p. 185. New York: Harper & Bros., 1962.

72. Washburne, "The Grade Placement of Arithmetic Topics," *op. cit.*, p. 656.

73. *Ibid.*, p. 643.

There is little systematic, formal research directed specifically at curriculum questions arising out of the Committee's recommendations. Johnson[74] viewed the recommended placement with favor, but Beall and Grossnickle[75] found it possible to teach "long division" at mental ages below those proposed by the Committee of Seven. MacGregor[76] reported that eleven-year-olds in Scotland scored more than one year above the norms on American tests, and this despite the fact that they had received no instruction for some of the items on the test. MacGregor believes that one reason for the difference is that in Scotland instruction in arithmetic begins at age five. There are still the questions: How early *can* instruction in arithmetic begin? How early *should* it begin?

Mental age does not seem to be a particularly useful index of readiness for whatever activity, process, or skill we are planning to teach. In a sense this fact has been realized even by those who propose minimal or optimal mental ages, for they generally list a whole host of other conditions that need to be taken into account for an accurate assessment of readiness. The continuance of the practice of reporting specific mental ages attests to the difficulty of giving up an idea that depends upon a simple technique for obtaining a single numerical index of readiness. It is time to search for other types of clues which will give more specific guidance to the teacher.

LEARNING SETS

Producing readiness.—The concepts of "maturity" and "maturation" seem to imply that "readiness" for some specific type of educational activity appears full blown in the course of time. Hymes, for instance, is quite opposed to the expression "building readiness"— these are "uncongenial terms."[77] There are others who disagree, urging that "reading readiness is not now left to chance and to time alone; it is *produced*."[78] Possibly we shall make better progress if

74. J. T. Johnson, "An Evaluation of Research on Gradation in the Field of Arithmetic," *Journal of Educational Research*, XXXVII (1943), 161–73.

75. See Brownell, "A Critique of the Committee of Seven's Investigations on the Grade-Placement of Arithmetic Topics," *op. cit.*

76. Gregor MacGregor, *Achievement Tests in the Primary School*. Scottish Council for Research in Education, Vol. VI. London: University of London Press, Ltd., 1934.

77. Hymes, *op. cit.*, p. 11.

78. Brownell, "Readiness for Subjectmatter Learning," *op. cit.*, p. 446.

we give less weight to the concept of maturation and emphasize more the notion that readiness depends upon appropriate stimulation and opportunity for relevant learning experiences and that practice and integration are essential to knowledge or skills.

There are examples in educational practice in which the latter point of view is being recommended and carried out. Mueller writes of "building algebra readiness in grades seven and eight."[79] He suggests that arithmetic may be taught so as to develop arithmetic concepts and to build readiness for algebra. For instance, the arithmetic teacher may emphasize "the factor point of view," "equation-type thinking" and "ordered pairs," and thus will prepare the pupils for ninth-grade algebra. In his description of the "Madison Project," Davis[80] points out that the major interest is in developing readiness for ninth-grade algebra by trying to assure that pupils have the necessary background skills, understanding, and motivation. To do this, those involved in the project determined what skills and techniques are basic to success in algebra and then attempted to teach them in the elementary grades so that they were well learned ahead of time by prospective algebra students. Brune[81] recommends the introduction of informal geometry in the lower grades, where the teachers should expect pupils to become actively curious and to discover relationships for themselves, in the course of which they should develop mathematical motivations that will help them in their later studies. For Brune, readiness is a function of adequate "mathematical maturity" and of emotional security that will permit the pupil to continue his studies. (What does Brune mean by "mathematical maturity"? Probably he does not refer to a biological budding of mathematical competence. More than likely he is thinking along the lines of readiness to be mentioned shortly, but to use the word here is to introduce ambiguity.)

Olander[82] used a special test to assess readiness for "signed num-

79. Francis J. Mueller, "Building Algebra Readiness in Grades Seven and Eight," *Arithmetic Teacher*, VI (November, 1959), 269–73.

80. Robert B. Davis, "The 'Madison Project' of Syracuse University," *Mathematics Teacher*, LIII (November, 1960), 571–75.

81. Irvin H. Brune, "Geometry in the Grades," *Arithmetic Teacher*, VIII (May, 1961), 210–19.

82. C. E. Olander, "The Use of a Readiness Test in Teaching a Unit on Signed Numbers," *School Science and Mathematics*, LVII (1957), 131–38.

bers." The test was prepared after an analysis of the operations, skills, and information required for manipulating signed numbers. Olander's notion of a diagnostic test to assess readiness for some specific activity is reasonable, was suggested some time ago, and is found in certain recent studies of the learning process. We are dealing here with what Woody[83] labeled "educational readiness" as contrasted with what he termed biological, psychological, and sociological readiness. It was Woody's contention that "educational" readiness is the heart of the educational process and that it is one type of readiness over which the teacher has a considerable influence. For example, arithmetic readiness depends upon the pupil's background of experiences, his control over the necessary language and language skills, his ability to read, and his ability to handle the fundamental facts.

Brownell[84] was thinking of this latter aspect of readiness in his discussion of "arithmetic readiness as a practical classroom concept." Teachers have to make a practical judgment about when to begin a new topic in arithmetic, basing their judgment upon their information about the total arithmetic program in their school, upon what has already been taught, and upon whatever evidence there is about the prospects for success. Even more specifically, for instance, readiness for two-place division will depend upon such matters as mastery of the simple division combinations, grasp of the idea and the process of division, skills in adding (including carrying), subtracting (with and without borrowing), and so on.

The scores on Brownell's diagnostic tests showed that the pupils were ready in varying degrees to take the next step economically and efficiently. The results point up several implications for readiness: (a) we ought to allow for a wide margin of flexibility in the grade placement of arithmetic topics if we are to provide for the range of individual differences in achievement; (b) we need to strive toward a closer approximation of a reasonable, feasible individualization of instruction; (c) we will probably be forced to compromise our judgments about whether or not to proceed because the conditions

83. Clifford W. Woody, "A General Educator Looks at Arithmetic Readiness," *Mathematics Teacher*, XXX (1937), 314–21.

84. William A. Brownell, "Arithmetical Readiness as a Practical Classroom Concept," *Elementary School Journal*, LII (September, 1951), 15–22.

for complete readiness in all its facets will not be satisfied for each pupil.

The method of analytical diagnostic testing is probably applicable to other subject matters. However, it may be noted, in addition, that evidence about readiness may be obtained, for instance, by observational and interview techniques. The boy who performed subtraction according to the following statement is not ready for subtractions involving large numbers. The question was: $17 - 8 = ?$ The boy's verbalization was $17 - 8$ is, let's see, $8 \times 2 = 16$, $17 - 16 = 1$, $8 + 1 = 9$, the answer is 9. To rely upon testing only is to lose opportunities to discover peculiarities or creativeness in processes.

The importance of the educational component of readiness has been recognized by various writers. Thus, the idea was included in the research and recommendations of the Committee of Seven,[85] but the importance of its role was often lost sight of because the reports sometimes failed to stress sufficiently the necessity for assessing educational achievement as well as mental age.

Learning sets and hierarchies: an experimental analysis.—Further understanding of the concept of educational readiness may follow from a consideration of such research as that dealing with "the acquisition of knowledge" by Gagné and others.[86] Gagné relates his research directly to the matter of transfer, and not even indirectly to questions of readiness,[87] although both method and results seem to be relevant since educational readiness as discussed above appears to involve transfer from lower- to higher-level activities and processes. It seems worthwhile, therefore, to outline Gagné's research in some detail.

First of all, we must know what Gagné means by the term "learning set": "Knowledge relevant to any given final task to be learned

---

85. Washburne, "The Grade Placement of Arithmetic Topics," *op. cit.*, and "The Work of the Committee of Seven on Grade-Placement in Arithmetic," *op. cit.*

86. Robert M. Gagné and N. E. Paradise, "Abilities and Learning Sets in Knowledge Acquisition," *Psychological Monographs*, LXXV, No. 14 (1961), 1–23 (Whole No. 518); Robert M. Gagné, John R. Mayor, Helen L. Garstens, and Noel E. Paradise, "Factors in Acquiring Knowledge of a Mathematical Task," *Psychological Monographs*, LXXVI, No. 7 (1962), 1–21 (Whole No. 526).

87. Learning theorists have given little, if any, attention to problems of readiness for learning.

is conceived as a set of subordinate capabilities called *learning sets*."[88]
Next, Gagné, thinking about self-instructional programs, theorizes
that "differences in rate of completion of a learning program are
primarily dependent upon the number and kind of learning sets (i.e.,
the 'knowledge') the learner brings to the situation, secondarily
upon his standing in respect to certain relevant basic abilities, and
not in any direct sense upon a general 'learning rate ability.' "[89] Acceptance of the theory implies that "a substantial proportion of the
variance in learning program performance is attributable to the attainment or nonattainment of learning sets relevant to the final task
which the program is designed to teach."[90]

Next, in order to test his theory, Gagné analyzed a self-instructional program on "solving equations," and proposed the hierarchy
of learning sets shown in Figure 1. The ovals at the bottom of the
hierarchy represent the "basic" ability factors which are relevant to
the learning sets which are shown arranged in levels of increasing
complexity. The data from 118 ninth-grade algebra students generally confirmed the theory, and weaknesses in the self-instructional
program may well account for some of the nonconfirmatory evidence. Here are two of Gagné's predictions that were verified:

1. Correlations of theoretically relevant basic abilities were higher than
those of irrelevant basic abilities with measures of final performance,
with transfer of training scores, with number of learning sets achieved,
and with rate of learning of the total program.
2. Instances of positive transfer to each learning set from subordinate
relevant learning sets were found to occur throughout the hierarchy
with proportions ranging from .91 to 1.00.[91]

In other words, the basic abilities postulated to be important for
the learning task were, indeed, related to the criterion measures, and
success at successively higher levels was dependent upon attainment
of the learning sets at the next lower level. We may consider that
we are here dealing with the phenomenon of transfer, but we also
propose that the research does investigate one aspect of readiness. In
this sense a pupil is ready for the materials at some given level if he
has attained the learning sets up to that level.

Gagné's research has a number of interesting features even though

88. Gagné and Paradise, *op. cit.*, p. 2.
89. *Ibid.*, p. 3.   90. *Ibid.*   91. *Ibid.*, pp. 17–18.

one may question parts of it. (These comments are relevant for investigators planning similar types of research on readiness.) On the negative side, the results might have been more satisfying if he had prepared his own program in terms of an analysis of the "knowledge and abilities" required for "solving equations" instead of rely-

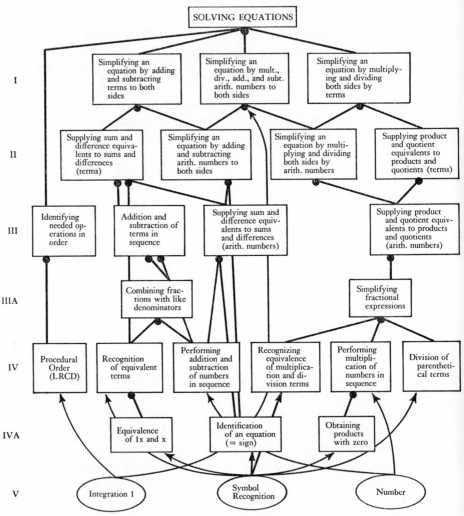

Fig. 1.—Proposed hierarchy of learning sets in a self-instructional program on "solving equations." (From Robert M. Gagné and Noel E. Paradise, "Ability and Learning Sets in Knowledge Acquisition," *Psychological Monographs*, LXXV, No. 14 [1961], 6.)

ing upon a ready-made program which turned out to be rather ineffective as judged by the results obtained on the criterion tests of
achievement, transfer, and attainment of learning sets. It seems unfortunate that he selected an instructional program using mathematical ideas and language that are, as he said, somewhat old-fashioned,
"judged against the standards of modern algebra texts."[92] One wonders, too, about the term "basic abilities used in reference to the
learning sets on the lowest rung of the proposed hierarchical ladder.
Thus, "number ability" (Fig. 1) is measured by tests of "addition,"
"subtraction," "multiplication," and "division"; and "integration"
by a test of "following directions." Why apply the term "basic" to
such learning sets? In what sense does "number" on level V represent
something *"basically"* different from "performing addition and
subtraction of numbers in sequence" at level IV? The learning set
designated by the term "numbers" can itself probably be stated as
a series of hierarchical levels. To say that "numbers" represents the
"simplest kind of things an individual must 'know how to do' in
order to progress up through the hierarchy" raises questions about
the meaning of such adjectives as "simple" and "complex" when
referring to a response.[93]

Gagné believes that the learning sets at level IV A are "almost as
simple as can be defined, for a human being."[94] Any algebra teacher,
however, knows that many pupils find difficulty with such sets as
these; and there are many college students who are not able correctly "to obtain products with zero." Just what is a "simple learning
set"? Does any item of "knowledge" have a specific inherent, intrinsic difficulty?

Despite these comments, Gagné's research is important to questions about theories and practices of readiness for learning. His
method of analyzing "complex" tasks, such as "solving linear equations," or "finding formulas for the sum of n terms in a number
series," and so on, appears to be the essence of any practical attempt
to determine pupils' educational readiness for some new process or

92. *Ibid.*, p. 5.

93. May we speak of differences in the complexity of the *response* "4" in
these situations: What is the sum of 2 and 2? What is the quotient when 3356 is
divided by 829? What is the solution of the equation $2x = 8$? of $x^2 - 4x - (x-4)^2 = 0$?

94. Gagné and Paradise, *op. cit.*, p. 5.

activity. The teacher must decide on the ultimate goal and must determine what subskills are necessary if a pupil is to progress smoothly and easily to the goal *by the methods and materials the teacher proposes to use*. This latter point is important, for there may well be a variety of means by which to reach the goal, and it may be necessary to have a specific set of steps for whatever hierarchical arrangement is to be used.

Learning sets and hierarchies and the curriculum.—There are many ways of organizing an introductory course in Euclidean geometry, each with its own hierarchies and its own patterns of educational readiness. Elementary-school arithmetic may be developed in any of a variety of sequences. The decimal system may be taught before the binary system; other systems may be introduced before the decimal system. One's decision about the sequence of topics affects what one will look for as evidence of readiness. The sciences may lend themselves to hierarchical analysis; but no doubt there are many sensible hierarchies. Again, then, what one regards as readiness will depend upon one's goals and one's means to those goals.

It may be, of course, that the type of analysis proposed is feasible for only certain types of subject matter, for instance, mathematics or science. Little of the curriculum in English and social sciences has been subjected to the systematic, logical, hierarchical type of analysis that appears appropriate for arithmetic, mathematics, and sciences. However, there are many sequences by which secondary-school English may be developed, and each sequence will have its own requirements for educational readiness. A given topic may have readiness specified in various terms depending upon the content already used, that to be used, and the instructional procedures to be employed.

When is a pupil ready to undertake the study of restrictive and nonrestrictive clauses? Is it possible, realistically, to assign this to some specific grade level or some optimal mental-age level? Again, what determines whether or not a pupil is ready for *Ode to Immortality?* When, in terms of readiness, shall we introduce the pupils to *Macbeth?* Does something akin to emotional readiness assume significance for these two latter questions? Is it reasonable to believe that all pupils aged fourteen years are ready in the sense that they have a common background of emotional experiences simply by reason of having lived for a common period of time? Probably not. Social experiences of children vary markedly, so that a reading of "Our Father, who art in heaven" arouses distinctly contrasting emotions in different children.

Much reading, whether in English or the social studies, requires the reader to construct meaning from words used figuratively, and many misunderstandings are traceable to unintended interpretation of figurative language. Just what does a speaker mean when he says, "My, but he is a big baby"? As we search for his meaning, we must take into account relevant experiences, the tone of the speaker, the situation in which the statement is made.[95] When is a pupil ready for the study of figurative language? The answer probably depends upon what figures are to be taught and what examples are used to teach pupils how to ferret out the meaning the writer is trying to convey. The concept of readiness in English and social studies may be even more complex than it is in mathematics or science.

Of course, the degree of readiness necessary for understanding a piece of prose or a poem also depends upon how much understanding is to be expected—for, after all, understanding is not an all-or-none affair; there are degrees of understanding. Here the teacher must make a decision, and the requirements by way of readiness are affected by that decision. The concept of hierarchies seems appropriate to a discussion of meaning and understanding, as seems apparent in Richards' statement that "the other words around a word are an important part [no more] of the sign-field. They can make us mistake one word for another, as proofreaders know; they can distort the very letters. That is a mistake at the humblest level of the hierarchies of interpretations through which we understand or misunderstand words."[96] If Richards is using the word "hierarchy" in the sense already discussed, and we believe he is, then the concept of hierarchy can be useful in an attempt to assess a pupil's readiness for the "next step" in English or in the social studies.

Meaning is not given by the writer or speaker; rather it is con-

95. I. A. Richards, *Interpretation in Teaching*. New York: Harcourt, Brace & Co., 1938.

96. I. A. Richards, "What Is Involved in the Interpretation of Meaning?" in *Reading and Pupil Development*, p. 50. Edited by W. S. Gray. Supplementary Educational Monographs, No. 51. Chicago: University of Chicago Press, 1940.

structed by the reader or listener. William James's amusing misinterpretation of what the boatman in *Lord Ullin's Daughter* expected to
receive for his services is an example:

> "I'll row you o'er the ferry.
> It is not for your silver bright,
> But for your winsome lady."[97]

James concluded that the boatman was to receive the lady as payment. (James, aged eight at the time, seems quite "mature.") If it is
easy to misinterpret such lines as those from *Lord Ullin's Daughter*,
how much easier it is to formulate a misinterpretation when language is used figuratively. Consider an example from *Troilus and
Cressida* (the desperately lovesick Troilus is answering Pandarus,
who has just been praising Troilus' sweetheart, Cressida):

> . . . thou answer'st, she is fair;
> *Pour'st in the open ulcer of my heart*
> *Her eyes, her hair, her cheek, her gait, her voice.*

What meaning is to be assigned to the italicized lines? What does
readiness for this type of reading involve?

Interpretation is easily conceived to be a type of problem-solving,
with all that such a process implies for readiness, including the pupil's language competence and background of experiences which are
intellectually and emotionally relevant. In order to build meaning
from the printed page the reader must take meaning to the page. For
instance, a pupil will not know what was happening when he reads,
"The keeper dusted the elephant," unless he has had some sort of
relevant experience. Of course, relevant experiences may be vicarious. Altogether too little is known about the intellectual and emotional requirements for much of the literature taught in the schools.
It is probably as true today as it was when James wrote: "In the last
resort, the teacher's own tact is the only thing that can bring out the
right effect."[98] James was not writing about readiness, but his words
are useful in that context; in many curricular matters teachers have
to rely upon their own teaching experiences and good judgment in
making decisions about the "when" of teaching specific topics, principles, or skills.

97. James, *op. cit.*, p. 107.   98. *Ibid.*

Concluding Statement

The concept of readiness has long been of interest to serious students of education. There can be little disagreement with the notion that pupils learn most effectively and efficiently when instruction is introduced at an appropriate time—neither too early nor too late but, rather, when they are ready. Disagreements arise, however, when we seek to determine what it is that produces readiness, and when we try to define readiness for particular curricular activities. Certain evidence concerning the nature of causation of readiness—a question of theory—can be traced to results from biologically oriented studies of structural modifications in the embryonic period, from "naturalistic" observations of motor activities, from observations of cognitive behavior of subjects supposedly deprived of opportunities for specific types of experiences, of subjects given "early" training, and of subjects living in a "normal" environment with neither "deprivation" nor "enrichment." Disagreements also arise when we try to measure readiness for specific instructional purposes—a question of practice. Readiness has been conceived as including such a variety of components, with limited interrelationships, that an index of general readiness is not very useful; an index of "average" readiness is likely to be more concealing than revealing.

The theoretic concept of maturation, itself a vague, generic term, became associated with that of readiness—to their mutual disadvantage. Structures, dependent primarily upon "maturation," must be developed to the point where they can function for any given type of learning activity; but this development, which primarily is the result of "maturation," is also dependent to some degree upon the use of structures themselves. A pupil cannot learn to read the printed page unless he is able to move his eyes in a rather regular and controllable manner; yet such discipline is, in some unknown degree, influenced by *using* the eyes and, so, of learning to use them better. Even so, structural specifications have not been, and probably cannot be, specified for each educational task; also, even if this were possible, the results would not likely be helpful practically. The concept of maturation has been linked to the concept of "critical moments" and "stages," and these notions in turn have implied, for certain educators, the doctrine of postponement, a doctrine which has come in for serious criticism in recent years.

One group of educators, enamored of the concept of mental "maturity," tried to use mental age (measured by intelligence tests) as the criterion for determining when a pupil is ready for some specified activity. Serious questions were raised about the usefulness of this index of readiness, but the concept received rather wide acceptance for a good many years and is still accepted in some quarters.

"Maturity" is a complex term, one that includes a great variety of characteristics—physical, social, emotional, anatomical, mental, and so on. The idea of "general" or average maturity, under these circumstances, can have only minimal significance. Further, each of such components of general maturity, as has been mentioned, is itself complex. For instance, mental age is a statement about the pupil's average performances on a variety of tasks. Two pupils may have identical mental ages, but they can have quite different patterns of scores on subtests contributing to mental age or to their total scores on an intelligence test.

The notion of maturation, including that of mental maturity, has not been particularly fruitful for educational planning. Probably a more useful notion is to be derived from an analysis of the knowledge and skills required for some new cognitive activity. The advantage of this particular approach has received attention primarily from investigators interested in arithmetic and mathematics. The method may be illustrated by considering what components by way of skills and knowledge a pupil must be able to recall, transfer, and apply if he is to be able to solve a quadratic equation. Once these components are known, they can be arranged in a hierarchy that proceeds from lower to higher levels of knowledge. Diagnostic tests can be developed to assess the pupil's preparation. Such a concept of "cognitive readiness" seems to offer considerable possibility for the improvement of instruction. Current research on "learning sets" is related to the analytic method just described and may provide a useful theory for studying educational readiness. The idea seems worthy of systematic consideration in curricular areas other than mathematics.

Of course, a pupil may have "cognitive readiness" and yet be deficient in certain aspects of "noncognitive readiness," as in the domains of emotion and motivation. And these latter are not easy to assess and provide for. Skinner[99] found it a simple matter to get his pigeons "ready" to acquire some new skill, such as turning figure-eights; all he had to do was to deprive them of food for some specific period of time. In other words, you can lead a horse to water, and you *can* make him drink—simply by deprivation.

Readiness for school learning has to take a more positive approach and provide "enrichment." Deprivation will not prepare a pupil to study directed numbers or democracy, or the Boston Massacre—indeed, we must provide for the necessary background knowledge rather than wait for time alone to produce readiness.

All this means that schooling, instruction, and education will not be of maximum effectiveness if we adopt either of two extreme views—that readiness for learning depends simply upon the passage of time or that it is ever present "at any age." We cannot simply wait for pupils to maturate. We must provide for, produce, or build, both cognitive and noncognitive readiness. In so doing we shall directly and deliberately improve teaching and learning.

99. B. F. Skinner, *Science and Human Behavior*. New York: Macmillan Co., 1953.

CHAPTER X

Creative Thinking, Problem-solving, and Instruction

J. W. GETZELS

All learning involves problems. What then do we mean when we distinguish between problem-solving and other forms of learning? Are these terms mere redundancies? Or is there a difference between learning to remember a date and learning to understand the meaning of a negative number? Between learning to apply a given formula and to conceive of a new relationship? Between learning to know the correct answer to an old question and to raise a new question about an old answer? And if there are differences among these, are there complementary differences in appropriate instructional method?

It is the peculiar circumstance that although there are numerous conceptions of learning, there are few systematic formulations of the cognitive problems found in the classroom, and virtually none regarding the nature of teaching. This chapter will consider: (*a*) the nature of cognitive problems in the classroom; (*b*) relevant conceptions of creative thinking and problem-solving; (*c*) the available experimental studies in stimulating originality, and the implications of these for teaching; and (*d*) a number of the salient instructional issues deriving from the preceding theoretical and empirical work.

On the Nature of Problems in Learning: Types of Cognitive Problems

The *Taxonomy of Educational Objectives* suggests a classification of intellective problems in the classroom by *type of learning objective*, and *skill required* as follows: knowledge, requiring recall; comprehension, requiring understanding of what is communicated; application, requiring the use of abstractions in concrete situations; analysis, requiring the dissecting of what is communicated; synthesis, requiring the organization of a pattern from separate parts; evaluation, requiring the judgment of a subject against a standard of appraisal.[1]

This suggested classification deals with *presented* problems. It omits from consideration and seems not to recognize in the classroom a significant group of problems we may call *discovered* problems. A different and perhaps more general classification to include *both presented and discovered problems* may be made if we look at the issues in terms of what is *known* and what is *unknown* in the problem-situation. From this point of view, we may identify the following types of problems:

1. The problem is given (is known) and there is a standard method for solving it, known to the problem-solver (student, experimental subject) and to others (teacher, experimenter) and guaranteeing a solution in a finite number of steps.

2. The problem is given (is known) but no standard method for solving it is known to the problem-solver, although known to the others.

3. The problem is given (is known) but no standard method for solving it is known to the problem-solver or to the others.

4. The problem itself exists but remains to be identified or discovered (become known) by the problem-solver, although known to the others.

5. The problem itself exists but remains to be identified or discovered (become known) by the problem-solver and by the others.

6. The problem itself exists but remains to be identified or discovered (as in 4 and 5) and there is a standard for solving it, once the problem is discovered, known to the problem-solver and to the others (as in 1).

7. The problem itself exists but remains to be identified or discovered, and no standard method for solving it is known to the problem-solver, although known to the others (as in 2).

8. The problem itself exists but remains to be identified or discovered, and no standard method for solving it is known to the problem-solver or to the others (as in 3).[2]

This list does not, of course, exhaust the possibilities, but enough has been said to suggest two salient points: (*a*) There is a group of problems, too often neglected by teachers and experimenters alike, in which the problem is not given but is discovered or "becomes

1. *Taxonomy of Educational Objectives*. Edited by Benjamin S. Bloom. New York: Longmans, Green & Co., 1956.

2. W. L. Libby, "Tools for Discovery of Problems and Their Solutions (Heuristics)." Center for Programs in Government Administration, University of Chicago (mimeographed).

known"; and (*b*) there is a range of problems involving various degrees of what is known and unknown, requiring various degrees of innovation and creativeness for solution.

In Type 1 problems a minimum of innovation or creativeness is required. The teacher teaches that the area of a rectangle is "side *a* multiplied by side *b*," and the student is required to "solve the problem": What is the area of a rectangle when $a = 3$, $b = 4$? The student need only plug the given data into the given formula or the known method to find the answer. Much, perhaps most, teaching is of this order. In problems of Types 2–8, the principle of solution, and perhaps even the essential question itself, must be discovered. An attempt at inventiveness, at "going beyond the information given," must be made. These problems are often avoided or turned into Type 1 problems by the teacher, and students do not acquire experience with the more creative or innovative aspects of learning.

Solving problems of Types 2–8 involves what is called "creative thinking." In a sense, the term "creative thinking," like innovative problem-solving, is a tautology. For these problems cannot be solved except through innovation or creativeness in however modest a degree. As Maltzman says: "There is no fundamental difference in the behavioral principle determining originality and problem-solving behavior. . . . Both involve the evocation of relatively uncommon responses, otherwise the situation would not be called a problem or the behavior original."[3] The terms are used only to distinguish the processes involved in working on problems of Types 2–8 from those involved in solving Type 1 problems (really "pseudo-problems") the solution of which is also commonly said to involve thinking and problem-solving.

A hard and fast distinction is sometimes made between "reasoning" at one extreme, primarily determined by objective criteria, and "imagining" at the other extreme, primarily determined by subjective criteria. Except perhaps for analytic purposes, such a distinction cannot be maintained, at least not for the problems with which we are concerned. Thinking, reasoning, imagining, reflecting, judging, conceiving, and problem-solving are close kin to each other

---

3. Irving Maltzman, "On the Training of Originality," *Psychological Review*, LXVII (July, 1960), 232. See also, Ernest R. Hilgard, "Creativity and Problem-solving," in *Creativity and Its Cultivation*, pp. 162 ff. Edited by Harold H. Anderson. New York: Harper & Bros., 1959.

when one is dealing with the "unknown." Nor will it do to apply the term "imagining" only to the arts, and the term "reasoning" only to the sciences. Is the formula $E = Mc^2$ less the product of "imagining" than, say, the "Moses" or the *Eroica*, and are they so much less the product of "reasoning" than the formula? To be sure, different standards of appraisal for achievement or of "proof" may be applied, but successful solution of the problems in either field requires something of novelty, originality, and creativity.

Conceptions of Thinking and Problem-solving

Although there may be agreement on what constitutes an act of original thinking or problem-solving as in the case of $E = Mc^2$, the "Moses," or the *Eroica*, there is the widest disagreement regarding the processes underlying the act. Conceptions of the processes derive from sources as diverse as logic, learning theory, developmental studies of children, factorial constructions of the intellect, and psychoanalysis. It is impossible to deal sensibly with instruction for creative thinking and for problem-solving without considering, however briefly, a number of these conceptions of the processes themselves.

LOGICAL-PHILOSOPHICAL CONCEPTS

Dewey's famous five "logically distinct" steps of the "act of thought" have been influential for a half-century. Succeeding each other in order, they are "(i) a felt difficulty; (ii) its location and definition; (iii) suggestion of a possible solution; (iv) development by reasoning of the bearings of the suggestion; (v) further observation and experiment leading to its acceptance or rejection; that is, the conclusion of belief or disbelief."[4] Although Dewey himself was at pains to point to the value of nonlogical "playfulness" in thinking,[5] the "logically distinct" five steps became particularly attractive to the educator, doubtless because they seem to provide an organized attack on problem-solving, and it was believed this attack could be sharpened through step-by-step training.[6] Latterly, however, analy-

4. John Dewey, *How We Think*, p. 72. New York: D. C. Heath & Co., 1910.

5. *Ibid.*, pp. 219 ff.

6. Merle W. Tate, Barbara Stanier, and Berj Harootunian, "Differences between Good and Poor Problem-solvers." School of Education, University of Pennsylvania, 1959 (mimeographed).

ses of problem-solving behavior have suggested that these formal steps might be more a statement of one type of "scientific method" than a description of how people think.

LEARNING THEORY CONCEPTS: UNI-PROCESSES AND DUAL-PROCESSES

Systematic consideration of thinking has come from the learning theorists. Stated in extreme terms, for uni-process theorists like Thorndike or Guthrie, thinking is the outcome of conflicting action tendencies from past associative learning and consists of selecting previous associations to try out in the new situation. The fundamental process is the same whether reproducing nonsense syllables, shooting clay pigeons, or playing chess. All behavior, no matter how apparently "novel" or "insightful," rests ultimately on stimulus-response principles.[7] As Thorndike put it, the same general laws that "explain how a child learns to talk or dress himself and why he gets up in the morning or goes to bed at night also explain how he learns geometry or philosophy and why he succeeds or fails in the most abstruse problems. . . ."[8]

For dual-process theorists like Wertheimer or Goldstein, associative learning and thinking cannot be considered on the same continuum. They distinguish sharply between "ugly thinking"—problem-solving based upon trial and error—and "productive thinking" —solutions based upon cognitive reorganization. Productive problem-solving begins when the thinker "realizes" the problem, i.e., when he sees the inner structure of the situation. The structural strains produce tensions in the thinker, and vectors are set up determining the steps to be taken to transpose the incomplete situation into one that is structurally complete. What is especially significant for instruction from this point of view is that the person "naturally" seeks the inner structure of a problem situation if he is unfettered by habits developed through training in blind association and "ugly" trial-and-error learning, i.e., in our terms, if he has not been restricted to an educational experience devoted exclusively to problems of Type 1 or, at best, Type 2.

7. H. F. Harlow, "Thinking," in *Theoretical Foundations of Psychology*, pp. 452–502. Edited by H. Helson. New York: D. Van Nostrand Co., 1951.

8. Edward L. Thorndike, *Human Learning*, p. 160. New York: Century Co., 1931.

DEVELOPMENTAL CONCEPTS: PIAGET

The most extensive work on the problem-solving processes of children has been done by Piaget. His early concepts—egocentrism, absolutism, syncretism, juxtaposition—are well-known and have been ably presented in a preceding yearbook of the National Society.[9] But his less familiar postwar work may ultimately be of greater significance for education. As before, Piaget conceives of the development of thinking as occurring in stages.[10] There is first the period of "sensori-motor intelligence" from birth to two years, during which language has not yet appeared, and the child can only perform motor actions. These actions have some of the features of intelligence but of an intelligence that is not yet operational.

From two to four years, there is a period of "pre-conceptual" thought, the character of which may briefly be described as follows: If adults reason either *de*ductively from the general to the particular or *in*ductively from the particular to the general, the child during this period reasons *trans*ductively from the particular to the particular.[11]

From four to seven years there follows a period of "intuitive" thought, which is thought that has not yet freed itself from perception. For example, when a child at this stage pours liquid or beads from one glass bottle to another of a different shape, he believes that the actual quantity is increased or decreased depending on the shape of the recipient bottle.[12]

The next period, seven to eleven years, is one of "concrete operations" during which the reasoning processes are logical but not altogether dissociated from the concrete data, complete conceptual generality not yet having been attained. In the final period of "propositional or formal operations," from eleven to fifteen years, the child attains complete conceptual generality and achieves the capac-

---

9. William A. Brownell, "Problem-solving," in *The Psychology of Learning*, pp. 415–43. Forty-first Yearbook of the National Society for the Study of Education, Part II. Chicago: Distributed by University of Chicago Press, 1942.

10. See, for example, Jean Piaget, *Logic and Psychology*. New York: Basic Books, 1957.

11. D. E. Berlyne, "Recent Developments in Piaget's Works," *British Journal of Educational Psychology*, XXVII (1957), 1–12.

12. Piaget, *op. cit.*, pp. 11–12.

ity for hypothetico-deductive reasoning. He is now able to accept any sort of data as purely hypothetical and to reason correctly from them. As Piaget himself puts it, "Instead of just coordinating facts about the actual world, hypothetico-deductive reasoning draws out the implications of possible statements and thus gives rise to a unique synthesis of the possible and the necessary."[13]

A large part of the information regarding the latter stage comes from a series of experiments by Inhelder, in which children were invited to discover for themselves, with the help of simple apparatus, elementary laws of physics. Children during the "intuitive" stage varied conditions haphazardly and observed what happened in particular cases without deriving any general principles. During the "concrete operations" stage, one factor at a time was varied and its effect noted. Not before the "formal operations" stage did the child plan truly scientific investigations, varying the factors in all possible operations in a systematic order. The instructional implications are unmistakable: Children with no previous instruction seem capable of learning scientific laws in this way with more zest and understanding than by traditional teaching methods. But timing is important—they are not able to do this before the formal operations stage has been reached.[14]

ON THE SOLUTION OF ALREADY ENVISAGED PROBLEMS VERSUS THE ENVISAGEMENT OF PROBLEMS FOR SOLUTION

The preceding formulations have been concerned mainly with "known" or presented problems. Here, to use Wertheimer's terminology, there is typically a given problem situation, S_1, and the thinking process moves it rationally to a solution situation, S_2. But what about situations which are not of the S_1-S_2 class? What about the situation where the problem itself, i.e., the S_1 is not given (is not known) but is *discovered?* Or what about situations when the S_1 plays little or no role, where the individual begins with an S_2 that is to be created?

Wertheimer himself recognizes these issues but is able to say little about them in the terms of his conceptualization of thinking. He can only comment: "The process starts, as in some creative processes in art and music, by envisaging some features of an S_2 that is to be cre-

13. *Ibid.*, p. 19.   14. Berlyne, *op. cit.*, p. 9.

ated. The artist is driven toward its crystallization, concretization, or full realization . . . (similarly with a mathematician who envisages the idea of a formula or of an equation)."[15]

But this formulation fails to deal exactly with the two questions touched upon but left unanswered, i.e., the source of the "envisaged S_2" and the source of the "drive" toward its "full realization." There is a difference between working on the solution to a problem that is presented and discovering a problem that needs solution. Much productive or creative thought is really of this second kind—i.e., discovering problems. And it is the processes involved in this kind of thought that we know least about from the point of view of either learning or teaching. Help for dealing with the issues here may be forthcoming from two very disparate modes of inquiry. One is the factor analysis of thinking, especially in its creative aspects, resulting in potentially heuristic categories and operationally useful instruments. The other is the psychodynamic formulation of creative thinking deriving from clinical analysis.

FACTOR ANALYTIC CONCEPTS: GUILFORD

Although there have been many factor analyses of intellectual behavior, in the area of creative thinking, Guilford's work has been most influential.[16] According to his analysis, intellectual behavior falls into two major classes—memory factors and thinking factors, the latter being the more numerous. Thinking factors can be further subdivided into convergent-thinking processes and divergent-thinking processes, a distinction of greatest importance that has not been sufficiently appreciated in psychology or education.

Intellectual production can be defined as the generation of new information from known information. Convergent thinking pertains to new information that is maximally determined by the known information, as in the case of Type 1 problems. Divergent thinking

---

15. Max Wertheimer, *Productive Thinking*, p. 197. New York: Harper & Bros., 1945.

16. See, for example, J. P. Guilford *et al.*, "A Factor-analytic Study of Creative Thinking. II, Administration of Tests and Analysis of Results," *Reports from the Psychological Laboratory*, No. 8 (Los Angeles: University of California, 1952); "A Factor-analytic Study across the Domains of Reasoning, Creativity, and Evaluation. I, Hypotheses and Description of Tests," *Reports, ibid.*, No. 11 (1954); "A Revised Structure of Intellect," *Reports, ibid.*, No. 19 (1957).

pertains to new information that is minimally determined by the known information, as in the case of Type 8 problems. In the one, the requirement is for a single already ascertained right response. In the other, a variety of responses involving "fluency," "flexibility," "originality," and "elaboration" may be called for.

Guilford argues that this distinction has profound implications for instruction. In his words,

> It [education] has emphasized abilities in the areas of convergent think-ing and evaluation, often at the expense of development in the area of divergent thinking. We have attempted to teach students how to arrive at "correct" answers that our civilization has taught us are correct. This is convergent thinking. We have also attempted to teach them to think critically, which means evaluation. This has been done very often within the limits of socially accepted standards, again with the emphasis upon one right answer. Outside the arts we have generally discouraged the development of divergent-thinking abilities, unintentionally but effec-tively. . . .[17]
>
> With the information that most of the creative thinking abilities are in the divergent-thinking category, the teacher can see opportunities to call for divergent thinking. In transmitting our culture to the younger generation, we naturally stress conventional answers to problems, hence we emphasize convergent thinking. In urging that we need more empha-sis upon divergent thinking on the part of students, I am not advocating that we attempt to create a generation of young rebels. It should be possible to teach appreciation for those things from the past that are good as well as to encourage students to see how things might be done better.[18]

PSYCHOANALYTIC CONCEPTS

It hardly seems necessary to apologize today for bringing Freud into the classroom or learning laboratory. Still, it is well to remem-ber that the first edition of Hilgard's *Theories of Learning* in 1948 carried altogether only four references to Freud for a total of per-haps a half-dozen sentences, and not a single psychoanalytic work was cited in a bibliography of several hundred items.[19] The 1950 Yearbook of the National Society for the Study of Education,

17. "A Revised Structure of Intellect," *ibid.*, p. 19.

18. J. P. Guilford, "Creativity: Its Measurement and Development," p. 24. An address presented to educators of Sacramento County, Sacramento, California, January 20, 1959 (mimeographed).

19. Ernest R. Hilgard, *Theories of Learning*. New York: Appleton-Century-Crofts, 1948.

Learning and Instruction, did not carry even one reference.[20] In the second edition of Hilgard's book, published in 1956, a full chapter of some forty pages was devoted to Freud, and over a dozen references were cited in the bibliography.[21] A similar development is under way in the area of thinking and problem-solving, especially in their more creative aspects, and, in fact, the suggestion has most recently been made that *"psychoanalysis is very largely a cognitive psychology."*[22]

In the area of problem-solving and thinking, as elsewhere, psychoanalytic theory is too complex and too little formalized for brief presentation. Nonetheless, several relevant points may be outlined in simplified fashion: (*a*) The basic cleavage in thought is that between two processes, an unconscious, arational *primary* process and an ego-controlled, rational *secondary* process. (*b*) The interaction between the two processes is conflictual, involving repression and defense. (*c*) Creative thought derives from an elaboration of the "freely rising" primary process fantasies. (*d*) It is when these unconscious forces become ego-syntonic that the occasion exists, in Freud's words, for "achievements of special perfection,"[23] i.e., creativity. (*e*) In short, the ultimate source of what we called the "envisaged new situation" is the same as that of dreams or play—in the primary process—but in "co-operation" (the term is Freud's) with the secondary process.

What about the source of the drive toward the "realization of the new situation"? The source is put in the vicissitudes of infantile sexual investigation, and the critical effect of early childhood experience on mental functioning is emphasized once again. The investiga-

20. *Learning and Instruction.* Forty-ninth Yearbook of the National Society for the Study of Education, Part I. Chicago: Distributed by the University of Chicago Press, 1950.

21. Ernest R. Hilgard, *Theories of Learning.* New York: Appleton-Century-Crofts, 1956 (second edition).

22. Ernest R. Hilgard, "Impulsive versus Realistic Thinking: An Examination of the Distinction between Primary and Secondary Processes in Thought," *Psychological Bulletin,* LIX (1962), 477.

23. Sigmund Freud, "The Unconscious," *Collected Papers,* Vol. IV, p. 127. London: Hogarth Press, Ltd., 1949. For a fuller discussion of the points briefly outlined in this section, see Jacob W. Getzels and Philip W. Jackson, *Creativity and Intelligence: Explorations with Gifted Students,* pp. 88–123. New York: John Wiley & Sons, 1962.

tion drive with which early sexuality is linked may undergo three fates: In one, investigation may share the same fate as the sexuality, i.e., repression, and curiosity becomes inhibited and free intellectual activity is restricted for life. In the second, the repression may be incomplete, and the suppressed sexual investigation comes back from the unconscious in the form of compulsive and cautious reasoning. In the third, "which is the most rare and perfect type,"[24] sexual repression takes place too, but investigation, not suffering the fate of the repression, is sublimated into curiosity with consequent pursuit of intellectual interests and creativity.

More recently, there has been a shift of interest from id to ego processes and a concomitant shift of emphasis in thinking from the role of the unconscious to that of the preconscious. It is now held that the ego may gain access to primary process thought by way of the preconscious without being overwhelmed by the unconscious as had previously been posited. The essentials of this position are given by Kris:

. . . ego regression (primitivization of ego functions) occurs not only when the ego is weak—in sleep, in falling asleep, in fantasy, in intoxication, and in the psychoses. This suggested . . . that the ego may use the primary process and not be overwhelmed by it. The idea was rooted in Freud's explanation of wit according to which a preconscious thought is "entrusted for a moment to unconscious elaboration" and seemed to account for a variety of creative or other inventive processes. . . .[25]

Rapaport formulated Kris' point most concisely as follows:

. . . many types of productive processes, from wit to art, and many other phenomena of inventiveness can be fully explained only if we assume that the ego regulates its own capacity to regression, that its organizing functions include the function of voluntarily and temporarily withdrawing cathexis from one area or the other, in order later to regain improved control.[26]

Kubie puts the issue even more sharply. He argues that where conscious processes predominate, thinking is rigid since the con-

24. Sigmund Freud, *Leonardo da Vinci: A Study in Psychosexuality*, p. 50. New York: Random House, 1947.

25. E. Kris, *Psychoanalytic Explorations in Art*, p. 312. New York: International Universities Press, 1962.

26. David Rapaport, *Organization and Pathology of Thought: Selected Sources*, p. 372. New York: Columbia University Press, 1951.

scious symbolic functions are anchored in literal relationships to specific (and known) conceptual and perceptual units. Where unconscious processes predominate, there is even more rigid anchorage—in this case to "unreality," i.e., to the unacceptable conflicts, objects, and impulses which have been rendered inaccessible to conscious introspection and to the corrective influence of experience.[27] Kubie states: "The uniqueness of creativity, i.e., its capacity to find and put together something new, depends on the extent to which preconscious functions can operate freely between these two ubiquitous concurrent and oppressive prison wardens."[28]

THE PARADOX OF CREATIVE THINKING: IMPULSE AND REFLECTION

This, then, is the paradox—a paradox difficult in any case, but especially difficult for the teacher: Despite the self-evident need for conscious effort and rationality in problem-solving, the development of reality-orientation and logic with age, and the required training in reflective forms of reasoning in school, mature creative thinking and innovative problem-solving entail, at least in some degree, a regression to playfulness, fantasy, and the arationality of primary process and childlike modes of thought. Hadamard, in his book *The Psychology of Invention in the Mathematical Field*, cites with approval a relevant and illuminating distinction between "cogito," meaning orginally to "shake together," and "intelligo," meaning originally to "select among."[29] Cogitation and intelligence: the one refers to letting one's ideas, memories, impulses, fantasies rise freely; the other refers to the superimposed process of choosing from among unanticipated combinations those patterns which have significance in reality.[30] The "cogito" component of creative thinking seems predominantly an impulsive or preconscious process, the "intelligo" component a predominantly reflective or conscious process.

In this respect, the accounts given by creative thinkers themselves of their thought processes are compelling. Poincaré, for example,

27. Lawrence Kubie, *Neurotic Distortion of the Creative Process*, p. 47. Lawrence: University of Kansas Press, 1958.

28. *Ibid.*, p. 45.

29. Jacques S. Hadamard, *The Psychology of Invention in the Mathematical Field*, p. 29. New York: Dover Publications, 1954.

30. Kubie, *op. cit.*, pp. 50–51.

tells the now familiar story of how he struggled with a mathematical problem to no conclusion and finally turned away from it to go on a geologic excursion. One day, while engaged in some other matters, the solution "appeared" in his mind. He writes of this and other similar experiences: "Most striking at first is this appearance of sudden illumination, a manifest sign of long, unconscious prior work. The role of this unconscious work in mathematical invention appears to me incontestable."[31] A. E. Housman writes of his poetic creation, ". . . there would flow into my mind, with sudden and unaccountable emotion, sometimes a line or two of verse, sometimes a whole stanza at once, accompanied, not preceded, by a vague notion of the poem which they were destined to form a part of."[32] Mozart states similarly, "Thoughts crowd into my mind as easily as you could wish. Whence and how do they come? I do not know and I have nothing to do with it. Those which please me I keep in my head and hum them; at least others have told me that I do so."[33] Einstein in the famous letter describing his thought processes says, ". . . this combinatory play seems to be the essential feature in productive thought—before there is any connection with logical construction in words or other kinds of signs which can be communicated to others. . . . Conventional words or other signs have to be sought for laboriously only in a secondary stage, when the mentioned associative play is sufficiently established and can be reproduced at will. . . . It seems to me that what you call full consciousness is a limit case which can never be fully accomplished. This seems to me connected with a fact called the narrowness of consciousness."[34]

Two features of these and many other such accounts are notable. One feature is the similarity of the descriptions in the arts and the sciences. As Bronowski puts it: "The discoveries of science, the works of art are explorations—more, are explosions, of hidden likeness. The discoverer or the artist presents in them two aspects of nature and fuses them into one. This is the act of creation, in which an original thought is born, and it is the same act in original science

31. Hadamard, *op. cit.*, p. 14.

32. Brewster Ghiselin, *The Creative Process: A Symposium*, p. 91. New York: New American Library of World Literature, Inc. (Mentor Book), 1955.

33. Hadamard, *op. cit.*, p. 16.

34. *Ibid.*, pp. 142–43.

and original art."[35] The second feature is the insistence upon the alternation of spontaneous and almost involuntary creation with conscious and rational effort. Sometimes the process begins with the conscious effort as in the case of Poincaré, which is then followed by a "sudden illumination"; sometimes the process seems to begin with a sudden illumination as in the case of Housman, which is then worked out by conscious effort. But always there is the alternation between the preconscious sphere, or what Galton called the "antechamber" of thought, and the conscious sphere, or what Galton called the "presence chamber" of thought.[36] When communication between the two is cut off, we have, in Eyring's words, the "genuine tragedy . . . presented by the brilliant mind with a critical faculty so far outrunning creative imagination that the unhappy possessor is forever condemned to bitter sterility."[37] Schiller, writing a generation before Freud to a friend who complained of his lack of creative power, said:

The reason for your complaint lies, it seems to me, in the constraint which your intellect imposes upon your imagination. . . . In the case of a creative mind, it seems to me, the intellect has withdrawn its watchers from the gates, and the ideas rush in pell-mell, and only then does it review and inspect the multitude. You worthy critics, or whatever you may call yourselves, are ashamed or afraid of the momentary madness which is found in all real creators, the longer or shorter duration of which distinguishes the thinking artist from the dreamer. Hence your complaints of unfruitfulness, for you reject too soon and discriminate too severely.[38]

The implications of these formulations for teaching seem quite clear. The premature censorship of ideas whether by the thinker himself or by the teacher as critic has inhibitory consequences for creative thinking and problem-solving. This is not to say that all ideas are relevant, or that relevant ideas are not founded in previous experience and knowledge or in periods of conscious preparation.

35. J. Bronowski, *Science and Human Values*, pp. 30–31. New York: Harper & Bros., 1956.

36. Hadamard, *op. cit.*, p. 25.

37. H. Eyring, "Scientific Creativity," in *Creativity and Its Cultivation*, *op. cit.*, p. 4.

38. Sigmund Freud, "The Interpretation of Dreams," in *The Basic Writings of Sigmund Freud*, p. 193. Edited by A. A. Brill. New York: Modern Library, 1938.

Of course the creative mathematician must know mathematics, the creative writer the fundamentals of rhetoric. And inspiration may in fact be 90 per cent perspiration. But the ever-present danger in the classroom is that the balance may be upset—"cogito" may too readily be sacrificed to "intelligo." Or to return to our different types of problem-situations, too much effort may be expended on Type 1 or even Type 2 problems, and not enough on the other more open-ended types of problem-situations.

MOTIVATIONAL CONCEPTS: STIMULUS-REDUCING
AND STIMULUS-SEEKING

The preceding conceptions of thinking and problem-solving are, for the most part, based on a homeostatic model that has dominated psychology and education for the past half-century.[39] According to this model, the organism is *driven* into activity by more or less noxious stimuli. It acts to rid itself of these stimuli in order to return to the satisfaction of rest and equilibrium. The organism is driven into exploration, thinking, problem-solving, and innovation as he is driven into other forms of behavior—food-seeking, for example. That is, *this* behavior is also the means of reducing painful excitation, tension, and conflict.

In recent years there has been a growing discontent with this homeostatic model and the drive concept of motivation. It appears that something important is neglected when drives alone are made the operating forces of behavior.[40] Exploration, problem-solving, and creative thinking may, indeed, be the means of reducing certain drives. But they are not only that. They may also be ends in themselves, the organism acting to seek stimulation as well as to avoid stimulation. The optimum state may not be passivity but activity, and although the organism may be threatened by what is strange, it is clearly often intrigued and challenged by what is new, and will go out of its way to encounter, explore, and master that which is intriguing and challenging. Once pointed out, the evidence for this comes

39. J. McV. Hunt, "Experience and the Development of Motivation: Some Reinterpretations," *Child Development*, XXXI (1960), 51.

40. R. W. White, "Motivation Reconsidered: The Concept of Competence," *Psychological Review*, LXVI (1959), 297. Our debt to this paper will be self-evident throughout this section.

from so many sources that it is surprising this view is not more firmly established in psychology and education.

One of the most obvious features of animal behavior, for example, is the tendency to explore the environment. As White points out: "Cats are reputedly killed by curiosity, dogs characteristically make a thorough search of their surroundings, and monkeys and chimpanzees have always impressed observers as ceaseless investigators."[41] Indeed, Butler[42] and Butler and Harlow[43] have shown that monkeys will learn a difficult task in discrimination when the only apparent motive is the opportunity to look out upon the entrance room to the laboratory. More than this, not only will animals explore for the sake of exploring but they will apparently solve problems for the sake of solving them. Harlow reports a series of studies demonstrating that viscerogenically sated monkeys will learn to unassemble a puzzle of some complexity with no other drive or reward than the privilege of unassembling it.[44]

Discontent with drive orthodoxy has not been restricted to investigators of animal behavior. Schachtel—and he speaks here for a growing number of psychologists like Maslow, Fromm, Erikson, and Rogers—argues that:

(1) The infant is not entirely helpless but shows from birth on steadily increasing capacities for active searching for satisfaction and for active discovery and exploration and that it enjoys these active capacities; and (2) that the child in many ways shows a promise which altogether too often is betrayed by adult man and his society and by the growing child itself when it yields to those forces and aspects of the culture, as transmitted by parents, teachers, and peers, which are crippling to its inherent potentialities.[45]

White goes further and argues that the central motive in the growth of children is not food satisfaction or thirst satisfaction or

41. *Ibid.,* p. 298.

42. Robert A. Butler, "Discrimination Learning by Rhesus Monkeys to Visual-Exploration Motivation," *Journal of Comparative and Physiological Psychology,* XLVI (1953), 95–98.

43. Robert A. Butler and Harry F. Harlow, "Discrimination Learning and Learning Sets to Visual Exploration Incentives," *Journal of General Psychology,* LVII (October, 1957), 257–64.

44. Harry F. Harlow, "Motivational Forces Underlying Behavior," in the Kentucky Symposium, *Learning Theory, Personality Theory, and Clinical Research,* pp. 36–53. New York: John Wiley & Sons, 1954.

45. Ernest G. Schachtel, *Metamorphosis,* p. 5. New York: Basic Books, 1959.

some other drive satisfaction but effective interaction with the environment—what he calls *competence motivation*.[46] He cites as one instance the readily observed "play of contented children." A child entirely satisfied viscerogenically does not remain at rest. As early as the first year it gives evidence of active exploration and even experimentation. The behavior is "directed, selective, and persistent, and it is continued not because it serves primary drives, which indeed it cannot serve until it is almost perfected, but because it satisfies an intrinsic need to deal with the environment."[47] If we may put it this way, there seem to be not only viscerogenic needs to be satisfied by satiation but neurogenic needs to be gratified by stimulation, i.e., needs for excitement, novelty, and the opportunity to deal with the problematic.

An interesting line of evidence bearing on this issue comes from studies of human behavior under conditions of so-called "stimulus deprivation," or perhaps better, "minimum stimulus-variation." To cite one of several experiments: Bexton, Heron, and Scott paid subjects "to do nothing." The subjects were well fed, the conditions were comfortable—except external stimulation was minimized. Few could endure this for more than two or three days. They developed a desire for stimulation that was almost overwhelming.[48] Hebb has directed our attention to common human activities like reading detective stories, skin-diving, or driving cars at high speeds which suggest a need to raise the level of stimulation.[49] In short, theory, observation, and experiment point to the conclusion: There seems to be an optimum level of activation and stimulation. Below this level, increase in stimulation is reinforcing. Above this level, decrease in stimulation is reinforcing.[50]

We are familiar enough with situations of excessive stimulation— for example, too great work loads, too many confusing social interactions, intellectual problems which are so complex as to seem in-

46. White, *op. cit.*, p. 318.   47. *Ibid.*

48. W. H. Bexton, W. Heron, and T. H. Scott, "Effects of Decreased Variation in Sensory Environment," *Canadian Journal of Psychology*, VIII (1954), 70–76.

49. See, for example, D. O. Hebb and W. R. Thompson, "The Social Significance of Animal Studies," in *Handbook of Social Psychology*, I, 551. Edited by Gardner Lindzey. Reading, Mass.: Addison-Wesley Publishing Co., 1954.

50. For a summary of the relevant theory and research, see White, *op. cit.*, pp. 313-15, and Hunt, *op. cit.*, pp. 494 ff.

soluble. The result is high *frustration* with consequent deterioration of behavior. But it is possible also to have too little stimulation, too little that is problematic. As White points out, interest requires elements of unfamiliarity, "of something still to be found out and learning still to be done."[51] This is the condition for creative thinking in the classroom as elsewhere. Below the optimal level of stimulation there is *boredom*, which is in effect also *frustration*—frustration as a consequence of too little that is problematic, too little opportunity to confront the new, to explore, and to experiment. The present danger in the classroom lies in this latter circumstance, for as we have already had occasion to observe, the Type 1 problem-situation with its paucity of "something still to be found out" is the all-too-usual context of teaching—a context that can be changed by putting into the curriculum and at the disposal of the teacher more open-ended types of problem-situations of the order of Types 2–8.

Experimental Studies of Teaching for Creative Thinking and Problem-solving

There has recently been a stir in education for a "new kind of teaching." Numerous articles and books have appeared arguing that present methods no longer meet the challenge of the new age. The call is for instructional methods (and materials) emphasizing the ability to see generalizations in specifics, to discover, to ask fruitful questions.[52] The newer courses of study at the elementary and secondary levels often include statements of such objectives as "To maintain and expand children's interest and curiosity through use of exploration in problem-solving activity as the basis of the learning process."[53] The newer teacher guides abound in such terms as insight, problem-solving, discovery, inquiry, originality, creativity.

In many ways this trend is to the good. But the new materials and

51. White, *op. cit.*, p. 314.

52. See, for example, Francis S. Chase and Harold A. Anderson, *The High School in a New Era* (Chicago: University of Chicago Press, 1958); Jerome S. Bruner, *The Process of Education* (Cambridge, Mass.: Harvard University Press, 1960); Herbert A. Thelen, *Education and the Human Quest* (New York: Harper & Bros., 1960); Joseph J. Schwab and P. E. Brandwein, *The Teaching of Science* (Cambridge, Mass.: Harvard University Press, 1962). For some counterarguments to "discovery" in "inquiry" teaching and learning, see D. P. Ausubel, "Learning by Discovery: Rationale and Mystique," *Bulletin of the National Association of Secondary-School Principals*, XLV (December, 1961), 18–58.

53. *Early Elementary Resource Guide in Science.* Kalamazoo, Mich.: Department of Instruction and Guidance, 1960.

methods are like those they are supposed to supersede in that they are based more on exhortation and testimonial than on empirical demonstration that *this* curriculum and *this* teaching method does indeed make *this* difference. While the new curriculum-makers and methodologists are exhorting the experimental approach to knowledge, they are not to any great extent submitting their own exhortations to experiment. We are not, of course, suggesting that what is being advocated is not worthwhile. There is no question that certain teachers do regularly and predictably produce in children learning phenomena along the indicated lines. But the basic experimental questions—What exactly is it that these teachers do that makes a difference? Can this be communicated to others? Can creative thinking and problem-solving be systematically taught in the classroom?—remain largely untouched. Rosenbloom recently told a Psychometric Society meeting:

> Much of the new development in the mathematics curriculum [and other curricula] comes from the attempt to incorporate in practical textbooks and teacher's guides the art developed by a few gifted teachers. When you try to analyze what we have tried to do, and to find out to what extent we have succeeded, you will be investigating processes which are virgin territory. I don't recognize them in your research literature.[54]

Although this charge is in the main valid, there are a number of lines of research in which certain tentative implications for instruction can be seen. There are first the implications of the studies of the processes of creative thinking themselves of the sort to which we have already referred. The work, for example, of Guilford and of MacKinnon with adults,[55] and of Getzels and Jackson[56] with children, suggests that teachers must distinguish between intelligence as measured by the I.Q. and creative thinking. As MacKinnon puts it: "There is increasing reason to believe that in selecting students for special training of their talent we may have overweighed the role of intelligence either by setting the cutting point for selection in the intellectual dimension too high or by assuming that regardless of

---

54. P. C. Rosenbloom, "Design of Curriculum Experiments in Mathematics." Address to the Psychometric Society, September 5, 1962. I am grateful to Professor Rosenbloom for permission to quote from the manuscript.

55. D. W. MacKinnon, "The Nature and Nurture of Creative Talent," *American Psychologist*, VII (July, 1962), 488–95.

56. Getzels and Jackson, *op. cit.*

other factors the student with the higher I.Q. is the more promising and should consequently be chosen."[57] More than this, the work of Getzels and Jackson[58] and of Torrance[59] also suggests that teachers tend to prefer in their classes students with high I.Q.'s, that is, with highly developed convergent thought processes, over the average student, but not to prefer students with highly developed divergent thought processes.

Virtually all accounts of the creative process agree that there must be openness in the creative person to new stimuli from without and to the acceptance of impulse from within. This suggests that the teacher must use caution in setting overly restrictive limits upon what those whom he is nurturing may experience and express. Discipline and self-control are necessary, and criticism is obviously important. But if we wish to encourage creative thinking, we must also provide opportunity for stretching the imagination and perceptiveness, discussing with students at least on occasion the most "divergent" and fantastic of ideas and possibilities. As MacKinnon says: "It is the duty of parents to communicate and of professors to profess what they judge to be true, but it is no less their duty by example to encourage in their children and in their students an openness to all ideas and especially to those which most challenge and threaten their own judgments."[60]

In addition to these inferences from studies of the creative process, there are certain implications that may be derived more directly from studies of teaching for creative thinking and problem-solving. Although these regrettably scant studies were usually done in the laboratory rather than in the classroom, and were often of indeterminate outcome, they do mark the possibility of systematic concepts and research in this area. In his paper "On the Training of Originality,"[61] Maltzman points out that although psychologists have done little experimental work on facilitating originality, nonpsychologists have been concerned with the problem for some time. Their suggestions may not be bound by scientific canons of evidence, but what they say is often in accord with accepted principles

57. MacKinnon, op. cit., p. 493.   58. Getzels and Jackson, op. cit.

59. E. Paul Torrance, Guiding Creative Talent. Englewood Cliffs, New Jersey: Prentice-Hall, Inc., 1962.

60. MacKinnon, op. cit., p. 493.   61. Maltzman, op. cit., 229–42.

of behavior. Mearns,[62] for example, in a book originally published in 1929 illustrates many techniques for inducing children to attempt original expression and to increase communication with their "secret unexpressed selves." He suggests that in order to encourage originality in the classroom, the teacher must not only provide a "permissive atmosphere" and shun "drill" but he must reinforce and manifestly approve efforts at originality when they occur.

Among others who have suggested methods for training in and testing of originality are Slosson and Downey in 1922,[63] and, more recently, Osborn, who argued that practice in "group ideation" or "brainstorming" will develop originality.[64] Apparently the first *experimental* attack on facilitating originality was made by Josiah Royce.[65] In one procedure his subjects were required to draw a series of figures unlike any they had ever seen; in another, his subjects were presented with a series of drawings and were required to draw figures as different as possible from each of the models. The results led Royce to conclude that these procedures may facilitate originality and that they correspond to conditions in society conducive to originality.

Maltzman and his colleagues carried out a series of carefully controlled experiments. Beginning with a suggestion by Guilford that originality as measured by tests of the "unusual response-type" might be related to solving "insight-type" problems, they performed two experiments.[66] In one, an attempt was made to determine whether a relationship could be found between originality, as so defined, and ability to solve Maier's two-string problem. In the other, an attempt was made to determine whether training in "unusual uses" for objects would facilitate the solution of the two-string problem in which these objects may be used. In the first study, sig-

62. Hughes Mearns, *Creative Power: The Education of Youth in the Creative Arts.* New York: Dover Publications, 1958.

63. Edwin E. Slosson and June E. Downey, *Plots and Personalities.* New York: Century Co., 1922.

64. Alex Osborn, *Applied Imagination.* New York: Charles Scribner's Sons, 1957.

65. Josiah Royce, "The Psychology of Invention," *Psychological Review,* V (1898), 113–44.

66. Irving Maltzman, L. O. Brooks, W. Bogartz, and S. S. Summers, "The Facilitation of Problem-solving by Prior Exposure to Uncommon Responses," *Journal of Experimental Psychology,* LVI (1958), 399–406.

nificant but low correlations were found for men but not for women. In the second, the training did improve the performance of women, but, although the direction of the effect was the same for men, the change was not statistically significant.

These studies were concerned with the relation between originality in verbal responses and problem-solving. Another series of studies was concerned directly with the facilitation of uncommon verbal responses. Maltzman, Bogartz, and Breger argued that, according to S-R theory, common responses to a stimulus are those which are dominant in the response hierarchy, and uncommon or original responses are those low in the response hierarchy.[67] Therefore, if a subject could be induced to give responses low in his hierarchy, the originality of his responses would be increased. Training of this nature might then produce a disposition to give uncommon responses in other situations.

One way of producing the desired effect is to present the same stimulus words repeatedly with instructions to give a different response each time. This was done, and a test list composed of words not encountered in the training list and Guilford's *Unusual Uses Test of Originality* were then given. In addition, a number of other variables including intermittent verbal reinforcement of uncommon responses and instructions to be original were introduced. The results showed that originality of associations to new words can be facilitated to a significant degree by training. Instructions to be original also produced an increase in originality. With respect to the *Unusual Uses* test, the training appears to have some effect, but the data require further analysis.

Maltzman, Simon, Raskin, and Licht followed up a number of the ambiguities in the afore-mentioned work, notably the question of whether the effects of the training would persist over time.[68] A delay of approximately one hour and of two days was interposed between the training and test situation for several control and experimental groups. A significant training effect was obtained on the word asso-

67. Irving Maltzman, W. Bogartz, and L. Breger, "A Procedure for Increasing Word Association Originality and Its Transfer Effects," *Journal of Experimental Psychology*, LVI (1958), 392–98.

68. Irving Maltzman, S. Simon, D. Raskin, and L. Licht, "Experimental Studies in the Training of Originality," *Psychological Monographs*, LXXVI (1960), 6 (Whole No. 493).

ciation and the *Unusual Uses* test, showing that the effects of originality training do tend to persist, at least under the given experimental conditions.

The inevitable question about all experimental work in originality may be put here also: Have these studies been dealing with originality at all? Maltzman's answer is firm:

> . . . it should be noted that the term "originality" as employed [here] refers to a particular kind of behavior measured by a specified operation under given conditions. If it is objected that this is not genuine originality, then it would be incumbent upon the critic to specify the latter behavior in equally operational terms so that it too may be subjected to experimental study.[69]

A group at the University of Buffalo recently used a "creative problem-solving course" given at that institution to ascertain the effect of training in Osborn's "brainstorming" technique on performance in problem-solving. Results of an initial investigation showed that the training did generalize to creative problem-solving and, indeed, tended to produce increments on a personality dominance scale.[70] A second investigation demonstrated the superiority of brainstorming instructions in problem-solving over the more usual instructions to "produce good ideas with a penalty for bad ideas."[71] Another experiment was designed to examine the same issue with untrained subjects and also to compare the effect of training in the "creative problem-solving course."[72] It was found that significantly more good ideas were produced under brainstorming conditions and that subjects trained in the "creative problem-solving course" produced more good-quality ideas. A final experiment examined the persistence of the effects produced by the "creative problem-solving course."[73] The subjects were an experimental group

69. *Ibid.,* p. 16.

70. Arnold Meadow and Sidney J. Parnes, "Evaluation of Training in Creative Problem-solving, *Journal of Applied Psychology,* XLIII (1959), 193.

71. Arnold Meadow, Sidney J. Parnes, and Hayne Reese, "Influence of Brainstorming Instructions and Problem Sequence on a Creative Problem-solving Test," *Journal of Applied Psychology,* XLIII (1959), 413–16.

72. Sidney J. Parnes and Arnold Meadow, "Effects of Brainstorming Instructions on Creative Problem-solving by Trained and Untrained Subjects," *Journal of Educational Psychology,* L (1959), 171–76.

73. Sidney J. Parnes and Arnold Meadow, "Evaluation of Persistence of Effects Produced by a Creative Problem-solving Course," *Psychological Reports,* VII (1960), 357–61.

composed of students who had completed the course eight months to four years before the experiment, and a control group composed of students who had registered, but were uninstructed, in the course. The experimental group outperformed two separate control groups on all measures of creative thinking used, including a number of the Guilford instruments. The researchers explain their positive results by the principle that brainstorming encourages the separation of the production if ideas from the evaluation of ideas so that novel hypotheses are not unduly inhibited.

Maltzman has critized these studies on a number of methodological grounds, including the perennial objection to classroom experiments that "there is the difficulty of assessing what the relevant variables are, whether it was the training in problem-solving per se, or the changes in motivation resulting from participating in a class and studying a procedure which explicitly claims to facilitate problem-solving."[74] Taylor, Berry, and Block are also skeptical of the group-brainstorming technique. The title of their research report gives the question to which their study was directed: "Does Group Participation When Using Brainstorming Facilitate or Inhibit Creative Thinking?"[75] They found that, as compared with twelve nominal groups (i.e., groups composed artificially of four individuals each who actually worked alone), the performance of twelve real groups (i.e., groups composed of four individuals each who actually worked together) was "markedly inferior" in the quantity, originality, and quality of ideas.

Torrance, in an experiment in teaching creative thinking at the primary-school level,[76] posed two problems: (a) whether children in the first three grades could be trained to use Osborn's principles for stimulating new ideas, and (b) what the effects of instructions to think of as many ideas as possible regardless of the quality of ideas would be, as compared with instructions to think of the most interesting, clever, and unusual ideas. He found that in the second and third grades, the trained children were consistently superior to the untrained children in all of his measures of creative thinking. A surprising finding was that instructions to produce a large number of

74. Maltzman, op. cit., p. 232.

75. Administrative Science Quarterly, III (1958), 23–47.

76. E. Paul Torrance, "Priming Creative Thinking in the Primary Grades," Elementary School Journal, LXII (1961), 34–41.

ideas without regard to quality resulted in fewer responses than instructions to produce interesting, clever, and unusual ideas. Torrance concluded:

Results of this experiment indicate that pupils in the primary grades, with the possible exception of the first, can in a short period be taught a set of principles that will enable them to produce more and better ideas than they would have without training. The results provide no support for motivating pupils in the primary grades to produce a quantity of ideas without consideration for quality.[77]

An instructional procedure proposed by Suchman for encouraging "autonomous thinking" is "Discovery or Inquiry Training." This technique is based on the rationale that learning through inquiry transcends learning which is directed wholly by the teacher or the textbook.[78] The experimental phase of the five-year project was designed to answer the questions: Does "inquiry training" produce measurable changes in the inquiry process in the ordinary elementary classroom? Does the learning of science concepts through "inquiry training" compare favorably with learning through the more usual expository teaching? The "inquiry training" took the following form: A motion picture posed a problem in physics, and the children were confronted with the question, "Why?" They could search for the solution only by asking the teacher questions answerable by "Yes" or "No." In effect, they had to formulate their own hypotheses and test these with questions taking the form of verbalized experiments.

The subjects were pupils in the fifth and sixth grades, the experimental group receiving "inquiry training" for a twenty-four-week period, the control group not. At the end of the training period, the two groups were tested on three kinds of growth: understanding of physics, information, and skill in the inquiry process. The results showed no significant differences in concept understanding and information, but a marked difference in favor of the experimental group in inquiry. Suchman is careful to point to the limitations of this initial study and to the negative nature of some of the results, but he is sufficiently encouraged by the results to say, "Our main

77. *Ibid.*, p. 41.

78. J. R. Suchman, "The Elementary School Training Program in Scientific Inquiry," p. 4. Urbana, Illinois: University of Illinois (mimeographed).

conclusion from the test results and from our experience with Inquiry Training in many classrooms is that the technique in its present form has a marked effect on the motivation, autonomy and question-asking fluency of children. They clearly enjoy having the freedom and the power to gather their own data in their quest for assimilation."[79]

Some Instructional Issues

It is evident that no *single* set of principles of instruction for creative thinking and problem-solving can be drawn from present theory and research. The theory is too diverse; the research too scant. It is, however, possible to raise a number of issues for general consideration and perhaps even for the guidance of teachers and investigators.

1. With respect to the cognitive problems of the classroom, a distinction can be made between *presented* problems and *discovered* problems. More than this, problems range from those making little demand to those making substantial demand for innovation and creativeness. What is the effect on the learner of the quantitatively different representation of these problems in the classroom?

2. There appear to be different stages of development in thinking from *sensorimotor* to *propositional* and *inventive* intelligence. How can the cognitive problems dealt with in the classroom be related to the developmental stages of the children?

3. Although such broad categories as *convergent* and *divergent* thinking do not exhaust the possibilities, they do suggest the existence of different styles of cognition. Indeed, there is some evidence for individual differences in the preference for one mode over another.[80] How do different styles of thinking affect the solution of different types of problems and the reaction to different modes of teaching?

4. There is a paradox in teaching for creative thinking. On the one hand, solving problems seems to require conscious effort, the possession of established facts, and rationality of attack—all aspects of *secondary-process thought*. On the other hand, creative thinking seems to entail at least a degree of regressive playfulness, impulse acceptance, and arationality—all aspects of *primary-process thought*.

79. *Ibid.*, p. 126. 80. Getzels and Jackson, *op. cit.*

How can instruction proceed in developing secondary-process thought without thereby irrevocably cutting the person off from all aspects of primary-process thought, and, conversely of course, how can encouragement in the acceptance of primary-process thought proceed without thereby derogating the significance of secondary-process thought?

5. The human being is not only a stimulus-reducing but a stimulus-seeking organism. He strives not only to master problems with which he is confronted but to confront problems in order to master them. There seems to be an optimum level of stimulation. Above this level, too much is problematic, i.e., too much is unknown. The consequence is frustration, and a decrease in stimulation is reinforcing. Below this level, too little is problematic, i.e., too much is known. The consequence is boredom, and an increase in stimulation is reinforcing. One condition of creative thinking in the classroom, as elsewhere, is an optimum balance of stimulation, i.e., between the known and the unknown. What is the nature of this balance for given students, teachers, and subject matter?

6. In response to the recent demand for "new kinds of teaching," two lines of instructional innovation seem to be developing. One line attempts to foster inquiry, discovery, and creative thinking in the classroom by revising the curriculum materials and teaching methods in the specific subjects taught. The other attempts to institute courses of instruction in inquiry, discovery, and creative thinking as such. Evaluation of the results of what is being done is as yet very rare indeed. But these attempts do raise once more the issue of learning sets and transfer. Can a set for inquiry, variability of response, and originality in thinking be taught, and if it can, is such set specific to the given subject in which it was learned or does it transfer to other subjects?

These are only illustrative issues. But, clearly, there is much more to be done. We have tended to look at teaching from the perspective of learning and thinking, so that statements about the practice of teaching derive from theory and research in learning and thinking. It may be advisable to change our stance for a while and look at learning and thinking from the perspective of the practice of teaching, the hope being that five years from now we may have along-side the dozen present treatises on "Theories of Learning" and "Theories of Thinking" at least one substantial treatise on "Theories of Teaching," or perhaps better on "Theories of Teaching-Learning-Thinking"—teaching, learning, and thinking all being seen as complementary activities within the same conceptual framework.

CHAPTER XI

Theories of Teaching

N. L. GAGE[1]

The thesis of this chapter is that theories of learning will have greater usefulness to education when they are transformed into theories of teaching. This thesis rests upon an assumption as to the present usefulness of learning theory in education and upon a distinction between theories of learning and theories of teaching. Let us examine each of these ideas.

First, the limited usefulness of learning theory in education has long been acknowledged. Estes, writing on "Learning" in the *Encyclopedia of Educational Research,* judged that "no convergence is imminent between the educator's and the laboratory scientist's approaches to learning," and he was able to report little progress "toward bridging the gap between laboratory psychology and the study of school learning."[2] Near the close of his *Theories of Learning,* Hilgard stated, ". . . It is not surprising, therefore, that the person seeking advice from the learning theorist often comes away disappointed."[3] Educational psychology textbooks usually include treatments of learning that draw in general terms upon learning theories. But these treatments bear only slight resemblance to the elaborations of the theories as portrayed in Hilgard's book.

Second, our thesis embodies a basic distinction between theories of learning and theories of teaching. While theories of learning deal with the ways in which an organism learns, theories of teaching deal with the ways in which a person influences an organism to learn.

1. The author is very grateful to Philip W. Jackson and Romayne Ponleithner for valuable editorial suggestions.

2. William K. Estes, "Learning," in *Encyclopedia of Educational Research,* p. 767. Edited by Chester W. Harris. New York: Macmillan Co., 1960 (third edition).

3. Ernest R. Hilgard, *Theories of Learning,* p. 485. New York: Appleton-Century-Crofts, 1956 (second edition).

To rephrase the thesis: Although theories of learning are necessary to the understanding, prediction, and control of the learning process, they cannot suffice in education. The goal of education—to engender learning in the most desirable and efficient ways possible—would seem to require an additional science and technology of teaching. To satisfy the practical demands of education, theories of learning must be "stood on their head" so as to yield theories of teaching.

In this chapter, we shall attempt to support this thesis by considering (a) the need for theories of teaching, (b) the need for analysis and specification of teaching in developing such theories, (c) some illustrative analyses and specifications of teaching, and (d) the kinds of research that might yield improved empirical bases for theories of teaching.

The Need for Theories of Teaching

That theories of teaching are needed in addition to theories of learning may seem in the main to require no argument. Yet, the development of theories of teaching has been neglected. In comparison with learning, teaching goes almost unmentioned in the theoretical writings of psychologists. Many signs of this disregard can be observed. For example, *Psychological Abstracts* contains large sections on laboratory learning and school learning but only a small section on teaching, and that within the section on "Educational Personnel." The *Annual Review of Psychology* usually includes a chapter on learning but seldom more than a few paragraphs on teaching. Volumes have been devoted to theories of learning, but not a single book deals exclusively with theories of teaching. Textbooks of educational psychology give much more space to discussions of learning and the learner than to methods of teaching and the teacher. *A Comprehensive Dictionary of Psychological and Psychoanalytical Terms* has three pages, containing 50 entries, concerned with learning but devotes only five lines to "Teaching" as follows: "The art of assisting another to learn. It includes the providing of information [instruction] and of appropriate situations, conditions, or activities designed to facilitate learning."[4]

4. Horace B. English and Ava C. English, *A Comprehensive Dictionary of Psychological and Psychoanalytical Terms.* New York: Longmans, Green & Co., 1958.

The reasons for the neglect of theories of teaching are in themselves of interest. Examining these reasons may help determine
whether such theories are possible of formulation and are desirable.

Art vs. science.—Sometimes the attempt to develop theories of
teaching is seen as implying the development of a science of teaching.
Yet, some writers reject the notion of a science of teaching. Highet
entitled his book *The Art of Teaching,*

> . . . because I believe that teaching is an art, not a science. It seems to
> me very dangerous to apply the aims and methods of science to human
> beings as individuals, although a statistical principle can often be used
> to explain their behavior in large groups and a scientific diagnosis of
> their physical structure is always valuable. . . . Of course it is necessary
> for any teacher to be orderly in planning his work and precise in his
> dealing with facts. But that does not make his teaching "scientific."
> Teaching involves emotions, which cannot be systematically appraised
> and employed, and human values, which are quite outside the grasp of
> science. "Scientific" teaching, even of scientific subjects, will be inade-
> quate as long as both teachers and pupils are human beings. Teaching
> is not like inducing a chemical reaction: It is much more like painting
> a picture or making a piece of music, or on a lower level like planting
> a garden or writing a friendly letter.[5]

Highet's argument would, of course, also militate against the development of a science of learning. His argument against a science of
teaching need not be considered to apply to a theory of teaching.
We should not equate the attempt to develop a theory about an activity with the attempt to eliminate its phenomenal, idiosyncratic,
and artistic aspects. Painting and composing, and even friendly
letter-writing and casual conversation, have inherent order and lawfulness that can be subjected to theoretical analysis. The painter,
despite the artistry immanent in his work, often can be shown by
students of his art to be behaving according to a theory—of color,
perspective, balance, or abstraction. The artist whose lawfulnesses
are revealed does not become an automaton; ample scope remains for
his subtlety and individuality. His processes and products need not
remain immune to attempts at rational understanding on the part of
critics and scholars.

5. Gilbert Highet, *The Art of Teaching,* pp. vii–viii. New York: Vintage
Books, 1955.

So it is with teaching. Although teaching requires artistry, it can be subjected to scientific scrutiny. The power to explain, predict, and control that may result from such scrutiny will not dehumanize teaching. Just as engineers can still exercise ingenuity within the theory of thermodynamics, teachers will have room for artistic variation on the theory that scientific study of teaching may establish. And for the work of those who train, hire, and supervise teachers, theory and empirical knowledge of teaching will provide scientific grounding.

Even if it had no practical value, a scientific understanding of teaching should still be sought. Like interstellar space and evolution, learning has been studied for its own sake. So teaching can be studied as a phenomenon of interest in its own right. Theories of teaching are desirable because of their practical value if it is forthcoming, but desirable in any case.

Presumed adequacy of learning theory.—The need for theories of teaching stems also from the insufficiency *in principle* of theories of learning. Theories of learning deal with what the learner does. But changes in education must depend in large part upon what the teacher does. That is, changes in how learners go about their business of learning occur in response to the behavior of their teachers or others in the educational establishment. Much of our knowledge about learning can be put into practice only by teachers. And the ways in which these teachers would put this knowledge into effect constitute part of the subject of theories of teaching. Our position is that practical applications have not been gleaned from theories of learning largely because theories of teaching have not been developed. The implications of learning theory need to be translated into implications for the behavior of teachers. Teachers will then act on these implications in such ways as to improve learning. Theories of teaching and the empirical study of teaching may enable us to make better use of our knowledge about learning.

Is there any room for theory of teaching? Or, on the other hand, is theory of learning and behavior so all-encompassing as to preclude any valid concern with theory of teaching? Hilgard pointed out that Hull "scarcely distinguishes between a theory of learning and a theory of behavior, so important is learning in his conception of behavior. . . . Hence the systematic aspects of learning theory have come to be important to all psychologists interested in more general theories."[6] Because teaching is a form of behavior, adequate theories of learning, or general theories of behavior, would, in this view, encompass teaching as well. But this view applies only to teaching considered as the "dependent variable," the thing to be explained. In this sense, the behavior of teachers will indeed be understood by the same theories that apply to the behavior and learning of pupils. The kind of theory of teaching with which we are concerned places the behavior of teachers in the position of "independent variables" as a function of which the learning of pupils is to be explained. That is, theories of teaching should be concerned with explaining, predicting, and controlling the ways in which teacher behavior affects the learning of pupils. In this perspective there is ample room for theories of teaching. Such theories would deal with a whole realm of phenomena neglected by theories of learning.

It might be objected that, with learning as the dependent variable, theories of teaching become only a subclass of theories of learning: a subclass in which the independent variables consist of the behavior and characteristics of teachers. Such a conception of theories of teaching seems altogether admissible within the thesis of this chapter; it would not change the major argument. Theories of teaching would still need to be developed as a substantial discipline, even if not co-ordinate with theories of learning.

The two kinds of theory must ultimately, of course, be strongly connected; theories of learning will have many implications for theories of teaching. But that is another matter. These implications will become clear as the study of teaching develops. As will be illustrated, the psychology of learning has much to offer the person who attempts to formulate the ways in which teaching proceeds.

THE DEMANDS OF TEACHER EDUCATION

Explicit concern with the theory of teaching should benefit teacher education. In training teachers, we often seem to rely on mere inference from theory of learning to the practice of teaching. Yet, what we know about learning is inadequate to tell us what we should do about teaching. This inadequacy is clearly evident in our educational psychology courses and textbooks. The irrepressible question

6. Hilgard, *op. cit.*, p. 2.

of students in educational psychology courses is, "How should I teach?" While they may infer a partial answer from a consideration of how pupils learn, they cannot get all of it in this way. Much of what teachers must know about teaching does not directly follow from a knowledge of the learning process. Their knowledge must be acquired explicitly rather than by inference. Farmers need to know more than how plants grow. Mechanics need to know more than how a machine works. Physicians need to know more than how the body functions. Teachers need to know more than how a pupil learns.

Teachers must know how to manipulate the independent variables, especially their own behaviors, that determine learning. Such knowledge cannot be derived automatically from knowledge about the learning process. To explain and control the teaching act requires a science and technology of teaching in its own right. The student of educational psychology who complains that he has learned much about learning and learners, but not about teaching, is asking for the fruits of scientific inquiry, including theories of teaching.

The Need for Analysis and Specification

How should work toward such theory proceed? In this section, we advocate the analysis and specification of teaching. Then we consider some sketches of what such analysis and specification might lead to.

THE MISLEADINGLY GENERIC TERM, "TEACHING"

As a concept, teaching sorely needs analysis. Such analysis should clarify the concerns of theories of teaching. For "teaching" is a misleadingly generic term; it covers too much. It falsely suggests a single, unitary phenomenon that may fruitfully be made the subject of theory development.

It may fairly be argued that learning theory has long been hung up on a similar fallacy. Because the term "learning" has been applied to an enormous range of phenomena, psychologists have been misled into believing that a single theory can be developed to explain all these phenomena. Animal learning in puzzle boxes and Skinner boxes, human learning of nonsense syllables and eyelid responses in the laboratory, and the learning of school subjects in classrooms have all been termed "learning." And, because all these activities have been given the same name, psychologists have attempted to account for all of them by a single, unified, general theory.

Yet, as is well known, after more than a half-century of effort, no such unification of learning theory has materialized. Research and theorizing on learning have had three main foci—animal learning, human learning in the laboratory, and human learning in the class-room. (In recent years, a fourth focus has developed: programed learning. In time this new development may strengthen the connec-tion between the laboratory and the school.) The various kinds of learning have not been embraced successfully by any single learning theory. And this failure may well stem from the false belief that a single term, "learning," guarantees that a single, universally applica-ble theory of learning can be found.

Some analogies to other processes may clarify this point. Medicine does not search for a single theory of illness or healing. Physicians long ago discovered that people can get sick in several basically dif-ferent ways, such as being infected with germs or viruses, having organic malfunctions, suffering traumatic impacts of energy, or ex-periencing environmental deprivations. And, rather than a general theory of healing, physicians use several different approaches, such as giving medicines, using surgery, improving environments, or changing diets.

Another example is "getting rich," which is, like learning, con-cerned with the acquisition of something. Getting rich also takes place in many different ways—inheriting, gambling, stealing, making profits, or earning wages—and no one has tried to develop a general, unified theory of how to get rich. The concept of "getting rich" simply has no scientific value; it covers too many different proc-esses. Perhaps we should consider the possibility that, as a unitary concept, school learning has no scientific value either, because it covers too many distinct phenomena and processes.

The same then might be said of teaching. The term "teaching" should not be taken to imply that teaching is a basic process to which a general theory may apply. For "teaching" embraces far too many kinds of process, of behavior, of activity, to be the proper subject of a single theory. We must not be misled by the one word, "teaching," into searching for one theory to explain it.

WAYS OF ANALYZING THE CONCEPT OF TEACHING

If this argument is valid, the concept of teaching must be analyzed to reveal processes or elements that might constitute the proper subject of theories. What kinds of analysis can be made? Several can be suggested.

First, teaching can be analyzed according to types of teacher *activities*. Teachers engage in explaining activities, mental hygiene activities, demonstrating activities, guidance activities, order-maintaining activities, housekeeping activities, record-keeping activities, assignment-making activities, curriculum-planning activities, testing and evaluation activities, and many other kinds of activities. If everything a teacher does *qua* teacher is teaching, then teaching consists of many kinds of activity. It is unreasonable to expect a single theory to encompass all of these.

Second, teaching can be analyzed according to the types of *educational objectives* at which it is aimed; examples of major types are affective, psychomotor, and cognitive objectives. Thus, teaching processes can be classified according to the domain of objectives to which they seem primarily relevant. When the teacher uses words to define, describe, or explain a concept, such as "extrapolation," his behavior may be primarily relevant to cognitive objectives. When he offers warmth and encouragement, we may consider him to be acting in ways primarily relevant to the affective domain. When he demonstrates the correct way to write a capital F, his behavior may be primarily relevant to psychomotor objectives. At any given moment, more than one of these domains of objectives may be affected. It may sometimes be difficult to distinguish the teacher's influence on cognitive change from his influence on affective change in pupils. So, when the teacher fails to explain something clearly, the pupil may become not only confused (cognitively) but discouraged (affectively) as well. Nonetheless, analyses of this kind may have strategic value. At any rate, we should not assume that a single theory of teaching will apply to all kinds of objectives.

A third way to analyze teaching stems from the notion that teaching can be viewed as the obverse, or "mirror image," of learning and therefore has *components corresponding to those of learning*. If the learning process can be analyzed into basic elements or components—let us use Neal Miller's "drive," "cue," "response," and "reward" as examples—then teaching can be analyzed similarly. Corresponding components of teaching might be "motivation-producing," "perception-directing," "response-eliciting," and "reinforcement-providing." For some elements of Miller's analysis of learning, there are well-established separate domains of theory, such as theories of motivation and theories of perception. Similarly, theories of motivating, perception-directing, response-eliciting, and rewarding, corresponding to such elements of the teaching process, may develop. In any event, it is questionable whether a single theory of teaching should be sought to encompass all these components of the teaching process.

A fourth way to analyze teaching, not entirely distinct from those already mentioned, derives from *families of learning theory*. These families may be illustrated by "conditioning theory," "identification theory," and "cognitive theory." Some theorists (e.g., Mowrer[7]) conceive learning, in all its forms, to be a matter of conditioning with punishment or rewards consisting of primary or secondary reinforcements associated with independent or response-dependent stimulation. Such a conditioning theory of learning may imply a corresponding kind of theory of teaching. Other theorists (e.g., Bandura[8]) emphasize that learning consists, at least in major part, of the learner's identification with a model, whom the learner imitates. In this case, a second kind of theory of teaching is implied. A third kind of theorist (e.g., Luchins[9]) holds that learning consists of the cognitive restructuring of problematical situations. Here, a third kind of theory of teaching is suggested.

It is conceivable that all three of these major families of learning theory are valid, for different kinds of persons learning different things in different situations. Any reductionism, or attempt to derive the other two from any one of these, may yield only a spurious parsimony. The three kinds of theory seem at present to be compatible,

7. O. Hobart Mowrer, *Learning Theory and Behavior*, p. 213. New York: John Wiley & Sons, 1960.

8. Albert Bandura, "Social Learning through Imitation," in *Nebraska Symposium on Motivation*. Edited by M. R. Jones. Lincoln: University of Nebraska Press, 1962.

9. Abraham S. Luchins, "Implications of Gestalt Psychology for AV Learning," *AV Communications Review*, IX, No. 5 (1961), 7–31.

in the sense that they at least do not lead to different predictions about the same data. Rather, they seem to have been developed to account for different data—for the learning of different kinds of things in different situations. If so, all three approaches to the development of theory of teaching should be of some value.

We have suggested the bases for four different analyses of teaching: (*a*) types of teacher activities, (*b*) types of educational objectives, (*c*) components of the learning process, and (*d*) families of learning theory. We have also suggested that no single theory of teaching should be offered that would attempt to account for all activities of teachers, would be aimed at all objectives of education, and would involve all components of the learning process, in a way that would satisfy all theories of learning. To comply with our call for specification, we should now at least sketch what a theory of teaching might be concerned with, if it is to become specific. To do so, we shall make various selections from among the products of our analyses.

Selection One.—From the teacher's activities, let us select the one called explaining, leaving aside for the moment the mental hygiene, demonstrating, and other activities. Of the types of objectives, let us choose to focus on the cognitive domain, and, even more specifically, on the student's ability to extrapolate trends beyond the given data. Of the components of the learning process, let us choose the perceptual, or the teacher's corresponding function of directing the student's perceptions to the salient part of his environment, which, in the present instance, consists of the kinds of trends in data that we want him to learn to extrapolate. And finally, of the families of learning theory in accordance with which we wish to derive a theory of teaching, let us choose the cognitive restructuring approach.

At this point, having made these choices, we should be in a better position to develop a theory of teaching. Having eliminated many realms of phenomena from our concern, we have cut the problem down to size. We may still be a long way from our goal, but not so far as before.

Of the several choices we have made, the most arguable one is that of the cognitive restructuring as against the conditioning or the identification paradigms of learning and, hence, of teaching. The cognitive restructuring paradigm of learning holds that the learner arrives at knowledge and understanding by perceiving the situation (the problem) before him and then rearranging it, through central cognitive processes, in ways that yield meaning of a rational, logically consistent kind. The teacher can engender this restructuring by pointing to, either physically or verbally, and by manipulating the parts of the cognitive configuration so as to make the structure he wants learned stand out as a kind of figure against the ground of irrelevancies and distractions. The teacher manipulates the cognitive field in accordance with laws of cognition—analogous to the laws of perception governing the constancies, groupings, and whole-qualities in visual and auditory stimuli. Then the pupil apprehends the cognitive structure to be learned. He can no more avoid learning in this instance than he can avoid seeing the phi-phenomenon (the appearance of motion when two lights are flashed in brief succession) under proper conditions.

This conception of teaching follows the metaphor of the manipulator of stimuli who *compels* perceivers to see the stimuli in certain ways. Following certain principles of, say, similarity and proximity, we can compel a person to see a configuration of dots as falling into rows rather than columns. Similarly, following certain principles of cognitive structure, the teacher can "compel" his students to understand the principles of extrapolation.

Can we justify the rejection of the conditioning and identification paradigms for this kind of teaching? The conditioning paradigm seems to fall short simply because such teaching does not proceed by successive approximation of responses to the objective, as is implied by the term "shaping behavior." The teacher does not get the pupil to move gradually toward correct extrapolating behavior by feeding him stimuli that gradually take on the form of the problem to be understood, eliciting responses that gradually approximate what is correct, and providing reinforcement appropriately along the way. Rather, the teacher can often produce the desired behavior all at once by judiciously restructuring the student's cognitive field.

As for the identification paradigm in this instance, it would hold that the teacher gets his results by being prestigious or positively cathected. Why do we reject this approach to understanding the teaching of a logically consistent set of ideas? The identification approach implies that prestigious models can succeed in teaching even logically inconsistent or invalid ideas. But it is unlikely that the model can get a learner to imitate behavior that the learner can plainly perceive to be logically or cognitively inconsistent. (Asch's conformity-producing group-pressure situations seem to produce mere compliance rather than learning, since much of the yielding disappears in private retests.[10]) Much of what we teach has an iron logic of its own; mathematics is a prime example. *To the degree that the content is logically structured*, the learner will be influenced by the structure rather than by his human model.

Selection Two.—Let us now try another fairly likely combination of the components resulting from our analyses. From the teacher's activities, let us select his mental-hygiene function. From the types of educational objectives, let us select one from the affective domain, such as the pupil's emotional security in the classroom situation. Of the components of the learning process, let us choose the motivational one, or the teacher's corresponding function of arousing in the pupil a desire to learn what the teacher wants him to learn. And finally, of the families of learning theory, let us choose conditioning.

For this particular selection of specifications, we should pay particular attention to the teacher's acts of rewarding the pupil's provisional tries. Dispensing praise and warmth, almost without regard to what the pupil does so long as it remains within classroom requirements, the teacher positively reinforces the pupil's efforts to comply with the teacher's demands for effort and activity. Basking in a shower of laudatory remarks and approving glances, the pupil gradually comes out of his shell. He shows evidence of improved security.

Why do we select the conditioning approach here and reject cognitive restructuring or identification? In this instance, what has to be learned has no particular cognitive structure. No set of logically organized ideas has to be grasped by the pupil. The goal of getting the pupil to feel secure enough to respond in the classroom cannot readily be achieved, as we all know, through any process of rational explanation or intellectual argument.

We reject the identification approach because the goal in this in-

10. David Krech, Richard S. Crutchfield, and Egerton L. Ballachey, *Individual in Society*, pp. 504–29. New York: McGraw-Hill Book Co., 1962.

stance is not to get the pupil to behave the way the teacher does. The kinds of emotional security and activity that the pupil should exhibit in the classroom cannot be achieved through a process of imitating the teacher's security and activity. Indeed, the teacher's confidence and high activity may be precisely what overwhelms the pupil and causes him to withdraw into nonparticipation. For this particular combination of (a) mental-hygiene activity, (b) affective objective, and (c) motivational component of the learning process, it is not the pupil's identification with the teacher that will bring about the security we want. It is rather the teacher's consistent reinforcement, by the conditioning paradigm of the teaching process, that will gradually "shape" the pupil's behavior into a form bespeaking emotional security.

Selection Three.—A third selection from the components of our analyses of teaching will illustrate a still different version of a theory of teaching. Suppose we select the teacher's demonstrating activities, aimed at psychomotor objectives, with special concern for the response component of the learning process. For example, let us consider the teacher's activity in demonstrating the proper way to write the capital letter *F* in attempting to teach handwriting. Here it seems appropriate to emphasize the identification-imitation paradigm of the teaching process. The teacher goes to the blackboard and writes the letter *F* with the motions that he wants his pupils to adopt as their own. The teacher's prestige makes his way of performing this task unquestionably correct in the eyes of his pupils. His pupils watch him do it and then do it themselves. Depending on the maturity of their psychomotor skills, their success may be complete or partial. But given sufficient maturity, the pupils will write the letter *F* with the motions that the teacher wants them to use. The pupils make responses matching those of the teacher. Their imitation involves combining responses into relatively complex new patterns solely by observing the performance of another person.

In this instance, let us again assume that what is to be learned has no necessary logic. Many different ways of writing the letter *F* could be defended on rational grounds. Thus, the teacher does not carry out his task by explaining the reasons for a particular solution of the problem of how to write the letter. He does not derive his solution by building on earlier conclusions or premises. He has no ideational structure for his pupils to incorporate into their own thinking. Hence, the notion of teaching by cognitive restructuring does not seem to apply to this particular form of teaching.

We reject the conditioning approach here because it would entail a highly inefficient kind of gradual approximation to the desired behavior. To proceed through a painstaking process of response differentiation and extinction, gradually reinforcing desired bits of writing behavior and extinguishing the undesired ones, would be a wearisome and ineffective undertaking. It seems better to characterize the teaching process in this instance as a matter of inducing imitation of what is demonstrated by a prestigious model with whom the pupil identifies.

The foregoing may not represent the most fruitful ways of analyzing the concept of teaching. Other analyses, yielding different components, are clearly possible. Other combinations of resulting components may be more interesting to other persons seeking to develop theories of teaching. The point is that some such analyses and choices must be made before the properly specified concern of a theory can be isolated. Otherwise, attempts to develop theories of teaching will founder on excessive generality. To avoid such analyses and choices is to assume that the single word *teaching* denotes a single process amenable to a single, general theory. That kind of assumption has led to the present chasm between the purportedly general theories of learning developed in psychological laboratories and the kind of learning that goes on in schools. Although learning the Morse code, learning political attitudes, and learning mathematics are all called "learning," they do not necessarily involve the same kind of process. And, because the teaching of all these things is called by the one name of teaching, it does not follow that a single theory of teaching will account for how the teacher does his work.

Connections between Theory and Research on Teaching

Theories not only reflect past experience but also shape future research. Often the main value of a theory lies in the new kinds of research it generates. Throughout the history of psychology, new empirical work, revealing new phenomena and processes, has followed upon new theories. Theories of motivation, perception, and learning have had this effect, and, similarly, the development of theories of teaching may stimulate new kinds of research with variables that have been neglected previously.

This kind of development can be seen in current research on programed learning. Many new variables have been given experimental attention in studies of programed learning as a result of the development of reinforcement theory. Prompting, construction versus selection of responses, overtness of response, and a variety of reinforcement techniques are now being studied. Some of these variables had been identified previously, but they now take new forms, more relevant to meaningful learning in classrooms.

What impact will the development of theories of teaching have on research? Only research effort will tell. But some conjectures may be warranted. Such conjectures are intended to stimulate explicit concern with theories of teaching of the kind urged in this chapter. Some of the new research movements briefly described below are already under way and serve as illustrations of promising developments.

Teaching as cognitive restructuring.—Theories of teaching as cognitive restructuring focus on the teacher's behavior as a manipulator of ideas. Such theories concentrate research attention on the intellectual structures that characterize what is to be taught. This emphasis was occasionally evident in the research on teaching done in the 1930's and '40's. Studies of cognitive development and learning, such as those by Piaget, have long been available. But manifestations of a growing concern with the teacher's role in fostering such learning have only recently begun to appear. As Ausubel and Fitzgerald put it, "The importance of cognitive structure variables has been generally underestimated in the past because preoccupation with noncognitive, rote, and motor types of learning has tended to focus attention on such current situational and intrapersonal factors as task, practice, drive, incentive, and reinforcement variables."[11]

Some recent research on teaching conceived as cognitive restructuring may be mentioned to illustrate the kinds of variables brought

11. David P. Ausubel and Donald Fitzgerald, "Meaningful Learning and Retention: Interpersonal Cognitive Variables," *Review of Educational Research*, XXXI (December, 1961), 500–510.

to the fore by such an orientation. Smith has directed a study[12] of the logical operations of secondary-school teachers and students; he and his co-workers have described and analyzed such logical operations as defining, designating, classifying, explaining, and evaluating.

Another kind of research concerned with cognitive variables in teaching is illustrated by the work of Runkel,[13] who was concerned with a relationship, termed "collinearity," between the teacher's dimensions of thought and those of his students. Collinearity differs from similarity in that it indicates whether the dimensions or factors used in evaluating a set of objects might be the same even though the rank order of the objects in the evaluations given by two persons might be quite different. For example, two persons might evaluate a number of suits of clothing on the same bases (color, cut, and price) as underlying dimensions, even though they assign quite different rank orders to the suits. Runkel found evidence that, the greater the collinearity of students and teachers, the higher the achievement of the students as judged by the teachers. The finding was attributed to better communication between teachers and students when their cognitive structures were collinear.

A third style of research on cognitive variables in teaching is exemplified in studies by Suchman, who has been developing methods of training children in scientific inquiry,[14] that is, methods of increasing the number of valid questions children ask in seeking explanations of elementary scientific phenomena demonstrated in a film.

A final example is provided by the work of Ausubel,[15] who used organizers (i.e., "advanced introductory material at a high level of abstraction, generality, and inclusiveness") to influence various attributes of cognitive structure and then ascertained the influence of

12. B. Othanel Smith and Milton O. Meux, with the collaboration of Jerrold Coombs, Daniel Eierdam, and Ronald Szoke, *A Study of the Logic of Teaching.* Urbana: Bureau of Educational Research, University of Illinois, 1962 (mimeographed).

13. Philip J. Runkel, "Cognitive Similarity in Facilitating Communication," *Sociometry,* XIX (1956), 178–91.

14. J. Richard Suchman, "Inquiry Training in the Elementary School," *Science Teacher,* XXVII (November, 1960), 42–47.

15. Ausubel and Fitzgerald, *op. cit.,* p. 505.

this manipulation on learning, retention, and problem-solving.

Teaching as model-providing.—As for research illustrating the identification approach to teaching, Bandura's recent work[16] seems noteworthy. He has conducted experiments dealing with (*a*) the effects on imitation of pairing a model with generalized reinforcers, (*b*) delayed imitation in the absence of the model, (*c*) the influence of the behavior of models in shaping frustration-reactions, and (*d*) the influence of social reinforcement and the behavior of models in shaping children's moral judgments. Bandura offers cogent arguments for greater concern with what we would characterize as teaching by model-providing than with teaching by conditioning.

Teaching as conditioning.—The conditioning approach to teaching has been studied extensively in recent years—primarily through research on teaching machines and programed learning. Krumboltz's review[17] organized recent findings under four headings: (*a*) evoking the desired response, (*b*) reinforcing the desired response, (*c*) maintaining and improving the desired response, and (*d*) eliminating the undesired response. To the degree that such research can be translated into implications or teacher behavior rather than merely the design and administration of programed learning materials, it will bear upon theories of teaching conceived according to the conditioning approach.

Summary

This chapter has developed the thesis that theories of learning will become more useful in education when they are transformed into theories of teaching. In support of this thesis, we examined the need for theories of teaching and sought to counter the arguments that teaching is an art and that learning theories make theories of teaching unnecessary. The demands of teacher education make theories of teaching especially important. In developing theories of teaching, a major step is analysis and specification. We offered analyses on the basis of (*a*) types of teacher activity, (*b*) types of educational objective, (*c*) components of the learning process, and (*d*) families

16. Bandura, *op. cit.*, pp. 256–64.

17. John D. Krumboltz, "Meaningful Learning and Retention: Practice and Reinforcement Variables," *Review of Educational Research*, XXXI (December, 1961), 535–46.

of learning theory. Then we examined several selections of components from these analyses to illustrate how theories of teaching might be formulated when they were aimed at different combinations of a, b, c, and d, above. The sketches of these selections indicate that no single, unified, general theory of teaching should be sought to account for the various processes by which teachers engender learning. Rather, a number of theories of teaching, corresponding to major families of learning theory, will be necessary. Finally, the various approaches to the development of theories of teaching will influence research on teaching. Such influence has already appeared in a number of research movements that can be classified according to the three families of theory of teaching employed in the earlier discussion: cognitive structure theories, identification theories, and conditioning theories.

CHAPTER XII

Reform Movements from the Point of View of Psychological Theory

PAUL WOODRING

Introduction

All educational programs presumably rest upon some sort of psychological theory, but, in the case of recent reform movements, the theory is implied more often than stated. Many of the new programs being tried, and the changes being urged, are planned and sponsored by individuals or groups who give scant attention to theories of learning and are concerned primarily with the security of the nation and with the continuity and advancement of the culture. There are some exceptions, however, and it is these that deserve the most attention here.

From the turn of the century until about 1930, educational theory and psychological theory were closely related. During these years the best known and most influential names in educational psychology were men who also had made important contributions to psychological theory: James, Dewey, Judd, and Thorndike.

After about 1930, educational psychology and general psychology grew farther apart. In many universities the department of educational psychology became a part of the school of education, while general psychology became a separate department. As a result there was a notable decline of communication between learning theorists and those most directly concerned with the preparation of teachers for the public schools.

The number of educational psychologists in the nation continued to grow rapidly, but many of the new group were educators first and only secondarily psychologists. They attacked practical problems directly and with less attention to basic research and theory than had been characteristic of the earlier group. In the schools of education, disparaging remarks about "rat psychologists" were frequently heard, while experimentally oriented psychologists were equally disparaging in their comments about educators.

During the late twenties and the thirties, the leadership in educational theory fell upon educational philosophers who, in most cases, were not psychologists. Some of the new group stressed individual development, while others wished to use the school as an instrument in social change, but none of them placed great emphasis on academic learning of the traditional kind. Many of them seemed prone to select, from the vast mass of psychological evidence, only such data as supported their theories and to reject the remainder.

During the thirties and forties the psychological underpinnings of education shifted away from functional psychology, associationism, and behaviorism and toward Gestalt psychology, field theory, organismic psychology, and psychoanalysis. These theories were never adequately synthesized, and the presentation offered in many courses in educational psychology became eclectic.

Educational psychologists, after Thorndike, were less interested in finding better ways of teaching the academic subjects and skills and more interested in the child's social and emotional adjustment and the general problems of growth and development. Although a few psychologists continued to investigate the problems of academic learning, the textbooks in educational psychology reflected the shift of emphasis, and many of the students preparing to become teachers gained the impression that a deep concern over the teaching of subject matter and skills was a little old fashioned and inconsistent with psychological evidence.

Meanwhile, many of the psychologists conducting research on individual differences became so involved in highly complex statistical manipulations that their work became unintelligible to classroom teachers, and, as a result, psychologists lost their influence in the school. During the same period, learning theorists became increasingly reluctant to draw conclusions about human learning, particularly classroom learning, from laboratory experiments with nonhuman species. Those who did draw conclusions were, in many cases, educators insufficently grounded in psychological theory, and as a result some questionable interpretations appeared in the educational literature. Perhaps partly as a result of this misinterpretation or over-interpretation of the evidence, educational psychology suffered a relative loss of prestige among psychologists, and it became more difficult for the colleges and universities educating large numbers of teachers to recruit first-rate psychologists to their staffs. The problem was compounded by the fact that many of those interested in the applied fields of psychology were, at this time, moving into the more remunerative fields of industrial and clinical psychology.

Most of the educational reforms of the first half of the twentieth century were loosely grouped together under the term "Progressive Education." Although it had its origins much earlier, this movement had its greatest influence between 1918 and 1935.

Progressivism in education rested in part upon new psychological evidence of the nature of the learner and of the learning process and in part upon new interpretations of the school as a social institution —interpretations which greatly expanded the school's role and required greater emphasis on social and recreational activities and on vocational preparation with a corresponding decline of emphasis on purely academic learning. There seems little doubt that during the progressive period the schools became more pleasant and attractive places for children.

After the mid-thirties Progressive Education, as an organized reform movement with identifiable leadership, went into decline, although the movement did not expire until two decades later. But from about 1935 until about 1955, there was nothing in American education that may properly be called a reform movement except at the local level.

During the war years there was little attention to educational improvement, except in the armed forces where it was found necessary to teach mathematics and foreign languages with great speed. After the close of World War II, the schools underwent two periods of sharp attack from the outside, and it was the second of these that prepared the way for the new reform movement—the one that engages us at present. The first attack, a political one best known as McCarthyism, reached its peak about 1952. Schools and teachers were charged with un-Americanism, and textbooks were searched for evidence of subversion.

The second wave of criticism was almost completely unrelated to the first, although it has sometimes been confused with it; and this confusion has made it easy for those defensive of the status quo to brand all educational critics "enemies of the schools." This second wave stemmed from different causes and was carried along by a totally different group of people. In this second attack, and in the debate that followed it, the great majority of academic scholars and intellectuals stood in opposition to the spokesmen for professional education. This wave was not an attack upon the schools or upon the principles of free public education. It was not an attack upon academic freedom or upon the right of a child to learn the whole truth. In a sense it was a defense of these things. It was an attack along a broad front upon a set of educational philosophies and practices which the critics believed had come to dominate our schools, and which, they believed, were false and dangerous.

Rightly or wrongly, psychologists were blamed for some of these philosophies and practices. They were held responsible for the greatly reduced emphasis on competition as a motive for learning, a symptom of which was the shift from grading on a competitive basis to a new kind of grade card on which the teacher attempted to grade the student's performance against his own potentialities. They were blamed for the alleged relaxation of discipline in the schools and for the new permissiveness. And, because, the "Life Adjustment Program" was confused in the public mind with psychological adjustment, psychologists were blamed for the loss of academic rigor found in these programs.

When these attacks came, psychologists, as distinct from the new breed of educational psychologists, made little effort to defend themselves, partly because academic and scientific psychologists had withdrawn themselves so far from the educational arena that they scarcely knew about the attacks on the schools. Educational practices were defended by educators who, in most cases, were not psychologists and who were unable to state clearly and forcefully the psychological principles on which education must rest.

It was the public debate which followed the second wave of educational criticism which laid the groundwork for the new wave of educational reform which came into being during the late 1950's and seems likely to reach a new crest during the present decade.

Unlike the progressive reforms of thirty years ago, which emphasized new goals and broadened responsibilities for the schools, the new reform movement emphasizes not ends but means. It consists of a series of proposals designed to promote more effective means of teaching and of learning. Consequently it ought, it would seem, to be based upon the best available evidence from psychological research, and its evaluation ought to incorporate the best procedures known to psychologists.

In a few cases, perhaps, it does. In more cases, however, the new programs are being promoted with imagination, flair, and enthusiasm but without a great deal of psychological sophistication. They are pushed by practical educators including a few vigorous school super-intendents and principals who are eager to meet the new challenges facing the schools and cannot wait until psychologists have com-pleted their research and have come to agreement about the proper theoretical basis for classroom learning. Some of them are familiar with the results of recent psychological research but are convinced that these results are not of great value to them in meeting their immediate problems. And they may be right.

The educational reforms of the present period fall roughly into five categories: technological innovations, new staffing patterns, program reorganization, curricular reforms stressing new content, and new programs for teacher education.

Technological Innovations

EDUCATIONAL TELEVISION

Of the technological innovations, educational television is un-doubtedly the one which so far has reached the largest number of learners, but it is also the one that bears relationship to basic psy-chological research. Although it is possible to make a sophisticated statement of the rationale for teaching by television, most of the impetus for the spread of the use of that technology has come from other sources. When psychologists have played a part, it usually has been limited to that of evaluating results.

The implied (but rarely stated) psychological basis for teaching by television is the hypothesis that learning occurs in response to an appropriate stimulus or stimulating situation and that a highly skilled and well-informed teacher may provide a more effective stimulus by way of a 21-inch screen than is provided by a mediocre teacher who is physically present in the classroom.

A considerable amount, indeed the major part, of classroom in-struction in the conventional school is provided by teachers who describe, explain, inform, clarify, exhort, and demonstrate, while children watch and listen, and, it is hoped, react in more complex ways. While this method, or assortment of methods, has been sharp-ly criticized by those who call it all "lecturing" and who believe it should be replaced by student discussions, the method continues to be used in many secondary schools and most colleges.

Television makes it possible for the teachers who use this method most effectively to bring their talents to a much larger number of students. Those who endorse educational television are convinced that a child will learn more about counterpoint, for example, by watching and listening to a discussion and demonstration presented by Leonard Bernstein backed up by the New York Philharmonic than he will by listening to his local music teacher backed up by a student pianist.

The evidence today is not likely to convince a skeptical scientist that it is safe either to accept or reject this hypothesis. But most of the arguments used in opposition to educational television rest upon no more scientific evidence than do those used in favor of it. Oppo-nents say that "children can't ask questions of the television teacher," which is true, but it is equally true that children cannot ask questions of the author of a textbook or a classic, and yet we have always assumed that a book can be an effective stimulus for learning.

The assumption, frequently voiced by opponents of television, that a child can learn only in an intimate environment in which he and the teacher can exchange views does not rest upon experimental evidence, nor does the view that physical distance between pupil and teacher is an important variable in learning.

Wherever the teacher may be, and whatever he may do, he is only a part of the stimulating situation to which the child responds, and it is obvious that the child learns not what the teacher says but what he, the child, does by way of response. It seems entirely possible that the question of whether the teacher is physically present in the classroom or only an image and a voice from a television set may not be very important psychologically—certainly many viewers of commercial television respond to their favorite singers and come-dians as very "real" people. But, before we can make firm decisions about the place of television in the classroom, we need better evidence than is now available.

Programed learning as it is used in teaching machines rests upon a firmer foundation than does educational television, or at any rate the rationale has been more clearly enunciated. The underlying principle is that of immediate reinforcement. In conventional classroom practice, reinforcement, either positive or negative, is rarely immediate and often almost nonexistent. The student writes a theme or completes a test paper which may not be returned to him for days or weeks. By the time it is returned he has forgotten why he made the responses he did and is interested only in the grade assigned to the paper. His oral contributions may occasionally be reinforced immediately by a smile or a frown from a teacher or a classmate, but often the pupil is far from clear about just what he has done that is right or wrong.

When he uses a teaching machine, or other device for programed learning, the learner is told immediately whether his response is right or wrong, and he cannot proceed to the next item until he gets it right. There seems little doubt that learning will be enhanced.

The subject of teaching machines and the theory of autoinstruction are discussed in much greater detail by Pressey and Lumsdaine in chapters xv and xvi of the present volume.

New Staffing Patterns

TEAM TEACHING

Of the new staffing patterns, team teaching is undoubtedly the most important, but it is misnamed. It might more appropriately be called "team organization and planning" because the teaching, at any given moment, usually is done by an individual rather than by a team.

Team teaching differs from subject-matter departmentalization in that the assignment of teacher roles often is not along subject-matter lines. Instead, one member of the team may take most of the responsibility for keeping records and consulting with parents, another may be responsible for the custodial aspects of elementary school-keeping, while a third teaches children to read. Each teacher does what he likes to do and can do best, and yet everything essential gets done.

Team teaching rests upon the assumption that great individual differences exist among teachers—even among teachers with similiar education and experience—and that these differences, whether genetic or environmental, are so firmly established by the time the prospective teacher begins his professional training that no program of teacher education will eliminate them even if it is believed that they ought to be eliminated. It follows that it is not feasible to require every certified teacher to play all the roles required of a teacher in a self-contained classroom and that the self-contained classroom ought to be replaced by a new kind of classroom organization with a new staffing pattern.

Most of the teaching teams include such subprofessional personnel as teacher-aides and secretaries, and it is assumed that many of the responsibilities normally assigned to a professional teacher can be discharged as well or better by a noncertified member of the team who receives a lower salary than that paid to teachers. Most of them also include apprentice teachers who serve a semester as a junior team member in lieu of practice teaching. Those responsible for the programs, and the university schools of education working with them, are convinced that such an internship provides a much better introduction to the profession than does the conventional period of student teaching.

An adequate evaluation of team teaching—or of the self-contained classroom which it is designed to replace—will require the establishment of a better criterion than has yet been applied. It will be necessary to measure long-term changes in the students as a result of experience in schools using the new as against the old staffing pattern. For a time, the Hawthorne effect will be at work. The variables obviously are many, and difficult to control. But until such a criterion is used, reliance must be placed on the judgment of professional people who are unlikely to agree about the outcomes.

THE DUAL PROGRESS PLAN

The Dual Progress Plan is a program for the improvement of learning in the elementary school based upon the psychological evidence as interpreted by a psychologist, George Stoddard. Although the plan is sometimes considered a special kind of team teaching, it differs significantly from other team-teaching programs.

From his evaluation of the evidence regarding individual difference in capacity for learning different subjects, Stoddard concludes that children who are grouped together in a homeroom where they study the language arts and the social studies should be regrouped for that part of the day when they are to study mathematics, science, music, and art. He concludes that progress in one subject should not be dependent upon progress in the others—that annual promotions from one grade to another based upon generalized achievement create unnecessary problems.

Stoddard further concludes, from the evidence regarding individual differences among teachers, that the teachers selected to teach English and social studies—"the cultural imperatives"—cannot be counted upon to be competent to teach mathematics and science any more than they can be expected to be proficient in music and art.

Under the Dual Progress Plan, the child spends half the school day in a homeroom with his social peers where he studies "the cultural imperatives." During the other half-day he is with children whose competence is similar to his own in mathematics, science, music, or whatever subject or activity is being engaged in. He may be in a very advanced class in mathematics and a retarded section in music, if such assignments are consistent with his abilities, and for each of these subjects he has a teacher selected on the basis of his special competence in that field. Because men, in our culture, are somewhat more likely than women to become proficient in mathematics and science, the teachers of these subjects, under Stoddard's plan, are likely to be men even in the primary grades, but the homeroom teacher who teaches English is more likely to be a woman.

The Dual Progress Plan is designed to provide improved academic instruction in all elementary subjects without impairing the child's opportunity for good social and emotional adjustment. The principles underlying it are fully described in Stoddard's book, *The Dual Progress Plan.*[1]

1. George D. Stoddard, *The Dual Progress Plan.* New York: Harper & Bros., 1961.

Program Reorganization

THE TRUMP PLAN

Program reorganization frequently requires new staffing patterns, but it also includes a manipulation of other variables, including time, space, equipment, and schedules. The most far-reaching proposals for reorganization of the secondary school are those of the Commission on the Experimental Study of the Utilization of the Staff in the Secondary School, a commission authorized by the National Association of Secondary-School Principals and supported by the Fund for the Advancement of Education. Because the length of the name of the commission exceeds the memory span of most readers, these proposals have come to be known as the Trump Plan, for J. Lloyd Trump who is Director of the Commission.

The Trump Plan has evolved over the past six years, and variations of it are being tried in more than fifty secondary schools located in all parts of the country. It has been described in various publications of the National Association of Secondary-School Principals.[2]

The Trump Plan calls for a complete reorganization of the secondary school. Class periods of the standard length are to be replaced by periods of varying length. The standard class size of 30 pupils is to be replaced by some very large lecture and demonstration classes and some small discussion groups. Laboratory activities and a considerable amount of individual work are provided. Use will be made of educational television and teaching machines. New buildings will be designed to facilitate the new organization, and the teaching staff will be organized on the team basis.

Nothing about the Trump plan appears to be in any way inconsistent with learning theory or with the known facts of individual differences among students and teachers—indeed, it appears to make much better provision for individual differences than does the con-

2. See J. Lloyd Trump and Dorsey Baynham, *Guide to Better Schools: Focus on Change* (Chicago: Rand McNally, 1961); J. Lloyd Trump, *Images of the Future: A New Approach to the Secondary School* (Washington: National Association of Secondary-School Principals, 1959); and *The Bulletin* (National Association of Secondary-School Principals), Vols. XLII, XLIII, XLIV, and XLV.

ventional plan of high-school organization. No doubt an excellent rationale, based on psychological principles, could be made for it, but, to this writer's knowledge, such a rationale has not yet been formulated and the plan appears to have developed independently of psychological theory.

THE CONANT PROPOSALS

The Conant proposals[3] for the improvement of the secondary school are much less far-reaching than the Trump proposals. Conant believes that the comprehensive high schools now found in the great majority of medium-sized cities already are doing a reasonably adequate job and that only two changes are necessary. First, the small high schools—those with a graduating class of fewer than 100 students—should be eliminated by consolidation; and, second, new and more rigorous programs should be provided for the academically talented where these are not already available.

Conant's recommendation that small high schools be eliminated is not based upon evidence that quality of instruction or of learning is closely related to size of school but, rather, on the practical consideration that a very small school cannot provide a wide variety of vocational and other elective offerings such as are necessary if each student is to graduate from high school with a marketable skill.

Conant's second proposal, that a more rigorous program be designed for the academically talented, indicates an acceptance of psychological evidence regarding individual differences in learning capacity, although the proposed program has no very obvious relation to learning theory. The decision to design a special program for those scoring in the top 15 per cent on tests of academic aptitude appears to have been a statesmanlike decision rather than one based primarily on scientific evidence. The line had to be drawn somewhere, and it was assumed that the lower it was drawn the more difficult it would be to hold the group to high standards. At an earlier stage in the development of his plans, Conant suggested that the line be drawn through a point one sigma above the mean, but this was rounded off as the top 15 per cent to make it understandable

3. James B. Conant, *The American High School Today*. New York: McGraw-Hill Book Co., Inc., 1959.

to the school-board members to whom *The American High School Today* was addressed.

The 15 per cent figure advocated by Conant is much smaller than the percentage of high-school graduates who now enter college. The Conant program for the talented appears to have been intended only for those students destined to enter colleges with the higher entrance standards—not for all potential college students. Conant's program for the other 85 per cent of high-school students requires more time in vocational courses than seems to be justifiable for the many students who plan to go to college, and will go, even though they do not fall within the highly talented group.

For the talented group, Conant recommends a program consisting of four years of mathematics, four of English, four of one foreign language, three of science, and three of social studies. This adds up to a number substantially larger than the number of courses now required for high-school graduation.

The decision to require more courses of the talented group and to emphasize a traditional academic program (presumably with improved course content) was based on the practical judgments of teachers, presidents, and admissions officers of the most highly selective colleges rather than upon any objective evidence that this program is the best possible preparation for college work or for a good life. The evidence from the Eight-Year Study appears to have been ignored in designing the curriculum.

In so far as there is a theory of learning behind the Conant program it appears to be the assumption that, if talented students are assigned the proper tasks and then rewarded for completing the tasks by grades, diplomas, and scholarships, they will learn much that they need to know. To psychologists such an assumption may seem unsophisticated, but this is the theory of learning that has been accepted by the great majority of classroom teachers down through the ages. And, in varying degrees, it has obtained results.

Conant is well aware, of course, of the importance of good teaching, teaching that emphasizes problem-solving and drawing conclusions from evidence. His recommendations to school boards do not include new ways of attracting or identifying such teachers, but when he was president of Harvard, Conant was responsible for the inauguration of the Master of Arts in Teaching program, which was designed to provide such teachers for the secondary schools.

THE NONGRADED SCHOOL

The nongraded, or ungraded, elementary school is another effort to adapt the school program to the facts of individual differences in learning capacity. Until about 1850 most of the nation's elementary schools were ungraded, but, as schools became larger as a result of urbanization, graded systems became the common practice. In such a system the child and his parents were led to believe that every child ought to climb the educational ladder at the rate of one grade per year and that the child who could not do so was a failure. As better evidence regarding the nature of individual differences was accumulated, it became obvious that such a system was appropriate only for children near the center of the distribution, but by that time the system of school grades had become so rigid that change was difficult and upsetting to teachers.

The nongraded system is an effort to get away from the rigidities of the graded system and to make it possible for each child to proceed through the school at his own best rate without introducing the concept of failure. A discussion of this system, and of the rationale behind it, may be found in *The Nongraded Elementary School* by Goodlad and Anderson.[4]

Curricular Reforms Stressing New Content

The great majority of elementary- and secondary-school teachers rely heavily on textbooks as a basis for the organization and presentation of subject matter. There are exceptions, of course. Vigorous and imaginative teachers, when free to do so, plan their own courses and make much use of materials aside from the text if it is easily available. Some may depart markedly from the organization of topics and the point of view of the author of the text. The great majority of teachers, however, find it easier to use the textbook (and the workbooks and teacher's guides that accompany it) as a basis in planning their courses. In many schools supplementary materials are not available in sufficient quantities for student use.

4. John I. Goodlad and Robert H. Anderson, *The Nongraded Elementary School*. New York: Harcourt, Brace & World, 1959.

The result is that those who have written the textbooks have played a major part in determining the curriculum. For more than half of the nineteenth century McGuffey, more than any one man, decided how reading should be taught and what selections from literature children should read in the elementary schools.

Until about 1930 the great majority of the textbooks used in high school were written by academic scholars who, in most cases, were university professors of science, history, mathematics, or languages and literature, and the content of high-school texts often was a simpler version of the history, science, or literature taught in college.

More recently, an increasing number of the widely used elementary textbooks have been written by committees. Often the committee has included one or more academic scholars, but other members have been curriculum consultants or other professional educators and not infrequently final decisions about content organization and style have been made in editorial offices. The result has been textbooks that are easily understood by children and are attractively made up with ample illustrations but that are less closely related than their predecessors to the world of scholarship.

For a quarter of a century—roughly from the early thirties until the late fifties—the academic scholars and scientists seemed to have lost interest in the content of elementary and secondary curricula. Then, as a result of the widespread criticism of the schools during the fifties, some of them again took a look at what was being taught below the college level. They were alarmed by what they found. They reported that many of the textbooks being used, particularly in mathematics and the sciences, were hopelessly out of date and unrelated to the most recent developments in those fields.

With foundation and governmental support, groups of distinguished physicists and mathematicians, working closely with educators and secondary teachers, set out to overhaul the content of the public school curriculum in their own disciplines. They were followed by other scholars and scientists from the fields of chemistry, biology, languages, and the social sciences. New textbooks, visual aids, supplementary reading materials, and laboratory apparatus have been prepared for the use of pupils and teachers, and teachers have been invited to summer institutes to learn to use the new materials and to be brought up to date in their subjects.

The impetus behind these new programs came from the need for improved content rather than from new approaches to the psychology of teaching. The theories of learning on which they are based are implied rather than stated. These theories are not new—they would have sounded familiar to James or Dewey—but they are psychologically sound. Each program provides a well-organized sequence of learning experiences, and the learner is provided with a wide range of stimulating materials, including books, visual aids, and laboratory equipment. The emphasis throughout is on problem-solving rather than on memory of facts. If the phrase "learning by doing" had not become a cliché, it could appropriately be applied to these programs, which emphasize well-motivated pupil activity planned in terms of an established goal.

New Programs for Teacher Education

During the nineteenth century the great majority of secondary-school teachers were educated in liberal-arts colleges where they studied the academic disciplines but learned little or nothing about the processes of teaching and of learning. During the same period, most of our elementary-school teachers were educated in normal schools where a considerable amount of attention was given to educational process but where the academic content presented was at an elementary level, consisting often of little more than a review of the subjects taught in the lower schools.

Since 1900 these two traditions have drawn more closely together, but the rapprochement has not been without a considerable amount of friction. The colleges and universities have admitted professors of education to their faculties but have not always welcomed them with enthusiasm. Between 1900 and 1930, most of the normal schools became degree-granting teachers' colleges, and since 1930 most of them have become general state colleges that offer the full range of academic courses, taught, in most cases, by faculty members holding graduate degrees in their various disciplines. Teacher education is no longer a thing apart but is now a segment of the mainstream of higher education in America. But conflicts between the normal-school (and teachers' college) tradition, with its emphasis on process, and the liberal-arts tradition, with its emphasis on intellectual content, still persist in universities and liberal-arts colleges as well as in the state colleges that once were normal schools.

Many of the new programs in teacher education had their origins in these conflicts and are designed to offer possible solutions. In 1936, James B. Conant, then president of Harvard, initiated a program for secondary-school teachers which incorporated many of the best features of both traditions. Carefully selected liberal-arts graduates were offered a one-year program of graduate work in which about half the time was spent in advanced study of a scholarly discipline and the other half in a sequence of professional courses or seminars for teachers. Each candidate also spent at least one semester as an intern in a secondary-school classroom, where his work was closely supervised. At the end of the year he was granted the Master of Arts in Teaching degree (MAT or AMT).

At first the new program grew slowly, but after the end of World War II, when the teacher shortage became acute, foundations provided scholarship funds, and the number of candidates greatly increased. Many other universities developed similar programs, and some colleges that did not award the MAT degree nevertheless incorporated some of its features into their programs for teacher education.

One of the assumptions underlying these programs is that an extended internship with closely correlated professional seminars will contribute more to a teacher's understanding of his job than the usual sequence of professional courses followed by a brief period of practice-teaching during the undergraduate period. The intern in an MAT program spends the full day in the classroom for at least a full semester and is perceived by the pupil as "the teacher" rather than "a practice teacher." He is also more likely to see himself as a teacher and to accept the responsibilities of his profession during the internship period.

Somewhat similar programs, leading to certification but not always to degrees, have been developed for older liberal-arts graduates, particularly older women whose children are grown. These, too, concentrate all the professional courses on seminars, and the practice-teaching or internship, in the fifth year. The professional seminars are specifically designed for highly selected mature students, and their content is at a more sophisticated level than that found in the professional courses commonly required of under-graduates.

Much of the criticism of these new programs has come from those educators who are convinced that professional education for teachers should begin during the undergraduate period and be spread over a considerable period of time. They see the concentrated fifth-year programs as, at best, a stopgap procedure for meeting the teacher shortage rather than as a better way of educating teachers.

The basic question is: "Will more effective teachers be produced by a program in which professional training is spread out over a period of years, or by a concentrated program following a four-year undergraduate program of liberal education?" Many educators have firm convictions on this subject but research has provided no convincing evidence on either side of the dispute. The evidence is inconclusive, both because we have no adequate criterion for teaching success and because the individuals selecting the two programs are not equivalent. The fifth-year programs select their candidates much more carefully (the fact that they are able to do so is one of their virtues), and they have proven to be more attractive to candidates of higher intelligence, superior scholarship, and, in general, of a higher cultural and economic level. If their graduates prove to be better teachers than the products of conventional undergraduate programs, this may well be the result of superior selection rather than of superior programs.

It seems apparent, however, that we need all the good teachers we can get, from whatever source, and equally apparent that older liberal-arts graduates, as well as younger ones who do not decide to become teachers until after they receive their A.B. degrees, provide an important source of supply. This being the case, it is necessary to provide a variety of ports of entry into the professional program in order that potential teachers who make a late decision to enter the profession will not be discouraged from doing so.

Conclusion

The search for the psychological principles and theories underlying recent reforms in education has proved to be discouraging because most of these reforms do not appear to rest upon clearly stated psychological principles. Most of these reforms seem to have arisen not from new psychological discoveries but rather from social and political pressures and from widespread public discontent with the state of our educational system and the quality of the results being achieved with children. Of the many current reforms, only the Dual Progress Plan and programed learning are closely related to psychological principles and were developed in large part by psychologists.

It appears that, with a few exceptions, the psychologists working at the frontiers of their science today have little interest in pedagogical problems and give them only peripheral attention. The result is that psychology no longer plays a very important part in determining the direction of educational experimentation. In many of the new reform programs, the role of educational psychologists has been limited to a consulting capacity and to evaluation. Other people, who are not psychologists, usually plan the course of action and make the important decisions. In many cases it is educational administrators rather than educational or psychological theorists who are taking the lead in striking out in new directions.

The current situation is regrettable. If the discoveries of psychologists are to be brought to bear on the problem of improving the condition of mankind, it is clear that education offers greater opportunities than any other field. This is true, both because all our people spend from 10 to 16 years in school and college, while a much smaller number are reached directly by psychologists working in other applied fields, and because learning, broadly defined, is the central problem in both psychology and education. In a very real sense, all education *is* applied psychology. If psychologists—the most able psychologists—neglect the field of education they will have missed their greatest opportunity.

REFERENCES

In lieu of extensive documentation of the text of this chapter, the following references are presented.

REFORM MOVEMENTS IN EDUCATION

BODE, BOYD H. *Progressive Education at the Crossroads*. New York: Newson & Co., 1938.

CREMIN, LAWRENCE A. *The Transformation of the School*. New York: Alfred A. Knopf, Inc., 1961.

DEWEY, JOHN. *Experience and Education*. New York: Macmillan Co., 1938.

——. *The School and Society*. Chicago: University of Chicago Press, 1899.

HANDLIN, OSCAR. *John Dewey's Challenge to Education*. New York: Harper & Bros., 1959.

RIESMAN, DAVID. *Constraint and Variety in American Education*. Lincoln: University of Nebraska Press, 1956.

WESLEY, EDGAR B. *NEA: The First Hundred Years*. New York: Harper & Bros., 1957.

WOODRING, PAUL. *A Fourth of a Nation*. New York: McGraw-Hill Book Co., 1957.

TECHNOLOGICAL INNOVATIONS

Automatic Teaching: The State of the Art. Edited by Eugene Galanter. New York: John Wiley & Sons., 1959.

GREEN, EDWARD J. *The Learning Process and Programmed Instruction*. New York: Henry Holt & Co., 1962.

HUGHES, JOHN L. *Programmed Instruction in Schools and Industry*. Chicago: Science Research Associates, 1962.

PRESSEY, S. L. "A Machine for Automatic Teaching of Drill Material," *School and Society*, XXV (May 7, 1927), 549–52.

——. "A Third and Fourth Contribution toward the Coming 'Industrial Revolution' in Education," *School and Society*, XXXVI (November 19, 1932), 668–72.

Programmed Learning and Computer-based Instruction. Proceedings of the Conference on Application of Digital Computers to Automated Instruction, Washington, D.C., 1961. Edited by John E. Coulson. New York: John Wiley & Sons, 1962.

SKINNER, B. F. "Teaching Machines," *Science*, CXXVIII (October, 1958), 969–77.

STODDARD, ALEXANDER. *Schools for Tomorrow: An Educator's Blueprint*. New York: Fund for the Advancement of Education, 1957.

Teaching Machines and Programmed Instruction. Edited by Edward Fry. New York: McGraw-Hill Book Co., 1963.

Teaching Machines and Programmed Learning. Edited by A. A. Lumsdaine and Robert Glaser. Washington: National Education Association, 1960.

NEW STAFFING PATTERNS AND PROGRAM REORGANIZATION

CONANT, JAMES B. *The American High School Today*. New York: McGraw-Hill Book Co., 1959.

GOODLAD, JOHN I., and ANDERSON, ROBERT H. *The Nongraded Elementary School*. New York: Harcourt, Brace & Co., 1959.

STODDARD, GEORGE D. *The Dual Progress Plan*. New York: Harper & Bros., 1961.

TRUMP, J. LLOYD. *Images of the Future*. Washington: National Association of Secondary-School Principals, 1959.

TRUMP, J. LLOYD, and BAYNHAM, DORSEY. *Guide to Better Schools: Focus on Change*. Chicago: Rand McNally Co., 1961.

NEW PROGRAMS FOR TEACHING EDUCATION

CONANT, JAMES B. *The Education of American Teachers*. New York: McGraw-Hill Book Co., 1963.

HODENFIELD, G. K., and STINNETT, T. M. *The Education of Teachers: Conflict and Consensus*. Englewood Cliffs, New Jersey: Prentice-Hall, Inc., 1961.

STABLER, ERNEST. "The Master of Arts in Teaching Idea," *Educational Record*, XLI (July, 1960), 228.

STINNETT, T. M. "The Teachers College Myth," *Journal of Teacher Education*, VII (December, 1956), 290, 366-70.

Teacher Education: A Reappraisal. Edited by Elmer R. Smith. New York: Harper & Row, 1962.

WOODRING, PAUL. *New Directions in Teacher Education*. New York: Fund for the Advancement of Education, 1957.

CHAPTER XIII

Some Theorems on Instruction Illustrated with Reference to Mathematics

JEROME S. BRUNER[1]

The following pages represent an attempt to develop a few simple theorems about the nature of instruction. I shall try to illustrate them by reference to the teaching and learning of mathematics. The choice of mathematics as a mode of illustration is not premised on the typicality of mathematics. For mathematics is restricted to well-formed problems and does not concern itself with empirical proof by either experiment or observation. Nor is this an attempt to elucidate mathematics teaching as such, for this would be beyond my competence. Rather, mathematics offers an accessible and simple example for what, perforce, will be a simplified set of propositions about teaching and learning. Moreover, there are data available from mathematics learning that have some bearing on our problem.

The plan is as follows. In the first section, some characteristics of a theory of instruction will be set forth. This is followed by a statement of some highly general theorems about the instructional process. The section that follows then attempts to convert these general propositions into workable hypotheses which are examined in the light of selected observations on mathematics learning. Finally, we conclude with some remarks on the nature of research in support of curriculum-making.

Nature of a Theory of Instruction

A theory of instruction is *prescriptive* in the sense that it sets forth rules concerning the most effective way of achieving knowledge or skill. By the same token, such a theory provides a yardstick for criticizing or evaluating any particular way of teaching or learning.

1. Mrs. Blythe Clinchy assisted in the preparation of this paper.

A theory of instruction is a *normative* theory. It sets up criteria and states the conditions for meeting them. The criteria must have a high degree of generality: for example, a theory of instruction should not specify in an *ad hoc* fashion the conditions for efficient learning of third-grade arithmetic. Rather, such conditions should be derivable from a more general view of mathematics learning.

One might ask why a theory of instruction is needed, since psychology already contains theories of learning and of development. But theories of learning and of development are descriptive rather than prescriptive. They tell us what happened after the fact: for example, that most children of six do not yet possess the notion of reversibility. A theory of instruction, on the other hand, might attempt to set forth the best means of leading the child toward the notion of reversibility. A theory of instruction, in short, is concerned with how best to learn what one wishes to teach, with improving, rather than describing learning.

This is not to say that learning and developmental theories are irrelevant to a theory of instruction. In fact, a theory of instruction must be concerned with both learning and development, as well as with the nature of particular subject matter; and there must be congruence among the various theories, all of which have a complementary relation to each other.

A theory of instruction has four major features:

1. A theory of instruction should specify the experiences which most effectively implant in the individual a predisposition toward learning— learning in general or a particular type of learning. For example, what sorts of relationships toward people and things in the preschool environment will tend to make the child willing and able to learn when he enters school?
2. Second, a theory of instruction must specify the ways in which a body of knowledge should be structured so that it can be most readily grasped by the learner. Optimal structure refers to the set of propositions from which a larger body of knowledge can be generated, and it is characteristic that the formulation of such structure depends upon the state of advance in a particular field of knowledge. In a later section, the nature of different optimal structures will be considered in more detail. Here it suffices to say that since the goodness of a structure depends upon its power for *simplifying information,* for *generating new propositions,* and for *increasing the manipulability of a body of knowledge,* structure must always be related to the status

and gifts of the learner. Viewed in this way, the optimal structure of a body of knowledge is not absolute but relative. The major requirement is that no two sets of generating structures for the same field of knowledge be in contradiction.

3. Third, the theory of instruction should specify the most effective sequences in which to present the materials to be learned. Given, for example, that one wishes to teach the structure of modern physical theory, how does one proceed? Does one present concrete materials first in such a way as to elicit questions about recurrent regularities? Or, does one begin with a formalized mathematical notation that makes it simpler to represent regularities later encountered? What results are in fact produced by the use of each? The question of sequence will be treated in more detail later.

4. Finally, a theory of instruction should specify the *nature and pacing of rewards and punishments* in the process of learning and teaching. Intuitively, it seems quite clear that as learning progresses there is a point at which it is better to shift away from extrinsic rewards, such as teacher's praise, toward the intrinsic rewards inherent in solving a complex problem for one's self. So, too, there is a point at which immediate reward for performance should be replaced by deferred reward. The shift rates from extrinsic to intrinsic and from immediate to deferred reward are poorly understood and obviously important. Is it the case, for example, that wherever learning involves the integration of a long sequence of acts, the earliest shift should be made from immediate to deferred reward and from extrinsic to intrinsic reward?

It would be beyond the scope of any single paper to pursue in any detail all of the four aspects of a theory of instruction set forth above. What I shall attempt to do here is to explore a major theorem concerning each of the four. The object is not comprehensiveness but illustration.

Predispositions

It has been customary, in discussing predispositions to learn, to focus upon cultural, motivational, and personal factors affecting the desire to learn and to undertake problem-solving. And indeed, such factors are of enormous importance. But we shall concentrate here on a more cognitive level: upon the predisposition to explore alternatives. For it is this predisposition that is often most affected by cultural and motivational factors.

Since learning and problem-solving depend upon the exploration of alternatives, instruction must facilitate and regulate the exploration of alternatives on the part of the learner.

There are three aspects to the exploration of alternatives, each of them related to the regulation of search behavior. They can be described in shorthand terms as *activation, maintenance,* and *direction.* To put it another way, exploration of alternatives requires something to get started, something to keep it going, and something to keep it from being random.

The major condition for *activating exploration* of alternatives in a task is the presence of some optimal level of uncertainty. Curiosity, it has been persuasively argued,[2] is a response to uncertainty and ambiguity. A cut-and-dried routine task arouses little exploration; one that is too uncertain may arouse confusion and anxiety, with the effect of reducing exploration.

The *maintenance of exploration,* once it has been activated, requires that the benefits from exploring alternatives exceed the risks incurred. Learning something with the aid of an instructor should, if instruction is effective, be less dangerous or risky or painful than learning on one's own. That is to say, the consequences of error—exploring *wrong* alternatives—should be rendered less grave under a regimen of instruction, and the yield from the exploration of *correct* alternatives should be correspondingly greater.

The appropriate *direction of exploration* depends upon two interacting considerations: a sense of the goal of a task and a knowledge of the relevance of tested alternatives to the achievement of that goal. For exploration to have direction, in short, the goal of the task must be known in some approximate fashion, and the testing of alternatives must yield information as to where one is with respect to it.

Structure and the Form of Knowledge

Any idea or problem or body of knowledge can be presented in a form simple enough so that any particular learner can understand it.

The structure of any domain of knowledge may be characterized in three ways, each affecting the ability of any learner to master it: (*a*) *the mode of representation* in which it is put, (*b*) its *economy,*

2. D. E. Berlyne, *Conflict, Arousal, and Curiosity.* New York: McGraw-Hill Book Co., Inc., 1960.

and (*c*) its *effective power*. Mode, economy, and power vary in appropriateness to different ages, to different "styles" among learners, and to the differences between subject matters.

Any domain of knowledge (or any problem within that domain of knowledge) can be represented in three ways: (*a*) by a set of actions appropriate for achieving a certain result (*enactive representation*), (*b*) by a set of summary images or graphics that stand for a concept without defining it fully (*ikonic representation*), and (*c*) by a set of symbolic or logical propositions drawn from a symbolic system that is governed by rules or laws for forming and transforming propositions (*symbolic representation*). The distinction can most conveniently be made concretely in terms of a balance beam, for we shall have occasion in a later section to consider the use of such an implement in teaching children quadratic functions. A very young child can plainly act on the basis of the "principles" of a balance beam, and indicates that he can do so by being able to handle himself on a see-saw. He knows that to get his side to go down farther he has to move out farther from the center. A somewhat older child can represent the balance beam to himself either by drawing or by a model on which rings can be hung and balanced. The "image" of the balance beam can be varyingly refined, with fewer and fewer irrelevant details present, as in the typical diagrams in an introductory textbook in physics. Finally, a balance beam can be described in ordinary English, without diagrammatic aids, or it can be even better described mathematically by reference to Newton's Law of Moments in inertial physics. Needless to say, actions, pictures, and symbols are differentially difficult for people of different ages, different backgrounds, different styles. Moreover, a problem in the law would be hard to diagram, one in geography lends itself to imagery. Many subjects, such as mathematics, have alternative modes of representation.

Economy in representing a domain of knowledge refers to the amount of information that must be held in mind and processed to achieve comprehension. The larger the number of items of information that must be carried to understand something or deal with a problem, the greater the number of successive steps one must take in processing that information to achieve a conclusion; hence, the less the economy. For any domain of knowledge one can rank summaries of it in terms of their economy. It is more economical (though less powerful) to summarize the American Civil War as a "battle over slavery" than as "a struggle between an expanding industrial region and one built upon a class society for control of federal economic policy." It is more economical to summarize the characteristics of free-falling bodies by the formula $S = \frac{1}{2}gt^2$ than to put a series of numbers into tabular form summarizing a vast set of observations made on different bodies dropped different distances in different gravitational fields. The matter is best epitomized by two ways of imparting information: one requiring carriage of much information, the other more a pay-as-you-go type of information-processing. A highly imbedded sentence is an example of the former ("This is the rat that the cat that the dog that the boy chased, teased, and killed"); the contrast case is more economical ("This is the boy that chased the dog that teased the cat that killed the rat"). Economy, as we shall see, varies with mode of representation. But economy is also a function of the sequence in which material is presented or the manner in which it is learned—over and beyond the optimum structure that can be achieved. The case can be exemplified as follows. Suppose the domain of knowledge consists of available plane service within a twelve-hour period between five cities in the Northeast—Concord, New Hampshire; Albany, New York; Danbury, Connecticut; Elmira, New York; and Boston, Massachusetts. One of the ways in which the knowledge can be imparted is by asking the student to memorize the following list of connections:

> Boston to Concord
> Danbury to Concord
> Albany to Boston
> Concord to Elmira
> Albany to Elmira
> Concord to Danbury
> Boston to Albany
> Concord to Albany

Now we ask, "What is the shortest way to make a round trip from Albany to Danbury?" The amount of information-processing required to answer this question under such conditions is considerable. We increase economy by "simplifying terms" in certain characteristic ways. One is to introduce an arbitrary but learned order —in this case, an alphabetical one. We rewrite the list:

> Albany to Boston
> Albany to Elmira
> Boston to Albany
> Boston to Concord
> Concord to Danbury
> Concord to Elmira
> Danbury to Concord

Search then becomes easier, but there is still a somewhat trying sequential property to the task. Economy is further increased by using a diagrammatic notation, and again there are varying degrees of economy in such recourse to the ikonic mode. Compare the diagram on the left and the one on the right.

When we come to a consideration of mathematics, it will be apparent that the form of presentation is probably a far more important determinant of economy than the nature of the mathematics itself.

The *effective power* of any particular way of structuring a domain of knowledge refers to the generative value of a set of learned propositions. In the previous section, rote learning of a set of connections between cities results in a rather inert structure from which it is difficult to generate pathways through the set of cities. Or, to take an example from a recent report by Donaldson,[3] children who are told that "Mary is taller than Jane, and Betty is shorter than Jane" are often unable to say whether Mary is taller than Betty. One can perfectly well remark that the answer is "there" in the logic of transitivity. But to say this is to miss the psychological point. *Effective power* will, to be sure, never exceed the inherent logical generativeness of a domain—although this is an admittedly difficult statement from the point of view of epistemology. In common-sense

3. Margaret Donaldson, *A Study of Children's Thinking*. London: Tavistock Publications, Ltd., 1963.

terms, it amounts to the assertion that grasp of a field of knowledge will never be better than the best that can be done with that field of knowledge. The effective power within a particular learner's grasp is what one seeks to discover by close analysis of how in fact he is going about his task of learning. Much of Piaget's research[4] seeks to discover just this property about children's learning and thinking. There is an interesting relationship between economy and power. Theoretically, the two are independent: indeed, it is clear that a structure may be economical but powerless. But it is rare for a powerful structuring technique in any field to be uneconomical. This is what leads to the canon of parsimony and the faith shared by many scientists that nature is simple: perhaps it is only when nature can be made reasonably simple that it can be understood. The power of a representation can also be described as its capacity, in the hands of a learner, to connect matters that, on the surface, seem quite separate. This is especially crucial in mathematics, and we shall return to the matter later.

Sequence and Its Uses

Instruction consists of leading the learner through a sequence of statements and restatements of a problem or body of knowledge that increase the learner's ability to grasp, transform, and transfer what he is learning. In short, the sequence in which a learner encounters materials within a domain of knowledge affects the difficulty he will have in achieving mastery.

There are usually a variety of sequences that are equivalent in their ease and difficulty for learners. There is no unique sequence for all learners, and the optimum in any particular case will depend upon a variety of factors, including past learning, stage of development, nature of the material, and individual differences.

If it is true that the usual course of intellectual development moves from enactive through ikonic to symbolic representation of the world,[5] it is likely that an optimum sequence will progress in the same direction. Obviously, this is a conservative doctrine. For when

4. Jean Piaget, *The Child's Conception of Number*. New York: Humanities Press, 1952.

5. Jerome S. Bruner, "The Course of Cognitive Growth," *American Psychologist* (in press).

the learner has a well-developed symbolic system, it may be possible to by-pass the first two stages. But one does so always with the risk that the learner may not possess the imagery to fall back on when his symbolic transformations fail to achieve a goal in problem-solving.

Sequencing must take into account the limited capacities of any organism to process information. In this sense, a sequence that begins economically will usually be advisable. This hypothesis is further premised on the assumption that more economically presented materials, learned first as a model, will serve to reduce the potential complexity of materials encountered later.

Exploration of alternatives will necessarily be affected by the sequence in which material to be learned becomes available to the learner. It is an empirical question as to when the learner should be encouraged to explore alternatives widely and when he should be encouraged to concentrate on the implications of a single alternative hypothesis. To this subject we return in the next section.

Reverting to the earlier discussion of activation and the maintenance of interest, it is necessary to specify in any sequence the level of uncertainty and tension that must be present to initiate problem-solving behavior and what is necessary to keep active problem-solving going. This again is an empirical question.

Optimum sequences, as already stated, cannot be specified independent of the criterion in terms of which final learning is to be judged. A classification of such criteria will include at least the following: (*a*) speed of learning, (*b*) resistance to forgetting, (*c*) transferability of what has been learned to new instances, (*d*) form of representation in terms of which what has been learned is to be expressed, (*e*) economy of what has been learned in terms of cognitive strain imposed, (*f*) effective power of what has been learned in terms of its generativeness for new hypotheses and combinations. Achieving one of these goals does not necessarily bring one closer to others. Speed of learning is sometimes antithetical to transfer or to economy. and so forth.

The Form and Pacing of Reinforcement

Learning depends upon knowledge of results at a time when and at a place where the knowledge can be used for correction. Instruction increases the appropriate timing and placing of corrective knowledge.

"Knowledge of results" is useful or not depending upon (*a*) when and where the learner is able to put the corrective information to work, (*b*) under what conditions such corrective information can be used, even assuming appropriateness of time and place of receipt, and (*c*) the form in which the corrective information is received.

Learning and problem-solving are divisible into phases. These have been described in various way by writers such as Wallas,[6] Dewey,[7] Woodworth,[8] Tolman,[9] Bruner,[10] Simon,[11] and Miller, Galanter, and Pribram.[12] But all the descriptions agree on one essential feature: that there is a cycle involving the formulation of a testing procedure or trial, the operation of this testing procedure, and the comparison of the results of the test with some criterion. It has variously been called trial-and-error, means-end testing, trial-and-check, discrepancy reduction, test-operate-test-exit (TOTE), hypothesis testing, and the like. These "units," moreover, can readily be characterized as hierarchically organized: we seek to cancel the unknowns in an equation in order to simplify the expression in order to solve the equation in order to get through the course in order to get our degree in order to get a decent job in order to lead the good life, and so on. Knowledge of results, it follows from this, should come at that point in a problem-solving episode when the person is comparing the results of his try-out with some criterion of what he seeks to achieve. Knowledge of results given before this point either cannot be understood or must be carried as extra freight in immediate memory. Knowledge given after this point may be too late to guide

6. Graham Wallas, *The Art of Thought*. New York: Harcourt, Brace & Co., 1926.

7. John Dewey, *How We Think*. New York: D. C. Heath & Co., 1910-1933.

8. Robert S. Woodworth, *Dynamics of Behavior*. New York: Henry Holt & Co., 1958.

9. Edward Chace Tolman, *Purposive Behavior in Animals and Men*. New York: Century Co., 1932.

10. Jerome S. Bruner, "The Act of Discovery," *Harvard Education Review*, XXXI (Winter, 1961), 22-32.

11. Herbert A. Simon, William James Lectures, Harvard University, 1963.

12. G. A. Miller, Eugene Galanter, and Karl H. Pribram, *Plans and the Structure of Behavior*. New York: Henry Holt & Co., 1960.

the choice of a next hypothesis or trial. But knowledge of results must, to be useful, provide information not only as to whether or not one's particular act produced success but also whether the act is in fact leading one through the hierarchy of goals one is seeking to achieve. This is not to say that when we cancel the term in that equation we need information as to whether it will all lead eventually to the good life. Yet there should at least be some "lead notice" available as to whether or not cancellation is on the right general track. It is here that the tutor has a special role. For most learning starts off rather piecemeal without the integration of component acts or elements. Usually, the learner can tell whether a particular cycle of activity has worked—feedback from specific events is usually quite simple—but often he cannot tell whether this completed cycle is leading to the eventual goal. It is interesting, in consequence, that one of the nonrigorous short cuts to problem solution, basic rules of "heuristic," stated in Polya's noted book[13] has to do with defining the over-all problem. To sum up, then, instruction uniquely provides information to the learner about higher-order relevance of his efforts. In time, to be sure, the learner must develop techniques for obtaining such higher-order corrective information on his own, for instruction and its aids must eventually come to an end. And finally, if the problem-solver is to take over this function, it is necessary for him to learn to recognize when he does not comprehend and, as Roger Brown[14] has suggested, to signal incomprehension to the tutor so that he can be helped. In time, the signaling of incomprehension becomes a self-signaling and equivalent to a temporary stop-order.

The ability of problem-solvers to use information correctively is known to vary as a function of internal state. One state in which information is least useful is when the learner is impelled by strong drive and anxiety. There is a sufficient body of research to establish this point beyond reasonable doubt—e.g., Postman and Bruner,[15]

13. György Polya, *How To Solve It*. New York: Doubleday & Co., 1957 (second edition).

14. Roger W. Brown, "From Codability to Coding Ability." Unpublished manuscript, Harvard University, 1963.

15. Leo Postman and Jerome S. Bruner, "Perception under Stress," *Psychological Review*, LV (November, 1948), 314–23.

Easterbrook,[16] Bahrick, Fitts, and Rankin,[17] and Longnecker.[18] Another such state has been referred to in the literature as "functional fixedness"—a problem-solver is, in effect, using corrective information exclusively for the evaluation of one single hypothesis that happens to be wrong. The usual example is treating an object in terms of its conventional significance when it must be treated in a new context— we fail to use a hammer as a bob for a pendulum because it is "fixed" in our thinking as a hammer. The studies of Maier,[19] Luchins,[20] Duncker,[21] and others all point to the fact that during such a period there is a remarkable intractability or even incorrigibility to problem-solving. There is some evidence to indicate that high drive and anxiety lead organisms to be more prone to functional fixedness—e.g., Bruner, Matter, and Papanek[22] and Bruner, Mandler, O'Dowd, and Wallach.[23] It is obvious that corrective information of the usual type, i.e., straight feedback, is least useful during such states and that an adequate instructional strategy aims to terminate the interfering state by special means before continuing with the usual provision of correction. In such cases, instruction verges on a kind of therapy, and it is perhaps because of this therapeutic need that one often finds therapy-like advice in lists of aids for problem-solvers, e.g., Hum-

16. J. A. Easterbrook, "The Effect of Emotion on Cue Utilization and the Organization of Behavior," *Psychological Review*, LVI (May, 1950), 183–201.

17. Harry P. Bahrick, Paul M. Fitts, and Robert E. Rankin, "Effect of Incentives upon Reactions to Peripheral Stimuli," *Journal of Experimental Psychology*, XLIV (1952), 400–406.

18. E. D. Longenecker, "Perceptual Recognition and Anxiety," *Journal of Abnormal and Social Psychology*, LXIV (1962), 215–21.

19. N. R. F. Maier, "Reasoning in Humans. I, On Direction," *Journal of Comparative Psychology*, X (1930), 115–43; "Reasoning in Humans. II, The Solution of a Problem and Its Appearance in Consciousness," *Journal of Comparative Psychology*, XII (1931), 181–94; "Reasoning in Humans. III, The Mechanisms of Equivalent Stimuli and of Reasoning," *Journal of Experimental Psychology*, XXXV (1945), 349–60.

20. Abraham S. Luchins, "Mechanization in Problem-solving—the Effect of *Einstellung*," *Psychological Monographs*, LIV, No. 6 (1942), Whole No. 248.

21. Karl Duncker, "On Problem-solving," *Psychological Monographs*, LVIII, No. 5 (1945), Whole No. 270.

22. Jerome S. Bruner, Jean Matter, and Miriam Lewis Papanek, "Breadth of Learning as a Function of Drive Level and Mechanization," *Psychological Review*, LXII (1955), 1–10.

23. Jerome S. Bruner, Jean Matter Mandler, D. O'Dowd, and Michael A. Wallach, "The Role of Overlearning and Drive Level in Reversal Learning," *Journal of Comparative and Physiological Psychology*, LI (1958), 607–13.

phrey,[24] who suggests that one turn away from the problem when it is proving too difficult.

If information is to be used effectively, it must be translated into the learner's way of attempting to solve a problem. If such translatability is not present, then the information is simply useless. Telling a neophyte skier to "shift to his uphill edges" when he cannot distinguish on which edges he is traveling provides no help; simply telling him to lean into the hill may succeed. Or, to take a more cognitive sphere, there is by now an impressive body of evidence that indicates that "negative information"—information about what something is *not*—is peculiarly unhelpful to a person seeking to master a concept—e.g., Hovland and Weiss,[25] Bruner, Goodnow, and Austin,[26] Wason and Jones,[27] and Hunt.[28] Translatability of corrective information can, in principle, also be applied to the form of representation and its economy. If learning or problem-solving is proceeding in one mode—enactive, ikonic, or symbolic—corrective information must be provided either in the same mode or in one that translates into it. The point is obvious, to be sure, but so often violated as to be pedagogically interesting. In mathematics particularly, one finds that teachers often provide information for correction in a highly symbolized notation when, in fact, the student is proceeding either without knowledge of the symbolic language used or by the use of some sort of approximate imagery. The result is incomprehension or defeat. Again, the matter of economy is obvious but also frequently overlooked. Corrective information that exceeds the information-processing capacities of a learner is obviously wasteful.

Finally, it is necessary to reiterate one general point made above in passing. Instruction is a provisional state that has as its object to

24. George Humphrey, *Directed Thinking*. New York: Dodd, Mead & Co., 1948.

25. Carl I. Hovland and Walter Weiss, "Transmission of Information concerning Concepts through Positive and Negative Instances," *Journal of Experimental Psychology*, XLV (1953), 175–82.

26. Jerome S. Bruner, Jacqueline Goodnow, and George A. Austin, *A Study of Thinking*. New York: John Wiley & Sons, 1956.

27. P. C. Wason and Sheila Jones, "Negatives: Denotation and Connotation," *British Journal of Psychology* (in press).

28. Earl B. Hunt, *Concept Learning: An Information-processing Problem*. New York: John Wiley & Sons, 1962.

make the learner or problem-solver self-sufficient. Any regimen of correction carries the danger that the learner may become permanently dependent upon the tutor's correction. The tutor must correct the learner in a fashion that eventually makes it possible for the learner to take over the corrective function himself. Otherwise the result of instruction is to create a form of mastery that is contingent upon the perpetual presence of a teacher.

Selected Illustrations from Mathematics

Before turning to the task of illustrating some of the points raised in the foregoing rather formalized account of the nature of instruction, a word is in order about what is intended by such illustration. During the last half-decade, much work has gone into the mathematics curriculum. One need only mention the curriculum projects that are better known to appreciate the magnitude of the effort—the School Mathematics Study Group, the University of Illinois Committee on School Mathematics, the several projects of Educational Services Incorporated, the Madison Project, the African Mathematics Project, the University of Maryland Mathematics Project, the University of Illinois Arithmetic Project, and the Stanford Project. From this vast activity, it would be possible to choose illustrations of virtually anything one wished to illustrate. Illustration in such a context in no sense constitutes evidence.

For the fact of the matter is that the evidence available on factors affecting the learning of mathematics is still very sparse. Research on the instructional process—in mathematics as in all disciplines—has not been carried out in connection with the building of curricula. Too often, psychologists have come upon the scene, armed with evaluative devices, only after a curriculum has already been put into operation. Surely it would be more efficient and more useful if embryonic instructional materials could be tried out under experimental conditions so that revision and correction could be based upon immediate knowledge of results.

By means of systematic observational studies—work close in spirit to the work of the ethologists, like Tinbergen,[29] and of Piaget[30]—in-

29. Nickolaas Tinbergen, *Social Behavior in Animals*. New York: John Wiley & Sons, 1953.

30. Piaget, *op. cit.*

vestigators could obtain information sufficiently detailed to allow them to discern how the student grasps what has been presented, what his systematic errors are, and how these are overcome. In so far as one is able to formalize the nature of the systematic errors and the strategies of correction employed in terms of a theory of learning or concept attainment, one is thereby enabled to vary systematically the conditions that may be affecting learning and to build these factors directly into one's curriculum practice. Nor need such studies remain purely observational. Often it is possible to build one's mathematics materials into a programed form—as in the work of Stolurow and Beberman[31]—and obtain a detailed behavioral record for analysis.

To make clear what is intended by a detailed analysis of the process of learning, an example from the work of Suppes[32] will be helpful. He has observed, for example, that the form $3 + x = 8$ is easier for children to deal with than the form $x + 3 = 8$, and while the finding may on the surface seem trivial, closer inspection shows that it is not. Does the difficulty come in dealing with an unknown at the beginning of an expression or from the transfer of linguistic habits from ordinary English, where sentences are easier to complete when a term is deleted from the middle than from the end of the sentence? The issue of where uncertainty can best be tolerated or the issue of the possible interference between linguistic habits and mathematical habits is certainly one worthy of careful and detailed study.

Let me turn now to some illustrations from mathematics that have the effect of pointing up problems raised in the theorems and hypotheses earlier presented. They are not evidence of anything, only ways of locating what might be worth closer study.[33]

31. L. M. Stolurow and M. Beberman, "Comparative Studies of Principles for Programming Mathematics," *Semi-annual Report*, 1962, University of Illinois, Urbana.

32. Patrick Suppes, "Towards a Behavioral Psychology of Mathematics Thinking." Unpublished manuscript, Stanford University, 1963.

33. For a closer discussion of some of the observations mentioned in what follows, the reader is referred to Jerome S. Bruner and Helen Kenney, "Representation and Mathematics Learning," *Child Development* (in press). The general "bias" on which these observations are based is contained in Jerome S. Bruner, *The Process of Education* (Cambridge: Harvard University Press, 1960) and in Bruner, Goodnow, and Austin, *op. cit.*

Rather than presenting observations drawn from different contexts, I shall confine the discussion to one particular study carried out on a small group of children, and to that study we turn now.[34] The observations to be reported were made on four eight-year-old children, two boys and two girls, who were given an hour of daily instruction in mathematics four times a week for six weeks. The children were in the I.Q. range of 120–130 and they were all enrolled in the third grade of a private school that emphasized instruction designed to foster independent problem-solving. They were all from middle-class professional homes. The "teacher" of the class was a well-known research mathematician (Z. P. Dienes); his assistant was a professor of psychology at Harvard who has worked long and hard on human thought processes.

Each child worked at a corner table in a generously sized room. Next to each child sat a tutor-observer trained in psychology and with sufficient background in college mathematics to understand the underlying mathematics being taught. In the middle of the room was a large table with a supply of the blocks and balance beams and cups and beans and chalk that served as instructional aids. In the course of the six weeks, the children were given instruction in factoring, the distributive and commutative properties of addition and multiplication, and finally in quadratic functions.

Each child had available a series of graded problem cards which he could go through at his own pace. The cards gave directions for different kinds of exercises, using the materials described above. The instructor and his assistant circulated from table to table, helping as needed, and each tutor-observer similarly assisted as needed. The problem sequences were designed to provide, first, an appreciation of mathematical ideas through concrete constructions, using materials of various kinds for these constructions. From such constructions, the child was encouraged to form perceptual images of the mathematical idea in terms of the forms that had been constructed. The child was then further encouraged to develop or adopt a notation for describing his construction. After such a cycle, a child moved on

34. We are grateful to Z. P. Dienes, Samuel Anderson, Eleanor Duckworth, and Joan Rigney for their help in designing and carrying out this study. Dr. Dienes particularly formed our thinking about the mode of presenting the mathematical materials.

to the construction of a further embodiment of the idea on which he was working, one that was mathematically isomorphic with what he had learned though expressed in different materials and with altered appearance. When such a new topic was introduced, the children were given a chance to discover its connection with what had gone before and shown how to extend the notational system used before. Careful, minute-by-minute records were kept of the proceedings, along with photographs of the children's constructions.

In no sense can the children, the teachers, the classroom, or the mathematics be said to be typical of what normally occurs in third grade. Four children rarely have six teachers, nor do eight-year-olds ordinarily get into quadratic functions. But our concern is with the processes involved in mathematical learning and not with typicality. But it seems quite reasonable to suppose that the thought processes going on in the children were quite ordinary among eight-year-old human beings.

ACTIVATING PROBLEM-SOLVING

One of the first tasks faced in this study was to gain and hold the child's interest and to lead him to problem-solving activity. At the same time, there was a specific objective to be achieved—to teach the children factoring in such a way that, as Gagné et al.[35] have recently put it, they would have this component skill in an accessible form to use in the solution of problems. It is impossible to say on the basis of our experience whether the method we employed was the best one, but in any case it appeared to work. The first task introduced was one having to do with the different ways in which a set of cubic blocks could be arranged as "flats" (laid out in rectangular forms on the table, not more than one cube high) and in "walls" and "buildings." The problem has an interesting uncertainty to it, and the children were challenged to determine whether they had exhausted all the possible ways of laying things out. Unquestionably, they picked up some zest from the evident curiosity of their teachers as well. After a certain amount of time, the children were encouraged to start keeping a written record of the different shapes

35. Robert M. Gagné, John R. Mayor, Helen L. Garstens, and Noel E. Paradise, "Factors in Acquiring Knowledge of a Mathematical Task," *Psychological Monographs*, LXXVI, No. 7 (1962), Whole No. 526.

they could make, and what their dimensions were. Certain numbers of cubes proved intractable to reforming (the primes, of course) and others proved combinable in interesting ways—that three rows of three cubes made nine, that three layers of these nine "flats" had the dimensions of 3 × 3 × 3, and so on. The idea of factoring was soon grasped and with very little guidance the children went on to interesting conjectures about distributiveness. The task had its own direction built into it in the sense that it had a clear terminus: How to arrange a set of cubes in regular two- or three-dimensional forms. It also had the added feature that the idea of alternatives was built in—

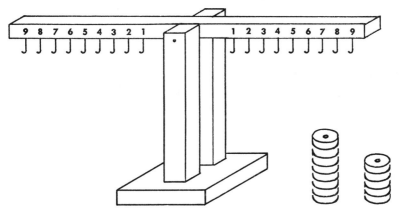

Fig. 1.—Balance beam and rings used in quadratic construction

What are the *different* ways of achieving such regularity? As the children gained in skill, they shifted to other ways of laying out cubes—in pyramids, in triangles where the cubes were treated as "diamonds," and so on. At this stage of the game, it was necessary to judge in any case whether the child should be let alone to discover on his own.

In a later section, when the balance beam is discussed, we shall see that the idea of factoring was further deepened by being applied to a "new" problem. I mention the point here because it relates to the importance of *maintaining* a problem-solving set that runs in a continuous direction. It is often the case that novelty must be introduced in order that the task be continued. In the case of the balance beam, the task was to discover the different combinations of rings that could be put on one side of the balance beam to balance a single ring placed on hook 9. In effect, this is the same problem as asking the different ways in which 9 blocks can be arranged. But it is in a different form, and the form seems to contain the ability for stimulating interest even though formally it is isomorphic to something else that has been explored to the border of satiety.

STRUCTURE AND SEQUENCE

We can best illustrate the points made in earlier sections by reference to teaching quadratic equations to the four children we studied. Each child was provided with building materials. These were large

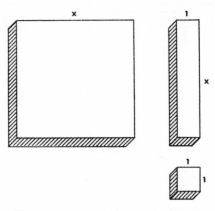

FIG. 2.—Three components for quadratic constructions

flat squares made of wood whose dimensions were unspecified and described simply as "unknown or x long and x wide." there were also a large number of strips of wood that were as long as the sides of the square and described arbitrarily as having a width of "1" or simply "1 by x." And there was a supply of little squares with sides equal to the width "1" of the strips, thus "1 by 1." The reader should be warned that the presentation of these materials is not as simple as all that. To begin with, it is necessary to convince the children that we really do not know and do not *care* what the metric size of the big squares is, that rulers are of no interest. A certain humor helps establish in the pupils a proper contempt for measuring in this context, and the snob appeal of simply calling an unknown by the name "x" is very great. From there on, the children readily discover for themselves that the long strips are *x* long—by correspondence. They take on faith (as they should) that the narrow dimension is "1," but that they grasp its arbitrariness is clear from one child's declaration of the number of such "1" lengths that made an *x*. As for "1 by 1" little squares, that too is established by simple correspondence with the narrow dimension of the "1 by *x*" strips. It is horseback method, but quite good mathematics.

The child is asked whether he can make a square bigger than the *x* by *x* square, using the materials at hand. He very quickly builds squares with designs like those in Figure 3. We ask him to record

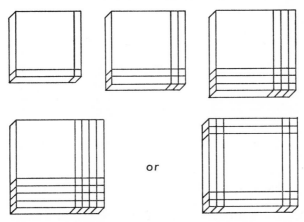

Fig. 3.—Squares of ever increasing size constructed with components

how much wood is needed for each larger square and how long and wide each square is.

He describes one of his constructed squares; very concretely the pieces are counted out: "an *x*-square, two *x*-strips and a one square" or "an *x*-square, four *x*-strips and four ones," or "an *x*-square, six *x*-strips and nine ones,". . . and so forth. We help him with language and show him a way to write it down. The big square is an "$x^\square$," the long strips are "1 *x*" or simply "*x*," and the little squares are "one squares" or "one by one" or better still simply "1." And the expression "and" can be shortened to "+." And so he can write out the recipe for a constructed square as "$x^\square + 4x + 4$." At this stage, these are merely names put together in little sentences. How wide and long is the square in question? This the child can readily measure off—an *x* and 2, or $x + 2$, and so the whole thing is $(x + 2)\square$. Brackets are not so easily grasped. And so the child is able to put down his first equality: $(x + 2)\square = x\square + 4x + 4$. Virtually everything has a referent that can be pointed to with a finger. He has a notational system into which he can translate the image he has constructed.

Now we go on to making bigger squares, and each square the child makes he is to describe in terms of what wood went into it and how wide and how long it is. It takes some ruled sheets to get the child to keep his record so that he can go back and inspect it for what it may reveal, and he is encouraged to go back and look at the record and at the constructions it stands for.

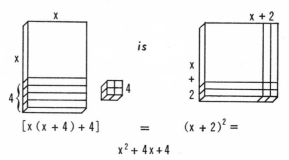

$$[x\,(x + 4) + 4] \qquad = \qquad (x + 2)^2 =$$

$$x^2 + 4x + 4$$

Fig. 4.—Syntactic exercise supported by construction

Imagine now a list such as the following, again a product of the child's own constructing:

$$
\begin{array}{lcllclclcl}
x\square & + & 2x & + & 1 & \text{is } x & + & 1 & \text{by } x & + & 1 \\
x\square & + & 4x & + & 4 & \text{is } x & + & 2 & \text{by } x & + & 2 \\
x\square & + & 6x & + & 9 & \text{is } x & + & 3 & \text{by } x & + & 3 \\
x\square & + & 8x & + & 16 & \text{is } x & + & 4 & \text{by } x & + & 4 \\
\end{array}
$$

It is almost impossible for him not to make some discoveries about the numbers: that the x values go up 2, 4, 6, 8 . . . and the unit values go up 1, 4, 9, 16 . . . and the dimensions increase by additions to x of 1, 2, 3, 4. . . . The syntactical insights about regularity in notation are matched by perceptual-manipulative insights about the material referents.

After a while, some new manipulations occur that provide the child with a further basis for notational progress. He takes the square, $(x + 2)^2$, and reconstructs it in a new way. One may ask whether this is constructive manipulation or whether it is proper factoring. But the child is learning that the same amount of wood can build quite strikingly different patterns and remain the same amount of wood—even though it also has a different notational expression. Where does the language begin and the manipulation of materials stop? The interplay is continuous. We shall return to this same example in a later section.

But what is now a problem is how to "detach" the notation that the child has learned from the concrete, visible, manipulable embodiment to which it refers—the wood. For if the child is to deal with mathematical properties he will have to deal with symbols per se, else he will be limited to the narrow and rather trival range of symbolism that can be given direct (and only partial) visual embodiment. Concepts such as x^2 and x^3 may be given a visualizable referent, but what of x^n?

Why do children wean themselves from the perceptual embodiment to the symbolic notation? Perhaps it is partly explained in the nature of variation and contrast.

The child is shown the balance beam again and told: "Choose any hook on one side and put the same number of rings on it as the number the hook is away from the middle. Now balance it with rings placed on the other side. Keep a record." Recall that the balance beam is familiar from work in factoring and that the child knows that 2 rings on 9 balances 9 on 2 or m rings on n balances n on m. He is back to construction. Can anything be constructed on the balance beam that is like the squares? With little effort, the following translation is made. Suppose x is 5. Then 5 rings on hook 5 is x^2, 5 rings on hook 4 is $4x$, and 4 rings on hook 1 is 4: $x^2 + 4x + 4$. How can we find whether this is like a square that is $x + 2$ wide by $x + 2$ long as before? Well, if x is 5, then $x + 2$ is 7, and so 7 rings on hook 7. And nature obliges—the beam balances. One notation works for two strikingly different constructions and perceptual events. Notation, with its broader equivalency, is clearly more economical than reference to embodiments. There is little resistance to using this more convenient language. And now construction can begin—commutative and distributive properties of equations can be explored: $x(x + 4) + 4 = x^2 + 4x + 4$ or $x + 4$ rings on hook x and 4 rings on hook 1 will balance. The child if he wishes can also go back to the wood and find that the same materials can make the design in Figure 4.

Contrast is the vehicle by which the obvious that is too obvious to be appreciated can be made noticeable again. A discovery by an eight-year-old girl illustrates the matter. "Yes, 4×6 equals 6×4 in numbers, like the way six eskimos in each of four igloos is the same as four in each of six igloos. But a venetian blind *isn't* the same as a blind Venetian." By recognizing the noncommutative property of ordinary language, the commutative property of a mathematical language can be partly grasped. But it is still only a partial insight into commutativity and noncommutativity. Had we wished to develop the distinction more deeply we might have proceeded concretely to a contrast between sets of operations that can be carried out in any sequence—like the order of eating courses at a dinner or of going to different movies—and operations that have a noncommutative order—like putting on shoes and socks, where one must precede the other. Then the child could be taken from there to a more general idea of commutative and noncommutative cases and ways of dealing with a notation, perhaps by identical sets and ordered identical sets.

We need not reiterate what must be obvious from this sequence. The object was to begin with an enactive representation of quadratics—something that could literally be "done" or built—and to move from there to an ikonic representation, however restricted. Along the way, notation was developed and by the use of variation and contrast converted into a properly symbolic system. Again, the object was to start with as economical a representation as possible and to increase complexity only when there was some way for the child to relate the presently complex instance to something simpler that had gone before.

What was so striking in the performance of the children was their *initial* inability to represent things to themselves in a way that transcended immediate perceptual grasp. The achievement of more comprehensive insight requires, we think, the building of a mediating representational structure that transcends such immediate imagery, that renders a *sequence* of acts and images unitary and simultaneous. The children always began by constructing an embodiment of some concept, building a concrete form of operational definition. The fruit of the construction was an image and some operations that "stood for" the concept. From there on, the task was to provide means of representation that were free of particular manipulations and specific images. Only symbolic operations provide the means of representing an idea in this way. But consider this matter for a moment.

We have already commented upon the fact that by giving the child multiple embodiments of the same general idea expressed in a common notation we lead him to "empty" the concept of specific sensory properties until he is able to grasp its abstract properties. But surely this is not the best way of describing the child's increasing development of insight. The growth of such abstractions is important. But what struck us about the children as we observed them is that they had not only understood the abstractions they had learned but also had a store of concrete images that served to exemplify the abstractions. When they searched for a way to deal with new problems, the task was usually carried out not simply by abstract means but also by "matching up" images. An example will help here. In going from the wood-blocks embodiment of the quadratic to the balance-beam embodiment, it was interesting that the children would "equate" *concrete* features of one with *concrete* features of another. One side of the balance beam "stood for" the amount of wood, the other side for the sides of the square. These were important concrete props on which they leaned. We have been told by research mathematicians that the same use of props— heuristics—holds for them, that they have preferred ways of imaging certain problems while other problems are handled silently or in terms of an imagery of the symbolism on a page.

We reached the tentative conclusion that it is probably necessary for a child, learning mathematics, to have not only a firm sense of the abstraction underlying what he was working on but also a good stock of visual images for embodying them. For without the latter, it is difficult to track correspondences and to check what one is doing symbolically. Here an example will help again. We had occasion, again with the help of Dr. Dienes, to teach a group of ten nine-year-olds the elements of group theory. To embody the idea of a mathematical group initially, we gave them the example of a four-group made up of the following four maneuvers. A book was the vehicle, a book with an arrow up the middle of its front cover. The four maneuvers were rotating the book a quarter turn to the left, rotating it a quarter turn to the right, rotating it a half turn (without regard to direction of rotation), and letting it stay in the position it was in. Each move was made from the position in which the book happened to be. They were quick to grasp the important property of such a mathematical group: that any sequence of maneuvers made could be reproduced from the starting position by a single move. This is not the usual way in which this property is described mathematically, but it served well for the children. We contrasted this elegant property with a series of our moves that did *not* constitute a mathematical group—indeed they provided the counter example themselves by proposing the one-third turn left, one-third turn right, half turn either way, and stay. It was soon apparent that it did not work. We set the children the task of making games of four maneuvers, six maneuvers, etc., that had the property of a "closed" game as we called it. A "closed" game is one in which the result of any combination of moves can be produced by a single move. They were, of course, highly ingenious. But what soon became apparent was that they needed some aid in imagery—in this case an imagery notation—that would allow them to keep track and then to discover whether some new game was an isomorph of one they had already developed. An isomorph, of course, is a game with identical moves in the formal sense, though they may be physically of a different kind. The prop in this case was, of course, the matrix, listing the moves possible across the top and then listing them down the side, thus making it easily possible to check whether each combination of pairs of moves could be reproduced by a single move. The matrix in this case is a crutch or heuristic and as such has nothing to do with the abstraction of the mathematical group, yet it was enormously useful to them not only for keeping track but also for comparing one group with another for correspondence. Thus, the matrix with which they started had the property of:

	s	a	b	c
s	s	a	b	c
a	a	c	s	b
b	b	s	c	a
c	c	b	a	s

s = stay
a = quarter-turn left
b = quarter-turn right
c = half-turn

Are there any four-groups with a different structure? It is extremely difficult to deal with such a question without the aid of this house-keeping matrix as a vehicle for spotting correspondence. What about a game in which a cube can be left where it is, rotated 180° on its verticle axis, rotated 180° on its horizontal axis, and rotated 180° on each of its four cubic diagonals? Is it a group? Can it be simplified to a smaller number of maneuvers? Does it contain the group described above?

In sum, then, while the development of insight into mathematics in our group of children depended upon their development of "example-free" abstractions, this did not lead them to give up their imagery. Quite to the contrary, we had the impression that their enriched imagery was very useful to them in dealing with new problems.

To sum up, we would suggest that learning mathematics may be viewed as a microcosm of intellectual development. It begins with instrumental activity, a kind of definition of things by doing them. Such operations become represented and summarized in the form of particular images. Finally, and with the help of a symbolic notation that remains invariant across transformations in imagery, the learner comes to grasp the formal or abstract properties of the things he is dealing with. But while, once abstraction is achieved, the learner becomes free in a certain measure of the surface appearance of things, he nonetheless continues to rely upon the stock of imagery he has built enroute to abstract mastery. It is this stock of imagery that permits him to work at the level of heuristic, through convenient and nonrigorous means of exploring problems and relating them to problems already mastered.

REINFORCEMENT AND FEEDBACK

With respect to corrective information, there is something particularly happy about the exercises we chose to use. In teaching quadratics by the use of our blocks and then by the aid of the balance beam, children were enabled by immediate test to determine whether they had "got there." A collection of square pieces of wood is aggregated in a form that either makes a square or doesn't, and the child can see it immediately. So, too, with a balance beam:

It either balances or it does not. There is no instructor intervening between the learner and the materials.

But note well that the instructor had to enter in several ways. In the first place, he determined within quite constrained limits the nature of the sequences so that the children would have the greatest chance of seeing the relation of what went before to what was up now. Whether we succeeded well in these sequences we do not know—save that the children learned a great deal of elegant mathematics in a fairly short time. What guided us was some sort of psychological-mathematical intuition, and, while that may be satisfactory for such engineering as we did, it is certainly not satisfactory from the point of view of understanding how to do it better.

We failed on several occasions, as judged by the lagging interest of a particular child, when we wanted to be sure that the child had really understood something. Our most glaring failure was in trying to get across in symbolic form (probably too early) the idea of distributiveness—that $a + (b + c)$ and $(a + b) + c$ could be treated as equivalent. One of our cleverest young pupils commented at the beginning of an hour, with a groan, "Oh, they're distributing the distributive law again." In fact, our difficulty came from a mis-judgment of the importance of giving them a symbolic mode for correcting ikonic constructions. We were too eager to be sure that they sensed the notational analogue of the factoring constructions they had been making and which they understood at the ikonic level so well that further construction was proving a bore.

We have few fresh observations to report on the matter of over-drive and anxiety. One of our pupils had a rather strong push about mathematics from his father at home. He was the child who, on the first day, had to demonstrate his prowess by multiplying two large and ugly numbers on the board, announcing the while, "I know a lot of math." He was probably our best student, but he made no progress until he got over the idea that what was needed was hard computation. It was he too who complained that the blocks used for quadratics *had* to have *some* size. But once he was willing to play with unknowns as "x," he showed considerable power. His father was our unwitting ally at this point for he told him that "x's" were from algebra, which was a subject most children took in high school.

Perhaps the greatest problem one has in an experiment of this sort is to keep out of the way, to prevent one's self from becoming a perennial source of information, interfering with the child's ability to take over the role of being his own corrector. But each classroom situation is unique in this way, as is each dyad of teacher and pupil. Some of the teacher-pupil pairs became quite notably charged with dependency; in others the child or the teacher resisted. But that is a matter beyond the scope of the present discussion.

Some Conclusions

A first and obvious conclusion is that one must take into account the issues of predisposition, structure, sequence, and reinforcement in preparing curriculum materials—whether one is concerned with writing a textbook, a lesson plan, a unit of instruction, or indeed, a conversation with didactic ends in view. But there follow from this obvious conclusion some rather nonobvious implications.

The type of supporting research that permits one to assess how well one is succeeding in the management of relevant instructional variables requires a constant and close collaboration of teacher, subject-matter specialist, and psychologist. As intimated earlier in these pages, a curriculum should be prepared jointly by the subject-matter expert, the teacher, and psychologist with due regard for the inherent structure of the material, its sequencing, and the psychological pacing of reinforcement and the building and maintaining of predispositions to problem-solving. As the curriculum is being built, it must be used as the material for testing in detail by close observational and experimental methods to assess not simply whether children are "achieving" but, rather, what they are making of the material and how they are organizing it. It is on the basis of "testing as you go" that revision is made. It is this procedure that puts the evaluation process at a time when and place where its results can be used for correction in the enterprise of making curricula.

Little save passing reference has been made to the issue of individual differences. Quite plainly, they exist in massive degree—in the extent to which children have problem-solving predispositions, in the degree of their interest, in the skills that they bring to any concrete task, in their preferred mode of representing things, in their ability to move easily through any particular sequence, and in

the degree to which they are initially dependent upon extrinsic reinforcement from the teacher. The fact of individual differences argues for pluralism and for an enlightened opportunism in the materials and methods of instruction. Early in this paper it was asserted,
rather off-handedly, that no single ideal sequence exists for any group
of children. The conclusion to be drawn from that assertion is not
that it is impossible to put together a curriculum that would satisfy
a group of children or a cross-section of children. Rather, it is that
if a curriculum is to be effective in the classroom it must contain
different ways of activating children, different ways of presenting
sequences, different opportunities for some children to "skip" parts
while others work their way through, different ways of putting
things. A curriculum, in short, must contain many tracks leading to
the same general goal.

Virtually all of the illustrations used in this paper have been taken
from mathematics, but there are some generalizations that go beyond to other fields. The first is that it took the efforts of many
highly talented mathematicians to discern the underlying structure
of the mathematics that was to be taught. That is to say, a mathematics curriculum could not be written but for the history and
development of mathematics. But even so glorious an intellectual
tradition as that of mathematics was not enough. For while many
virtues had been discovered for numbers to the base 10, students
cannot appreciate such virtues until they recognize that the base 10
was not handed down from the mountain by some mathematical
god. Rather, it is when the student learns to work in different number bases that the base 10 is recognized for the achievement that it
is. By analogy, one could as easily argue that simply because gram-
marians have a grammar for English that also works for Latin or
German or Spanish, it does not follow that the flat-out presentation
of that system will automatically help the student in his writing or
speaking. And though historians have traditionally worked in the
framework of an inviolate cronology, it does not follow that presenting history in this way is the best means of activating zestful
problem-solving in the student.

Finally, a theory of instruction seeks to take account of the fact
that a curriculum reflects not only the nature of knowledge itself
but also the nature of the knower and the knowledge-getting proc-

ess. It is the enterprise *par excellence* where the line between subject matter and method grows necessarily indistinct. A body of knowledge, enshrined in a university faculty and embodied in a series of authoritative volumes, is the *result* of much prior intellectual activity. To instruct someone in these disciplines is not a matter of getting him to commit results to mind. Rather, it is to teach him to participate in the process that makes possible the establishment of knowledge. We teach a subject not to produce little living libraries on the subject but, rather, to get a student to think mathematically for himself, to consider matters as a historian does, to embody the process of knowledge-getting. Knowing is a process, not a product.

CHAPTER XIV

The Analysis of Reading Instruction: Perspectives from Psychology and Linguistics

JOHN B. CARROLL

Introduction

The purpose of this chapter is to deal with the problem of the application of psychological theory, not by a discursive general discussion, but by the exploration of a concrete case, namely, the teaching of reading. Despite the large amount of research and expository writing in the field of reading, the nature of reading as behavior has still not yet been accurately described in the light of knowledge from the two most relevant disciplines, psychology and linguistics. For it is not psychological theory alone that is needed for fruitful theoretical analysis of a field of instruction, but also knowledge and principles from other relevant disciplines, most obviously those related to the subject matter of instruction.

The first part of the chapter presents a fairly detailed analysis, from both psychological and linguistic standpoints, of the behavior we call *reading*. The remainder of the chapter considers some ways in which the teaching of this behavior may profit from psychological theory and experimentation. This latter discussion will be woven around a point of view concerning the nature of instruction and its analysis.

The Specification and Psychological Analysis of Reading Behavior

LANGUAGE, SPEECH, AND READING

Reading behavior, even though not completely understood in all its aspects, is descriptively not as complex as it has sometimes been depicted. Reading must be defined in the context of a proper understanding of the nature of language and its actualization in spoken or written messages in a particular language or dialect.

A language may be defined as "a structured system of arbitrary vocal sounds and sequences of sounds which is used, or can be used, in interpersonal communication by an aggregation of human beings, and which rather exhaustively catalogs the things, events, and processes in the human environment."[1] The system inherent in a language derives essentially and primarily from the sequence of articulated, heard sounds in *spoken* utterances or messages.

The speech communities of many languages have developed conventional systems whereby spoken messages can be recorded in written, visual form. Not all the features of spoken messages are normally represented in the writing system (although special transcription systems can be devised to represent all the meaning-bearing elements of spoken messages), but enough of them are symbolized to permit competent speakers of the language (who can also read) to reconstruct the spoken form of a written message in most of its important features. Writing systems usually contain certain elements of their own which do not correspond explicitly to anything in spoken messages, e.g. paragraphing, punctuation, capitalization, and different ways of writing items which are phonemically identical (as *hair—hare*). Many written messages are composed, transmitted, and read with very little involvement of overt speech, but *construction of a spoken form is always possible.*

The behavior we call *reading* may be described as the perception and comprehension of written messages in a manner paralleling that of the corresponding spoken messages. That is to say, just as speakers of a language can comprehend spoken messages, persons who have learned to read can comprehend written messages. Comprehension of spoken and of written messages are not entirely independent processes, however. Save for the case of an individual who learns to read a foreign language before he learns to understand it— and there is considerable doubt about what "reading" can mean in such a case—learning to read a language depends not only upon the ability to understand the spoken form of a language but also upon the ability to reconstruct the spoken forms of written messages. In

1. John B. Carroll, *The Study of Language*, p. 10. Cambridge, Massachusetts: Harvard University Press, 1953.

"reading aloud," it is evident that the individual can make this reconstruction. In "silent reading"—even at very high rates and without detectable subvocal activity—it is reasonable to assume that comprehension occurs in response to some kind of internal representation, however abbreviated or fragmentary, of a spoken message. The reader does not respond solely to visual symbols; he also responds to some sort of reconstruction of a spoken message which he derives from the written message. In interpreting the comprehension of written messages, we must draw upon whatever we can find out about the comprehension of spoken messages.

The activity of reading can, therefore, be analyzed into two processes: (*a*) on the basis of the written message, the construction or reconstruction of a spoken message or of some internal representation of it; and (*b*) the comprehension of messages so constructed. It is of the greatest importance to consider these processes separately, even though typically they may occur virtually simultaneously, for different psychological and linguistic problems are involved in each of them.

Nevertheless, nothing said here should be taken to imply that these two processes—speech reconstruction and the apprehension of meaning—should be separated in procedures of teaching. There is evidence, in fact, that the teaching of the mechanics of speech reconstruction (techniques of word recognition) is best done with materials which are maximally meaningful to the learner, e.g., words that are labels for things of interest to the learner or very simple sentences that convey an interesting or useful message.

THE SPEECH REPERTOIRE

In what follows, we shall be concerned solely with the processes by which a child learns to read the written form of his native language.

The reconstruction of spoken messages from written messages depends upon the development of the speech repertoire as a whole and particularly on the ability to recognize features of the spoken language system that correspond in some way with features of the writing system. By the age of beginning school, the normal child has acquired, largely out of awareness, most of the basic phonology and grammar of his language, as well as a substantial vocabulary. In other words: (*a*) He can discriminate (respond differentially) to all or nearly all of the phonemes of his language, and (usually) produce these phonemes with fair accuracy. (*b*) He can understand and produce all the major sentence types of his language; in fact, his sentences are often more varied and complex than those found in the usual primer. (*c*) His vocabulary is numbered well into the thousands.[2]

At the same time, it must be recognized that children vary widely in their speech repertoires. Children who have difficulty with the discrimination or the production of phonemes will generally experience difficulty in learning to read until these handicaps are no longer present. Some children have learned a dialect of English which is markedly substandard or at variance with the dialect of the teacher, so that they do not make the same phonological or grammatical distinctions as the teacher. Some children have limited vocabularies because they come from intellectually impoverished environments.

PHONEMICS, GRAPHEMICS, AND PHONICS

If reading as a subject matter has a "content," that content is the relation between the structure of spoken messages and the system of marks or symbols used to represent these messages. Strangely enough, this content is rarely discussed (save in the most general terms) in textbooks on the teaching of reading and its psychology. There is no comprehensive compendium or description of the relationship, although large parts of it are now available.[3] To make matters worse, writers on the teaching of reading have often failed to make appropriate distinctions or to use proper terminology when discussing the writing system of English, which they characterize as "unphonetic." Linguistic scientists, who are the authorities in these matters, reserve the term *phonetics* for the study of the purely acoustic and articulatory aspects of speech sounds in languages. *Phonemics* is their term for the study of the ways in which certain

2. Nevertheless, children's vocabularies have sometimes been overestimated. See Irving Lorge and Jeanne Chall, "Estimating the Size of Vocabularies of Children and Adults: An Analysis of Methodological Issues," *Journal of Experimental Education* (in press).

3. Eleanor M. Higginbottom, "A Study of the Representation of English Vowel Phonemes in the Orthography," *Language and Speech*, V (April–June, 1962), 67–117.

classes of sounds are distinctive sound units (*phonemes*) in particular languages. Just as phonemes are the minimal sound units in a language, *graphemes* are the minimal visual symbolic units in a writing system. And just as phonemes may occur in certain ranges of free or conditional variation in actual utterances, graphemes (alphabetic letters, digits, punctuation marks, and the like) may appear in variant forms (upper and lower case, different type faces, different handwritten shapes, and so on). English orthography utilizes an alphabetic principle whereby the relationship between speech and writing can be most easily described in terms of correspondences between graphemes and phonemes.

These correspondences, in English, are more regular than irregular, contrary to the impression often given. It may be estimated that a computing machine could be programed to "translate" a printed text into phonemes with better than 95 per cent accuracy even without building into the computer program information about irregularly spelled words. The program would simply incorporate a large number of rules for translating graphemes in conjunction with other graphemes in their immediate environments. Now, the number of such rules might be much larger than the number it would be feasible to embody in a procedure for teaching reading to children, but many of them are of considerable power. There is evidence, in fact, that mature readers behave as if they had acquired a large number of these rules.[4]

These considerations allow us to give an intermediate criterion of reading behavior: An important stage in the development of reading behavior is reached when the learner has mastered the important grapheme-phoneme correspondences which help in the reconstruction of spoken from written messages. At this stage, the learner may be said to have "broken the code" of English orthography. Further development in reading involves increasing facility in the use of this code.

WORD RECOGNITION AS PROBLEM-SOLVING

Let us focus attention on that phase of the reading process which we have described as the reconstruction of spoken messages. For a

---

4. Eleanor J. Gibson, J. J. Gibson, Anne Danielson, H. Osser, and Marcia Hammond, "The Role of Grapheme-Phoneme Correspondence in Word Perception," *American Journal of Psychology*, LXXV (December, 1962), 554-70.

variety of reasons, the natural unit for this process of reconstruction is the *word;* that is, messages are in general reconstructed word by word even though skilled readers are able to apprehend and reconstruct groups of words simultaneously.

In the fullest sense of the term, recognition of a printed word is the reconstruction of the corresponding spoken word (or some internal surrogate thereof) and the apprehension of whatever meaning would be contained in the spoken word (or the particular meaning conveyed by a particular spelling).

In the mature reader, word recognition occurs extremely rapidly and unhesitatingly. This process of rapid recognition is not well understood. Research evidence suggests that frequency of past experience is an important factor in speed of recognition, but this does not guarantee that word recognition is not based on a highly speeded recognition of higher-order grapheme-phoneme correspondences. In any case, the goal of reading instruction should be to produce rapid recognition facility for as many words as possible. In the mature reader, it is perhaps true, astounding as it may seem, that reading is based upon a capability of instantly recognizing thousands or even tens of thousands of individual word patterns, almost as if words were Chinese characters not structured by an alphabetic principle.

Nevertheless, it must be emphasized that whole-word perception is dependent upon perceptions of parts—even rather small details of a pattern. One may guess that differences between such easily confused pairs as *unclear* and *nuclear* can be reliably perceived at tachistoscopic speeds not very far from normal thresholds for words of similar length and frequency. There is little evidence that mature readers use "word-shape" (the general outlines of a word) as a cue for word recognition; it is doubtful that use of this cue should be an objective of the teaching of reading. Rather, beginners need to learn to perceive individual letters as details of word patterns.

When the beginning reader meets a word with which he is unfamiliar, that is, one that he cannot recognize instantly, the process of word recognition may be regarded as a case of problem-solving. Various cues are available to him; sometimes certain cues will very quickly allow him to arrive at a proper reconstruction of a word; at other times, cues must be used to suggest a series of possibilities. In this case, the learner must essentially go into a "search-routine," testing out each one of the possibilities until a satisfactory one is found. The case will vary, of course, depending upon whether the spoken word and its meaning happen to be in the child's speech repertoire. It will also vary depending upon what kind of information is available to allow the child to confirm his guess—whether, for example, there is sufficient context to test the correctness of a guess.

This analysis suggests that the process of learning to read involves the building up in the learner of a "set" to expect not only variety in the kinds of word recognition problems he will meet but also (and particularly) ambiguity in the cues available to him. For example, letter-shapes in handwriting (and sometimes in print) are often ambiguous; grapheme-phoneme correspondences are in some cases highly ambiguous (e.g., initial GE- or GI- yield "hard" or "soft" *g* with about equal frequencies); whole words are sometimes ambiguous, as when they are homographs (e.g., READ = /riyd/ or /red/); and context may yield only partially reliable information.

Some suggestions may be made toward the further specification of cues available for word-recognition. For the present purposes, it seems useful to discuss four classes of cues, forming successive levels of a hierarchy.

Letters (*graphemes*).—The weight of experimental evidence suggests that a pattern can be more easily recognized when the individual has learned to recognize the distinctive parts of the pattern. The distinctive parts of printed words are, of course, the letters composing them. The beginning reader must be able to discriminate and recognize the graphemes commonly found in texts. The variant forms of each grapheme (e.g., upper- and lower-case forms; printed and cursive forms; etc.) must be recognized as belonging to a single class. The ability to say the names of graphemes should be a goal of instruction, not only because this affords a method of testing recognition but also because the names are useful in other phases of instruction. At the same time, the learner must understand that the names of graphemes are not in every case useful cues for the letter-sound correspondences, to be discussed next.

Letter-sound correspondences (*"phonic cues"*).—Because of the alphabetic principle underlying English orthography, letters or combinations of letters standing in printed words can be cues to the phonemic constituents of the corresponding spoken words. For convenience, let us call these "phonic cues." In learning to make use of them, the beginning reader must become aware[5] that a spoken word is a sequence of sounds and that the left-right order of letters in writing corresponds to this temporal sequence, though not always in a one-to-one match. He should also become aware of the structure of syllables, the general pattern being [C] V [C], where C stands for a consonant or consonant cluster, and V for a vowel or diphthong, and where the brackets denote that the element inclosed may or may not be present. With regard to the actual use of phonic cues, the goal is *not* to have the learner acquire formally stated rules concerning letter-sound correspondences but to teach habits of responding to letters and letter-combinations in terms of those correspondences which occur with sufficient frequency in English orthography to make them fairly reliable cues. Because the correspondences quite frequently are different for the initial consonantal material and for the remainder of a syllable, it is useful to deal with these components separately. (In fact, it may often be useful to deal with the second component, the -V [C] material of a syllable, in terms of pattern recognition; examples of high-frequency patterns are -AM, -AME, -AIM, with transfer to similar patterns -AT, -ATE, -AIT.)

Intra-word context cues.—In dealing with polysyllabic words, it is often possible for the beginning reader to reconstruct the word by parts; commonly occurring syllables like UN-, -CEPT-, and -TY will come to be recognized instantly and supply a kind of context for suggesting the possibilities to be tested for the rest of the word.

Larger-context cues.—The context of a given word consists of the other parts of the total message in which it stands. Normally, this context is verbal, but it may also be pictorial or graphic. Context may place certain limitations upon the range of possibilities which may occur in the place of the given word. The limitations are partly of a grammatical and partly of a semantic nature. For example, the context may enhance the probability that a certain word in a sentence is a noun and the name of a fruit ("He picked a _____ off the tree and ate it"). The learner must be taught to use the context

5. In speaking of the learner's "becoming aware" of such a fact, we do not mean that he needs to be taught the formal verbal statements we use here; we are describing things which we believe normally even a young child can become aware of in the sense of coming to have his perceptions organized or structured in a certain way.

to suggest the range of possibilities within which he organizes the "search routine" mentioned earlier, but he must also be taught to select only those possibilities which conform to the phonic cues also available. He must also become aware that there are certain cases in which the context is diacritical for the proper reconstruction of the spoken counterpart of a word. For example, to reconstruct the spoken form of "He made a bow," more context is needed than is given.

THE READING TASK BEYOND WORD RECOGNITION

Even if the reader properly reconstructs the spoken counterpart of each word in a printed text, he may not necessarily comprehend the total message. He may "call off" the words as if they stood in a list and fail to apprehend the manner in which the message would normally be uttered with its linguistic features of stress, intonation, and juncture. There is a "set" or "attitude" to be taught, to the effect that printed texts correspond to spoken utterances and that part of the task of reading is to infer the most probable spoken utterance pattern for each sentence. The child must be taught the skill of putting the separate words together as a total utterance. He must learn not only to read aloud, with acceptable spoken utterance patterns, but also to read silently, with the normal overt utterance being represented in a kind of inner speech. His silent-reading speed must be accelerated as much as may be consistent with comprehension and the nature of a particular reading task (reading for details, skimming, searching for information, etc.). Further, the reader must learn the significance of such "para-graphemic" features of printed texts as punctuation, paragraphing, change of type font, tabular arrangement, and so forth.

READING COMPREHENSION

Comprehension, whether of speech or writing, is a process not completely understood and difficult to describe briefly, in any case. It can be described linguistically as a process of comprehending morphemes (minimal meaning units) and the grammatical constructions in which they occur. The lexical meanings of morphemes can be stated in terms of objective referents and their attributes and relationships; the meanings of grammatical constructions can be described in terms of structural relationships among persons, things, and/or events in spatial and temporal configurations. The native speaker of a language normally acquires a wide range of both lexical and grammatical meanings without their having been explained to him. Problems of reading comprehension appear to arise mainly when texts contain lexical, grammatical, or ideational materials which happen to be outside the reader's repertoire.

It is sometimes said that reading is a process of apprehending thought. This can also be well said of listening; there is no difference in principle between speech and writing with respect to the intellectual demands they make.

We shall have to leave the analysis of reading behavior at this point, recognizing that there are further aspects of reading behavior which need to be provided for in the curriculum: critical judgments, evaluation of argumentation, literary appreciation, and so on. For now, it will have to stand as an article of faith that these aspects can be specified in behavioral terms, at least to the extent of identifying the classes of stimuli (e.g., types of reading material) which might be expected to evoke certain kinds of responses.

Problems of Psychological Theory in Behavioral Description

It can hardly be claimed that reading is not a ready target for the application of psychological theory. The very attempt to describe reading behavior inevitably requires the use of numerous terms requiring further theoretical analysis—terms like "perception," "recognition," "internal surrogates of speech behavior," "comprehension," and "meaning response." It raises deep theoretical problems: How shall we define the stimulus, identify equivalent stimuli, isolate units of response, or identify common elements in performances? Through lack of space, we shall have to be content merely to call attention to such problems. We shall give short shrift to problems of perception and proceed to some remarks about the analysis of responses.

For present purposes, let us entertain the view that behaviors can be specified in terms of the classes of stimuli and responses involved, and that they can be classified into one or more paradigms amenable to theoretical and experimental treatment. "Terminal behavior," i.e., behavior exemplifying the final goals of instruction, will be viewed as being achieved by passing through a course of development in which component, prerequisite behaviors are learned and gradually automatized to the extent that they go from overt, observable status to covert, unobservable status. In this sense we may speak of such things as "internal surrogates of speech behavior."

It is recognized that, in an activity of such a generalized character as reading, the number of separate responses to be learned (let us call them "items") may be very large and that any really detailed, "fine-grained" specification of them might require major research efforts. These separate items are viewed as not being completely independent of one another; they are regarded as being composed of subsidiary elements which may generalize or transfer to sizable classes of other items to be learned. For example, in early stages of reading instruction, letter discriminations are prerequisite for later stages; certain grapheme-phoneme correspondences are learned which generalize to large classes of items. The various items to be learned in order to read offer many examples of structure and organization.

The further behavioral specification of reading behavior requires detailed identification of the stimulus-response relationships to be learned. Some of the more important classes of these are as follows:

Stimulus	*Response*
(1) Isolated graphemes (classes of visual symbols)	.... Identifying response, e.g., saying the "name" of a letter
(2) Particular graphemes or grapheme combinations in words	.... Phonemic responses, e.g., articulations of particular phonemes, linked to other phonemes
(3) Printed words	.... Spoken reconstruction (overt or covert)
(4) Spoken words (overt or covert)	.... Meaning responses
(5) Sentences or broader contexts	.... A delimited class of lexical or grammatical meanings to fit into a particular position in a sentence
(6) Any word not recognized	.... "Search-routine" to explore possibilities suggested by phonic, intra-word context, or larger context cues

Still other kinds of stimulus-response relations could be listed; for example, the phonemic responses of the second line of the table above could be regarded, in turn, as stimuli for associated words containing these phonemes or similar phonemes to be used in the "search-routine" listed in the last line. Each kind of stimulus-response relation could be studied and specified in further detail.[6]

For theoretical, experimental, and instructional purposes it is useful to attempt to sort these stimulus-response relations into precise paradigms of learning. Many of those involved in reading appear to fit the paradigm of what Skinner has called the discriminative operant.[7] These are the cases in which a response that already exists in the repertoire of the individual is put under the control of a discriminative stimulus by being reinforced only when it occurs upon the presentation of the stimulus. For example, saying a letter name like "you" can be regarded as an operant which is put under the control of the grapheme U; interestingly enough, the meaning response "second person pronoun" which might in other contexts be made to this letter name is virtually extinguished. This, at any rate, is a fairly clear case of a discriminative operant, as are also the stimulus-response relations in items (2), (3), and (6) of the above tabular arrangement.

The cases in items (4) and (5) are not so clear because they involve "meaning" responses. The psychological analysis of such responses is currently one of the most active fields of investigation,[8] and it is too early to draw conclusions. Meaning responses *can* be analyzed as discriminative operants, but the work of Staats and Staats[9] suggests that they have many of the characteristics of responses governed by the laws of classical conditioning. The problem of "meaning" touches also on the problem of concept-formation, which is the target of another active field of investigation.

It is possible to take the position that, in teaching, it will not much

6. For example, one phase of an experimental program at Cornell University concerns the perception and identification of graphemes. See E. J. Gibson, J. J. Gibson, A. Danielson, and H. Osser, "A Developmental Study of the Discrimination of Letter-like Forms," *Journal of Comparative and Physiological Psychology*, LV (December, 1962), 897–906.

7. B. F. Skinner, *Science and Human Behavior*. New York: Macmillan Co., 1953.

8. See, for example, *Verbal Learning and Verbal Behavior*. Edited by Charles N. Cofer. New York: McGraw-Hill Book Co., 1961.

9. Carolyn K. Staats and A. W. Staats, "Meaning Established by Classical Conditioning," *Journal of Experimental Psychology*, LIV (July, 1957), 74–80.

matter whether a given stimulus-response relation follows one paradigm or another, for it could be argued that the behaviors involved
are so complex that in any setting there will be at least some elements
that follow whatever paradigm is the basis for a teaching operation.
Further, since a good part of teaching is essentially "telling" (i.e.,
giving verbal directions concerning some state of affairs or course of
action), the learner will often be able to "program" his activities in
accordance with whatever paradigm is actually involved. For example, telling a person to memorize a series of associations is tanta-
mount to asking him to program his own learning. Nevertheless,
greater precision and efficiency in learning may come through experimental analysis of the components of reading instruction in
terms of paradigms of learning.

It would be a gross oversight not to mention problems of motivation and task orientation. Reading is a mode of response in a special
kind of communication system paralleling that of speech. The learner
will not maintain active orientation toward the task of learning to
read unless he is reinforced for it, either extrinsically or intrinsically.
The individual must have a reason for wanting to learn to read, and
he must find pleasure and satisfaction, either immediately or ultimately, in this activity. His capacity for consciously organizing and
directing his own learning processes, when he is well motivated,
must not be underestimated.

Theory-based Instructional Procedures

The planning of instruction in the light of psychological theory
requires that we step back a moment to view in perspective the task
to be learned.

Reading behavior, like any complex skill, consists of a large number of separate learnings to be acquired. These behaviors—responses
to particular classes of stimuli, sets, attitudes, and the like—must be
learned one by one or, if that is not possible, in sets that are small
enough to allow some occasion, however brief, when each separate
thing to be learned occupies, so to speak, the foreground of the
stage. One function of a program of instruction is to organize all the
learnings so that they can be acquired in this one-by-one, sequential
fashion in an efficient manner. At the same time, the program allows
the learner to start with those learnings which are closest to the

learnings he brought with him to the task and upon these gradually build new responses which take him nearer and nearer to the desired terminal behavior.

Actually, the number of responses that may have to be learned in order to "break the code" of English orthography is not large; this much can be acquired in two or three months by bright children, and in an even shorter time by adults who happen to be illiterate in English. Later stages of reading development may take longer because they involve learning to recognize thousands of words, learning to concentrate on the meanings of paragraphs with highly involved thought development, and so on.

Psychological theory can be brought to bear on the learning of such an activity as reading in two ways:

a) It can provide information as to the nature of each act of learning and the conditions affecting it. Each act of learning contains, in microcosm, the whole of the problem of learning. It brings into play the question of what paradigm or paradigms of learning may be in operation. Any or all of the variables that might conceivably affect any one act of learning are potentially in the ascendant. Some of these variables, of course, reside in the effects of other learnings.

b) It can formulate an "economics of learning"; that is to say, a theory and a practical art for selecting optimal rates and orders of presentation when there are several or a large number of items to be learned. It is reasonable to suppose that the acquisition of new responses throughout the course of development of an activity, with so many component parts and with such an interweaving of relations of prerequisites among these parts as reading, is a process that can proceed at different rates and with different degrees of success, depending upon the degree to which the successive items to be learned are introduced in an optimal order and at an optimal rate.

Theory and experimentation in psychology have been centrally concerned with the first of these problems. For example, Skinner's account of learning is essentially an account of how a given response is acquired and maintained. This emphasis is justified, probably, by the hope that the complete accounting for any given unit of learning can be extrapolated to the case of units in numbers greater than one. For example, Estes' probabilistic model, concerned with the probability that a given item will be learned on a given occasion, can be successfully generalized for series of items; the resulting equations provide a good fit for certain kinds of paired-associate data using multi-item lists.[10]

Further development is needed, either on purely empirical or rational grounds, toward a model for the learning of multiple items which would take account of retroactive and proactive inhibition and other factors affecting learning. Some years ago, Thurstone[11] showed that in a variety of experimental situations the learning time required per item increases approximately as the square root of the number of items to be learned. Whether this finding has practical significance for organizing presentation rates of items needs to be determined.

Faced with the problem of teaching a series of behaviors which are interrelated by the kind of prerequisiteness that is illustrated in reading behavior, the psychologist is tempted to suggest that efficiency of learning can be optimized if adequate account is taken of these prerequisite relations. But he is not even sure that optimizing is necessary or feasible. Perhaps it is the case that the learner will inevitably sort out for himself what he can best learn at any given time. After all, the child learns to speak without having the learning "programed" for him. (This begs the question, however, of whether children could learn to speak more rapidly under special regimens.) Some children seem to be able to learn to read simply by being "read to" while looking at the lines of printing. Some studies of programed instruction suggest that different orders of presentation have alarmingly small effects. Thus, of what help is it to "program" the order of presentation of the various components of reading behavior? Why not simply present a variety of words and their pronunciations and allow the child to infer grapheme-phoneme correspondences for himself, or whatever he wants to infer, for that matter? Essentially, of course, this is what is done in some kinds of contemporary reading instruction, but, in an effort to remedy the presumed inefficiency

10. W. K. Estes, "Growth and Function of Mathematical Models for Learning," in *Current Trends in Psychological Theory*, pp. 134-51. Pittsburgh: University of Pittsburgh Press, 1961.

11. L. L. Thurstone, "The Relation between Learning Time and Length of Task," *Psychological Review*, XXXVII (January, 1930), 44-53.

and failures of such a system, there are other systems which lay great stress on the programing of letter recognition and the development of grapheme-phoneme correspondences. At the present time, there is no adequate theoretical or empirical basis for deciding among these or other systems.

The present writer believes strongly that a proper analysis of reading behavior, such as attempted here, should make it possible, along with appropriate research studies, to develop an efficient program of reading instruction. A clear, logical, and experimental analysis of what kinds of learnings are prerequisite to other behaviors and of the setting in which each new learning should take place would be required. For example, research in the field of reading does not enable us to say with certainty in what order the various processes in word recognition are best learned. To what extent is grapheme recognition prerequisite to the recognition of the whole pattern of a word? To what extent is it feasible to teach grapheme-phoneme response habits in the earliest phases of word-recognition practice? If this *is* feasible, should early teaching of grapheme-phoneme correspondences be based only on a selection of highly regular correspondences, or should the child be presented with a certain degree of irregularity and variety in order to condition him to the full range of irregularity in English orthography? These and many other questions arise from the kind of psychological and linguistic analysis of the task of reading that has been attempted in this chapter.

For the most part, current systems of reading instruction have not been based on the kind of approach to reading behavior adopted here. Much of the research on reading, even when methodologically sound, has been of little use because the teaching procedures examined by the research were not thoroughly sound. Further, the measuring instruments employed usually have been of the sort that yield only gross assessments; one searches in vain for a study of the speed with which children acquire a mastery of grapheme-phoneme correspondences, for example.

A further difficulty stems from the overnormativeness of much research in reading instruction. By this we mean that research studies have been more concerned to study the characteristics of existing learning situations than to determine the effects of novel regimens of instruction. After we read that Vernon "held that children cannot infer the course of action in a picture until they are nine or ten years of age"[12] it may come as a shock to learn that O. K. Moore at Yale University has been able to teach ordinary children to read at age three or four and to produce their own newspaper by age six. Similarly, Dolch and Bloomster's study[13] has been widely quoted to the effect that children cannot make phonic generalizations before a mental age of seven; the fact is that this study did not concern itself with any effort to *teach* these phonic generalizations, but only with whether children could infer them for themselves in a particular kind of testing situation. Research studies are needed to determine optimal procedures by which the various behaviors identified in our analysis can be taught to children at various chronological or mental ages, and the parameters of such learning should be determined.

Generally, we believe that teaching becomes a relatively straightforward and simple operation, once an adequate analysis of the behavior to be taught has been made and a program of instruction has been planned which features each separate item to be learned in its proper order and in its proper behavioral setting. A direct rather than an indirect approach is to be taken. For example, a proper strategy for increasing vocabulary is to determine students' vocabulary needs by appropriate diagnostic testing, then proceed to teach the items identified, one by one, at some appropriate rate of introduction. This may be hard work for both teacher and students; it may be difficult to cover as much ground as might be desired, and there is always the danger of lagging motivation.[14] But if the objective is firmly fixed in mind, the foregoing procedure seems to be a better strategy than making the quasi-mystical assumption that vocabulary can "automatically" be acquired by any student who does wide reading. Even if wide reading is recommended (as it may very well be, on its own merits) for vocabulary development, there are

12. The quotation is from David H. Russell and Henry R. Fea, "Research on Teaching Reading," in *Handbook of Research on Teaching*, chap. xvi. Edited by N. L. Gage. Chicago: Rand McNally Co., 1963.

13. E. W. Dolch and Maurine Bloomster, "Phonic Readiness," *Elementary School Journal*, XXXVIII (November, 1937), 201–5.

14. A. W. and C. K. Staats believe that many difficulties in reading are to be accounted for by the intensity and "aversiveness" of the training. [See their article, "A Comparison of the Development of Speech and Reading Behavior," *Child Development*, XXXIII (December, 1962), 831–46.]

definite procedures that ought to be recommended to students regarding how they can best profit from their reading.

The preparation of instructional materials and teaching procedures is a task that requires countless decisions. It is not possible to base all of them on directly relevant research findings; intuitive guesses, based both on experience in teaching and on psychological theory, must be made at every turn. Techniques of "programed instruction," in which performance is tested very frequently during a program, offer the possibility of testing some of these decisions efficiently.

An area that demands much detailed investigation is that of individual differences—in "readiness," in rate of learning under instruction, and in modes of learning. Determining readiness should be regarded as a process of assessing the repertoire of responses (speech and otherwise) possessed by a child when he is about to undertake some new step in learning to read. A child is to be regarded as ready to learn to read, for example, when he is found to possess the responses that have been determined to be prerequisite for this learning; if he is not ready in this sense, steps should be taken to attempt to teach him the relevant prerequisite responses. Children cannot be diagnosed as "slow learners" except on the basis of carefully prescribed propaedeutic teaching procedures which still fail to produce desired results. Teachers and experimentalists should keep in mind, also, the possibility that children possess different patterns of aptitudes for reading and that these differences in aptitude can be used to prescribe different procedures of teaching.

As stated at the outset of this paper, an attempt has been made to show how psychological theory can deal with the practical problems of teaching in one area of the curriculum—reading. It is hoped, however, that the illustration will suggest the way to similar efforts in other curricular areas.

CHAPTER XV

Autoinstruction: Perspectives, Problems, Potentials

SIDNEY L. PRESSEY

Autoinstruction is probably the most publicized, most exploited, possibly most errant, and potentially most valuable of all contributions of American psychology to education.

Early Work—to About Ten Years Ago

Educational toys with feedback are to be found in patent files reaching back at least a hundred years, but it seems generally recognized that systematic work on "teaching machines" began some forty years ago, with the exhibition of such a device by the writer at the 1925 meetings of the American Psychological Association. There followed some dozen journal reports by the writer and his students and a number of theses under his direction.[1] All this work had certain common features which related to major interests of the time, such as objective measurement, the "psychology of the school subjects," and diagnostic and practice tests which brought these two types of work into collaboration. Efforts were being made not only to score objective tests mechanically but also to perform other tasks similarly. Thus, Clark Hull devised a machine for computing correlations, and the writer well remembers an evening spent with him, discussing the great potentialities of mechanical aids in both research and instruction. Also at this time there was substantial research regarding college teaching.

1. Sidney L. Pressey, "A Simple Apparatus Which Gives Tests and Scores—and Teaches," *School and Society*, XXIII (March 20, 1926), 373–76; "A Machine for Automatic Teaching of Drill Material," *School and Society*, XXV (May 7, 1927), 549–52; and "A Third and Fourth Contribution toward the Coming 'Industrial Revolution' in Education," *School and Society*, XXXVI (November 19, 1932), 668–72. Others of these papers will be cited later. All are excerpted or abstracted in *Teaching Machines and Programmed Learning*, pp. 32–93 (Edited by A. A. Lumsdaine and Robert Glaser. Washington: National Education Association, 1960).

In view of interests and activities of the time, it is not strange that all the early teaching machines used objective items—and thereby possessed advantageous qualities now so neglected that they should be briefly mentioned. The writer's 1925 device showed a four-choice question in a window and had four keys. If the student thought the second answer correct, he pressed the second key; if he *was* right, the next question was turned up. If the second was not the right answer, the initial question remained in the window, and the learner had to try until he found the right one. Meanwhile, a cumulative count of all tries was kept. This count not merely yielded a record; it aided the learner by keeping before him knowledge of progress and goal. And two experiments, in which the learner was required to go through each "teach-test" until he made a perfect score, suggested that he *was* aided by this knowledge.[2] Since the machine made it possible for a student to go through a thirty-question teach-test in as little as five minutes and since setting back the machine to start again was a simple matter, guided progress to a perfect score was both easy and challenging.

Two unique features of this first machine had promise that is still unrealized. The first was a simple mechanical arrangement—simply lifting a lever completely reversed the action and provided a very convenient, self-scoring, record-keeping, testing device. A new question was turned up regardless of which key was pressed, but only right responses were counted. A test could thus be injected at any point in a series of teaching run-throughs. Intermittent reinforcement was thus provided: A learner might be put through a difficult teach-test several times; then the lever could be shifted, and he would get no cues as to the correctness of his responses, but a record would be kept of them.

The second unique feature was a simple attachment (for the testing) that made possible the placing of a reward dial at any desired goal-score which, if attained, automatically gave the student a candy lozenge. This was not simply a "toy" feature. A variety of rewards or recognitions could thus be automatically and immediately given

2. James K. Little, "Results of Use of Machines for Testing and for Drill upon Learning in Educational Psychology," *Journal of Experimental Education,* III (September, 1934), 59–65; A. L. Stephens, "Certain Special Factors Involved in the Law of Effect," *Absracts of Doctoral Dissertations,* No. LXIV, pp. 505–11. Columbus: Ohio State University Press, 1953.

for attaining goals, which could be progressively raised or adjusted to each learner's capacity or progress—to maximally motivate the learner or to experiment with regard to motivation.

These features of the writer's 1925 machine have been described not simply because of historical interest but because they illustrate possibilities in automation which have since been neglected but which are of likely value. A very important value was exemplified in the device described in "A Machine for Automatic Teaching of Drill Material" (see footnote 1). The apparatus was so ordered that, in successive times through a teach-test, only those items would be returned on which an error had been made the previous time through. (The device could be set for one, two, or three no-mistakes on each item, according to the standard which one desired should be achieved.) And the machine reported in the article "A Third and Fourth Contribution toward the Coming 'Industrial Revolution' in Education" (see Footnote 1) in yet different ways aided students in learning and the instructor in teaching: The machine marked on each answer-card each item on which a mistake had been made, printed on the card the total number of errors, and kept a cumulative record of the number of errors made by the class on each item, so that after the close of an automatized lesson the instructor could note at once those items causing most trouble and could immediately focus instruction upon them. Meanwhile, the writer's former student, Hans Peterson, and his brother had devised "chemo-sheets" on which the student checked his choice of answers to multiple-choice questions with a swab, finding that wrong answers immediately turned red and right ones blue. Later the writer extensively experimented with a "punch-board" (into which, through a cover-paper, a student punched with his pencil, finding that it went deeper when he found the right answer). He also devised a selective-review apparatus using cards—later greatly improved by another former student.[3] By 1932, devices had been reported exemplifying a wide range of potentials for automation in instruction.

3. J. C. Peterson, "The Value of Guidance in Reading for Information," *Transactions of the Kansas Academy of Science*, XXXIV (1931), 291–96; S. L. Pressey, "Development and Appraisal of Devices Providing Immediate Automatic Scoring of Objective Tests and Concomitant Self-Instruction," *Journal of Psychology*, XXIX (April, 1950), 417–47; Leslie J. Briggs, "Two Self-instructional Devices," *Psychological Reports*, IV (December, 1958), 671–76.

The value of such devices was promptly investigated and found substantial. Thus, Little's very careful and adequate research (see footnote 2) used modifications of the writer's 1925 and 1932 apparatus as part of the regular class procedure throughout a quarter course; the investigation involved fourteen sections, with instructors rotated; subjects in experimental and control sections were paired on the bases of a pretest and general ability; end-tests included both objective questions, different in form and content detail from the autoinstructional material, and essay-type questions; and complete distributions of results were presented. The writer knows of no recent research more adequately designed than this of thirty years ago. And the results clearly evidenced the value of the devices. Using a largely similar design, the writer later (1950) provided more specific evidence that autoinstruction, using objective items, did cause learning which did spread or transfer, was greater with immediate feedback than with feedback delayed a day, and was found to last at least two months. Autoinstructional materials were used to reduce or even (with able students) to eliminate all regular class meetings, the able students working only in an autoinstructional laboratory and finishing the twelve-weeks' course in six weeks with superior grades.

The outcomes being good and the materials inexpensive and supplementary to established matter and methods rather than competitive with them, why did this early autoinstruction not take hold? As has been said often recently, the basic reason probably was that the educational world was not yet ready for any such innovation. But there was another factor. The major part of this early work was done during the worst of the Great Depression; then, there were no funds for innovations (the writer financed most of his apparatus-building out of his own pocket), and, with thousands of teachers unemployed, any possibility of creating technological unemployment was to be avoided.

Recent Work—the Last Ten Years

As already mentioned, the earlier work developed out of research in educational measurement, the "psychology of the school subjects," and instructional methods; recent work seems impatient of such research and apparently often ignorant of it, deriving instead from the laboratory, especially the animal laboratory. Thus, the first book reporting the current movement begins with a long review of relevant literature leading to the flat statement that "educators have not done the systematic, controlled type of study that is needed to reveal general principles of learning efficiency."[4] In Skinner's two initial major papers in the field, he is sweepingly critical of educational practice and theory and derives the applications of his own work thereto especially from his research with pigeons.[5]

Skinner's concepts are highly plausible and consistent; his applications of them to educational materials and methods are congruent and striking. Schooling involves multitudinous bit-learnings; in arithmetic alone, 50,000 is a "conservative estimate." For reinforcement to be most effective, it must be immediate. Errors in learning are to be avoided so far as possible, since an error once made tends to be repeated; therefore, each step must be made easy enough that an error will be unlikely. Since seeing an error may lead to its acceptance and, also, since recall rather than discrimination is the objective, multiple-choice items are taboo. In terms of all this, with extraordinary boldness he then attempts revolutionary changes in both educational methods *and* materials. In place of textbooks or like matter, there will be numerous "frames" or units of subject matter, each easy enough that the right response will be highly likely. There is provision for immediate "constructed" response appraised at once as to correctness. That his principles may call for very numerous units, indeed, does not dismay him; "at five or six frames per word, four grades of spelling may require 20,000 or 25,000 frames."

To provide that each frame in the planned sequence will be presented and responded to and that the right response will be reinforced, simple apparatus was devised. Most common was a box-like container housing a roll of paper on which were the frames, each in

4. *Automatic Teaching: The State of the Art*, p. 14. Edited by Eugene Galanter. New York: John Wiley & Sons, 1959. That the search of the literature on which the above generalizations was made may not have been very wide is suggested by the fact that, of the 58 titles in the bibliography, 29 were of articles published in the *Journal of Experimental Psychology*. No reference was made to the *Journal of Educational Psychology*, the *Journal of Educational Research*, or the Yearbooks of the National Society for the Study of Education.

5. B. F. Skinner, "The Science of Learning and the Art of Teaching," *Harvard Educational Review*, XXIV (Spring, 1954), 86–97; "Teaching Machines," *Science*, CXXVIII (October 24, 1958), 969–77. These papers are also in *Teaching Machines and Programmed Learning*, *op. cit.*, pp. 99–113 and 137–58.

turn being exposed through a window to the student; beside this was another window exposing another roll of paper (or part of the same one) which provided space for writing the one- or two-word constructed answer. Turning a knob or pushing a lever turned up the roll to show the right answer and the next frame, which was to be dealt with in the same way. But since box and roll can be expensive as well as a bother to load and care for and require a considerable amount of space, the programed book soon became the more common device. In it a page showed a frame, such as, "A doctor taps your knee (patellar tendon) with a rubber hammer to test your _____." The student wrote on a separate sheet of paper the word he thought should be filled in, then turned the page to find that the word called for was "reflexes"—and to find there also the next question.[6] Such, in brief, are the mechanisms used commonly in Skinnerian linear programs. But increasingly it has been emphasized that the kind of device—whether box and roll or programed book—is relatively minor; the important thing is the programing. Is each frame so artfully phrased, with hints and prompts, that the student will surely "emit" the desired "constructed" word or two? Does the difficulty of the frames proceed on such a gentle gradient that the learner never stumbles? To make a program better is primarily to make it easier, and one well-known psychologist has suggested that the function of all such autoinstructional devices is transitional and temporary: to bring about writing which proceeds at so gentle gradients of thought that no aids of any kind will be needed and all students will proceed without difficulty.

Crowder's materials are different from those described with respect to origin (technical training programs in the armed services), mode of response, and versatility in their use.[7] A frame may be a whole paragraph, presented on the screen of a mechanical "tutor," and following the paragraph a question with several possible answers from which the student chooses one by pressing a particular button. If his choice is correct, the next question in order is shown on the

6. This item is the first frame of James G. Holland and B. F. Skinner, *The Analysis of Behavior: Programmed Instruction.* New York: McGraw-Hill Book Co., Inc., 1961.

7. Norman A. Crowder, "Automatic Tutoring by Intrinsic Programming," in *Teaching Machines and Programmed Learning, op. cit.,* pp. 286–98.

screen. But if his choice is wrong, he may be shown explanatory matter and given a subseries of questions designed to explain his error to him. That is, the program "branches" this way or that, according to each student's need. A somewhat similar procedure is used in "Tutor Texts" or "scrambled books"; the top half of a page may present a problem and the lower half lists several possible answers, each followed by the number of the page to which the learner, who has chosen a particular answer, is to turn. If he chooses the right answer, he finds on that page the next question; if he chooses a wrong answer, he finds on the page to which he turns a chiding explanation of his error and is sent back to try another.

A variety of other devices and types of program is now available.[8] But practically all of these in the past ten years have been "autopresentational" devices or procedures, in marked contrast to the earlier devices, which attempted only to elucidate or instruct with regard to what had been read in text or other initial source.

What happens when attempts are made to make a teaching-machine roll or programed or scramble book take the place of both textbook and teacher? Two recent surveys of evaluative investigations report findings which seem to have almost no effect at all on what these programers are doing. Thus, Silberman has reported that most findings indicate no difference between constructed and multiple-choice responses in the furtherance of learning—as is congruent with the success of objective items in the autoinstruction of ten or more years ago. Further, Silberman found that overt responses were no better than covert responses—or, in effect, no response at all. In short, one can learn from "silent reading." Further, "Beyond demonstrating that a carefully written set of materials will teach if a student will spend enough time studying them, we have little unequivocal evidence for principles of programed instruction." And Gagné reports uncertainties about even such a cardinal concept as reinforcement.[9]

8. James D. Finn and Donald G. Perrin, *Teaching Machines and Programmed Learning: A Survey of the Industry*. Washington: National Education Association, Technological Development Project (Occasional Paper, No. 3), 1962. (U.S. Office of Education, OE-34019, 1962.)

9. Harry F. Silberman, "Self-teaching Devices and Programed Materials," *Review of Educational Research* XXXII (February, 1961), 179–93; Robert M. Gagné, "Military Training and Principles of Learning," *American Psychologist*, XVII (April, 1962), 83–91.

Repeatedly, mention is made that constructed items take more time than objective items, any response more time than no response, many steps more time than fewer steps. And if one critically examines well-known programs, cumulating difficulties appear which go beyond those discussed in the reviews which have been cited. For example, the Holland-Skinner programed book[10] has 54 frames, on eight pages, in its first "set." This means 54 page-turnings, 6 of them from page 8 back to page 1, and 54 writings of "constructed" responses—and in this total process presumably many instances of putting down a pencil and picking it up again to write the response on a separate sheet. As the authors note, about 23 minutes, on the average, are required to read some 1,100 words by this process. To assure that the program was sufficiently easy and cued for emitting only the right constructed response, it was made very wordy and repetitive. The writer was able to formulate in 360 words a succinct statement which colleagues agreed carried all the content of the 1,100 words (except for two questionable examples); this succinct statement was read in a median time of one and a half minutes by students in a section of a beginning course in psychology, and they did as well on an essay quiz on the contents of the set as another section which had been through the set in the manner prescribed by Holland and Skinner.

Their programed textbook has some 1,940 frames, but the total number of page-turnings is nearer 2,500 because there are 23 exhibits to which there must be turnings in dealing with frames which follow them. And the extent of the awkwardness in use is not fully realized until review is attempted: The exhibits are not in the table of contents; there is no index; and attempts at selective use have only the list of sets and parts at the beginning for guidance. But this is much more than is possible with a teaching-machine roll; only by turning it back (if possible) or through again may it be reviewed, and selective review is impossible. In a busy school, bulk would seem a not entirely negligible item. The afore-mentioned programed book has only about one-third as many words on a page as the usual book, i.e., three pages are required to present what a text would present in one. But a machine roll may be worse. Recently the writer received, as a bonus for a five-dollar purchase at a supermarket, a

10. Holland and Skinner, *op. cit.*

"teaching machine" made of pasteboard and about the size of a 500-page volume; the accompanying blurb offered twenty additional volumes of this "modern miracle" at $1.29 each. The program sealed into the bonus volume could have been put, in usual textual form, in a six-page folder.

Current Problems

Surely, in view of faults in current materials that have been noted and of evidence of their failure to meet the high expectations set for them, it is time that we give a long, hard look to both those materials and the theories on which they are based—instead of simply trying to improve the materials in terms of their theory or even rushing to make the most of current interest before it fades.

If (as indicated by findings previously noted and by a great variety of other evidence) one *can* learn from silent reading without overt responding, the need for fragmenting matter into many little frames disappears, and the question arises as to what, for purposes of autoinstruction, a unit for learning may be. Obviously, the unit will vary according to the maturity of the learner and the complexity of the subject matter but even in elementary school, learnings are structured and an important part of the learning consists of finding one's way about in it all. To take an obvious example, Chicago is learned about as both a place on the map and a center of commerce; classification of matter in the geography text is both a fact of the subject matter and a convenience for the learner, and the text is used both for initial study and for reference. Even somewhat larger "frames" in current programs may be false to the facts of the subject and a gross inconvenience. More often, presentation of matter with structure in a form convenient for both initial survey and later review and reference seems desirable, as does also the placing of the task of the day in relation to what has been and is to be learned. In short, there are values in a book.

In a textbook, a laboratory manual, or other material, autoinstructional matter could be inserted (or made available on a separate sheet) when needed. When should this be done? Perhaps in going through a laboratory exercise or in working on a problem, the autoinstruction could lead the learner through in little steps, as a child is led in a current, orthodox program. But, at least above the lower grades, most learning is for larger understanding. It seems generally agreed that a speaker should be heard through, before questioning him. In a well-organized book, written at a level suitable for its users, elucidative autoinstruction might well be most effective and integrative if placed at the end of each chapter. Or there might be little clusters of autoinstructional items at whatever places in a chapter they seem to be needed. Experienced teachers will know fairly well (and informal experimenting and check-up "quizzes" will show more definitely) when and where such material is needed; points where help is needed can be located with greater precision in such subjects as arithmetic or science.

As mentioned earlier, objective items have been found to be as learning-producing in a given time as are "constructed" write-in questions. If autoinstruction is to be used not to present but, rather, to assure understanding in silent reading (or understanding of educational films or other instructional media), the objective item would seem especially appropriate. This item can specify the likely misunderstanding and contrast it in sharp juxtaposition to the right one. The great value and convenience of objective items can thus be realized. Objective items may be either scattered through a reading or placed at the end; either way, responses can be checked on a separate chemo-sheet very expeditiously, and the sheet can also be used to guide selective review.

One very important issue relating to objective items has been almost completely neglected: An objective item designed for use in instruction should be developed in very different fashion from an item designed for use in measurement. It has been suggested in a preceding paragraph that the item should be elucidative or corrective in a process of study-reading for understanding. It is to be considered good in the degree to which it is thus corrective or elucidative. And not only each question, but each alternative in each question, should be evaluated in these terms. For such evaluation, a very straightforward procedure may be used: An item of information or understanding appears in a pretest at the beginning of a course, is dealt with by an objective, autoinstructional item when relevant in the course, and then appears in the final examination. A control class has pre- and end-tests; but the autoinstructional item is omitted. A notably clear and humorous autoinstructional item was found by one of the writer's students to be responsible for a 74 per cent greater gain on the part of the autoinstructional group as compared with the control group on the final examination. But three other autoinstructional items, also studied, showed two or three percentage points *less* gain for the autoinstructed than that achieved by the control group—primarily because the items were too easy and a little confusing. And in the best item, further analysis showed that one alternative was so easy as to bring about no learning.[11]

On twelve out of thirty items thus appraised, the gains of the experimental (autoinstructed) group were 20 per cent or more greater than those of the control group not having any autoinstruction. Every one of the twelve most effective items had at least one alternative so rarely chosen or contributing so little gain that it could be eliminated; it was concluded that for autoinstruction, three-choice items were better than those presenting four or more choices. It seemed clear that autoinstructional material consisting entirely of items thus selected should be a greater aid to learning than the usual multiple-choice matter constructed as if it were for testing. And the greater value of items such as those advocated over items in orthodox programing would seem clear. In current, orthodox programing, the item is supposed to be so easy that at least 95 per cent get it right (no room for gain); wrong answers cannot be presented (and cannot be identified as wrong); and the right response is only as clear and attention-getting as the student can hastily, with the aid of hints and cues, formulate by himself.

The foregoing discussion involved part of an evaluation of the use of autoinstruction in certain sections of a large university course, which were compared with other classes or sections taught in the "usual" fashion. What "usual" is may be ill-defined, but the big practical issue is: Does the use of a teaching machine or pro-

---

11. R. S. Jones, "Integration of Instruction with Self-scoring Measuring Procedures," *Abstracts of Doctoral Dissertations*, No. LXV, pp. 157–65. Columbus: Ohio State University Press, 1954. The writer's point of view and suggestions as to methods and devices have been more fully presented in two recent papers: "Basic Unresolved Teaching Machine Problems," *Theory into Practice*, I (February, 1962), 1–6, and "Teaching Machine (and Learning Theory) Crisis," *Journal of Applied Psychology*, XLVII (February, 1963), 1–6. The chapter by Lumsdaine in this volume recognizes the need for a broader concept of "programing" than usual a few years ago, but would seem so to extend the meaning of the term as almost to include any planned instructional matter.

gramed book result in more learning or save more time than the use of commonly used material and methods? In the afore-mentioned evaluation, autoinstruction was made routine in the experimental sections throughout the course; first gains from novelty interest had time to recede into minimal importance, boredom from burdensome routine had time to appear; and the gains that were more than temporary were the base of appraisal. Inasmuch as the total experimental design was sufficiently normal to educational situations, the outcome might be thought of as having some application in such situations. To a distressing degree, this has not been true of many investigations in this field.

Rather a composite picture of such undertakings appears to be somewhat as follows: Small groups of students (much smaller than a usual class) are paid well to go to a room which is not a classroom, in a building which is not a school, to do a special bit of learning in a strange way for undisclosed purposes, under the direction of a stranger so well subsidized that neither equipment nor time costs are important. In terms of social situation, motivation, setting, task, direction, and resources, such undertakings are so distant from educational realities that applications from them are uncertain. Whatever the justification for such special laboratory-type projects earlier, autoinstruction has now moved into the schools, and its usefulness there under usual circumstances for outcomes as usually determined should be a first basis of appraisal. When used enough to become routine, what is pupil attitude toward programed books and various autoinstructional devices? What is teacher attitude? As an everyday problem, how much of a chore may it be to get out this or that set of autoinstructional materials, to supervise the use of it, and to put it away? What are the results in terms of the examinations and tests commonly given to grade the progress of students in these courses?

In very practical ways, usual instruction should be compared not only with orthodox, many-little-frames, "constructed response" autoinstruction but also with such objective-item autoinstruction in the guidance of reading-study processes as suggested in the preceding paragraphs. After two or three months, what is pupil reaction to write-in versus chemo-card responding? Has a selective-review apparatus in arithmetic perhaps grown in pupil favor? What are the results on the usual tests and examinations? Also, how do variations in usual methods of instruction compare in such an experimental design? There is now much interest in independent study at both college and secondary-school levels. To what extent do various types of autoinstruction stimulate and guide independent work—and how tolerable is it in long-continued (not merely novelty) use?[12]

The special nature of autoinstruction makes it important that we consider the problem of transfer. Does filling in the correct word in thousands of frames dealing with punctuation, grammar, and sentence structure actually improve written English? How much does practice in an autoinstructional language laboratory improve "real-life" use of the language? In a highly subsidized trial in such a laboratory, each student in his separate booth listened to the machine saying a word or phrase in French, tried saying it and listened to himself, and tried again. When the writer asked if the students ever talked to each other or the instructor, the answer was "No"! In instrumentation the laboratory was fascinating; and in potential usefulness, promising; but methodology for realization of that potential seemed lacking; also lacking was any plan for determining whether and how much converse with real people was thus aided. More generally, to what extent does a student, from going through many hundreds of frames, emerge with some sense of the organization of the ideas thus presented seriatim without structure? Or, to take another special type of instruction, to what extent and in what ways might autoinstructional devices and materials be used in safety education, and *are* accidents thereby reduced?

In short, it is believed that current problems call for a co-ordination of earlier and later types of work in the field and the relating of them to congruent educational research. (*a*) If there can be learning from reading without responding, to what extent does the early work in adjunct autoinstruction again become important, and to what extent is research on methods of reading and study important? (*b*) If objective items may be used, what may be the relevancy of the early work in autoinstruction involving the use of such items? Also, to what extent might that type of use be improved, in the

12. Samuel Baskin, "Quest for Quality: Some Models and Means," *New Dimensions in Higher Education*, No. VII. Washington: U.S. Office of Education, Division of Higher Education, 1960.

light of research regarding problems in school learning and intensive analysis of the autoinstructional efficiency of each item such as has been described above? (c) As autoinstruction moves from the laboratory into the schools for continuing use there, how does this special type of instruction stand up in practical, hard-headed evaluations? (d) A special methodology involves special problems of transfer: Are these problems recognized? Have they been dealt with? What appear to be the outcomes? These seem to be problems now little recognized by many who are active in the field. But work on them will (the writer believes) enlarge rather than restrict the usefulness of the concept of autoinstruction—and enlarge also concepts of learning in both psychology and education.

Larger Issues

As pointed out earlier, work of the past eight or ten years in autoinstruction has been dominated by learning theory derived directly from experimentation with animals. And so in great part has been all American psychological theorizing regarding the nature of learning processes. But the recent research in autoinstruction shows such theory is not paying off. One can learn without responding, can learn from mistakes—human, meaningful learning proceeds in ways and at a rate transcending animal learning, The writer ventures the declaration that an all-important basic fault in the grand strategy and whole trend of American research and theory regarding learning is here come to most bizarre and unfortunate fruition. The most influential portions of that research and theory are based on the false "generalization from comparative studies that there are no differences, except quantitative ones, between the learning of lower mammals and man," while the all-important fact is that "at the human level there have emerged capacities not approached by the lower animals. . . . Language in man is perhaps the clearest of the emergents." Further, "the ceiling of ability itself may be modified by training"; by "acquiring appropriate linguistic or mathematical tools," problems otherwise impossible can be solved.[13] Surely that now-taken-for-granted-but-really-marvelous skill, silent assimilative reading, is such a tool. Perhaps the research involving programing

13. Ernest R. Hilgard, *Theories of Learning*, pp. 460–61. New York: Appleton-Century-Crofts, 1956 (second edition).

may enlarge concepts regarding learning. Perhaps autoinstructional devices may—especially if the objective item returns to respectability—facilitate research on learning.

Perhaps, at the same time, educational research may contribute in very important ways to the reconstitution of learning theories. As Brownell showed over thirty years ago, "reinforcement" is not an adequate concept in explaining even so apparently elementary learning as children's first acquaintance with number. Simply telling primary-school youngsters that $2 \times 3 = 6$ did *not* bring about learning of that number combination. These sturdy little empiricists had not merely to be told, they had to be shown—as by putting out two sets each of three pennies and demonstrating that they do, indeed, count to six. They had similarly to verify and to differentiate: that $2 + 3 = 5$ and $3 - 2 = 1$. As Piaget and others have described their development, children gradually develop a number system or a cognitive schema such as of space and causality; and they do this not by so crude a rote process as the accretions of bit learnings stuck on by reinforcements but by progressive processes of cognitive integration and clarification.[14] Moreover, reading-study processes may be brought into relation to these larger theories.

Though largely critical, the preceding discussion has really argued that autoinstruction is a concept much broader and very much more varied in its potentialities than is at this writing recognized by orthodox "programers." Teaching machines may aid children in their first acquiring of a reading vocabulary, their first forming of number ideas—not as rote learnings but with an artfully formed series of "number pictures" to develop number concepts. Drill in arithmetic or grammar may be so aided—not simply by reinforcings but by cognitive integratings and clarifyings. What the writer has called adjunct autoinstruction may assist in the use of all media of instruction—textbooks and other printed matter, educational films, and television. Moreover, if objective items are permitted to replace write-in responses to a large extent, then at one stroke, autoinstruc-

14. William A. Brownell, *The Development of Children's Number Ideas in the Primary Grades* (Supplementary Educational Monograph No. XXXV. Chicago: University of Chicago Press, 1928); Jean Piaget, *The Construction of Reality in the Child* (New York: Basic Books, 1954); David P. Ausubel, "A Subsumption Theory of Meaningful Verbal Learning and Retention," *Journal of General Psychology*, LXVI (1962), 213–24.

tion will be enormously facilitated and made more incisively effective. The prediction is ventured that in a few years the rejection of the objective item by Skinnerian programers will be seen as one of the most odd and perverse episodes in American psychology. The writer has seen *no* evidence that, with meaningful autoinstructional matter, wrong alternates mislead or discriminative tasks aid *only* discriminative learning—or that, using such items, they may not be few and incisive rather than many and dull-easy. As it is, programing may be saddled for ten years with voluminous, clumsy, thousand-frame, write-in programs soon to be discarded, but with one more mark against psychologists as theory-bound and impractical.

Not only will many fewer objective items, made in terms of their effectiveness in fostering learning as described earlier, accomplish much more but devices such as chemo-sheets and key machines will return to their rightful place. It is a strange phenomenon that the teaching-machine movement seems now, in many quarters, to have repudiated the machine. The writer persists in the conviction that devices—often "hardware"—should be and ultimately will be an integral and a major feature of "autoinstruction."

Exploitings and Potentials

In 1962, under the auspices of the United States Office of Education, "the first major exhibit of teaching machines and programed-instruction procedures, valued at $78,227, began a nationwide tour with a premier in Washington."[15] And a bulletin from the same office, early in 1962, reported that 123 teaching machines were in production or development, commercially priced as high as $5,000.00, and that 630 programs, running as long as 16,000 frames, were or shortly would be available.[16] Many millions of dollars are being invested in what has been advertised as "the greatest educational advance since the invention of printing"; and hundreds of psychologists and educators are rushing into the field. Yet the review of that field in the preceding pages would surely suggest that it is still not well marked out; basic concepts and methods are still in question, results are still often doubtful—a report of a recent subsidized investigation includes the strange and certainly not highly promising

15. *NEA Journal*, December, 1962, p. 5.
16. Finn and Perrin, *op. cit.*

conclusion that "no student was penalized in his level of achieve-ment because of having used programed materials"! The statement in the first sentence of this chapter would seem justified: that auto-instruction is, indeed, publicized, exploited, and possibly errant.

But there is also evidence that autoinstruction may aid pupils to better work and reduce the required hours of teaching time. If hampering concepts regarding "programing" can be discarded, if autoinstruction can be brought into teamwork rather than into com-petition with other instructional media, and if labor- and time-saving objective devices can be made use of, as they much warrant, then there may be realization of a notable advance in methodology, great-ly aiding both teacher *and* student to a degree vitally important in this time of tidal enrolments, lengthening curricula, and shortages and burdening of teachers.

CHAPTER XVI

Educational Technology, Programed Learning, and Instructional Science

A. A. LUMSDAINE[1]

Education and Technology

We have been hearing a good deal for the past few years about "educational technology," and likely we shall be hearing a great deal more about it in the coming years. The interaction of education and technology is a bi-directional one: technological advances in society not only pose new requirements for education but also offer new resources.

NEW EDUCATIONAL REQUIREMENTS POSED BY TECHNOLOGICAL CHANGE

Advances in physical-science and biological-science technology, ranging from the microscope to the space capsule and from the control of disease to the impact of automation on the spectrum of required occupational skills, obviously change the requirements for the job that education must do. These changing requirements are an increasing source of concern to professional educators as well as to the lay public.[2] However, the changed educational *needs* imposed by technological developments in society have, as such, little direct

1. The preparation of this paper was aided by research conducted with the support of the Cooperative-Research and Educational-Media Branches of the United States Office of Education, Department of Health, Education, and Welfare.

2. For implications of automation for educational *needs* and of technological tools as *means* for education, see respectively: G. E. Arnstein, *Automation: The New Industrial Revolution* (Washington: National Education Association, October, 1962, mimeographed); James D. Finn, Donald G. Perrin, and Lee E. Campion, *Studies in the Growth of Instructional Technology, I, Audio-visual Instrumentation for Instruction in the Public Schools, 1930–1960* (Technological Development Project, Occasional Paper No. 6. Washington: National Education Association, 1962).

implication for the *means* whereby these needs are to be met. Despite their importance, we shall, therefore, be relatively little concerned in this paper with implications of technological change, per se, for the requirements of education. However, the implications of educational technology as a source of new tools for improving instruction are central to our present concern.

TECHNOLOGICAL DEVELOPMENTS AS EDUCATIONAL RESOURCES

It seems to have gone largely unnoticed that the concept of technology as a resource for education is actually two quite distinct concepts. These need to be differentiated, even though the two are *de facto* often functionally interrelated. Both of these concepts of "educational technology" (or "instructional technology") have important relations to learning and behavior theory, on the one hand, and to educational practice on the other.

*Educational technology*₁.—The first meaning of educational technology refers to the application of physical-science and engineering technology to provide mechanical or electro-mechanical tools, instrumentation, or "hardware" which can be used for instructional purposes. This is the principal sense in which the term has been used by Finn and other spokesmen for the "audio-visual education" movement and by the electronic communications industry.[3] In this sense, the reference is generally to the use of equipment for presenting instructional materials, such as still and motion picture projectors (silent and sound), tape recorders (including the special arrangements employed as a "language laboratory"), television, "teaching machines," and, most recently, computer-based teaching systems.

*Educational technology*₂.—In the second sense, educational technology does not concern hardware, as such, but refers rather to a "technology" in a generic sense, as a derivative or application of an underlying science—somewhat as the technology of engineering relates to the science of physics or the technology of medical practice to the underlying biological sciences.[4] The focus of the present

3. James D. Finn, "Automation and Education, II, Automatizing the Classroom," *Audio-Visual Communication Review*, V (Spring, 1957), 451–67; James D. Finn, "Automation and Education, III: Technology and the Instructional Process," *Audio-Visual Communication Review*, VIII (Winter, 1960), 5–26; Finn, Perrin, and Campion, *op. cit.*

4. Arthur W. Melton, "The Science of Learning and the Technology of Educational Methods," *Harvard Educational Review*, XXIX (Spring, 1959), 96–

yearbook suggests the status of the science of behavior, especially learning theory, as a primary "underlying science" from which applications to a technology of instruction might be anticipated. However, potential contributions of other kinds of theorization to instructional practice also have been discussed—for example, theories of communication and cybernetics,[5] perceptual theories,[6] and branches of logistics or economics concerned with the utilization of instructional personnel and equipment.[7]

These two basic kinds of educational technology can interact in the design and use of instrumentation to provide better control over the learning situation, by providing a richer array of stimulus material (for example, through motion pictures), and also by providing for interaction between the responses of the learner and the presentation of instructional material.

Other technological contributions to education.—The second kind of educational technology ("technology$_2$") might also be considered as one aspect of a broader concept of "psychotechnology," referring to application of the science of psychology to practical human affairs. Not all such applications, of course, are primarily concerned with education: psychotherapy, personnel selection, and "human engineering" are obvious examples. Furthermore, there are aspects of psychotechnology not deriving from learning and behavior theory which have important educational applications. Examples are the application of psychometrics to aptitude and achievement testing and of statistical method and experimental design—deriving basically from the mathematics of measurement and probability the-

---

106. (Abstracted in *Teaching Machines and Programmed Learning*, pp. 658–60. Edited by A. A. Lumsdaine and Robert Glaser. Washington: National Education Association, 1960.)

5. George Gerbner, "Toward a General Model of Communication," *Audio-Visual Communication Review*, IV (Summer, 1956), 171–99; Wilbur Schramm, "Procedures and Effects of Mass Communication," in *Mass Media and Education*, pp. 113–38 (Fifty-third Yearbook of the National Society for the Study of Education, Part II. Chicago: University of Chicago Press, 1954).

6. "Perception Theory and AV Education," *Audio-Visual Communication Review*, X (September–October, 1962), Supplement No. 5 (Edited by Kenneth Norberg).

7. J. Lloyd Trump, *Images of the Future: A New Approach to the Secondary School*. Urbana, Illinois: Commission on the Experimental Study of the Utilization of the Staff in the Secondary School, 1959.

ory—to the analysis of educational data. A further illustration is the application of "task-analysis" concepts to the design of curricula (see chaps. ii and vii).[8]

Technological Contributions to Instruction

APPLICATIONS OF PHYSICAL SCIENCE AND ENGINEERING
ARTS TO INSTRUCTIONAL RESOURCES

Among the contributions which physical-science technology has contributed to teaching, one should not overlook the fundamental importance of the early advances represented by the invention of paper and, later, of movable type. These basic technological "break-throughs" made feasible the use of printed materials as instruments of teaching, thus removing the need for dependence on the individual teacher's oral discourse with a student or group of students as a sole channel of education. Further major technological advances were the invention of photography and lithography, adding picto-rialization to the economically mass-producible resources of in-struction. These advances were augmented by the capability for using projected pictures (based on developments in optics and illu-mination, as well as photography) through the development of vari-ous forms of slide or transparency projectors, the camera lucida, and the opaque projector; later, sound recording, silent and sound-synchronized motion pictures; and, quite recently, the electronic audio-visual transmission apparatus of television.[9] Figure 1 is a dia-grammatic representation of some interrelations between contribu-tions from physical and behavioral science and educational tech-nology.

Motion pictures and, later, television not only "brought the world to the classroom" in the sense of providing otherwise unavailable visual resources but also made feasible the multiplication of the audi-ence that might profit from the talents of the superior teacher. They also provided special presentation techniques (e.g., animation, over-lay, and photomontage) and permitted close-up views to give each

8. References herein to numbered chapters not otherwise designated are to chapters in this yearbook.

9. L. Paul Saettler, *History of Instructional Technology*, Vol. II, *The Techni-cal Development of the New Media*. Technological Development Project, Oc-casional Paper No. 2. Washington: National Educational Association, 1961 (mimeographed).

student a "front seat" or "over-the-shoulder" view of a process which an instructor is demonstrating.[10]

DEVELOPMENT OF EQUIPMENT AND MATERIALS RELATED TO EDUCATIONAL NEEDS AND PSYCHOLOGICAL THEORY

To what extent have developments in instructional hardware and materials for their use (technology$_1$) been influenced by educational

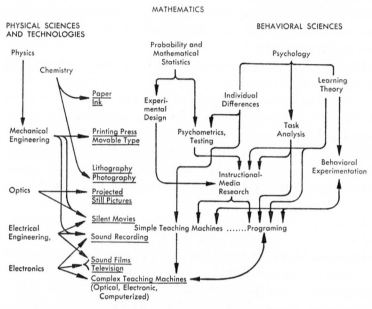

FIG. 1.—Some of the interrelationships among developments in physical and behavioral sciences related to educational technology.

requirements and, particularly, by behavioral-science research and learning theory (technology$_2$)?

Audio-visual devices and materials.—The development of motion-picture projection equipment and of television transmission and receiving equipment occurred almost entirely without reference to

10. Some experimental evidence on such factors is presented in Sol M. Roshal, "Film-mediated Learning with Varying Representations of the Task: Viewing Angle, Portrayal of Demonstration, Motion, and Student Participation," in *Student Response in Programmed Instruction,* pp. 155–75. Edited by A. A. Lumsdaine. Washington: National Academy of Sciences, National Research Council, 1961 (Distributed by Office of Technical Services, U.S. Department of Commerce; Publication No. AD281936).

education (much less to learning theory). This is particularly evident in the case of television; for motion pictures the situation is historically a bit less clear, since Edison evidently conceived the motion-picture projector initially as an educational tool.[11] However, its major development and technical perfection were conducted primarily by and for the benefit of the entertainment industry; only when technically perfected was much use made of the motion picture as an instructional instrument. Even the development of 16-mm. and, later, 8-mm. equipment was only partly stimulated by classroom-instruction possibilities, being largely aimed also at amateur application or "home movies."

Historically, the audio-visual media have been used primarily for group or "mass" presentation, without explicit regard to individual differences in learning ability. Their use is by no means so limited, as we shall see, but is related to the fact that development of projection equipment appears to have been carried out largely in terms of imitating, on a reduced scale, the properties of the theatrical projector. Only quite recently has a beginning been made to incorporate features in projection equipment that facilitate more flexible use by teachers and students.

Guidelines for the use of instructional films have stressed their roles as *aids* to teaching rather than as self-contained sequences of instruction. However, there has been an increasing tendency of late to construct films designed to stand alone as independent instructional media.[12] On the other hand, concurrent with this later trend is the recent increase in the feasibility of using film sequences as aids for the classroom teacher and as study materials for individual students—application made more practical by the development of such devices as self-threading 8-mm. cartridge-loading projectors. These developments go hand in hand with an increase in the number of very short films which range from a few seconds to a few minutes in length and which are suitable for instructional purposes. Additional features making film more effective for individual instruction include provision for stopping a filmed demonstration to

11. Saettler, *op. cit.*

12. For example, Harvey E. White, *Introductory Physics.* Wilmette, Illinois: Encyclopaedia Britannica Films, Inc., 1957. (Comprises 162 half-hour 16-mm. sound films.)

provide a still image at full illumination before proceeding to the next sequence.[13]

Rationale and uses of A-V media.—Another noteworthy characteristic of audio-visual media, as they customarily have been employed, is that they are almost exclusively used as vehicles for presenting stimulus materials, with little explicit attention to the response aspect of the stimulus-response paradigm of learning (see chap. ii). Porter[14] has noted this limitation in contrasting such stimulus devices with stimulus-*response* devices like the memory drum and the teaching machine. However, this limitation is not a necessary one and, at least at the research level, combinations of the audio-visual media with various forms of response-registering devices have recently been given increasing attention for both group and individual instruction.[15]

A great impetus to the use of motion pictures for instruction was given by the extensive employment of training films during World War II. The development of films for military instruction on a large scale during the war and, subsequently, for general education was based in large part on the concepts of the value of mass presentation of demonstrational material and of using such techniques as animation and dramatic or story-telling devices for expository purposes. This development occurred almost exclusively without reference to express inputs from theories of learning as developed by psychologists. Indeed, it could be argued that most of the development of audio-visual materials was relatively little influenced by *any* very precise theoretical notions. While such concepts as that of getting

13. See A. A. Lumsdaine, "Partial and More Complete Automation of Teaching in Group and Individual Learning Situations," in *Automatic Teaching: The State of the Art,* pp. 147–66 (Edited by Eugene H. Galanter. New York: John Wiley & Sons, Inc., 1959); A. A. Lumsdaine, "Teaching Machines and Self-Instructional Materials," *Audio-Visual Communications Review,* VII (Summer, 1959), 163–81. (Reprinted under title, "Teaching Machines: An Introductory Overview," in *Teaching Machines and Programmed Learning, op. cit.,* pp. 5–22.)

14. Douglas Porter, "A Critical Review of a Portion of the Literature on Teaching Devices," *Harvard Educational Review,* XXVII (1957), 126–47. (Reprinted in *Teaching Machines and Programmed Learning, op. cit.,* pp. 114–32.)

15. Lumsdaine, "Partial and More Complete Automation of Teaching in Group and Individual Learning Situations," *op. cit.,* pp. 149–52; *Student Response in Programmed Instruction, op. cit.,* pp. 1–3; George L. Gropper and A. A. Lumsdaine, *The Use of Student Response To Improve Televised Instruction: An Overview* (Studies in Televised Instruction, Report No. 7. Pittsburgh: American Institute for Research, 1961).

closer to the reality base of Dale's "cone of experience"[16] may have influenced the *acceptance* of audio-visual aids, they seem to have had less effect on film design and to have led to relatively little experimental research. It is also difficult to find ways in which other forms of communication models or related theory have been explicitly made a basis for empirical research or for determining the directions along which audio-visual materials have developed.[17] In the main, such theorization seems to have been introduced more as a *post hoc* rationalization for audio-visual instruction than as a direct contribution to the design of instructional materials or hardware.

Teaching machines and programed instruction.—This history of the development of audio-visual hardware, primarily independent of educational requirements, and of group-instruction media, largely independent of psychological theory, contrasts strikingly with the situation in more recent developments of teaching machines and programed-instruction sequences. The initial developments by Pressey in the late 1920's illustrate this change toward greater dependence on theory as do also the more recent developments which followed the impact of Skinner's work at Harvard and military research on response factors in the use of films.[18] Even though Pressey's devices initially emphasized the automation of testing rather than of instruction, it was evident that they incorporated principles of learning enunciated by psychologists—the major emphases being on active participation, immediate confirmation, and individual progression

16. Edgar Dale, *Audio-Visual Methods in Teaching*, p. 43. New York: Dryden Press, 1954 (revised).

17. For discussion of such models, see Schramm, *op. cit.*; Gerbner, *op. cit.*; and "The Changing Role of the Audiovisual Process in Education: A Definition and a Glossary of Related Terms," TDP Monograph No. 1, *Audio-Visual Communication Review*, XI (January–February, 1963), Supplement No. 6 (Edited by D. P. Ely). Concerning the need for audio-visual theory, see Charles F. Schuller, "AV Theory Is Essential: How Do We Build It?" *Audiovisual Instruction*, VII (September, 1962), 436–37. Growing recognition of the relevance of psychological learning theories for the design of audio-visual media of instruction is evidenced by such publications as Neal E. Miller *et al.*, "Graphic Communication and the Crisis in Education," *Audio-Visual Communication Review*, V, No. 3 (1957), Special Issue; and "Learning Theory and AV Utilization," *Audio-Visual Communication Review*, IX (January–February, 1961), Supplement 4 (Edited by Wesley C. Meierhenry).

18. Concerning convergence of influence of Skinner's work and that of the military programs, see Wilbur Schramm, *Programed Instruction*, pp. 44–45 (New York: Fund for the Advancement of Education, 1962); also, *Teaching Machines and Programmed Learning, op. cit.*, pp. 257–64.

adapted to the capabilities of individual learners (see chap. xv). The development of programed-learning sequences during the past few years illustrates a practical development representing a large investment, directed toward a major change in educational practice[19] which has, to a large extent, grown directly out of the concern of psychologists with theory and experimentation on learning.

Early in the development of programed-learning materials for individual student use, there appeared a number of specific attempts to provide rules for constructing such materials.[20] Thus far it is difficult, by contrast, to find such precepts being used to guide the construction of the more traditional kinds of instructional materials except in the *research* literature.[21] The main development of instructional films and televised programs also has thus far largely ignored the use of empirical data for testing and improving the effectiveness of program sequences. Quite the contrary has been true of the development of individual learning programs, where very considerable (even though as yet far from optimal) use of empirical data as a basis for revision has been a conspicuous feature of the practical development almost from the very outset.[22] However, it seems likely that empirically verifiable programing rules will increas-

19. Schramm, *Programed Instruction, op. cit.,* pp. 5–11.

20. For examples of such rules, see: David J. Klaus, "The Art of Auto-Instructional Programming," *Audio-Visual Communication Review,* IX (March–April, 1961), 130–42; B. F. Skinner and James G. Holland, *The Use of Teaching Machines in College Instruction: Final Report* (New York: Fund for the Advancement of Education, 1958; also in *Teaching Machines and Programmed Learning, op. cit.,* pp. 159–72); Lloyd E. Homme and Robert Glaser, "Problems in Programming Verbal Learning Sequences" (Paper read at American Psychological Association Convention, 1959; in *Teaching Machines and Programmed Learning, op. cit.,* pp. 486–96).

21. For example, see M. A. May, "Verbal Responses to Demonstrational Films," in *Learning from Films,* pp. 168–80 (Edited by Mark A. May and Arthur A. Lumsdaine. New Haven, Connecticut: Yale University Press, 1958); Fred D. Sheffield and Nathan Maccoby, "Summary and Interpretation of Research on Organizational Principles in Constructing Filmed Demonstrations," in *Student Response in Programmed Instruction, op. cit.,* pp. 117–31.

22. For example, see James G. Holland, "A Teaching Machine Program in Psychology," in *Automatic Teaching: The State of the Art, op. cit.,* pp. 69–82; James G. Holland, "Teaching Machines: An Application of Principles from the Laboratory," in *Teaching Machines and Programmed Learning, op. cit.,* pp. 215–28; and Susan R. Meyer, "Report on the Initial Test of a Junior High-School Vocabulary Program," in *Teaching Machines and Programmed Learning, op. cit.,* pp. 229–46.

ingly be developed in the future for film and TV instruction, and that provision will be made for greater use of test data for improving program effectiveness.[23] This could help greatly to increase the potential of these media for group instruction up to the inherent limits set by a fixed rate and sequence in group presentation.

EXPERIMENTAL RESEARCH ON INSTRUCTIONAL MEDIA

Prior to the recent concern with programed instruction, by far the largest amount of experimental research on instructional media was conducted in the context of instructional films which, because of their reproducible character, have important potentialities both as objects of research and as vehicles for research on instructional variables.[24] In most respects, however, this research has only scratched the surface of prevailing ignorance concerning the operation of variables which govern the effectiveness of instruction. Much of the research, up to the past five years or so, was conducted under a few major programs or projects, mostly with federal support from military agencies.[25] Perhaps the most concerted single series of inquiries made thus far was pursued in the context of a basically stimulus-response orientation, with special reference to factors which control student response during learning.[26] The extent to which such research programs have influenced the production of films for classroom teaching is difficult to assess. Doubtless there has been some influence, but most of the research was not closely integrated with the activities of production agencies, and to a considerable extent the main stream of instructional-film and TV production has con-

23. See Gropper and Lumsdaine, *op. cit.*

24. The most recent and comprehensive survey is that by A. A. Lumsdaine, "Instruments and Media of Instruction," in *Handbook of Research on Teaching*, pp. 609–54 (Edited by N. L. Gage. Chicago: Rand McNally & Co., 1963). Prior summaries include: Charles F. Hoban, Jr., and E. B. Van Ormer, *Instructional Film Research, 1918–1950* (Pennsylvania State University Instructional Film Research Program. Port Washington, New York: U.S. Naval Training Device Center, 1950; Technical Report No. SDC 269-7-19); Miller *et al., op. cit.*; W. H. Allen, "Audio-Visual Communication Research," in *Encyclopedia of Educational Research*, pp. 115–37 (Edited by C. W. Harris. New York: Macmillan Co., 1960).

25. These programs are described in Lumsdaine, "Instruments and Media of Instruction," *op. cit.*, pp. 605–9.

26. See *Student Response in Programmed Instruction, op. cit.*, especially the studies by Sheffield, Maccoby, and co-workers (chaps. ii–ix, pp. 13–131).

tinued without much direct influence from the results of experimental research.[27]

Research on variables influencing the effects of instructional media has been stimulated greatly during the past four or five years by the impetus of concern with programed instruction which resulted from the influence of Skinner's 1954 and 1958 papers and, to a lesser extent, from military research programs, particularly that of the Air Force Personnel and Training Center (see chap. vii). The expansion of such research on instructional media has been faciliated in recent years by the considerable amount of financial support made available by major foundations and from federal sources, especially the United States Office of Education's Cooperative Research and Educational-Media programs.

The sponsorship of the Lumsdaine and Glaser sourcebook on teaching machines and programed learning by the National Education Association's Department of Audio-visual Instruction in 1960 made possible the presentation to large segments of the educational world the papers of Skinner and his associates as well as the early studies of Pressey and some of the military research on training. Together with a number of popular articles on teaching machines, this publication may have marked a real turning point in the concern of the professional education community for the applicability of the theory and experimental science of learning to practical problems of instruction. However, it is likely that these sources of information would have had much less influence had there not been a growing volume of instructional materials in the form of programs, developed initially by psychologists and later by educators, available for commercial sale to schools. As the writer has previously noted, "We should not expect the conclusions and principles derived from . . . research to find their way into educational and training practice unless we make the translation ourselves or develop a systematic technology through which such translation may be effected."[28] The actual construction and experimental tryout of programed-learning ma-

27. Much the same statement can be made about the development of "hardware" training devices by military agencies and industry, where systematic research by psychologists began only as a sort of small sideshow following massive and costly programs of device development.

28. Lumsdaine, "Instruments and Media of Instruction," *op. cit.*, p. 670.

terials applicable to school curricula provide a very direct bridge between learning theory and application in the classroom.[29]

"Programmed Learning" and "Programed Instruction"[30]

Some major concepts underlying these two terms seem likely to represent a truly revolutionary development in educational history.[31] They also constitute a crucial interface between learning theory and the development of educational practice. However, the terms are not easy to define, and such definitions as have been offered are sometimes inconsistent or overly restrictive. A source of confusion is the tendency to identify some particular kind of program as synonymous with the term "program" or to fasten on some particular feature of current programs as a principal identifying characteristic.[32]

SKINNER'S INFLUENCE; THE CONCEPT OF PROGRAMING

Historically, the term "program," as applied to a sequence of instruction presented by a teaching machine, derives from the 1954 and 1958 papers of Skinner, whose influence has, directly or indirectly, guided the mainstream of developments in programed instruction during the later 1950's and early 1960's.[33]

Skinner's work stimulated many experimental psychologists to become interested in applying S-R theory and experimental techniques to practical problems of instruction. The nature of his influence can be indicated by noting some important characteristics implied in the concept of programing. To begin with, Skinner and most others associated with programing developments emphasized the three characteristics also exemplified in Pressey's devices—namely, frequent response, immediate correction or confirmation, and progres-

29. See Melton, *op. cit.*; also, Lumsdaine, "Instruments and Media of Instruction," *op. cit.*, pp. 586–87, 670.

30. For a commentary on the prevailing inconsistency in spelling of these terms, see editorial note in *Contemporary Psychology*, VII (1962), 354.

31. Schramm, *Programed Instruction, op. cit.*

32. See the characterization given by Pressey in chapter xv, which is more restrictive than the definition here proposed.

33. B. F. Skinner, "The Science of Learning and the Art of Teaching," *Harvard Educational Review*, XXIV (1954), 86–97; "Teaching Machines," *Science*, CXXVIII (October 24, 1958), 969–77 (Reprinted in *Teaching Machines and Programmed Learning, op. cit.*, pp. 99–113 and 137–58); "Why We Need Teaching Machines," in *Cumulative Record*, pp. 182.01–182.02 (Edited by B. F. Skinner. New York: Appleton-Century-Crofts, 1961).

sion at an individual rate (see chap. xv). A crucial, new concept introduced by Skinner was the idea that any educational subject matter could be regarded as an accumulative repertoire of behavior which could be analyzed logically and behaviorally into a number of small "steps" representing increments of successive approximation to final mastery. Another basic concept was that an optimal sequence of steps could be developed and refined on the basis of detailed records of the responses made by typical students to a preliminary version of an instructional program.

This concept of empirically developed programs meant not only that the progress of any one student through a program could be regarded a successive approximation to mastery of the subject but also that successive revisions of the program, based on feedback from students to the programer, could be regarded as successive approximations to an ideal learning sequence. A corollary was that the size and sequencing of the steps could be such that the student need seldom make an error, since potential errors could be anticipated and headed off before they were reached. Another implicit corollary is that optimal sequencing, applicable to many students, can often be better determined through psychological analysis of the stimulus and response features of the learning task, together with empirical development based on responses of typical students, than by the efforts of any one student to sequence his own activities.[34]

ESSENTIAL VERSUS SECONDARY ASPECTS OF THE PROGRAMED-LEARNING CONCEPT

In the writer's opinion, the afore-mentioned concepts are more central to the importance of programing than are the differences between Pressey and Skinner on the importance of students composing their own answers rather than depending on transfer from multiple-choice responding.[35] It is easy to lose sight of fundamental aspects of the rationale of programed learning, which emerge from the

34. That such effective management of learning is not necessarily easy to achieve is suggested by such studies as: J. Jepson Wulff and David L. Emeson, "The Relationship between 'What Is Learned' and 'How It's Taught,'" in *Student Response in Programmed Instruction*, op. cit., pp. 457–70; Slater E. Newman, "Student vs. Instructor Design of Study Method," *Journal of Educational Psychology*, XLVIII (October, 1957), 328–33; see also chapter xv.

35. See chapter xv; Skinner, "Teaching Machines," op. cit., p. 140.

general orientation to which Skinner has given the most impetus, because of the tendency to identify certain aspects of theory or format as definitive of this major trend in programing.

Some of the numerous aspects with respect to which different conceptions of programed instruction vary include: (*a*) stress on

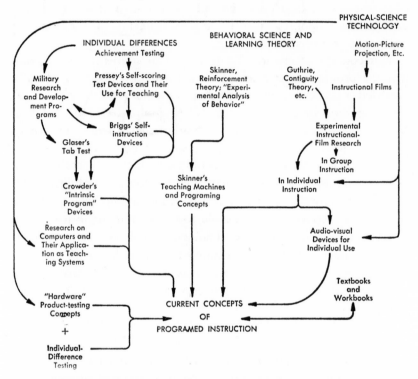

FIG. 2.—Converging streams of influence affecting present concepts and practices in programed instruction.

the notion of reproducibility or control of learner behavior; (*b*) degree of individualization of rate and/or sequence of instruction in accordance with the responses of the learner; (*c*) theoretical *vs.* empirical bases for program development; (*d*) the need for, and feasibility of, specifying instructional objectives in behaviorally stated terms; (*e*) the extent to which a program purports to take responsibility for managing the attainment of specified objectives *vs.* leaving it largely up to the student to manage his own learning activities; and (f) stress on instrumentation *vs.* stress on program content. Some of these differences stem from historical trends identified in Figure 2.

Generic definition of "program."—How can we most usefully define what we mean, in essence, by a "program"? Perhaps the most satisfactory general definition is as follows: *An instructional program is a vehicle which generates an essentially reproducible sequence of instructional events and accepts responsibility for efficiently accomplishing a specified change from a given range of initial competences or behavioral tendencies to a specified terminal range of competences or behavioral tendencies.* Such a definition has a minimum of restrictive connotations and can encompass most of the forms of programs that have been proposed. It makes no particular theoretical presuppositions and does not even require individual progress or overt response by the learner as part of the definition (though these characteristics may turn out to be theoretically or experimentally deducible as consequences of the general definition). Thus, a variety of program types and styles is admitted, which may differ in terms of using larger or smaller steps, varying amounts and kinds of student response, and any number of forms or combinations of "linear" paths or types of contingent alternative or "branching" sequences. However, it is evident that, in some sense at least, the definition implies a programed sequence of learner *behavior*, not merely a reproducible set of stimulus materials.[36]

A program is presequenced and implies a *presentation* to the student, not just a source of material to which the student may expose himself. A program thus has a beginning and an end; to borrow a phrase from computer programing, it has a start order and a stop order. The crucial aspect of this conception of programing is expressed by the "programer's credo" that if the student doesn't learn, the programer hasn't taught. This is the fundamental acceptance of responsibility for the management of learning—for trying to see to it that the student does learn and taking the blame for his failures. In an ideal program, the "stop order" occurs only when the student

36. Cf. a similar definition by Susan M. Markle in "The Changing Role of the Audiovisual Process in Education," *op. cit.,* p. 64, and the somewhat more restrictive characterization of programs by Schramm, *Programed Instruction, op. cit.,* pp. 1–3.

shows either that he has mastered the capabilities which are the program's objectives or that he is basically incapable of doing so.

Empirical guidance of programing.—If we consider programs in the generic sense proposed above and do not limit our attention to particular features which are the focus of Pressey's objections (see chap. xv), a strong argument for programing is that it leads to the study of stimulus-sequence conditions that promote effective learning. Since the existing state of the art does not permit predicting an optimal sequence on the basis of theory, an essential aspect of any program is some form of self-correction through feedback to the program, leading to cumulative revision based on programing errors revealed by students' responses to preliminary forms of a program. These responses include students' errors made on the individual "frames" of a program as well as later test data that may be correlated point by point with specific portions of the program. (This form of self-correction should be distinguished from that provided by a "branching" program in which decision points, based on errors of individual students but not made by other students, are used as the occasion for altering the sequence for a particular student.)

A sense in which progressive improvement may be conceived in the development of the art of programing (as distinct from the development of a single program) is successive approximation, through cumulative experience and research on programing variables, to the ability to write an initially very effective program sequence. It seems apparent that thus far we have taken only a few steps toward this goal, but it is the belief of many that the goal may ultimately be a realizable one. This belief is based on the reproducibility and control provided by instructional programs, particularly when used with suitable "teaching-machine" instrumentation, which make them very effective vehicles for experimental research leading to validation of instructional programing principles that can eventually comprise a science of instruction. (Such validation ultimately implies experiments in which the "subjects" in an experiment are a sample of programers—rather than just samples of students—and the experimental variable is instruction in the use of one or more programing principles.) Some illustrative experimental results relevant in the development of programing principles are discussed in a later section.

It should be emphasized that existing programs at best only approximate the potentiality for the kind of control over learning which could realize a goal of guaranteed mastery for all qualified students; many current programs are likely to be no more effective than alternative kinds of material. Indeed, some current "programs" merely follow the general superficial format implied by a particular rationale of programing, without meeting either the theoretical assumptions or empirical requirements which are supposed to be exemplified. A conspicuous shortcoming is the lack of sufficient try-out and revision, but there are also many other obvious failings in some existing programs, including inadequate analysis of the subject matter and inept use of what seem at present to be the more promising techniques of prompting, "vanishing" (see pp. 395 ff.), and feedback to the learner.

VARIATIONS IN CONCEPTIONS OF INDIVIDUAL LEARNING PROGRAMS

Individual learning programs are being produced in a wide variety of forms, and an increasing number of styles are emerging, employing various novel techniques. The fact that these initially tended to cluster around two or three main types should not blind us to the possibilities of almost infinite variation. An advantage of the definition proposed is that the *means* whereby educational ends are sought are not restricted to any particular form, provided we satisfy the condition of reproducibility and accept responsibility for trying to effect a specifiable change in behavior.

"Branching" variations.—Programs that are being experimented with depart, in varying degrees, from conventionalized "Skinner" or "Crowder" patterns of programing (see chap. xv, p. 359). Thus, there is an increasing tendency to combine "small-step" constructed-response programs with various forms of "branching," to employ mixed modes of response (e.g., both written and multiple-choice), to use a variety of auxiliary displays, and so on.[37] Numerous forms of branching have been experimented with, including complex computer-mediated branching sequences.[38] Thus, the tendency to er-

37. E.g., H. H. Shettel, D. Angell, and A. A. Lumsdaine, *Final Report: Self-Instructional Programs for SAGE System Operators.* Pittsburgh: American Institute for Research (Report No. AIR-C11-61-FR-2252), 1961.

38. Some such branching programs use, on occasion, the preference of the student as a basis for choosing among alternative pathways. See, for example: J. C. R. Licklider, "Preliminary Experiments in Computer-aided Teaching," in

roneously limit "branching" to the particular style of "intrinsic" programing with branching after every frame, originated by Crowder,[39] seems to be declining.[40]

"Adjunct" and "module" programs.—The general concept of programing, which implies learning through behavioral control by a program, readily encompasses "adjunct" (supplementary) programs that follow other forms of instructon, as recommended by Pressey in chapter xv. The question is not one of either-or but of degree. In some cases it may be hard to draw the line between "small-step" programs with extensive auxiliary "panel" material[41] and relatively free-study situations with autoinstructional materials serving as a frequent review. The basic question really is this: At what points is what degree of specifiable control over the student's learning to be provided—by the teacher, by the program, by the device that presents the program, and by the student himself?

"Module" or short-segment programs which can be interspersed

Programmed Learning and Computer-based Instruction, pp. 217–39 (Edited by John E. Coulson. New York: John Wiley & Sons, Inc., 1962); and William R. Uttal, "On Conversational Interaction," in *Programmed Learning and Computer-based Instruction, ibid.*, pp. 171–90.

39. Norman A. Crowder, "Automatic Tutoring by Intrinsic Programming," in *Teaching Machines and Programmed Learning, op. cit.*, pp. 286–98.

40. Actually, in the original programs for Skinner's disc machine (Skinner, "Teaching Machines," *op. cit.*) at least two kinds of "branching" were employed, namely drop-out of mastered items and use of instructions for selective review of discs. Pressey's second machine [S. L. Pressey, "A Machine for Automatic Teaching of Drill Material," *School and Society*, XXV (May 7, 1927), 549–52] also dropped out mastered items. For further discussion of similarities and differences between Skinner-type and Crowder-type programs, see A. A. Lumsdaine, "The Development of Teaching Machines and Programmed Self-Instruction," in *New Teaching Aids for the American Classroom*, pp. 136–73 [Stanford University, California: The Institute for Communication Research, 1960. (Abstract in *Teaching Machines and Programmed Learning, op. cit.*, pp. 653–54.)]. Allowing the student the "branching" option of calling for additional prompts has been employed experimentally by D. Angell and A. A. Lumsdaine, *A Study of Subject-controlled Partial Cueing in Paired-Associate Learning* [Palo Alto, California: American Institute for Research, 1961. (Report No. AIR-C14-9/61-SR4.)] and is incorporated in the "Didak" machine described in Skinner, "Why We Need Teaching Machines," *op. cit.*

41. A "panel" means an auxiliary display used with, and referred to in, a program. See Skinner and Holland, *op. cit.*, pp. 161–62; "The Changing Role of the Audiovisual Process in Education," *op. cit.*, p. 62. For an example, see Susan M. Markle, L. D. Eigen, P. K. Komoski, *A Programed Primer on Programing* (New York: Center for Programed Instruction, 1961).

between other forms of instruction to cover limited, specific units rather than entire courses are likewise compatible with the given definition of a program, provided the initial and terminal capabilities of the student are determined by suitable measurement. In applying this definition to a program which is *supplementary* (following other instruction), we need not specify fully the nature of the prior instruction if we specify the student's competence at the end of the prior instruction and, hence, his inital competence at the beginning of the program sequence. However, even the quite broad definition of a program that has been proposed is not compatible with the use of programs as *complementary* to concurrent instruction *of an unspecified sort*. In such use, there is the problem of knowing what accounted for the terminal behavior, at least unless this behavior is isolated by means of a controlled experiment to make possible the identification of the effective contribution of the program itself. Even with such experimentation, the results may be of little use for prediction unless the nature of the "other" instruction is also so fully specified that, in effect, it also acquires the properties of a parallel "program" (as it has been defined in this chapter).

Programed learning as a set of events.—We may even include the reading of a conventional textbook passage, *under specified conditions*, as a form of "program" if we are willing to submit such a "program" as accepting responsibility for teaching. However, in order to do so, the *use* of the text must be in some sense "programed," so that the vehicle of instruction is a specifiable set of events rather than remaining as an inert "thing" to be used in some unreproducible, uncontrolled manner. The same consideration applies logically also to the use of "programs" in the commonly more restricted sense of the term: Except to the extent that the conditions of a program's use may be "built in" through some kind of instrumentation, we need a specification of how the program is assigned and used, not merely an identification of the program *material* itself. A program needs to be thought of as generating a set of *events*, from which we can predict learning; a concept of programed learning that implies a specification of behavioral events on the part of the learner is more powerful than a concept of programed instruction that connotes only a set of materials or stimuli.

S-R ORIENTATION IN PROGRAMING

A basic emphasis in the progamed-learning orientation is on theorization conceived in terms of what the student *does,* reflecting Dewey's emphasis on learning by doing as well as the S-R orientation of the behavioral laboratory. This response-oriented point of view contrasts with conceptions of teaching or communication which concentrate primarily on the stimulus properties of a "message" which students "receive," and which tend to assume that what the student is told he then knows.[42] Emphasis on the study of student behavior, particularly as applied in the testing of programs and their cumulative revision, would make it seem likely, a priori, that thoroughgoing application could scarcely fail to produce, eventually, learning materials of superior effectiveness—both in the case of individually paced programs and of fixed-pace presentations, such as films and television.

Roles of student response.—In connection with this response-oriented point of view, attention should be given to several quite different functions of students' overt responses. In addition to the use of response data for revising a program, these functions include: (*a*) identifying a response which can be explicitly reinforced; (*b*) giving practice in making the response—most clearly important where response learning rather than merely association of an already learned response to new stimuli is required; (*c*) providing a basis for regulation of the sequence of the program—that is, to mediate "branching," either step by step or by longer segments; and (*d*) controlling the student's reading or observing through the selection of response requirements[43] so that the student must read or observe effectively in order to make an acceptable response. The best selection of those responses which are to be performed overtly in a program may differ considerably, depending on which of these functions the response is meant to serve.

Implicit responses.—An S-R model (see chap. ii) can apply theoretically not only to overt response but also to implicit or "covert" responses, such as those involved in reading or in "thinking an answer" required by a program. An extreme position sometimes ex-

42. Skinner, "Why We Need Teaching Machines," *op. cit.*
43. Skinner and Holland, *op. cit.,* p. 163.

pressed is that the student will learn only the responses which he overtly performs. Literally interpreted, this seems indefensible, since it is obvious that individuals do learn from silent reading and listening (cf. chap. xv, pp. 360 ff.). However, making the provisional assumption that the student should respond explicitly to everything which he is to learn may be a useful heuristic in writing a program. Experimental inquiry concerned with the effectiveness of overt and covert responding calls attention to the importance of a better understanding of implicit responses and of theorization, such as Sheffield's[44] on perceptual responding in serial tasks and Cook and Kendler's[45] on mediating responses in the learning of paired-associate material.[46]

Applicability of S-R reinforcement and contiguity principles.—A dualism between points of view stressing reinforcement following the to-be-learned response as against a Guthrian contiguity paradigm has been noted by Hill (see chap. ii). The latter viewpoint, leading to stress on prompting and the manipulation of cues preceding a response, appears to the writer to be more closely related *de facto* to programing operations and to "rules" of programing that have been enunciated,[47] even though an operant-conditioning paradigm, stressing reinforcement following the response, is often pointed to as the principal theoretical model for programed learning.

The writer has argued elsewhere[48] for more attention to a contiguity theory of the type generally advocated by Guthrie (see chap. ii) and pointed to a need for more of the kind of theorizing done by Sheffield.[49] The practical service of such theory in relation

44. Fred D. Sheffield, "Theoretical Considerations in Learning of Complex Sequential Tasks from Demonstration and Practice," in *Student Response in Programmed Instruction, op. cit.,* pp. 13–32.

45. John Oliver Cook and Tracy S. Kendler, "A Theoretical Model to Explain Some Paired-Associate Learning Data," in *Symposium on Air Force Human Engineering, Personnel, and Training Research,* pp. 90–98. Edited by Glen Finch and Frank Cameron. Washington: National Academy of Sciences, National Research Council, 1956.

46. See also John Oliver Cook, "From Audience Participation to Paired-Associates Learning," in *Student Response in Programmed Instruction, op. cit.,* pp. 351–66.

47. Lumsdaine, "Some Theoretical and Practical Problems in Programmed pp. 136–41. See, also, David Zeaman, "Skinner's Theory of Teaching Machines," in *Automatic Teaching: The State of the Art, op. cit.,* pp. 167–76.

48. *Ibid.,* pp. 137–43.   49. Sheffield, *op. cit.*

to programing is that it keeps attention focused on the learner's responses in relation to the controllable conditions of stimulation. As Hill has noted in chapter ii, contiguity theory makes the assumption that the necessary and sufficient condition for any learning to occur is temporal contiguity of cue and response. This position has been assumed from the outset by such theorists as Guthrie and Sheffield, and more recently a similar view has been adopted by Spence and by Estes (cf. pp. 35 ff., 40 ff.). The writer also adheres to this view; however, as noted in a previous discussion,[50] there are some crucial classes of responses needed in education for which it is difficult to identify cues that can be used to elicit the responses consistently. Especially important here is the class of responses involved in "paying attention" or "keeping at" the task of studying. It is for such classes of behavior that one might expect the manipulation of reinforcement schedules to be practically most useful. From this point of view, the difference in applicability of operant and elicited-response paradigms lies not per se in the kind of response to be learned but, rather, in the practical availability of an antecedent stimulus for eliciting the response that it is desired to condition.[51] Another possible way of saying this is that the important difference between emphasis on reinforcement schedules and a contiguity-theory emphasis on prompting conditions is a difference in the kind of instructional control over learning that is practicable in various situations, rather than per se a difference in basic requirements for learning.

Some Research Evidence Bearing on a Science of Instruction

Interrelations among theory, research, and practice are complex, as indicated in many parts of this yearbook. The practical relevance of a theory of learning lies in its efficacy for guiding the preparation of learning programs so as to reduce the amount of sheer trial and error (and hence cost) needed to arrive at an effective instructional product. In this sense the statement applies that "nothing is as practical as a good theory." However, general theories applicable to all forms of learning will probably need to be supplemented by inter-

50. Lumsdaine, "Some Theoretical and Practical Problems in Programmed Instruction," *op. cit.,* p. 139.

51. This contrasts with the position taken by Mowrer, reported by Hill in chapter ii.

mediate-level principles based on theorization dealing with specific kinds of learning situations in order to provide more specific guidelines for particular programing decisions.[52] Not only do such principles need to be validated through experiment but the programing decisions to which they lead will generally have to be further verified through empirical tryout of specific programs, as has been emphasized (p. 386), just as do similar theory-based decisions in, say, aeronautical engineering or preventive medicine.[53]

In this section, a few illustrative empirical results relating to principles at an intermediate level will be considered. Such experimental evidence as we thus far can marshal bearing on theoretical factors in instruction seems to come primarily from experiments on instructional media, conducted under controlled yet realistic conditions, rather than from less structured "naturalistic" experimentation with classroom-teaching "methods" or, on the other hand, from experiments conducted in highly artificial psychological-laboratory learning situations. This fact seems relevant to the question of whether a science of instructional programing, dealing with intermediate-level principles, needs to be developed as such—or whether implications of more general learning and behavior theory can ultimately suffice as a foundation from which a technology of practical programing principles can be directly derived.[54]

52. See Lumsdaine, *Student Response in Programmed Instruction, op. cit.,* p. 498.

53. The need for empirical data as a basis for assessing programs has been stressed by Rothkopf on the basis of what he has termed the "immature" status of theories of programing, and is reflected in the conclusion by the Joint Committee on Programed Instruction of the American Education Research Association, American Psychological Association, and the Department of Audiovisual Instruction of the National Education Association that the only defensible standards for assessing the effectiveness of specific programs at the present time must be on the basis of data from empirical tryouts. (This does not, of course, preclude adherence to principles of programing as rules of thumb in the construction of any particular program.) See Ernst Z. Rothkopf, "Criteria for the Acceptance of Self-Instructional Programs," in *Improving the Efficiency and Quality of Learning,* pp. 30–38 (Edited by Arthur E. Traxler. Washington: Educational Records Bureau and American Council on Education, 1961); and "Criteria for Assessing Programed Instructional Materials" (1962 Report of the Joint Committee on Programed Instruction and Teaching Machines, American Educational Research Association, American Psychological Association, and Department of Audiovisual Instruction, National Education Association), *Audiovisual Instruction,* VIII (February, 1963), 84–89.

54. Melton, *op. cit.; Student Response in Programmed Instruction, op. cit.,* pp. 497–500.

CONTINGENT GENERALIZATIONS AND A SCIENCE OF INSTRUCTION

The need for and probable character of such intermediate-level principles in the development of a science of instruction rests in part on the proposition that, in view of the complexity of human learning and the diversity of human learning tasks, we can expect to find relatively few universal generalizations that hold for all classes of instructional objectives, all classes of learners, and all conditions of instruction. Rather, what is likely to be most needed is a series of *contingent* generalizations that take account of the interactions of variables. Experimentally, this position argues for factorial experiments in which two or more variables are studied in combination, so that qualifications on a generalization can be determined, and we may validate contingent generalizations of the form: "Under condition A, result one is obtained, whereas under condition B, result two is obtained."[55] However, this stress on contingent generalizations does not imply the use of large, multifactor "shot-gun" experiments; on the contrary, the writer has argued[56] that relatively simple, more sharply focused experiments seem likely to be more productive.

A good example of contingent generalizations based on a simple factorial experiment is found in the differential results obtained in an experiment by Sheffield on the effects of a "one-sided" persuasive communication (which omitted arguments favoring the opposite conclusion) and a "two-sided" argument (which drew the same conclusion but nevertheless mentioned the opposing arguments).[57] The one-sided presentation was more effective in changing the opinions of those listeners who were favorably predisposed at the outset toward the conclusion being advocated, whereas the two-sided argument was the more effective in the case of those who were initially negative toward the advocated point of view. A similar differential conclusion was drawn from an instructional experiment reported by

55. This view was advocated in Carl I. Hovland, Arthur A. Lumsdaine, and Fred D. Sheffield, *Experiments on Mass Communication,* pp. 8–9. Princeton, New Jersey: Princeton University Press, 1949. See also, Lumsdaine, "Instruments and Media of Instruction," *op. cit.,* pp. 602–3.

56. Lumsdaine, *Student Response in Programmed Instruction, op. cit.,* p. 500; "Instruments and Media of Instruction," *op. cit.,* p. 604.

57. This experiment was reported by Hovland, Lumsdaine and Sheffield, *op. cit.,* pp. 201–27.

Maccoby, Michael, and Levine.[58] They were concerned with the question of whether effects of practice exercises interpolated between segments of a film were confined to the material practiced or also had a motivational carry-over to other, unrelated material contained in the same program. Such motivational carryover was found when the learners' extrinsic level of motivation was low but not when it was increased by the incentive of the students being told they would be tested at the end of the film.[59]

PROMPTING, "SMALL STEPS," AND "VANISHING"

Emphasis on prompting has been supported on the basis of results obtained by Cook[60] and collaborators, showing consistent superiority in paired-associates tasks for "prompting" over "confirmation" conditions.[61] Results obtained by Angell and Lumsdaine[62] showed, however, that a *mixture* of prompted and unprompted trials was more effective than complete prompting throughout—a finding consonant with the basic rationale for vanishing of cues as well as with

58. Nathan Maccoby, Donald N. Michael, and Seymour Levine, "Further Studies of Student Participation Procedures in Film Instruction: Review and Preview, Covert Practice, and Motivational Interactions," in *Student Response in Programmed Instruction, op. cit.*, 295–325.

59. An often-overlooked formal requirement for establishing a contingent generalization of this general character is that the *difference* in the incidence of the phenomenon be shown to be reliably greater under condition A than under condition B, rather than merely that the phenomenon be found under condition A and not demonstrated under condition B. (This condition was met in the above-cited experiment by Sheffield but was not fully met in the experiment reported by Maccoby, Michael, and Levine, *ibid.*, see esp. pp. 321–22.)

60. Cook, *op. cit.*

61. The term "prompting" is used here in a generic sense, referring to any initially adequate stimulus for eliciting the desired response; this is distinguished from Skinner's more restricted usage (B. F. Skinner, *Verbal Behavior*, pp. 255–58. New York: Appleton-Century-Crofts, 1957), which excludes direct copying. The terminology adopted by Briggs (Leslie J. Briggs, *A Survey of Cueing Methods in Education and in Automatic Programs*, p. 4. Pittsburgh: American Institute for Research, May, 1960. Report No. AIR-314-60-IR-106) is exactly the opposite of Skinner's, restricting prompting—as distinguished from "cueing"—to direct copying. The term "vanishing" (cf. Skinner, "Teaching Machines," in *Teaching Machines and Programmed Learning, op. cit.*, p. 146) is used here as synonomous with "fading." See Markle's definitions of these terms in "The Changing Role of the Audiovisual Process in Education: A Definition and a Glossary of Related Terms," *op. cit.*, pp. 131–35.

62. David Angell and A. A. Lumsdaine, "Prompted and Unprompted Trials versus Prompted Trials Only in Paired-Associate Learning," in *Student Response in Programmed Instruction, op. cit.*, pp. 389–98.

the more general argument that we must somehow prepare the learner to cope with an unprompted criterion situation.[63] It seems likely that a fruitful field for further experimental inquiry on principles of programing will concern gradients for the vanishing or withdrawal of prompts.[64]

The notion of introducing suitable prompts wherever needed, followed by their gradual withdrawal ("vanishing"), is closely related to the notion of using small (in the sense of easy) steps in an instructional program; however, possible confusion in conceptualization may arise owing to the use of several different meanings of the term "small steps."[65] A related fact is that some experiments have tended to confound "size of step" (in one or more senses) with number of steps, or total length of program.[66] The most direct independent variation of step size thus far has been in the case of procedural learning, notably in the studies reported by Maccoby and Sheffield.[67] In their studies, length of demonstrational segments (and hence temporal proximity *vs.* remoteness of prompts for the imitative performance of each succeeding step in a serial task) was

63. For further discussion, see *Student Response in Programmed Instruction, op. cit.*, pp. 479–83; Angell and Lumsdaine, "Prompted and Unprompted Trials Only in Paired-Associates Learning," *op. cit.*; David Angell and A. A. Lumsdaine, *Retention of Material Presented by Autoinstructional Programs Which Vanish and Which Do Not Vanish Verbal Cues* [Palo Alto, California: American Institute for Research, 1962. (Report No. AIR-C14-8/62-TR)].

64. A. A. Lumsdaine, "Response Cueing and 'Size-of-Step' in Automated Learning Programs." Paper read at the American Psychological Association Convention, 1959. (Printed in *Teaching Machines and Programmed Learning, op. cit.*, pp. 517–39, under the title "Some Issues concerning Devices and Programs for Automated Learning.")

65. *Ibid.*, p. 532.

66. Examples are found in J. E. Coulson and H. F. Silberman, *Results of an Initial Experiment in Automated Teaching* (Santa Monica, California: System Development Corp., 1959; also in *Teaching Machines and Programmed Learning, op. cit.*, pp. 452–68); and J. L. Evans, R. Glaser, and L. E. Homme, "A Preliminary Investigation of Variation in the Properties of Verbal Learning Sequences of the 'Teaching Machine' Type," in *Teaching Machines and Programmed Learning, op. cit.*, pp. 446–51.

67. Nathan Maccoby and Fred D. Sheffield, "Theory and Experimental Research on the Teaching of Complex Sequential Procedures by Alternate Demonstration and Practice," in *Symposium on Air Force Human Engineering, Personnel, and Training Research, op. cit.*, pp. 99–107; Nathan Maccoby and Fred D. Sheffield, "Combining Practice with Demonstration in Teaching Complex Sequences: Summary and Interpretation," in *Student Responses in Programmed Instruction, op. cit.*, pp. 77–85.

systematically varied without altering the length or content of the total instructional material. Short steps were found to be generally more effective than long steps for initial learning, with some evidence also supporting the theoretical expectation, in line with the concept of vanishing, that initial use of short steps followed by progressive lengthening of steps would lead to the best performance in a later test situation.

RETENTION AS RELATED TO PROGRAMING THEORY AND ASSESSMENT

Theoretical as well as practical interest in delayed-retention measures goes beyond a concern with merely determining whether differences produced by programs persist after an interval of time. For example, analysis of another experiment by Sheffield showed that in some instances effects of an indoctrination program on attitudes showed an actual increase, or "sleeper effect," with the passage of time, whereas in other cases the decrease consonant with expected forgetting was found.[68] Similarly, in a recent experiment by Rothkopf,[69] differences in the effects of program variations which showed up only after a considerable retention interval were found for identification learning (basically, paired-associates) in a technical subject matter (electrical resistor codes). He compared rote drill on paired associates, similar drill using mnemonics, and programed instructional materials that employed "vanishing" (as implemented by a so-called "Ruleg" pattern[70]). Rothkopf failed to find any evidence of appreciable differences in immediate retention but found marked differences favoring the programed over rote instruction when retention was measured after a number of weeks.

A somewhat analogous result concerning the value of "vanishing"

68. Which of these would occur was, further, found to be partly predictable on the basis of individuals' intellectual characteristics and their initial opinions; see Hovland, Lumsdaine, and Sheffield, *op. cit.*, pp. 182–200.

69. Ernst Z. Rothkopf, "Programed Self-Instructional Booklets, Mnemonic Phrases, and Unguided Study in the Acquisition of Equivalences," in *Journal of Programed Instruction*, I (1962), 19–28.

70. The "Ruleg" (rule-example) concept involves sequences in which, typically, a rule plus an example is used as the basis for prompting the student's completing a further, incomplete example; in later frames, these prompts are withdrawn one at a time until the student is able to respond appropriately without prompting. See Evans, Glaser, and Homme, *op. cit.* (Abstracted in *Teaching Machines and Programmed Learning, op. cit.*, 619–20.)

has been reported by Angell and Lumsdaine[71] in comparing the effects of two forms of a program to teach a short-cut method for squaring two-digit numbers.[72] In one form of the program, vanishing of prompts was used in accordance with current practices that prevail in much linear-style programing. The other program was substantially identical, except that prompts were deliberately continued throughout the program. The results failed to show evidence of any significant differences in terms of immediate testing, but the vanishing program was significantly superior when retention was measured a week or so later. (An instructive, if perhaps only analogical, parallel may be noted between these results and those obtained in laboratory-learning experiments, with both humans and lower animals, on "partial" or intermittent reinforcement. Like vanishing, this involves omission of the unconditional or reinforcing stimulus on some of the trials, and it is in general superior to 100 per cent reinforcement primarily with respect to rate of extinction rather than with respect to rate of acquisition.) It is evident that such results are not only of interest in relation to theory but also can affect decisions concerning suitable time intervals between instruction and testing in the conduct of applied research studies for assessing the effectiveness of specific programs.

TASK VARIABLES

The emphasis on contingent generalizations that has been noted suggests a possible basis for reconciliation between Gagné's contention that the most applicable principles for the design of training programs are to be found in principles of task analysis (see chap. vii, pp. 171 ff.) as against the position of those who would seek the main basis for instructional programing in principles deriving from learning theory. The writer would suggest that these two kinds of orientation can be reconciled in terms of theorization which states relationships among stimulus and response variables as contingent

71. Angell and Lumsdaine, "Retention of Material Presented by Autoinstructional Programs Which Vanish and Which Do Not Vanish Verbal Cues," *op. cit.*

72. These were experimental modifications of a program by James L. Evans, "Squaring Two-digit Numbers Ending in 5," in *Programmed Learning: Evolving Principles and Industrial Applications,* pp. 85–87. Edited by Jerome P. Lysaught. Ann Arbor, Michigan: Foundation for Research on Human Behavior, 1961.

principles that take explicit account of the characteristics of specific learning tasks. Thus, the importance of an analysis of task characteristics can figure not only in the identification of what it is that has to be learned, but also as a basis for relating the cue-discrimination characteristics and response requirements of a particular task to the program sequences needed to teach it most effectively.

This approach is exemplified in the theoretical analysis presented by Sheffield[73] based on contiguity learning principles, and investigated experimentally in studies by Sheffield, Maccoby, and collaborators dealing with the phasing of practice in relation to the size and placement of demonstration sequences in teaching procedural tasks.[74] These were analyzed as a function of task-organization features, such as contextually similar "natural units," and testing of differential predictions was possible with respect to, for example, several aspects of the whole-learning, part-learning problem as affected by particular characteristics of a given task. One such contingent generalization was that both the identification of optimum practice units and the temporal arrangements in which such units are utilized will depend on the degree and kind of inherent task organization. This was shown by Sheffield[75] to follow from the consideration that the arrangement of practice and demonstrational segments needs to reconcile the potentially competing requirements of reducing intraserial interference and of integrating subsequences into total-task performance.

On the other hand, it may also be profitable to seek for generalizations that have considerable invariance regardless of superficial differences of subject matter or type of instructional objective. For example, the general principle of anticipating undesired response tendencies has been noted as a common problem in effective persuasion and in heading off incipient error tendencies in teaching perceptual-motor or symbolic skills.[76] Similarly, theorization may ex-

73. Sheffield, *op. cit.*

74. Summaries by Sheffield and Maccoby in *Student Response in Programmed Instruction, op. cit.,* 117–31; more detailed reports by Sheffield, Maccoby, Margolis, and others on pp. 87–116 of the same volume; see also the learning-task analysis in experiments by Wulff and Emeson, *op. cit.*

75. Sheffield, *op. cit.*

76. Concerning error probabilities in skill learning, see Abram Amsel, "Error Responses and Reinforcement Schedules in Self-Instructional Devices," in *Teach-*

tend to variables which apply in common to more than one class of tasks as ordinarily defined in terms of such gross characteristics as manual versus verbal tasks. For example, Sheffield and Maccoby[77] have noted that the principles of task organization encountered in the serial learning of mechanical-assembly tasks would appear to be much the same as those which may apply to the organization of a lecture.

Concluding Comments: A Science and Technology of Programed Learning

The potential for both empirical and theory-guided improvability inherent in the concept of programed learning suggests that the limits for its attainment are far from having been reached as yet. One of the important influences of Skinner's work has been to foster a shift away from experimental studies which merely observe conditions under which learning and forgetting take place, and toward a greater emphasis on the management of efficient learning conditions designed to bring about desired forms of behavior.

The attempt to develop instructional materials not only to serve as a vehicle for testing hypotheses but also to attain a high degree of instructional effectiveness tends to generate provisional "rules" for effective programing of instruction, which can be implemented in experimental materials even though these rules are not tested directly within the confines of a given programing project.[78] Such working guidelines need to be translated into hypotheses that can be subjected to experimental test if a genuine science of instruction is to evolve.

Such a science of instruction can help to undergird not only an educational technology of programing principles but also the development of better specifications for the design of instructional hardware, ranging from simple teaching-machine components to complex computerized systems. It seems likely that this development will

---

ing Machines and Programmed Learning, op. cit., pp. 506–16. Concerning anticipation of undesired response tendencies in designing a persuasive communication, see Hovland, Lumsdaine, and Sheffield, *op. cit.,* p. 203.

77. Sheffield and Maccoby, *op. cit.*

78. Examples of such rules are to be found in May, *op. cit.,* pp. 176–78, and in Sheffield and Macoby, *op. cit.,* pp. 129–31.

generally require the formulation of theory-oriented contingent generalizations, with task and learner characteristics as modifying parameters in terms of which hypothesized cue-response relationships are differentially predicted. It also seems likely that these relationships must, in considerable part, both be based on and lead to an improved knowledge of the functioning of implicit responses in human learning from instructional programs. In addition, the fruitfulness of S-R contiguity theory and reinforcement-manipulation paradigms needs to be further delineated in terms of classes of learning tasks which differ with respect to the initial degree to which desired responses can be predictably elicited by available cues.

Finally, it may well be re-emphasized that differences in present conceptions and forms of programing, as well as their current theoretical rationales, are less important than the basic conviction that instruction is amenable to systematic description and improvement through experimental inquiry.[79] Such inquiry needs to be directed both to the development of a theory and science of instruction, as a long-range goal and as a shorter-range goal, to the development of an improved technology for perfecting and describing the performance characteristics of particular programs in contributing to behaviorally specified instructional outcomes.

79. This conviction reflects the position expressed in Lumsdaine and Glaser in *Teaching Machines and Programmed Learning, op. cit.*, p. 564.

CHAPTER XVII

A Perspective on the Relationship between Learning Theory and Educational Practices

ERNEST R. HILGARD

The relationship between learning theory and educational practices is that between any pure science and its technological applications. In the process of application something more than the theory is always involved. Thus, one does not move directly from astronomy to navigation without concern for tides, prevailing winds, and the location of lighthouses; investigations of heredity in fruitflies do not lead immediately to applications in animal husbandry without concern for the resistance of cattle to disease, the desirable characteristics determined by the market, and many other considerations; advances in the chemistry of fuels do not automatically determine whether a manufacturer will favor compact cars or full-sized ones, with engines in the front or in the rear. It is no different with educational practices, for these practices are determined by educational objectives, by the demands of mass education, by community resources, as well as by the teachings of psychology. In this chapter, I propose to examine some aspects of the contribution of learning theory and of experimentation on learning to the technology of education. This whole yearbook is in some sense in answer to the same questions, so that this overview merely restates what has been said in different ways in what has gone before.

Some Faulty Conjectures

First, I should like to dispose of some assertions which, if not often made, are sometimes implied.

1. *"We cannot expect to have instruction scientifically based as long as learning theorists are not in agreement."* If one were unable to proceed without a learning theory upon which all agreed, the sit-

uation would indeed be frightening. At least two things need be said. For one thing, the disagreement among theorists may be in respect to the interpretation of a set of facts upon which, as facts, all agree; in this case, the issue often is not one to trouble the practical person at all. Thus rewards may control learning in a given situation and be interpreted in contiguity terms, in reinforcement terms, or in information terms. While eventually the correct interpretation might make some difference, it often makes little difference at the present stage of technology. Thus Lumsdaine points out that *fading* in programing can be supported by Guthrie's contiguity theory, although it is advocated by Skinner as in accord with his theory of *shaping* through reinforcement. Second, the technology of instruction rests on much more than learning theory.

2. *"Once learning theory is in order, the principles of instruction will flow from it."* Technology must respect theory, in that it cannot violate fundamentally established principles, but theory never dictates technology directly. Learning theory will not dictate instructional practices any more than the principles of thermodynamics dictate whether airplanes shall be driven by propellers or jets.

It is only at the most advanced stages of theory construction, and usually after considerale interplay with technology, that greater reliance comes to be placed upon theory. Thus, computations of the orbits of space vehicles make use of advanced theory; at the same time the materials used, the fuels employed, and the like, have in them a large measure of empiricism.

3. *"The learning theorists are quarrelsome, but psychological experimentation is sound. If we know the experimental literature, then we can base our instruction upon it."* This is a tricky matter, for several reasons. For one thing, experiments are often guided by (and limited by) theory. That is, a test of a given theory is usually conducted with the constraints appropriate to that theory, and may not be fair to other theories that would favor different constraints. Hence, the facts do not "speak for themselves." For another, experimentation goes on at various levels and at various degrees of relevance to educational practices. Even those experiments which appear to be most closely related to instruction may not be generalizable to other instructional situations. Ignorance of the literature is not, therefore, the trouble in trying to apply learning theory to education.

4. *"Because we can't wait for the learning theorist to finish his job, and because learning theory will not in any case tell us what to do, we might as well ignore the learning theorist."* Things are not as white or black as this; learning theory is quite likely to be useful even if it is not directly determinative of practice. One can think of other parallels. Historians, for example, despair of finding general lessons of history, yet they argue fervently that a political leader is better off if he is informed about history, for he can, in fact, learn something from it. Learning theory is likely to produce some economy in educational experimentation by suggesting directions in which answers can be sought, thus saving a wasteful empirical search. In the end, a practice must work, but if we guide our search for workable practices by theoretical considerations, we may save a great deal of time and effort along the way.

5. *"Psychologists know plenty about learning; educators know the problems of the schools. If only we could get them together, to talk to each other, most of our problems would be solved."* How many half-truths there are! Collaboration is needed, but its terms have to be specified. A few week-end conferences between psychologists and educators are not going to do the trick. The collaboration must be on long-range investigations, in which the search is conducted together. We do not know the best specifications for team research, but a variety of skills and experiences have to be brought together among people who understand each other as they face a common task. They have to learn from each other, so that part of the synthesis goes on in individual minds.

6. *"Teaching is an art, and we can learn more from good teachers than from any experiments we are likely to design, or from what any psychologist says about teaching."* Of course we can learn from skilled teachers, and it is true that some good instructional practices are invented rather than discovered in a laboratory. As Woodring points out in chapter xii, many reform movements in education are essentially inventions, without much benefit of psychological theory. But to throw away all the possibility of improving instruction through carefully designed studies would be like returning medical practice to the prescientific physician because we still value the bedside manner.

These assertions are highlighted to show that a problem exists and that we should try to think as clearly as we can about it in our attempt to establish a sounder relationship between theory and research in psychology and educational practices.

Steps on the Road from Pure-Science Research to Established Educational Practices

In order to avoid the sharp distinction between pure and applied research, I find it convenient to break up the stages from the "purest" of research on learning to the most "applied" research (that concerned with the adoption of an approved practice) into six steps according to their relevance to the educational enterprise. Three of these are placed within the "pure science" end of the continuum, three of them in the "educational technology" end, as shown in Figure 1. The steps are abstracted from what is, in fact, a continuum; any one investigator may work at once upon several of the steps, or in the areas in which the steps shade into each other. The roles become increasingly diverse as the steps become farther apart. While the diagram is self-explanatory, its two halves call for some added comments.

PURE-SCIENCE RESEARCH ON LEARNING

By pure-science research is meant that which is guided by the problems which the investigator sets himself, without regard for the immediate applicability of the results to practical situations. This does not mean that the investigator has no practical interests, or that he does not want his results used; it is only that he is patient and uses the methods and procedures appropriate to the topic on which he works. Within learning research we may divide the stages of relevance to learning into the following three, expanding somewhat the left three boxes of Figure 1.

Pure-Science Research in Learning

Step 1. Research on learning with no regard for its educational relevance, e.g., animal studies, physiological, biochemical investigations. Learning in the flatworm and learning in the rat with transected spinal cord classify here.

Step 2. Research on learning which is not concerned with educational practices but which is more relevant than that of Step 1 because it deals with human subjects and with content that is nearer

PURE RESEARCH			TECHNOLOGICAL RESEARCH AND DEVELOPMENT		
Not Directly Relevant	Relevant Subjects and/or Topics	School-relevant Subjects and Topics	Laboratory, Classroom, and Special Teacher	Tryout in "Normal" Classroom	Advocacy and Adoption
Step 1	*Step 2*	*Step 3*	*Step 4*	*Step 5*	*Step 6*
Animal Mazes, Eyelid Conditioning, Pursuit Learning, etc.	Human Verbal Learning, Concept Formation, etc.	Mathematics, Reading, Typing, etc.	Programed Instruction; Language Laboratory, in Early Stages	Results of Step 4 Tried in Regular Setting	Manuals and Textbooks Prepared; Teacher Training Undertaken

FIG. 1.—Steps in research on learning—pure research to technological development

to that taught in school, e.g., nonsense syllable memorization and retention. The principles being tested are likely to be theoretical ones, such as the relative importance of proactive and retroactive inhibition.

Step 3. Research on learning that is relevant because the subjects are school-age children and the material learned is school subject matter or skill, though no attention is paid to the problem of adapting the learning to school practices, e.g., foreign language vocabulary learned by paired-associate method with various lengths of list and with various spacing of trials.

These three steps of relevance all classify as pure-science research because the problems are set by the investigators in relation to some theoretical issues and do not arise out of the practical needs of instruction. Of course there may be bridges from any pure-science project to a practical one: perhaps drugs discovered in brain studies of rats may aid remedial reading, studies of interference may suggest intervals between classes or what should be studied concomitantly, and language-vocabulary results in a pure context may guide language acquisition in schools. The main point is that the scientist has not committed himself to relevance. He may even disavow it, in line with a cult of pure science that seems to have been developing. According to this view, something is valuable precisely because it is remote from application; so long as it is precise, it does not matter how trivial it is. This is a faulty conception of pure science, and for the investigator to escape responsibility for the relevance of his work by falling back upon this "pure science" is as likely to be a sign of weakness as of strength.

The three steps of relevance are well illustrated by the substance of several chapters in this yearbook. Work going on at Step 1 is well summarized in the chapters by Hill (chap. ii) and Pribram (chap. iv); Step 2 is well illustrated by Underwood's chapter (chap. vi); although Carroll moves between Steps 3 and 4, the bulk of his evidence I would classify as falling within Step 3 (chap. xiv).

A further word on Step 3 is in order. The best work will be done at this stage by combining the skills of the subject-matter specialist with those of the experimenter upon learning. I have in mind combining the work of linguist and psychologist, as in the use of Hockett's linguistic analysis by Gibson, Gibson, Danielson, and Osser,[1] and in the combination of experts in mathematical learning theory and linguists in the work of Suppes, Crothers, Weir, and Trager.[2]

A brief characterization of the report by Suppes and others will be useful in showing some of the characteristics of Step 3 investigations. The authors consist of a logician sophisticated with respect to mathematical models, a psychologist whose work lies particularly in the field of mathematical learning, and two linguists. The studies, which concern the teaching of the Russian language, used actual language students, working in the familiar setting of the language laboratory in one of the local junior high schools. The material to be studied was prepared with the aid of a linguist familiar with the structure of the Russian language, so that certain conjectures about linguistics could be studied at the same time that learning theory was being investigated. The discriminations called for were real ones—Russian words being spoken into the tape by someone fluent in Russian. Contrast this with the usual preparation of a list to be memorized in the laboratory! Without going into detail, let me indicate the kinds of things that come from such a study:

1. Linguists have offered some conjectures about which combinations of phonemes can be most easily identified and how easily allophones can be recognized. (An allophone is a phoneme that is acoustically a variant: the phoneme that is represented by the letter *p* in English is not equally explosive in *speech*, *peach*, and to*p*most. Hence these three *p*'s are allophones.) The investigation gave evidence that most of the conjectures of the linguist were indeed correct. A native speaker has no trouble in hearing two allophones as the "same" phoneme, but the student hearing a foreign language has a great deal of trouble, and in constructing a good program these details are important.

2. The effort to work up by small steps from the easier combinations to the more difficult ones, which seemed plausible enough from the theory of programing, turned out not to be advantageous. The students who received random presentations from the start did somewhat better than those who had the orderly progression from easy to difficult.

1. Eleanor J. Gibson, J. J. Gibson, A. Danielson, and H. Osser, "A Developmental Study of the Discrimination of Letter-like Forms," *Journal of Comparative and Physiological Psychology*, LV (December, 1962), 897–906.

2. Patrick Suppes, E. Crothers, Ruth Weir, and Edith Trager, *Some Quantitative Studies of Russian Consonant Phoneme Discrimination*. Stanford, California: Stanford University, Institute for Mathematical Studies in the Social Sciences, Technical Report No. 49, September 14, 1962.

3. The mathematical model that proved to fit these data best was a two-stage model, as though learning took place in two jumps from no learning through an intermediate stage to mastery.[3] What this means in terms of the underlying processes is not yet clear; it may mean that first comes a stage of discriminating the stimuli and responses, and then a stage of connecting them.

My reason for placing this investigation at Stage 3 is that it is essentially a pure-science project, concerned with phoneme-allophone discrimination, on the one hand, and mathematical models of learning, on the other. Its relevance to classroom learning comes about because of its choice of subjects, laboratory conditions, and subject-matter. It is close to the technology of instruction but is not yet designed to indicate just how Russian should be taught. The order of presentation (increasing difficulty *vs.* random difficulty) is the most technologically relevant of the suggestions coming from the study, but this has to do with only a small aspect of learning Russian and requires more substantiation before it can be generalized. At the same, time, it is fairly obvious that experimentation closely related to the instructional task is likely to bear educational fruit more quickly than experiments classifiable within Steps 1 and 2.

APPLIED OR TECHNOLOGICAL RESEARCH AND DEVELOPMENT

We are ready to consider what happens on the right-hand side of Figure 1, in the steps having to do with applied- rather than pure-science research. The steps may be described as follows:

Technological Research and Development

Step 4. Research conducted in special laboratory classrooms, with selected teachers, e.g., bringing a few students into a room to see whether or not instruction in set theory or symbolic logic is feasible, granted a highly skilled teacher.

Step 5. A tryout of the results of prior research in a "normal" classroom with a typical teacher. Whatever is found feasible in Step 4 has to be tried out in the more typical classroom, which has limited time for the new method, and may lack the special motivation on the part of either teacher or pupil.

Step 6. Developmental steps related to advocacy and adoption. Anything found to work in Steps 4 and 5 has to be "packaged" for wider

3. It will be recalled that Restle (chap. v) illustrated the use of a one-stage mathematical model.

use, and then go through the processes by which new methods or procedures are adopted by those not party to the experimentation.

It is evident that the mood has changed in the transition from pure-science research to technological research, although the distinction between Steps 3 and 4 may be slight under some circumstances, as indeed in the experiment by Suppes and others used in illustration of Step 3.

The steps in technological research and application have been spelled out in similar ways, with some other distinctions, by Glaser in chapter vii, by Gage in chapter xi, and by Lumsdaine in chapter xvi; nearly all chapters have given some attention to these issues.

If one were to review the relationship between experimentation on learning by psychologists in its relation to education over the past several decades, it would be fair to say that too much of the research has rested at Steps 1 and 2 to be educationally relevant; educational psychologists, too, have tended to work at this end of the spectrum and then to jump, by inference, to Step 6, without being sufficiently patient about Steps 4 and 5. In this respect the introduction of programed learning has been helpful, because of the serious concern both with the structure of subject matter and with the individual learner for whom the program is designed.

It is fruitful to compare educational measurement with the psychology of learning according to the steps of Figure 1. Educational measurements have been improved through the "pure-science" researches in statistics, theory of scaling, factor analysis, and so on; at the same time, the arranging of materials and the development of norms have been very careful, so that the better intelligence and achievement tests are well prepared and well accepted. Until the advent of the teaching machine there was little such processing of teaching materials, except for some rather spurious use of word counts in editing spellers and readers. A psychological speculation was for many years permitted to guide practice in the production of teaching materials, without the serious tryouts that would have been given to educational measurement materials. One consequence is that the prestige of educators who worked in the area of measurements was of high order among their psychological colleagues, while this has not been as true of those working in the field of learning. There are signs that this is now changing; what the steps of Figure 1 say, among other things, is that there are important tasks to be done all along the way. Many indicators point to a much healthier situation today than a few years ago in that the attention of scholars is being attracted to all steps along the way from pure science to technological application.

A Set of Strategies for Integrating the Psychology of Learning with the Technology of Instruction

Dividing the spectrum of pure and applied research into the six steps, three "pure" and three "technological," is descriptive of a problem, but it does not prescribe a program, except to invite good work all along the line. I wish to consider the same set of problems from a slightly different vantage point: the strategies that are involved with the aim of emerging with a scientifically based technology of instruction.

STRATEGY OF DISCOVERY AND INVENTION

Discovery is the task of pure science, and the scientist in his laboratory must be free to perform this task in his own way. From the point of view of education, we need to make the approach in the spirit of pure science but need to direct it to relevant contents. There is no reason why we should not seek to have more experimentation on school children in the learning of subject matters or necessary skills or the kinds of problem-solving that are likely to go on in school.

While assigning *discovery* to the pure-science end of our continuum of relevance, we must not overlook *invention*, which is by no means limited to scientists. Some promising advances in education have come about as the inventions of skilled teachers, and a technology of instruction needs to examine and conserve the values of these inventions. I think, for example, of the augmented Roman alphabet being tried out in England in order to gain the advantages of a purely phonetic reading and writing in English. This seems to be meeting with great success; I should call it an invention rather than a discovery. One might say the same of O. K. Moore's use of an electric typewriter with beginners in reading and writing. Pure scientists are inventive in the realm of ideas but not always in the realm of technologies. As one of my colleagues is fond of pointing out, an Einstein does not take out patents; an Edison does. We need both kinds, and this is an added reason why the psychologist whose work is to be relevant to education needs to be close to educators and teachers.

STRATEGY OF DEVELOPMENT OF METHODS, MATERIALS, AND PROCEDURES

At another level of science, this time applied science, we need those who will be concerned with the utilization of the discoveries and tested inventions from the investigations that have been described. This is not a matter of taking some principle and applying it in cookbook fashion to the subject matter of schools. We have had too much of this in the past. For example, when Thorndike emphasized the significance of word counts as giving order to what is taught in reading, the very plausible notion that the more frequent words should be taught first became a fetish in the construction of some elementary-school readers. This was a scientific aid to textbook construction, to be sure, but the further steps in development were not taken. Whenever they *were* taken it was found that, in context, pupils could learn words that were considered too difficult on the basis of the frequencies from word counts. Now there is a kind of revolt against the artificiality that has crept into the substance of much of our reading material, and an effort is being made to revitalize it.

As soon as the more practical step is taken seriously, it becomes obvious that the psychologist cannot work alone. There is a structure to knowledge, so that later steps depend in part upon earlier ones. There are discriminations to be made. Theories gain their support from selected facts of a particular kind, so that what kinds of facts are taught may establish the readiness for theoretical interpretations. Much of this lies outside the psychology of learning and in the realm of the subject-matter expert—the mathematician, the physicist, the biologist, and sociologist, the historian, the artist, the musician, the linguist. The serious interest being taken in the schools today by the scholars within the various disciplines is encouraging, but they can no more go it alone than the psychologists can go it alone. The emphasis upon the intellectual in education is fine, but it can easily produce, in new form, the old misunderstandings that gave rise to exaggerated theories of formal discipline. The subject-matter specialist is likely to think that his material is fundamentally so interesting that as long as it is arranged logically, and is comprehensible, the psychological problems will take care of themselves. This is no more true today than it ever was. This subject-matter expert has an essential role, but his collaboration with the learning expert is equally essential.

As long as the experimenter upon learning used artificial tasks, such as mirror-drawing, finger-mazes, pursuit rotors, and lists on memory drums, he could suit his own convenience; once he decides to program symbolic logic or the Russian language or the appreciation of poetry, he has additional constraints upon him. He finds it necessary to collaborate not only with subject-matter experts but to make use of the experience of skilled teachers. One of the first lessons of program development is this: A good program is not developed out of the mechanics of program construction or out of familiarity with the psychology of learning; it is not developed out of subject-matter expertness, nor through the sheer artistry of an able teacher; it requires the collaborative effort contributed by the various expertnesses. Once a reasonably promising program is developed, it has to be tried out in a classroom, perhaps a laboratory-type classroom, but with real school children taught by a real teacher. Then, before the development is completed, it has to be tried out in a regular classroom, where other obligations also exist. A teacher has many responsibilities, and children have diverse interests; whatever is new has to be fitted in somehow within an existing set of classroom procedures. These steps are all rather foreign to the typical experimental student of learning, but they are essential if the educational program is to be sound. I would argue for a division of labor and prestige, so that those who take on the developmental task are recognized and honored for the ingenuity they display, which must be at least equal to that of the pure scientist.

STRATEGY OF INNOVATION

In something as complex as a school system, we need another level of research strategy, which I shall call *the strategy of innovation*. The best of equipment may lie idle, the best of resources remain unused, the best of techniques sabotaged, if there is not care in introducing the new methods or new materials to all concerned. Once the pure-science principles have been established and the applications validated in practice schoolrooms, the more widespread adoption is by no means guaranteed or, if the adoption is forced there is no assurance that the desired results will be forthcoming. Abstractly, the steps of innovation are clear enough: Provide (*a*) a sound research-based program, validated in tryout, (*b*) the program packaged in such a way as to be available, as in good textbooks, supplementary readings in the form of pamphlets, films, programs for teaching machines, and guides for the teacher, (*c*) testing materials by which it can be ascertained if the objectives of the program have indeed been realized, with appropriate normative data on these evaluative instruments, (*d*) in-service training of the teacher to overcome the teacher's resistance to something new and to gain his enthusiastic acceptance of the program as something valuable as well as to train him in its use, and (*e*) support for the program from the community, school boards, parents, and others concerned with the schools.

It is my feeling that we have not done very well in appraising carefully our strategies of innovation. We have sometimes gone overboard for the novel and untried, just to keep up with the Joneses ("we have teaching machines, too"); at other times we have been very resistant. Commercialism and vested interests enter in unpleasant ways, sometimes supported, unfortunately, by fractions of the educational profession itself. Here, then, is a task calling for wisdom and sensitivity. The psychological contributions may come more from social psychology than from the psychology of learning, because the processes are those of social control and attitude change; but unless there is serious concern about the appropriate ways in which to bring innovation about, schools are likely to be the victims of whims, rather than the heirs of the best tradition we can establish through co-operative effort.

There are some specific suggestions that might be given consideration. It would be desirable, for example, for every school system, of whatever size, to have somewhere within it a school building, or at least a set of schoolrooms, devoted to in-service training of teachers and to innovation; these are on-going matters important at the community level and cannot be left to teacher-training colleges or universities. Both children and teachers could be rotated through these rooms in order to try out innovations before there is firm commitment to them. Thus, a few teaching machines or closed-circuit television projectors could be tried out without investing in them for a whole school system; teachers could have a voice in saying whether or not they wanted the new devices, or in selecting among various possibilities. Usually no harm would be done in waiting for a while if teachers were not ready, for methods imposed on teachers are unlikely to prove successful. Some of the innovations to be tried out might be those of successful local teachers themselves, here given the opportunity to show their colleagues how they do it in their own classrooms. Members of the school board and representatives of the parents could be brought in also to see things being tried out. The principles of tryout before acceptance, of choice by those who are to use the method, seem to me sound ones. If the new methods are indeed good, they will find acceptance.

The remarks that I have made reduce to this: In order to build a sound bridge from the experimental studies of learning to the classroom, we need a series of steps, for applied science consists of more than applying principles to practice. The main points are that in the research and development phases a collaboration is called for between psychologist, subject-matter specialist, and teacher; beyond this, careful consideration has to be given to techniques of innovation. If we achieve success in integrating these phases, we will move toward that improvement of education which will be satisfying to us all.

Postscript: Twenty Years of Learning Theory in Relation to Education

ERNEST R. HILGARD

It is of some interest to compare the content and emphases within the chapters of this yearbook with those of its predecessor that appeared twenty-two years ago.[1] The chairman of that yearbook committee, T. R. McConnell, served as a member of the committee for this one, and his comments have been helpful throughout. This note is appended at his suggestion.

The purposes and scope of the two yearbooks are somewhat different, partly because of the differences in the preoccupations of the psychological and educational professions then and now. In the day of the earlier yearbook, theories associated with the great names tended to be major points of dispute, and an effort to present the theories clearly, and to call attention to their complementary characters and to the possibilities of reconciling them seemed highly desirable. The 1942 yearbook was remarkably successful in this. The three theories chosen (conditioning, connectionism, and Gestalt) received able exposition by advocates within each camp. Thus, Guthrie summarized his conditioning theory, and Hull his, in chapters that remain very useful introductions to these viewpoints. Lewin's chapter on the field theory of learning is his only concise and comprehensive statement of his views on learning. It is of interest to have the contrasting chapters on connectionism by Sandiford (a purer Thorndikeanism) and by Gates (a more functionalistic and Woodworthian variety). The Gestalt chapter by Hartmann, unfortunately, represents the kind of extremism that, in part, led to the decline of interest in Gestalt. McConnell's reconciliation was entirely sensible. From the standpoint of the present, one notes the

1. *The Psychology of Learning.* Forty-first Yearbook of the National Society for the Study of Education, Part II. Edited by Nelson B. Henry. Chicago: Distributed by University of Chicago Press, 1942.

omission of Skinner, whose *Behavior of Organisms* (the major statement of his views) was at the time already four years old, and of
Tolman, whose major work had appeared ten years earlier. One can
never predict which existing positions are going to come into later
prominence and which will decline in favor. The whole emphasis
on mathematical models is, of course, a later one, and psychoanalytic
theories have come to the fore and declined during the interim. The
revival of physiological interest (Pribram, chap. iv) is also noteworthy. In the present yearbook, the later histories of the major
earlier viewpoints have been treated in the chapters by McDonald
(chap. i), Hill (chap. ii), and Hilgard (chap. iii), with some additional references in the chapters by Underwood (chap. vi), Lumsdaine (chap. xvi), and others, but the yearbook is not preoccupied
with the major viewpoints toward learning, for the era of the "great
debate" among the major theories is over.

There is far greater concern in this yearbook with the professional problems of developing psychological methodologies that will
be used collaboratively to deal with basic problems of education.
This preoccupation is shown in the several chapters dealing with
educational technology, in the concern with a psychology of teaching, in the review of the meaning of readiness as it affects school
practices, and in the other chapters that focus on concrete problems
of educational reform and instruction. The earlier yearbook also had
a section entitled "Implications for Education" consisting of six
chapters. Rereading of these chapters suggests that there is a tendency today to assume that we are starting fresh and to fail to give due
consideration to what has gone before. For example, a number of experiments on mathematics teaching, many generated by Gestalt
principles, were used as illustrations in the 1942 yearbook. These
have been entirely ignored by Bruner in chapter xiii of this yearbook,
though many of them are consonant with his views. Several of the
chapters in the 1942 yearbook make one see how little we have advanced in the two decades since they were written. We find, for
example, Brownell deploring the neglect of Piaget because ". . .
Piaget's studies seem to provide the most illuminating single description of the way in which children attain power in problem-solv-

ing."[2] The current upsurge of interest in Piaget's views shows how strange is the march of history.

Yet, I believe it is fair to say that most of the implications for education were derived in the earlier yearbook from what I called, in chapter xvii of the present volume, experiments in Stages 1, 2, and 3, rather than in Stages 4 and 5. In other words, the educational implications are more often than not hortatory: Because thus and so are true about learning, the teacher ought to do thus and so.[3] The flavor of the present yearbook can more nearly be summarized in the alternate form of statement: because this appears to be true about learning, we ought to see whether or not, in the actual context of the classroom, teachers can be helped in their dealing with students to implement these principles with the aid of appropriately designed materials and training in their use, supplemented with tests to see whether or not the desired advances are indeed forthcoming. In other words, we believe that scientific psychology of learning has the obligation to go all the way from theory to practice, using criticized data in every step. This involves a division of labor, of course, but with collaborative effort and mutual good will all along the line.

2. William A. Brownell, "Problem Solving," in *The Psychology of Learning*, p. 428.

3. See in this connection, Robert I. Watson, "A Brief History of Educational Psychology," *Psychological Record*, XI (1961), 209–42.

Index

Ability grouping as means of motivation, re-examination of, 188–89

Achievement, pupil personality and conditions favorable to, 200–204

Achievement interaction between teaching method and pupil personality, determination of, 204–5

Addictionance and dissonance, questions raised by experiments of, 91–92

Adey, W. R., 105, 106

"Adjunct" and "module" programs, discussion of, 388–89

Aims, Dewey's conceptions relating to, 12–13

Air Force Personnel Training Research Center (AFPTRC), reports of, 161, 162

Aircraft Observer Research Laboratory, development of training aids by, 161

All-or-none learning theory: application of, in determining optimal rate of instruction, 125–31; application of models based on, 121; determination of optimal size of class by use of model based on, 121–25; discussion of, assuming continuous time, 117–20; progress of groups in, on items 1, 2 . . . n, illustrated, 114

Allinsmith, Wesley, 204

American Psychological Association, 15, 354

Ames, Louise B., 217, 218

Amidon, Edmund 202

Analysis, emphasis on, in current research, 135

Anderson, Harold H., 200

Anderson, Robert H., 298

Angell, David, 395, 398

Anxiety: effect of classroom situation on, 195–96; effect of, on achievement, 196–97, 205

Anxious students, type of instruction suitable for, 207

Apperception, theory of, displaced by concept of interest, 58

Aptitudes, theoretical structure for research in, 158

Armament Systems Personnel Research Laboratory, major concerns of, 162

Armed Services Technical Information Agency (ASTIA), publications in, 154

Army's Human Resources Research Office (HumRRO), 177, 178

Asch, Solomon E., 203, 279

Association(s): concept of an, 136–40; conditions for establishment of, between verbal units, 137; conditions of, 140–41; definition of an, 137–38; formation of, in all-or-none theory, 138–39; forward and backward, 137–38; nature of problem of, 90

Association by contiguity, Guthrie's acceptance of, as basic law of learning, 40–41

Associative process, limitations of role of motivation in, 145

Audio-visual devices and materials, discussion of, 375–77

Audio-visual media, rationale and uses of, 377–80

Austin, George A., 318

Ausubel, David P., 283

Autoinstructional materials: branching in, 359–60; nature of, 358–59; *see also* Teaching machines; Programed instruction; Programed texts; etc.

Avoidance learning, interpretation of, 39

Baer, Donald M., 185

Bagley, William C., quoted, 17

Baker, Charles T., 204

Bandura, Albert, 185, 276, 284

Beall, Ross H., 227

Beberman, M., 320

Behavioral organization, concept of gradients in relation to, 217–18

Behavioral science, misservice of certain emphases of, to education, 79

Beilin, Harry, 198

Berlyne, D. E., 186

Berry, Paul C., 263

Bexton, W. H., 256

Bilodeau, Edward A., 164

Bilodeau, Ina McD., 164

Bingham, Harold C., 59

Biological Sciences Study Group, 189

Block, Clifford H., 263

Bloomster, Maurine, 225, 352

ing for, 257–65; Gestalt influences on, 62–63; Guilford's factor analytic concepts of, 247–48; identification of, as major area of research in learning, 134–35; importance of corrective functions in, 319–33; instructional issues in relation to, 265–67; interests of S-R psychologists in, 74–75; modes of procedure in, 318; present impact on, of various influences, 75; psychoanalytic concepts in, 248–51; *see also* Creative thinking; Thinking

Proctor, Virginia H., 199

"Productive thinking": line of inquiry growing out of Wertheimer's work on, 64; work of Wertheimer in field of, 63

Program(s): branching variations of, 387–88; description of types of, 358–60; generic definition of, 385–86; variations on conceptions of, 387–89

Programed books: criticism of, 362–63; nature of, 360–61; *see also* Programed instruction; Programed instructional materials; Programed texts

Programed instruction: discussion of development of, 378–80; Skinner's concepts relating to, 358–59

Programed instructional materials, criticisms of, 359–60

Programed learning: differences between Pressey's and Skinner's concepts of, 383; discussion of, in relation to educational reform, 292; essential aspects of concept of, 383–87; provision in, of techniques for maintaining performance, 92; relation of improvement in, to development of a science of education, 400–401; *see also* Programing, etc.

Programed texts: bases for proper use of, 88; dangers in, 362–63

Programing: applicability of S-R reinforcement and contiguity principles in, 391–92; corollaries of Skinner's concepts of, 383; criticisms of, 364–65; discussion of larger issues of, 367–68; objective *vs.* constructed items in, 357, 363–64; role of student's responses in, 390; Skinner's concept of, 382–83; S-R orientation in, 390; *see also* Programed learning; Programed instruction

Programing theory, retention as related to, 397–98

Progressive Education, origin and influence of, 288

Progressivism: beginnings of, 14; rise of, 6

Prompting, definition and discussion of, 395–96

Psychoanalytic theory, problem-solving in relation to, 249–51

Psychological concepts, loss of currency through disproof, neglect, and transformation, 56–59

Psychological theory(ies): bearing of, on learning to read, 349; characteristics essential to, 124–26; development of equipment and materials as related to, 375–80; Dewey's influence on, 10–13; era of conflicts of, 17–23; influence of, on educational theory, 1–5; *see also* Learning theory

Punishing behavior, effect of, on teacher influence, 194–95

Pupils: means by which instructor learns what is familiar and comprehensible to, 84–85; teachers' concern for orienting reactions of, 85

Pure-science research, description of steps from, to educational practice, 405–11

Rapaport, David, 250

Raskin, Simon D., 261

Readiness: Brownell's discussion of, 229; building of, 227–28; complexity of concept of, 210–12; concept of developmental stages, in relation to, 220–22; discussion of, in relation to types of subject matter, 234–35; discussion of, in perceptual terms, 80–85; discussion of nature and causation of, 237; implications of, for interpretation, 235–36; importance to education of knowledge of processes of, 80; learning sets in relation to, 229–36; maturation as factor in, 215–17; mechanisms that function in, 88–89; mental age as estimate of, 225–26; new approaches needed in, for school learning, 239; studies of timing in relation to, 222; views of possibility of building of, 228–29

Reading: application of psychological theory to, 345–48; process of learning, 342

Reading behavior: analysis of, 336–45; analysis of, as basis for instruction in reading, 351–52; description of, 337–

INFORMATION CONCERNING THE NATIONAL SOCIETY FOR THE STUDY OF EDUCATION

1. PURPOSE. The purpose of the National Society is to promote the investigation and discussion of educational questions. To this end it holds an annual meeting and publishes a series of yearbooks.

2. ELIGIBILITY TO MEMBERSHIP. Any person who is interested in receiving its publications may become a member by sending to the Secretary-Treasurer information concerning name, title, and address, and a check for $8.00 (see Item 5), except that graduate students, on the recommendation of a faculty member, may become members by paying $6.00 for the first year of their membership. Dues for all subsequent years are the same as for other members (see Item 4).

Membership is not transferable; it is limited to individuals, and may not be held by libraries, schools, or other institutions, either directly or indirectly.

3. PERIOD OF MEMBERSHIP. Applicants for membership may not date their entrance back of the current calendar year, and all memberships terminate automatically on December 31, unless the dues for the ensuing year are paid as indicated in Item 6.

4. DUTIES AND PRIVILEGES OF MEMBERS. Members pay dues of $7.00 annually, receive a cloth-bound copy of each publication, are entitled to vote, to participate in discussion, and (under certain conditions) to hold office. The names of members are printed in the yearbooks.

Persons who are sixty years of age or above may become life members on payment of fee based on average life-expectancy of their age group. For information, apply to Secretary-Treasurer.

5. ENTRANCE FEE. New members are required the first year to pay, in addition to the dues, an entrance fee of one dollar.

6. PAYMENT OF DUES. Statements of dues are rendered in October for the following calendar year. Any member so notified whose dues remain unpaid on January 1, thereby loses his membership and can be reinstated only by paying a reinstatement fee of fifty cents.

School warrants and vouchers from institutions must be accompanied by definite information concerning the name and address of the person for whom membership fee is being paid. Statements of dues are rendered on our own form only. The Secretary's office cannot undertake to fill out special invoice forms of any sort or to affix notary's affidavit to statements or receipts.

Cancelled checks serve as receipts. Members desiring an additional receipt must enclose a stamped and addressed envelope therefor.

7. DISTRIBUTION OF YEARBOOKS TO MEMBERS. The yearbooks, ready prior to each February meeting, will be mailed from the office of the distributors, only to members whose dues for that year have been paid. Members who desire yearbooks prior to the current year must purchase them directly from the distributors (see Item 8).

8. COMMERCIAL SALES. The distribution of all yearbooks prior to the current year, and also of those of the current year not regularly mailed to members in exchange for their dues, is in the hands of the distributor, not of the Secretary. For such commercial sales, communicate directly with the University of Chicago Press, Chicago 37, Illinois, which will gladly send a price list covering all the publications of this Society. This list is also printed in the yearbook.

9. YEARBOOKS. The yearbooks are issued about one month before the February meeting. They comprise from 600 to 800 pages annually. Unusual effort has been made to make them, on the one hand, of immediate practical value, and, on the other hand, representative of sound scholarship and scientific investigation.

10. MEETINGS. The annual meeting, at which the yearbooks are discussed, is held in February at the same time and place as the meeting of the American Association of School Administrators.

Applications for membership will be handled promptly at any time on receipt of name and address, together with check for $8.00 (or $7.50 for reinstatement). Applications entitle the new members to the yearbook slated for discussion during the calendar year the application is made.

5835 Kimbark Ave.   HERMAN G. RICHEY, *Secretary-Treasurer*
Chicago 37, Illinois

PUBLICATIONS OF THE NATIONAL SOCIETY FOR THE STUDY OF EDUCATION

NOTICE: Many of the early yearbooks of this series are now out of print. In the following list, those titles to which an asterisk is prefixed are not available for purchase.

POSTPAID
PRICE

iii

POSTPAID
PRICE

Distributed by
THE UNIVERSITY OF CHICAGO PRESS, CHICAGO 37, ILLINOIS
1964